D1042136

Benedicte Valentiner

BEDTIME AND OTHER STORIES
FROM THE
PRESIDENT'S GUEST HOUSE

*Mrs. V's memoirs of service
to four U.S. Presidents*

Benedicte Valentiner
Bedtime and Other Stories from the President's Guest House

Copyright 2011

Manufactured in the United States of America. All rights reserved.
No part of this book may be reproduced in any form or by any
electronic or mechanical means including information storage and
retrieval systems without permission in writing from the publisher,
except by a reviewer, who may quote brief passages in a review.

ISBN: 978-0-9835760-0-6
Library of Congress Control Number: 2011912160

Edited by Warren Sloat

Cover design and cover photo by Andrew Neighbour,
www.medianeighbours.com

Layout and typesetting by Julie Melton, The Right Type,
www.therighttype.com

Logo design by Luise Valentiner,
www.triggerpress.co.uk

Website design by Bette Ridgeway,
www.ridgewaystudio.com

Contact the Publisher:
www.chregonpress.com

Contact the Author:
www.benedictevalentiner.com

*Photos are courtesy of The Ronald Reagan Presidential Foundation and Library;
The George Bush Presidential Library; The William Jefferson Clinton Presidential Library; The George W. Bush White House; The U.S. Department of State;
various embassies; Lynn Hornor Keith and the author's private collection.*

10 9 8 7 6 5 4 3 2 1

TABLE OF CONTENTS

for

THE BLAIR HOUSE STAFF

past, present and future

with admiration and respect

BLAIR HOUSE

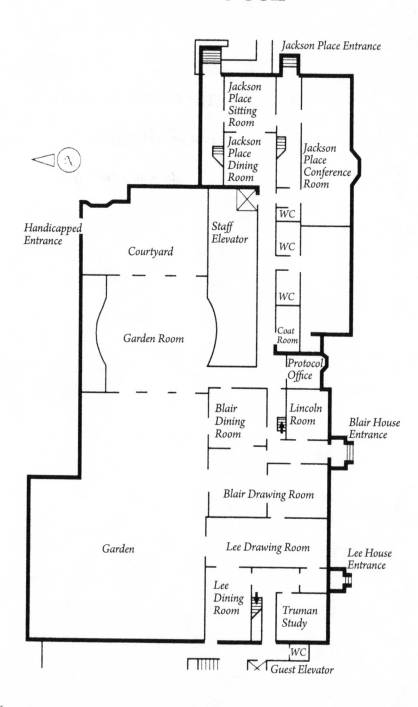

Jackson Place Entrance

Jackson Place Sitting Room

Jackson Place Dining Room

Jackson Place Conference Room

Handicapped Entrance

Courtyard

Staff Elevator

WC

WC

WC

Garden Room

Coat Room

Protocol Office

Blair Dining Room

Lincoln Room

Blair House Entrance

Blair Drawing Room

Garden

Lee Drawing Room

Lee House Entrance

Lee Dining Room

Truman Study

WC

Guest Elevator

PROLOGUE

On the first night of Boris Yeltsin's visit in September 1994 our two security officers on duty got a bigger adventure than they could ever have imagined.

At about 12:30 am Officers Paul Besett and Michael Cooney saw on their computer screen an astonishing sight. Clad but sparsely, having forgotten to put on his pajamas, the mighty President of the Russian Federation was briefly dressed as he negotiated the back stairs with the certainty of a person who had a directional problem.

He was stoned out of his skull – and he was almost naked.

Our security officers were glued to the computer screen. At the bottom of the circular emergency staircase going from the dressing room in the Primary Suite and leading to the New Executive Office building's garage, they saw Boris Yeltsin trying to open the garage door and nearly jumping out of his briefs from fright as it gave off a loud signal. Then the security officers lost him on the screen. Frantically they called the USSS Command Post to alert them that "their man" was loose in the house. And when they turned away from the screen they had another shock.

There was Boris Yeltsin in the flesh – and such a lot of it too – holding on for dear life to the door frame of their office. Without a word, he bowed gravely to them and staggered out, rolling around the corner into the Leslie Coffelt Room. This room, named for the security guard who gave his life defending President Harry S Truman during an assassination attempt by Puerto Rican Nationalists on November 1, 1950, was set aside as a down-room for the Metropolitan Police and USSS uniformed police so that during their strenuous and long hours protecting our visitors they could come in out of the cold and refresh themselves. During that particular night there were thirty sitting around when Yeltsin turned up.

"There is a drunken Russian in here," someone casually said to which another one replied:

"This is not a drunken Russian.

It's B o r i s Y e l t s i n!"

AUTHOR'S NOTES

"All the world's a stage, and all the men and women merely players:
They have their exits and their entrances."

William Shakespeare

I was nine when my grandmother made an apron and little cap for me, and I became the official waitress of my parents. My interest in hospitality had started at a very early age when I hung around the kitchen learning from and helping my mother in setting the stage for their frequent parties. Around six I graduated to opening the front door, taking coats and welcoming their guests, and just loved the ebb and flow of visitors. The waitressing lasted until one day when, serving my father, he kissed my cheek; I stormed into the kitchen, tore off my apron, and declared I was through because "the men would not leave me alone." Unknown to me at the time, the service I delivered at my parents' table in Copenhagen, Denmark would in Washington D.C. be known as "French service" and the hospitality industry would become my calling. Already back then, the part that I had assigned myself in my parents' home and the skills I honed became second nature to me and foreshadowed the role I would later play in the U.S. President's Guest House. I discovered early on how I thrived on the excitement and stimulation of being in other cultures, and pursued my hotel career around Europe until my parents got posted to Washington D.C. where I arrived as an immigrant in March 1963.

I fell in love with America, with its energy and enthusiasm, its generous spirit and openness; living in this vibrant and constantly changing society I was forced to be on my toes; in America one works hard, with long days, short vacations, and less than perfect benefits – but the stimulation, the challenges, the rewards can be enormous; the contrast to Denmark with its more sedate pace and its incremental changes was great. Everything here seemed possible. I never looked back and I never fell out of love with America.

My American journey, touched upon in the book, led me to the ultimate hotel job in the world – that of general manager of the U.S. President's Guest House, Blair House.

Blair House, located diagonally across from the White House in Washington D.C., is a complex of four historic townhouses and a large addition, comprising one and one half city block, a total of 70,000 square feet distributed on four floors and a full basement. It is the nation's B & B and its mission is to provide hotel accommodations to the official foreign guests of the United States president. Only chiefs of state, such as queens, kings, or presidents, and heads of government, such as prime ministers, may stay here at the specific invitation of the U.S. president.

The original Blair House was built in 1824, when the Federal City took shape, and much in new construction went up around the White House and the Capitol Building. Many of the new buildings were designed by the architect Benjamin Henry Latrobe whose design undoubtedly set the scale and size for Blair House, built in the Classical Revival style, today's nucleus of the President's Guest House. The first owner of the building, in those days comprising two stories and a basement (later in the century two more stories were added), was the first U.S. Army Surgeon General, Dr. Joseph Lovell, a Boston physician and Harvard Medical School graduate, and his wife and eleven children. In 1836 the fever killed Dr. and Mrs. Lowell and the house was bought by Francis Preston Blair.

Mr. Blair, a Kentucky gentleman, had arrived in Washington some years earlier with President Andrew Jackson and his administration. Mr. Blair was an open and vocal supporter of the president, and was invited to come to Washington to be editor of the pro-administration newspaper, the GLOBE. Blair became a close and trusted advisor of Andrew Jackson and was part of the president's kitchen cabinet. Mr. Blair also founded the Congressional Globe, a daily report of the proceedings in the U.S. Congress, which later became the Congressional Record, still being published today. The drawing rooms of Blair House became a political salon for the powerful and illustrious of its day. Not only was Francis Preston Blair influential in the city's political life, but two of the three Blair sons developed a taste for same.

Together the three played significant roles in bringing Abraham Lincoln to power, in creating the Republican Party, and generally in the advice rendered at the highest level.

The Blairs in the mid 1840s moved to the country, buying property in Maryland. Legend has it that Francis Preston Blair and his daughter, Elizabeth, were riding in the country side about a mile from the district line when his thirsty horse, Selim, found a beautiful natural spring bubbling up through mica rock, giving the rock the appearance of being lined with silver. Blair built a summer house there and named it Silver Spring. His son Montgomery also built a home near the spring naming it Falkland. For the next seven years distinguished tenants at Blair House included the Secretary of the Navy, George Bancroft, who established the U.S. Naval Academy at Annapolis, as well as the Secretary of the Interior, Thomas Ewing, whose daughter Ellen in the rear drawing room married a young soldier by name of William Tecumseh Sherman, later to become famous as a Union general in the Civil War.

During the spring of 1861, three days after the attack on Fort Sumter, South Carolina, which began the Civil War, Colonel Robert E. Lee of the U.S. Army was asked to come to Blair House. There, in his office, now called the Lincoln Room, Francis Preston Blair, on behalf of President Lincoln, offered him the command of the Union forces. Colonel Lee refused, and within three days had resigned his commission in the U.S. Army and joined the Confederacy, not wishing to be forced ever to invade his beloved Virginia. (Years later, in 1958, the Daughters of the Confederacy donated a painting of General Lee to Blair House, and, I was told, had a conniption when they heard this portrait was placed in the Lincoln Room!)

Mr. Blair built the red brick Lee House next door in 1857 for his daughter Elizabeth and her husband, Samuel Phillips Lee, a cousin of Robert E. Lee, who was serving the Union as a naval officer and who rose to become an admiral, another example of how the Civil War divided families. Mr. Blair himself, despite his deep roots in the South, and as a close friend of and at times an emissary of President Lincoln to Jefferson Davis, was so convinced of the legality and necessity of keeping the states together that he wholeheartedly supported the Union's objectives.

His older son, Montgomery Blair, gave up a position on the

Missouri Supreme Court to move to Washington, first to be defending counsel for the famous former slave, Dred Scott, before the U.S. Supreme Court, and then to take the appointment of postmaster general in Mr. Lincoln's cabinet. He was so successful that he almost retired the staggering debt of the postal service which at the time was larger than the national debt. He also created the international postal system and he brought postal services to the rural areas of America by having the railroad carry post offices on their trains. The younger son, Frank Blair, was a congressman from Missouri, credited with persuading the powers that be to keep Missouri in the Union on the eve of the Civil War. He also was a general in Tecumseh Sherman's army.

During the Second World War, the country's involvement in the affairs of the world increased dramatically, and international visitors traveled from afar to confer with the United States government. It was customary then for the president's guests to spend the first night at the White House, and then to take up residence at a hotel. Congress was most unwilling to put up appropriations for a guest house, despite the many requests from the U.S. Department of State. However, the desperation of Eleanor Roosevelt to get the visitors out of the White House prompted a giant effort. Blair House came on the market in 1941 after the death of Gist Blair, Montgomery Blair's second son and owner of the house. It is alleged the money for the purchase of Blair House was put up by Averell Harriman, distinguished diplomat and public servant, who also assisted with the purchase of the Lee House, up for sale in 1943.

The two houses remained unconnected for some years, but were occupied immediately by a succession of official visitors. While the Lee House came on the market void of any furnishings, the Blair House came with a considerable collection of furniture, silver, porcelain – all the objects that a family collects over the years, lovingly and randomly. Since the government took over, the family and other generous Americans have donated furniture and other items to both houses, including some of the Blair and Lee heirlooms.

For close to four years, starting in 1948, the Blair and Lee Houses were in effect the White House of the United States. President Harry S Truman and his family agreed to move back across the street to Blair House, vacating the White House for a while for a much needed major restoration. He and his family had lived at Blair House for the first three months of his presidency to give Mrs. Roosevelt time to vacate her home of many years after the death of her husband, Franklin D. Roosevelt. The Trumans remained there for 3 years and 4 months before the White House restoration was completed, living in the Blair House, using the Lee House for office space, and, cleverly, connecting the two houses. During his first three months there Mr. Truman drafted the Marshall Plan, which brought Germany and the rest of Europe back from the devastation of the Second World War. When in the longer residence he wrote the Truman Doctrine, and was persuaded by his secretary of state Dean Acheson to send troops to Korea. His Cabinet Room, the Lee Dining Room, was also the setting for his poker games.

On November 1, 1950 a Puerto Rican nationalist organization stormed the house to assassinate President Truman. I was told by one of his security guards that the president was hanging out his bedroom window (today's Eisenhower Room) watching the bullets whizzing around until pulled to safety. Another security guard, Leslie Coffelt, lost his life in defense of his president. A plaque commemorating this event is placed on the wrought iron fence just below and west of the Blair front door. Every year on November 1, a small detail from the U.S. Secret Service Uniformed Police holds a ceremony and places a wreath by the plaque. The family of Leslie Coffelt donated their mementos of his service, and, with a generous stipend from the Truman Scholarship Foundation, Blair House turned the downstairs security down-room into a memorial for him.

The two neighboring Victorian houses at Jackson Place around the corner were bought by the government in the early 1970s to add more office space to what was becoming a very busy presidential guesthouse. At the time, administered by the General Services Administration, the U.S. government's landlord, the whole complex was sinking into a decline and closed early May 1982 to overnight visitors, only continuing functions. Within the next six months, acknowledging the importance of the complex, both as historic buildings and national treasures and as tools of American foreign policy the U.S. Congress appropriated 8.9 million for the reconstruction and renovation of the complex. A National Council for the Blair House Restoration was created under the leadership of the Honorable Anne Armstrong, former ambassador to the Court of St. James; the council raised more

than five million dollars in cash or gifts-in-kind to be used for beautification. Heavily involved were the U.S. Chief of Protocol for President
Reagan, Selwa Roosevelt, and the Curator of the Diplomatic Reception Rooms, Clem Conger. Two notable interior decorators, Mark
Hampton and Mario Buatta, were hired with Hampton, the specialist
in the Federal period, doing the Blair and Jackson Place Houses, and
Buatta, known as the Prince of Chintz, the Lee House and the new
primary suite. The complex was reopened April 25, 1988 by President Ronald Reagan and Mrs. Reagan who for six years of their eight
year tenure in the White House had had to put up their official guests
in hotels.

From early 1988 until the end of July 2001, I was its general manager, its chatelaine and, to some, its soul. Known to official Washington and other world capitals as Mrs. V I was the impresario and stage
manager of an exclusive theatre; the resident cast was our 21 permanent State Department employees; the guest actors an assortment of
kings, queens, princes, an emperor and empress, presidents and prime
ministers and their acolytes. Around them hovered a supporting cast
comprising the hierarchy of the U.S. government, starting with our
president and secretary of state. All of us played out a multitude of
scripts with no rehearsals and few repeat performances.

I invite the reader to attend performances featuring leaders from
the world's 191 sovereign states: the royalty, presidents, prime ministers, and their entourages whose skills as well as posturing, occasional pomposity and thieving will amaze. The reader will participate
in a State Visit; peep in on top-level meetings on Middle East peace
when our delicious meals were the only subject on which the participants agreed; learn how the Blair House staff prepared, organized and
rendered service to the nation's distinguished official foreign guests
at this historic, charming and beautiful guest house, and come back-
stage with me, where, in truth, "everything is otherwise." Many world
events of the momentous years from 1988 to mid 2001 unfolded
behind the curtain and security of this unique house, thus continuing
its long tradition of participation in our nation's history.

Blair House is considered an arm of U.S. foreign policy. It is
administered by the U.S. Department of State, the staff is Protocol
Office employees, and I, as general manager, reported directly to the
U.S. chief of protocol, an appointee of the U.S. president. I served

four U.S. presidents, five administrations, and six secretaries of state over thirteen years and four months. I hosted 200 visits of presidents, prime ministers, kings and queens, and had to remain 467 nights at the house; my staff and I served close to 200,000 meals and snacks, 13,500 people above and beyond overnight and other guests toured the house, and I personally handled and arranged half million stems of flowers.

My position was unique. While other presidential guest houses in the world exist, I have it on the best of authority – our distinguished guests who have stayed in all of them – that there is none like Blair House.

The stage is now set;
All the props are in place;
I raise the curtain
and
I invite the reader to meet the movers and shakers – the actors – of our world.

THE CAST

I. *RONALD W. REAGAN, U.S. PRESIDENT*
George P. Shultz, U.S. Secretary of State
Selwa "Lucky" Roosevelt, U.S. Chief of Protocol

II. *GEORGE H.W. BUSH, U.S. PRESIDENT*
James A. Baker, U.S. Secretary of State 1989-1992
Lawrence Eagleburger, U.S. Secretary of State 1992
Joseph V. Reed, U.S. Chief of Protocol 1989-1991
James G. Weinmann, U.S. Chief of Protocol 1991-1992

III. *WILLIAM J. CLINTON, U.S. PRESIDENT*
Warren Christopher, U.S. Secretary of State 1993-1996
Madeleine Albright, U.S. Secretary of State 1997-2000
Molly Raiser, U.S. Chief of Protocol 1993-1996
Mary Mel French, U.S. Chief of Protocol 1997-2000

IV. *GEORGE W. BUSH, U.S. PRESIDENT*
Colin Powell, U.S. Secretary of State
Donald B. Ensenat, U.S. Chief of Protocol

Benedicte Valentiner	General Manager
Mike Coughlin	Project Manager
Don Blake	Security Guru
Sam Castleman, Randy Bumgardner	Deputy General Managers
Russell Cronkhite, Ian Knox	Executive Chefs
Greg Uhlein, Kym Gibson, Paul Akerboom, Ian Knox	Assistant Chefs
Jose Fuster	Head Butler
Smile Saint-Aubin, Antonio Rodriguez	Assistant Butlers
Jemma Rennie	Head Housekeeper
Lynn Keith, Tabitha Bullock	Administrative Officers
Teresinha Diaz	Parlormaid
Marinete Saias, Magna Cajina	Chambermaids
Agustinha Dos Santos, Vel Xirocotas	Laundresses
Frankie Blair, Sean Irby	Housemen
Cassandra Stone, Mary Williams, Candace Shireman	Curators
Julian Pike, Carolyn Parker, George Wilks, Brent Hancock	Facilities Managers
Lionel Harrison, Velma Newman	Custodial Staff
Luisa Salvi	Special Part-Timer
Bill Evans, Roy Bauman, Paul Rogers, Rodrick Waters and their gallant staff:	Security Chiefs

Darren Bailey, E. Besell, Paul Bessett, Michael Cooney, Donald Cossar, Mr. Crawford, Victor Freeman, Kenneth J. Gibson, Charles Le King, Albert Livingston, Ed Rosado, Da Silva, F. Smegelsky, Jacquet Thompson, Chris Thomson, Renzo Torchiani

ACT I

RONALD W. REAGAN
The President

***

GEORGE P. SHULTZ
The Secretary of State

***

SELWA "Lucky" ROOSEVELT
The Chief of Protocol

CHAPTER 1

BLAIR HOUSE RAISES ITS CURTAIN

*"Her voice was ever soft, gentle and low,
an excellent thing in woman."*

William Shakespeare

"General Secretary Gorbachev, if you seek peace, if you seek prosperity for the Soviet Union and Eastern Europe, if you seek liberalization, come here to this gate! Mr. Gorbachev, open this gate! Mr. Gorbachev, tear down this wall!"

It was early June 1987, and President Ronald Reagan had just hurled that challenge over the Berlin Wall to Secretary Mikhail Gorbachev, only one of the momentous events that were happening all over the world.

It was an exciting time, but I was but a spectator. I followed the stirring events carefully, but at what seemed to me a great distance. True, I was in Washington and working for a United States Senator, a job that to an observer might appear to be in the thick of world changing activities. I greatly respected my boss, Sen. Pete V. Domenici (R-N.M.), and when I first went to work for him the job actually did seem involving. I created his Division of Communications and then took charge of it, supervising the staff that handled his letters to constituents, newsletter mailings, and computer operations. For the past year I had also been his office manager. But after over six years the tasks had begun to be altogether too repetitious for me, and I was itching to do something different. Maybe, I thought, I should return to my first love: the international hotel business.

But how to get out?

I examined my choices. I had discreetly put out feelers with friends in the international community such as the World Bank, IMF, and the Inter-American Development Bank, but my background was too checkered and just not the right fit.

Then a telephone call energized my efforts to move on with my life. It was midnight, but my friend Neb sounded as cheery as if the day were new. "Benedicte," he said, "I am in town for a meeting and return home tomorrow, but Prue would never forgive me if I did not call you first." My friend since 25 years, Neboysha Brashich, a Foreign Service officer, at this time headed the U.S. AID effort in Belize.

Neb asked how I enjoyed my work for Senator Domenici. "Neb," I responded, "I am so bored by the parochial issues of New Mexico – how can I get myself back into the international world, preferably something to do with the hospitality industry?" I was not as callous about my beloved home state of New Mexico as I sounded, but six plus years with the Senator, dealing entirely with state and constituent issues, had left me weary and dull. "To use an analogy, Neb, I was asked to design a car, build a car, test drive a car, market a car, and now that I am maintaining that damn car, I have discovered I am not a maintenance person."

Neb arranged for an introduction to John St. Denis at State who concluded that with my varied international background, my proficiency in many languages and my ease with different cultures, I would fit well in the Protocol Office of the Department of State. When my international background and my extensive hotel experience were mentioned to Chuck Angulo, Executive Director of the Protocol Office, Chuck immediately exclaimed: "Blair House!"

Blair House, the President's Guest House, was the very private complex of four historic buildings across from the White House. It was so exclusive that only Chiefs of State and Heads of Government ever received an invitation from the President to stay there. President Harry S Truman and his family lived there for more than three years during a major White House restoration.

The restoration of this beautiful complex had begun six years earlier, long before I became involved in it. The federal government acquired it at the end of World War II to house the President's foreign visitors, and in the years that followed the four old houses gradually sank into a state of genteel shabbiness, with peeling paint, holes in ceilings and floors, and aging and unreliable plumbing, heating and electricity. In the spring of 1982 government officials decided that the complex was not just a vital adjunct of foreign policy but a national treasure; a bipartisan Congress appropriated $8.6 million to restore and renovate the four buildings, and construct a new fifth building to house a small ballroom and a safer primary suite. During the six years that it took to complete the project, official foreign visitors were accommodated in hotels around Washington.

Chuck Angulo and I hit it off right away. His office walls sported gorgeous huipiles from Guatemala where he had been stationed and where my mother and I had experienced the devastating earthquake in February 1976. Only halfway through our hour long discussion did we get around to my resume, and his search for a person to manage Blair House, which was to reopen within the next six months. The general manager was not well and not expected to stay on. Did I have any problem with timing? I could wait as long as it took, I said. He asked me to keep in touch on a monthly basis, which I did.

My chances, when I looked at them realistically, didn't look promising. I knew <u>no one</u> in the decision-making process who could speak up on my behalf. My only chance at the job was on merit and my hotel experience; but I did have one other advantage: Chuck Angulo showed himself to be a fine ally and supporter. He later told me that after meeting me, a couple of times a month he put my resume on the desk of Chief of Protocol Lucky Roosevelt, who invariably pushed it away asking him why he continued to press this resume upon her.

In January 1988 Chuck told me they were close to a development. When the manager resigned her position the search for a replacement began, and I was in contention. Chuck's persistence had paid off, and Ambassador Roosevelt interviewed me in early February. When I was called back for a second interview in her office, this time with a roomful of senior protocol staff, it was clear that the moment of truth had arrived.

I carefully put myself together. During my first meeting with Ambassador Roosevelt, I dressed all in black and white; for this critical return engagement I wore my Cynthia Howie power dress with checks of burgundy and navy, long navy leather boots, a lovely pink pearl necklace that my parents gave me as a 25th birthday present, and my grey Persian Lamb fur coat. I was dressed for success. I looked calm and elegant, competent and focused as I arrived.

Inside, however, inside I was quaking.

Chuck Angulo met me at the State Department entrance with Mike Coughlin, a distinguished Foreign Service officer, the Blair House project coordinator. Mike would become my mentor, leading me through the labyrinth of government paperwork and complications for the next two years. Both men strongly felt that the Blair House general manager should not be a political appointment. "Blair House needs continuity, Mrs. Valentiner," Mike stressed during our five-minute walk in the State Department foyer. "The manager must remain when the administration changes." I made a mental note to bring the subject up during the interview and to cite the importance of an institutional memory in the staff collective.

Then it was show time. I kept a tight rein on my composure as I entered the room, the focal point of all eyes. After introducing me to her closest associates, Ambassador Roosevelt noted that although she had already had a similar conversation with me a week earlier, she was inviting me to talk about myself, my background, my life and experiences, and my interests for a second time.

"Although I am American by choice," I began, "I remain so deeply grateful that I was born and raised in a small progressive nation like Denmark." I told them about my wonderful, supportive parents and my two brothers. My father was an officer of the Royal Danish Navy. He died an Admiral in 1972. My parents were very hospitable and with many foreign visitors English was a common language. From an early age I was hanging around the kitchen learning how to cook, how to serve, how to lay a table and how to give a party. Having been born in the beginning of the Second World War, I vaguely remember the German occupation of my country; both my parents were in the Resistance. Although I graduated from high school and later Copenhagen Business School in Denmark, I was fortunate to spend two and a half years, beginning at age 14, in Stockholm, Sweden, where my father was Danish Naval Attache. I was 15 when I met and was mesmerized by the first female executive of a major Swedish hotel, thus paving the way for my career choice. "I never wavered in this goal, every chance I got I took extra courses, worked abroad, making me able to cope in six languages." I worked during holidays in the hotel and restaurant business in Scotland and Switzerland; and when my father was posted to Washington in 1963 as Naval Attache, Danish representative to NATO's Standing Group and SACLANT I jumped at the chance to work for American hotels.

The seven years I worked for the International Director of Sales at the Shoreham Hotel in Washington D.C. were among the happiest in my life. My boss was German born Ruth S. Hamory – my mentor, fairy godmother and beloved friend till her death (in 2007.) Without her guidance through the maze of the American business practices, I would have failed miserably.

Washington D.C. was a sleepy town back then, with few good restaurants and not much theatre and music. To compensate for the cultural void our social life was elegant and sophisticated, and everyone entertained at home. My large circle of friends included many in the diplomatic corps. Every party I gave in my one-bedroom apartment on 29th Street was a mini United Nations. I prepared all the food myself, served it, and gave parties from eight to sixty guests, including ambassadors and admirals, colleagues of my father, who felt obligated to keep an eye on me after his return to Denmark in 1966.

In 1968, I told my audience, on the night of Robert Kennedy's assassination in Los Angeles I tore up my application for U.S. citizenship in a fit of fury. I wanted nothing to do with this violent and intolerant country any longer, having lived here during the assassinations of John F. Kennedy and Martin Luther King, whose murder set off rioting and looting in the streets of Washington. It took me a year to reassess my desires and to reapply for citizenship. Consequently I have always felt that I was baptized by fire as an American citizen.

"I married Lieutenant Colonel Kent Carnie, a falconer, in 1969," I continued. When he retired from the U.S. Army in 1972 we went to Iran to study and band birds of prey for the Shah's government – in between we hawked in Scotland, and lived six months in Spain. We traveled with a wirehaired dachshund, Napoleon, starting my own continuous ownership of that breed.

It was clear that I was holding the interest of the group, several of whom knew the Middle East and its tradition of falconry.

And I continued my saga. We lived in San Miguel de Allende, Mexico, for two years where I learned to weave and then settled in Santa Fe, New Mexico, where, I went on, "I maintained a weaving studio, worked in an art gallery, and for five years worked for the Minority Whip of the State House of Representatives which for me was a continuing lesson in citizenship. When Kent and I divorced, and we remain dear friends, I returned to Washington to work for Senator Domenici."

As I finished there were few questions, so that the session was more like a one-woman show. I felt that they were deeply interested in a life with so many chapters. I was confident that my career matched the job description perfectly. I was exhausted, but my anxiety had turned to elation with an adrenalin high coursing through my veins.

Everything, it seemed, had fallen into place perfectly with an uncanny precision. They were certainly attentive; Mike Coughlin commented afterwards that "they were mesmerized." Right after the interview, riding over with the ambassador, Mike Coughlin took me to see Blair House from the inside for the first time, an additional sign that I was being seriously considered for the job.

At that moment, February of 1988, the basic renovations were in place, and a new building that housed the Garden Room and the Primary Suite was finished. The exterior, however, still looked like a construction site – a tangle of chain-link fences, dug-up sidewalks, and warning signs. Only the basement entrance was open. Mike and I walked up the inside stairway to the first floor. The furnishings were sparse, most still packed up, but the first thing I noticed was glorious wallpaper, spread out in sections on the floors of the Blair Dining Room and Rear Drawing Room. This exquisite work of art, with gorgeous scenes of trees, flowers and exotic birds on a brilliant emerald green background, hand-painted on several layers of rice paper in mid-18th century China, had been exported to England, and until the late 1950s had decorated walls at Ashburnham House near Westminster. After restoration in Hong Kong it was sold at an auction in New York to Douglas Dillon, Secretary of the Treasury in the Kennedy cabinet, who gave it to the Lee House, along with a notable collection of furniture and carpets.

The craftspeople I met that day included Craig Maue and Craig Littlewood, master restorers of antique chandeliers. The two Craigs were dissecting the chandeliers, carefully restoring each facet to its former glory. "Never use liquid cleaning spray on the chandeliers," said the Craigs. "Just feather-dust them, and bring us back annually for restoration and maintenance."

As Mike walked me through the house, I saw what a daunting project the restoration was. Some furniture back from storage was waiting to be shipped out for reupholstering; a thousand storage boxes, stacked high in various pantries, were waiting to be unpacked; every room was filled with workmen and their tools, dust and debris. The size of the complex, 70,000 square feet over five stories in four old houses and one new building, boggled my mind imagining myself its chatelaine. The official count was 109 rooms.

Shortly after, Chuck Angulo asked me to name a reference in the Senator's office. No longer could I keep this quest of mine a secret. I suggested Angela Raish, the Senator's personal assistant, who had become a friend, and as her husband, Robert Raish, was a Captain USN Ret., we had found common ground in our backgrounds as well.

I found Angela in the Senator's office. "Angela, you have always told me to get out of here, to get on with my life," and I asked if she would feel comfortable recommending me for a position when Chuck Angulo of the Department of State called. "Of course, Benedicte, and what is this position?"

"General Manager of Blair House."

She staggered back, and exclaimed: "Benedicte, there are people in this town that would <u>kill</u> for that job."

When Angulo called, Angela elaborated not only on the way I carried out my responsibilities for the Senator, but – having been a guest in my home often – how I personally lived and entertained. Her glowing recommendation helped send me on my way.

A few days later, Ambassador Roosevelt called to offer me the position, subject to a security check. In mid-March, while my top security clearance at the State Department was being processed, my boss on the Hill detailed me over to Blair House, per special request of Ambassador Roosevelt who needed me well in advance of the gala opening on April 25. In his typical low-key fashion, Senator Domenici wished me luck and expressed sadness at my departure. I thanked him for permitting me to start right away at Blair House while still on his payroll. "It is no problem at all, Benedicte," he said. "Just be sure that your work up here gets done as well." So for the next six weeks I maintained a nightmarish schedule, stopping in Domenici's office a couple of nights a week after a full day at Blair House, and working weekends at both places.

I had no help from my assistant manager. During the six weeks of scrubbing and cleaning and unpacking, she assigned herself to looking after the President's infrequent foreign visitors, still being put up in hotels. So the maids and I, in large aprons, unpacked boxes as fast as they came out of storage, particularly, thinking of the forthcoming gala, searching for ashtrays and lamps. As we were not able to find enough closet space or to figure out when and if we would use certain pieces, we had taken to hide the porcelain and other promising goodies in weird places.

I was appalled to find electrical stoves and ovens in the Blair House kitchens. "There are no chefs alive who would want to cook on electricity – they want gas," I protested. Blair House Executive Chef Russell Cronkhite, on board a month earlier than me, was fully in accord. Forgetting about or blissfully unaware of the requirement to get everything cleared through the bureaucratic maze, he sprang into action. Without consulting with the Protocol Office, he called the Washington Gas Co. to talk about switching to gas. The company was thrilled to hear from us, especially because Blair House in earlier days had cooked with gas. Chef also persuaded the Hobart Company to exchange the electric ovens and stoves it had donated to the Blair House Restoration Fund for gas ovens and stoves.

All of this was done without contacting the State Department entities that oversee purchasing – a misstep that brought on a climate of strife, adversity and animosity with some of our colleagues at State that lasted for years. Chef had acted innocently, and with the best intentions, but in dealing with government bureaucracy the learning curve for both Russell and me sometimes curved in the wrong direction. However, at this time he prevailed, and as a gift the Washington Gas Co. restored our four exterior gas lamps, and donated gas for them in perpetuity. Three days before the gala, the gas lamps were lit, marking the unofficial beginning of a new era in the history of Blair House. While waiting for the exchange of the equipment, however, we had no functioning kitchen for opening night, and had to rely on caterers then and for some months thereafter. As of September, with the kitchens up and running, we started preparing all meals ourselves, and in the process gained a reputation for excellence.

In the period leading up to the gala reception, the staff slowly took shape. Ambassador Roosevelt had carefully put it together, and I had only to hire some of the maids, and later some housemen. The head butler did not get security clearance until June. We were a small team but we delivered. Much of our effort was devoted to daily upkeep and cleaning up after the workmen. In the larger Blair Pantry we unpacked and inventoried the newly donated crystal and china from the Lenox Company and silver tableware from Tiffany, and made storage decisions.

The pantry was long, narrow and impractical. Finding a solution put me into a tug-of-war with the General Services Administration (GSA), a federal agency in charge of the government's buildings, over my request for 16 more shelves and 700 cup hooks.

Mr. Payne called me.

"What do you need seven hundred cup hooks for, lady?" he asked.

"Mr. Payne, how good of you to return my call, I am most appreciative," I countered. "Have you been able to see the entire house yet? I would be so pleased to show it to you, and afterwards we can discuss the few extras I need here."

I walked Mr. Payne from the top of the fourth floor, through bedrooms, bathrooms, drawing and dining rooms of the four houses, through kitchens and storerooms, and ended my tour in the Blair Pantry. My staff had opened the boxes of coffee and tea cups, demitasse, and soup cups, 700 in all, and had laid out samples of each kind for his perusal.

He got my message – and I got my 16 shelves and 700 cup hooks.

Ambassador Roosevelt frequently called. "What, Mrs. V, have you unpacked today?" she would ask. "I am coming over tonight so we can put out objets d'art in the bedrooms." At first I told her in detail what we had unpacked in the Blair Pantry, and gave my opinion of where those newly-unpacked pieces ought to go. I learned quickly that such suggestions were not appreciated as our chief of protocol took tremendous pride in making such decisions herself. I learned to ask her casually where she intended to work that evening, after which Head Housekeeper Jemma Rennie and I would show her only the objects that we thought fit that area.

Workmen were in and out every day, bringing in a constant stream of telephones, carpeting, furniture, and boxes. One day when Ambassador Roosevelt turned into the Front Office on the basement level, a man carrying a carpet, hard on her heels, accidentally hit the sprinkler head in the ceiling just outside the door. Bedlam ensued, with greasy, dirty, and foul-smelling water pouring out of the ceiling, barely missing Ambassador Roosevelt. When the fire alarm went off, the security officers and the GSA personnel knew where to turn off the water and how to deal with the emergency. I would not have known what to do. The incident made me realize how interdependent we were, and how important it was to foster a spirit of teamwork among the staff. Meanwhile, our chief, enveloped in mink, remained standing like a statue in water, most seriously put out. I did not dare laugh. The poor carpet man, a regular at the house, was so ashamed that he disguised himself with dark glasses, and hid behind doors whenever he saw Ambassador Roosevelt.

One day a GSA carpenter invited me to watch as he chipped away at the fireplace mantel in the Truman Study. His skillful prodding and scraping slowly revealed an exquisite design hidden beneath several layers of paint. This mantel, circa 1902 and attributed to the great Gilded Age architect Stanford White, had been brought with President Truman from the White House. He and his family moved in here in November 1948 while the White House was gutted and rebuilt, a restoration that took three years and four months. The mantel came from the bedroom of Edith Roosevelt, wife of President Teddy Roosevelt. Blair House "forgot" to return it, and the mantel remains at Blair House, with the design now outlined in gold.

Interestingly, when Congress made the $8.6 million appropriation, care was taken that the funds cover only structural renovation. No government money was to be used for interior décor or furnishings. Congress didn't want to pay for fancy frills.

As a supplement to the federal appropriation, more than $5 million of gifts-in-kind and in cash were donated by generous American citizens and corporations. This relationship between government and the private sector is unheard of elsewhere in the world, and I always took great pride in pointing it out to our visitors. These donations were raised through the efforts of the National Council for the Restoration of Blair House, headed by the Honorable Anne

Armstrong, U.S. Ambassador to the Court of St. James during the Ford Administration.

Around midday on the day the council members were going to be honored by a presidential gala, I had just come downstairs when I heard for the millionth time the barking, grating, ever-demanding, never-satisfied voice of my boss, Ambassador Roosevelt.

"Mrs. V!"

The previous hour the head housekeeper and I had checked and double-checked the first floor, making sure that every surface was dusted, every bulb lit, every pillow puffed up, and everything was arranged perfectly.

Our eyes had to be especially sharp, for this was to be the big curtain-raiser for the revered old structure on Pennsylvania Avenue. Only hours later the lights would blaze from every window as President and Mrs. Ronald Reagan hosted a gala reception to celebrate its long-awaited reopening after six years of renovations. As I walked slowly through the main floor I wondered, whenever I caught a glimpse of the White House through the south windows, whether the Reagans, getting ready for this night to come, might be feeling just the least bit excited too.

The day-long preparations for the big event had drained my energies. I was pooped, and a little snack would provide a lift. I knew our chef had put out sandwiches for the staff in the Front Office. So I slipped downstairs to the basement called the ground floor. It's the part of the complex that only few of our guests see, and it's extensive, for Blair House consists of a four-building complex, and the subterranean ground floor extends unbroken under all of them. It houses offices, staff lounges, kitchens and security command posts.

On that afternoon of April 25, 1988, in the last year of the second Reagan presidency, I was six weeks into my job as general manager of Blair House, an assignment that looked to be the biggest challenge of my life. It would make me an actor in helping to advance the foreign policy of the United States – a minor role, of course, but not an insignificant one. Meals and lodgings for the Prime Minister of the United Kingdom, the President of the USSR, the modern mandarins of China, every cog in the diplomatic apparatus of the world would be entrusted to my care. When they came from the four corners of the earth to see the President they would be staying here, often with a sizable entourage of assistants and advisors. The administration did not want to bear any diplomatic displeasure because the chicken was rubbery or the bed lumpy. Every whim would be indulged not just within reason but actually beyond. My job would be to pamper our guests shamelessly at America's most prestigious bed and breakfast.

I was ready for that task, but what I longed for at that moment was a few minutes of peace and quiet and food. Yet just as I rounded the corner to the passage outside the offices, the voice that of all voices I least wanted to hear had rung out of the silence.

"Mrs. V!"

I headed towards the source of the voice, and found her sitting at the administrative officer's desk, less chipper than usual, picking at a sandwich and looking just as fatigued as I felt after the arduous labor of preparing the 70,000 square foot complex for the opening.

Her stress and tension had to be even greater than my own. Selwa "Lucky" Roosevelt had been working on the renovation for six years, since shortly after President Ronald Reagan had appointed her the Nation's Chief of Protocol.

The well-dressed ambassador, of Lebanese descent and a Roosevelt by marriage, was a small, good-looking, dark-haired woman with enormous brown eyes and beautiful skin. But her voice – ah, that voice – had been the bane of my existence for the last six weeks. It was a curse, an affliction from which I rarely could escape. It pursued me and my staff, incessantly throwing instructions, commands, requests, and questions at us at the most unexpected moments. We heard it during five-hour ordeals while trailing behind its owner, giving us endless directives on the movement of furniture, placement of china and crystal, ordering of the hundreds of items required to run a five-star hotel – followed by the unavoidable repeat of the instructions, as well as changes in what had already been decreed.

I had two sources of temporary relief. One was the answering machine I had hooked up to my home telephone bringing me some hours of escape from Mrs. Roosevelt's constant, nagging intrusion into my existence. And, since I was for a while still an employee of the U.S. Senate, and thus could still return to those duties if I chose, I took some solace in ducking into my bathroom off my office, where I could shake my fists to the ceiling, and whisper: "I do not have to take this anymore."

I was exhausted. I had not been able to sleep the previous night – tossing and turning with dreams of what could go wrong at the gala. Personally other things ranked higher – like sorting through and stowing away thousands of objects coming back from storage; making decisions on everything from telephones to disposing of unwanted items ("de-accessing" is the government term) and the ensuing battles with the Associate Curator; cataloging the new gifts of linen and china; and generally bringing order out of chaos. On the other hand I knew that Ambassador Roosevelt and her staff in the Protocol Office for years had envisioned this night as a milestone in Blair House history. The last thing I wanted was criticism, problems, or questions. The past six weeks, no matter how exciting or stimulating or challenging, had been anything but a bed of roses, and I did not need any more of Ambassador Roosevelt's input, which, however instructive or useful, was never complimentary. Was I passing muster? It was hard to tell.

So I was surprised, almost stunned, when she smiled at me.

"Mrs. V," she said, "I threw you in the water – and you swam."

Thus today I found myself installed at Blair House, ready, willing, and – cross my fingers – able to live up to expectations. I was not yet in charge, however. Ambassador Roosevelt was leaving no part of the planning to someone whom she had not worked with before; the Ceremonial staff of the Protocol Office was in command of the overall party planning, while I was responsible for the sparkling conditions of the house brought about by my staff. And my focus was totally on order, not on frills. This date was a deadline for me, rather than what the rest of the Protocol staff called The Event. Preparing and planning was much more important and enjoyable to me than were the events themselves, a point of view that set me apart from the Protocol people.

The guests, invited to wander throughout the entire house, were oblivious to the fact that it was like Aladdin's Cave under many beds, many treasures hidden from view by the beautiful bedspreads and bed skirts. The flowers were prepared by florist friends of the ambassador's, a joy that I would later assume; all the lamps were turned on, the caterers had set up buffets and bars everywhere covered with flowered tablecloths and votive candles, and left to me was hoping that my staff would remain where they had been assigned; and to figure out what to wear. I was woefully short of a presidential wardrobe, but for the occasion I did have a rather rich-looking turquoise Thai silk suit. Everyone on the Protocol staff was dressed beautifully and expensively and with make-up to die for, as was the jewelry worn by the guests.

When the deputy chief of protocol relieved me at my post by the entrance door, I was dispatched to join my staff in the Blair Drawing Room to meet President and Mrs. Reagan. After the assassination attempt on his life they never walked anywhere, so they arrived by limousine at the 700 Jackson Place entrance, avoiding the press stationed outside in Pennsylvania Avenue and enabling them to see more of the renovation by means of a walk through the two Jackson Place houses. Ambassador Roosevelt escorted them to our brand new guest book, inscribed in blue and gold by the Protocol Office calligrapher, and laid out for them on the desk outside the office which later was to be used by Protocol staff during visits. Randy Bumgardner, a young Protocol Visits Officer, later handpicked by me to become my deputy, who had been assigned a million tasks by Ambassador Roosevelt associated with the renovation, was rewarded for all his work with the responsibility of handing the pen to President and Mrs. Reagan. Then the Reagans entered the Blair Drawing Room to meet their presidential guest house staff, and I got my first glimpse of this famous couple.

Ambassador Roosevelt introduced me and I was greeted charmingly, congratulated and wished great luck by Mrs. Reagan, dressed in a simple and sleek black dress wearing a three string pearl necklace and matching bracelet. The President, in a dark suit with a red silk tie, was taller than I had imagined. Although wearing his usual crooked grin, he seemed less personal than his wife. Each staff member had a photo taken with both of them. And then we were shooed out, back to our assigned posts. This small ceremony took four minutes. I'd have loved to find out how this particular choreography had been written up for the President by his advance team.

Ambassador Roosevelt and I had met with President Reagan's advance people shortly before the gala. In modern government circles no high-ranking administration official ever goes anywhere until his advance people work out all the details. Every move is planned in advance, charted and checked for maximum effect. If it's a presidential or vice-presidential visit, U.S. Secret Service (USSS) agents are also part of the advance party to check out the security of the location.

The itinerary is then passed on to the White House Communications Agency (WHCA), White House media people, the president's (or vice-president's) personal staff (bearers of the tea bags and spare tie in case of a spill), the personal physician, and the carrier of the black bag – with instructions for the launching of nuclear weapons.

This was my first experience with advance people. Dealing with White House personnel can be daunting, but dealing with White House advance people – because of their inflated sense of power and importance – can be overwhelming.

Every step and every move of the President this evening was choreographed in advance. The hours that it took for the advance team to debate, discuss and disagree with the suggestions of Ambassador Roosevelt boggled the mind. Finally, after what seemed like the most comical attention to tiny details ever seen, they all reached agreement. Every step that President Reagan would take was counted, measured, and – the advance team made clear – had to be strictly adhered to. Even the single step he would take to get on the riser in the Garden Room for his speech was discussed at length; it had to be of a specific height, no variation allowed. The leader of the advance team, a man in his forties, walked and counted every single step himself, so this could be relayed to the President and no doubt learned by heart; I wondered how a grown man could do this for a living! Later I would observe that neither the first George Bush nor Bill Clinton carried advance preparations to such silly extremes.

President Reagan, on the other hand, was completely programmed. Although the minute planning of every detail seemed excessive at the time, I have since wondered whether it had anything to do with the cruel disease that took his mind, and may have been in its early stages then.

I kept away from the Garden Room during President Reagan's speech to the National Council. Such occasions were for guests, not staff members. And this evening, in particular, was surely to be savored by those who had devoted so much of their time to it. A high point for me was again meeting Robin Chandler Duke, wife of Angier Biddle Duke, former chief of protocol and former U.S. ambassador to Spain and Denmark. Both were intimately connected with the history of the house. During her husband's tenure as chief of protocol in the beginning of the 1960s she had presided over the only other full scale restoration of the President's Guest House, at that time consisting only of the Blair and Lee Houses. Robin Duke was vice chair of the National Council for the Restoration of Blair House.

When Robin Duke entered the Lee House, she casually looked past me, and, disregarding my outstretched hand, ignoring my words of welcome, and oblivious to my introduction of myself, charged past me, shrieking at the top of her voice: "my chairs, my beautiful chairs, you kept my chairs."

In the early sixties she had commissioned chair covers in blue on cream to adorn the 18 dining room chairs in the Lee Dining Room. The design was the grape leaf motive of the china export porcelain collected by the Blairs and Lees when these families owned the two houses. Robin Duke had conceived the brilliant idea to ask the wives of the cabinet secretaries of President Kennedy to embroider them. Each chair was marked with a small plaque listing which lady had embroidered the cover; for example Mrs. Lyndon B. Johnson had made one, as had Mrs. Dean Rusk and Mrs. Robert Kennedy, the wives of the vice president, the secretary of state, and the attorney general respectively. Similarly, "Prince of Chintz" Mario Buatta, entrusted with redecorating the entire Lee House, had created an elegant and emphatically blue Lee Dining Room, using as much of its historic pieces as possible.

Years later when I showed Eunice Shriver, the sister of President John F. Kennedy, through Blair House I commented as we reached the Lee Dining Room: "You recall of course when Robin Duke asked the wives of President Kennedy's cabinet secretaries to embroider these chairs and your own sister-in-law, Ethel Kennedy, did one of them?"

Mrs. Shriver looked at me incredulously: "Ethel – Ethel cannot set a stitch – she sent it to the nuns."

Mrs. Reagan returned several times to Blair House, gracious and relaxed, and always appreciative of small kindnesses. She beamed when our kitchen presented her with a "CARE" basket of special cookies, without nuts, to take back to the President. Nancy Reagan was beautifully dressed and coiffed, but alarmingly thin. Her women friends were the same: thin, massaged to death, nipped and tucked, face-lifted, with thin and breakable legs, and all decked in gold jewelry during the day, and something glittery during the evening. They looked expensive but not particularly healthy.

Publicity about Blair House continued into the fall. Ambassador Roosevelt had issued the decree that all inquiries should go through her State Department office. I grew up in a family tradition that "your name must never appear in the press except at birth, marriage and death," so that suited me fine. During the four days between the gala of President Reagan and Secretary George Shultz' diplomatic reception the newspapers broke the story about the gala and reopening of the house. There was a tiny blurb about me as the new general manager; a slightly longer story about the restoration and Ambassador Roosevelt. But the story that got the most space was a look at the professional life of our Executive Chef. The ambassador had specifically asked the Washington Post journalist to call Russell, as she could not remember all the details of his background and, as he told me later: "the journalist and I just got talking, Mrs. V." A celebratory lunch hosted by the ambassador at her club for her senior staff on the day this article was published is etched on my mind. The chief of protocol and some of her female staffers, furious about the publicity bestowed on Chef, raked their sharp fingernails over the (fortunately absent) Russell, calling him pompous and puffed with self-importance. While these words were somewhat justified regarding his demeanor it was certainly not a correct assessment of his character. But, was I ever grateful for having warranted just a few lines!

And then there was a story about our toilet paper.

We used two kinds of toilet paper, one for the working staff, and a better and softer variety for guests. Inadvertently the less desirable, scratchier kind was placed in the first floor ladies' room. Peggy Coopersmith, a renowned Democrat with a stellar reputation at the highest level, was the recipient of the scratches, and had innocently mentioned it in fun. Naturally the press picked it up. One happy consequence, however, was an annual generous donation from her to the Blair House Restoration Fund, designated for "soft tissue."

Although articles in the Washington Post Sunday Magazine, Architectural Digest and Southern Living were accurate and inoffensive, we remained careful around the press.

By the end of the second Reagan administration Blair House was once again hitting on all cylinders. All of the staff played a part in that but most of the credit goes to Lucky Roosevelt. She was perfectly suited to bring it off. Married to Archie Roosevelt, a grandson of President Teddy Roosevelt, she had pursued a career in journalism while accompanying her husband to several extended Central Intelligence Agency assignments in the Middle East and Spain. Through the Roosevelt family connection she knew everybody who mattered in American political and diplomatic life, and she knew what was required to deal with the highest echelon of international society. She was hard working, tenacious, creative, imperious, tough as nails, and very direct, capable of banging heads together, as well as nails into the walls, and, frequently, driving everyone, including me, bananas. I had great respect for her and I love this story: while beset with a difficult restoration problem, she charged into the office of a high ranking State Department official (and I really, really want this person to have been Secretary of State George Shultz), banged her hand on his table and said: "The trouble with you people here is that none of you have any balls."

Without the energy she generated, this grand project would have fallen flat. Few others would have had the nerve, temerity and perseverance to do the necessary bargaining, placating, cajoling, and persuading the people with decision-making power at the White House, Department of State, General Services Administration, Congress, Secret Service, Diplomatic Security and the city government of Washington.

This daughter of Lebanese immigrants may have been the only chief of protocol with the courage, foresight and tolerance to hire an immigrant with an accent, me, to manage Blair House. She was perfectly aware of the chance she was taking, awareness implicit in the comment she made to me several times: "You are now playing in the big league, Mrs. V."

If, as Angela Raish told me, there are people who would kill for the job, I don't condone the act but I understand the temptation. Being the general manager of Blair House is big-league. Historic events occurred here. The people who made world-shaking decisions were within arm's reach. I saw these movers and shakers in their public moments as well as their more private and less guarded moments. It was often the little things said and done, things of which the public was unaware, that illuminated their real character and their values. Over the next 13 years I would see very influential people do wonderful little things, and other very influential people do things that were not so wonderful.

I didn't know during those early months that I would be at Blair House for more than 13 years. I couldn't imagine then how much there was to learn about running the world's most diplomatically significant bed and breakfast, nor how that learning would give me the experience and confidence that would help me to do the job better. In working with advance people, for example, I learned not to let them push me around. I would take charge of the situation, ask what the team wished to accomplish, what they expected of us, and then I would suggest how we could best meet their needs. While dealing with up to 40 advance people, representing as many as ten different entities, would remain challenging, I discovered that my take-charge approach worked, and that they were grateful for the expertise which I and my staff could provide.

Early on in my stay I was frequently asked how I ended up as general manager of Blair House. The question was often shaded with an ever-so-slight inference that I must have known someone important, that I could not possibly have done it on my own merits. Not a flattering inference, but that's hyper-status-conscious Washington for you. I would tell them the truth: that I had turned up at the right time by sheer chance, that I was lucky, that circumstances and events favored me. Ambassador Roosevelt put it another way, maintaining that "it was Fate which brought you to me, Mrs. V."

But I believe in my heart, even more intensely than on the day I was interviewed for it, that this job, which called on all my skills and experience, was the work I was born to do.

CHAPTER 2

OUR FIRST VISITS

"There is nothing which has yet been contrived by man, by which so much happiness is produced as by a good tavern or inn."

Dr. Samuel Johnson

She appeared on the small landing, directly above me, and smiled. Dressed in a two piece gold and pink long silk dress, her hair coiffed to perfection, she was so impressive that I could not help myself, but blurted out: "I know, Prime Minister, it is quite inappropriate for me to say so, but you look absolutely smashing." She chuckled. "It is <u>never</u> inappropriate to say so," said Margaret Thatcher, The Right Honorable The Prime Minister of The United Kingdom of Great Britain and Northern Ireland, as she walked down the stairs to begin her gala evening at the White House, an emotional and heartfelt occasion hosted by Ronald Reagan in honor of the world leader he was closest to in terms of philosophy and ideology. She was also, in November 1988, the last official visitor of our President.

Prime Minister Thatcher had arrived the preceding evening at Andrews Air Force Base (AAFB) outside Washington D.C., duly received by Secretary Shultz. Two military helicopters carried the principal party to the Washington Monument, and five minutes later they were turned over to my care. The preparations, as always, were detailed but made considerably more difficult by the hands-on personal involvement of the chief of protocol. Ambassador Roosevelt did not yet really trust her Blair House staff to do a visit on our own, as we had only been assembled some nine months before.

Emotions those last months were slightly out of control. But, I was, at least, grateful that I had been allowed to deal directly with the advance team from Whitehall. Little details such as Prime Minister Thatcher requiring a drink tray permanently set up in her suite with Scotch and wine, and having a hairdresser at the ready, was useful information.

I was a bit apprehensive during their advance visit. When the house closed for restoration it was decided to greatly expand the existing buildings. Until 1982 the Primary Suite was the Eisenhower Room, facing Pennsylvania Avenue, and the connecting Library. Also the Secret Service, responsible for the safety of the world's leaders while in this country, was not happy with the suite's exposure to a busy street. In the restoration of the President's Guest House a two storied building to house a ballroom and a new primary suite was built on the north side of the complex, dividing the Garden and undetected from the street and filled with George II and George III furniture, generously donated by the Heathcote Foundation. The reason for my predicament was the second Primary Suite bedroom, meant for the spouse of the principal guest; it was decorated like a flower garden – from the silk moiré on the walls and the George III canopied tester bed to the embroidered carpet on the floor and flower prints on the walls. When the decorators and decorating committee had to decide how the new suite should look, they had taken into account that most governments, regrettably, were still headed by men. So they decided to make the primary bedroom somewhat masculine and the second bedroom the more feminine. I apologized to the Brits expressing the hope that Dennis Thatcher would not feel too out of place. "I can put sheets on with green monograms, but that is as much as I can do to de-feminize it," I said. But I was reassured when the team leader replied: "Oh, Dennis will be very much at home here. On a recent visit to the Arab Peninsula, he was put up in the pink marble harem quarters and as he absolutely roared with laughter over this you have no need to worry."

Prime Minister Thatcher, fighting a nasty cold during her entire stay, was hard working, with long days and short nights. She worked in the Library where Jose brought her hot tea with lemon and the occasional Jack Daniels, while Mr. Thatcher sipped Chivas Regal. She went through four television interviews one morning, starting at 7 am, going from site to site. My staff had been up half the night to assist the four major television station crews with their set-ups in the Jackson Place Houses. All set ups required two substantial arm chairs, two small tables with water, jug and glass, and flower arrangements. Mrs. Thatcher was groomed to perfection, looking as relaxed as if she had just been on vacation, and made a big impression on everyone by being considerate, appreciative, and on time. I had expressed surprise the first morning when she was the first one to come downstairs, to which she replied: "Never keep anyone waiting."

I was rather awed by one of her visitors. Dr. Andrei Sakharov, physicist, father of the hydrogen bomb, and later civil rights advocate, and in the eyes of the West certainly one of the Soviet Union's great heroes, was under medical treatment in the States at this time. Our security was in twitters when their equipment started to beep, triggered by Mr. Sakharov as he passed the Jackson Place Houses on his way to the front door. I wondered if he was full of chemical substances from his years as a scientist, or perhaps as a result of his treatment as I could smell him coming up the stairs. Shabbily dressed, he looked sick with a white pasty like face, but had such kind eyes. Andrei Sakharov died a year later.

The British Embassy's press secretary writing the prime minister's speech to President Reagan at the State Dinner asked if I had any anecdote which might have a bearing on the occasion. "How about the British influence on the White House to find a presidential guest house?" Delighted, he begged: "Pray tell all."

Early one December morning in 1941, shortly after the Japanese attack on Pearl Harbor, Eleanor Roosevelt came out of her bedroom at the White House, to find her least favorite house guest, a burly figure clad in a dressing gown, holding a cigar in one hand, and it is alleged, a brandy glass in the other, pacing up and down the corridor outside President Franklin D. Roosevelt's bedroom. She was annoyed and said: "Mr. Churchill, what ARE you doing here at this hour?" Whereupon Prime Minister Winston Churchill exclaimed that he MUST see the president right away. But Mrs. Roosevelt would have none of it; "Mr. Churchill, you have parted from the President only three hours ago, you cannot see him now, and you must go back to bed." Mrs. Roosevelt, worried about the health of her husband, did not appreciate Mr. Churchill keeping her husband occupied during the oddest hours. The idea was planted that she needed a guesthouse – and soon. Shortly after the Blair and Lee Houses came on the market, and a new tradition was started.

This anecdote went over well, as expected, but as Mrs. Thatcher had far too much she wished to say to President Reagan, it was only used 2 ½ years later when Queen Elizabeth, during the State Dinner in her honor, inserted it in her speech to President Bush.

While we reopened in April 1988, our first visit only happened the following September. Ambassador Roosevelt decided to have a lunch for her French counterpart, a distinguished French diplomat, advancing the visit of François Mitterrand, President of the Republic of France and Madame Mitterrand. Chef, beaming in his newly finished state-of-the-art kitchen, prepared a feast which not only brought forth raves of delight from our guests, but a statement typical of their proud race: "Your Chef must be French!"

During my walk-thru with the French I realized that I was not yet tuned in sufficiently to the ins and outs of the leaders of the world and had not quite grasped that President and Madame Mitterrand absolutely loathed one another.

They could not share the Primary Suite even just to change their clothes.

Suitable accommodations for Danielle Mitterrand would have to be found elsewhere in the house. My first suggestion of the Foreign Minister's suite on the third floor, consisting of a large sitting room, bedroom and bath, was rejected – the suite being appropriated for the president's chief of staff, and, I suspect, not isolated sufficiently from the French president. They settled on the rooms on the second floor of the Lee House, Room 25 for Madame Mitterrand, a junior suite, consisting of a charming bedroom with a four poster bed, a small sitting room and large bathroom, and two adjoining rooms for her staff. They requested the door into the rest of the house be closed at all times.

Ambassador Roosevelt, meanwhile, during my walk with the French team, had remained behind downstairs to discuss carpeting with Harold Keshishian, co-owner of Keshishians, dealers of oriental carpets. Harold Keshishian would become a valued and helpful member of our extended Blair House family. When I ushered our French guests into the Lee Drawing Room, Mr. Keshishian was in the process of correcting the placement of a carpet and our gallant chief of protocol was on hands and knees instructing him what to do. While the bemused French chief of protocol was sipping a glass of sherry, and quite possibly not believing his eyes, Ambassador Roosevelt ignored him, intent upon the task at hand. Nothing stood in the way of getting the house perfect, not even lunch guests.

Typical also was her detailed involvement in the one meal we would serve President Mitterrand during his fourteen hour visit to Washington. We had set a beautiful table for ten in our historic Lee Dining Room for his four course lunch. Following the custom in that administration, Jose had prepared finger bowls with plates and doilies on a serving table in the Lee Hallway from where he would serve this lunch. Being short of space on that table the bowls, already filled with water and a bud of impatiens from our Garden were on a tray; the plates with the doilies were stacked next to them, ready to be assembled quickly. Ambassador Roosevelt arrived, not only worried about President Mitterrand running late, and thus keeping President Reagan waiting across the street, but also ready to pounce on the arrangements which Jose, with my blessing, had worked out would best suit his delivery of service. While President Mitterrand was enjoying a fine lunch ten feet away, Ambassador Roosevelt proceeded to rearrange our set-up, over our whispered and vehement protestations. I do not exaggerate that it was touch and go as to whether Jose would stay and serve the remainder of the lunch. Fortunately, and quite possibly with great foresight, my Assistant Manager Sam Castleman walked in and without any fuss, in his quiet and charming fashion, carried Ambassador Roosevelt away to advise him on matters of some urgency up in the attic. And within a year I nixed the use of finger bowls after a foreign guest spooned his dessert into the water.

Our French guests departed at midnight. The following morning my staff and I met with Mrs. Roosevelt for an overview of the visit. We, especially our Head Butler and Executive Chef, were still basking in the glow of yesterday's visit, our first as a team, as after the lunch, the maître d'hôtel of the Élysée Palace in Paris, the man who managed President Mitterrand's household, put his arms around Jose and me, saying: "Never has my president eaten as well – as fast." Somewhat arrogantly President Mitterrand chose to be late for his White House meeting while enjoying a particularly fine four course meal which Jose served as quickly as possible. The luncheon only took 38 minutes, a record we would never break in my time.

So, it was a shock first to get a rather stern critique by the ambassador of everything that had happened the day before, items of which we were completely unaware and including "making" the French president late for his White House meeting. "Never keep our President waiting," I had been instructed. As I had no illusions as to my powers of persuasion, especially in forcing this particularly ice cold and distant leader of France to leave if he did not want to, and would undoubtedly experience similar situations in the future I vowed this would never happen again.

I would from then on ask the foreign chief of protocol to get his/her charge off on time instead.

And why had a television set been left inside the Primary Suite closet? The latter I could have explained if I had chosen to. I had gone up to meet the valet, who arrived by an earlier plane, and, to my surprise, discovered a large television stowed away in the Primary Closet. My first reaction was to have it quickly removed, but for the fact that the valet, during his unpacking, already had arranged President Mitterrand's socks in a neat row on its top. So I chose to ignore it, trusting that the president himself would have no reason to inspect the closet. While we were still digesting all this criticism, Ambassador Roosevelt threw us this bomb: "And why, may I ask, is there a hole in the door in Room 25?"

There were not one, but two holes in the door to Danielle Mitterrand's bedroom, where the antique door knob and keyhole used to be.

Trying to reconstruct when these items could have been removed we agreed it could only have been after Madame Mitterrand had left the house and during the hours when her staff was packing up. In addition, not one of the amenity items was left in any bathroom. This gift from Elizabeth Arden of creams, lotions, perfumes, eau de cologne, after-shave, and Lagerfeld soaps is put out for our guests' enjoyment, but we did not expect a clean sweep of all for our first visit which did not even include an overnight. We also lost some of our beautifully monogrammed towels. Undoubtedly, some households in Paris shortly thereafter were nicely equipped, to include a precious antique door knob and a keyhole. Some years later, before President Jacques Chirac's visit I penned a note to our new chief of protocol, voicing my fear of a repeat of the above, noting the fact that I had no spare antique door knobs and keyholes any longer in the attic.

Soon more opportunities for learning came; our second visitor was Moussa Traore, President of the Republic of Mali, here for a state visit. While I was fortunate to have Sam Castleman as deputy general manager, a former protocol visits officer with several years experience, none of us, apart from the dubious fourteen hour visit of the French, knew how a full visit was managed at the greatly expanded complex. Where would the president have his meetings? How did we handle the photo opportunity in our precious drawing rooms? Where would he eat? Where would the delegation eat? With press conferences no longer permitted, would we be able to accommodate television interviews?

Sam and I winged our way through the Mali visit, and worked out, using this lovely group of people as our guinea pigs, how the house was best used for the various functions. Moussa Traore was at the time one of Africa's most senior chiefs of state, having been in power for some twenty years. During the following years, meeting other of the world's autocratic leaders, I would find that no one seemed as gentle as he did, or as patriarchal. At night he established himself with his wife and entourage, some 16 of them, in the Lee Drawing Room. He held court, magnificently attired in his African white or turquoise embroidered kaftans, at the Garden end of the room, on the camelback sofa with his back to the curtains. He was so splendid, looked as if he was painted into the sofa which from then on was dubbed the Power Sofa. This particular spot became the focal point for most meetings held by our principal visitor and invited guests, and was the photo background most used. The enthusiasm which I felt for these modest and gentle people was also shared by my staff. Only sixteen stayed with us with the remaining delegation members in hotels, but everyone gathered for meals at the house. And, they made a point of asking if they might take with them the nice soaps we put out for them!

We also had our first experience with a Korean visit during the last months of the Reagan era. Blair House was going to be a pit stop for Roh Tae Woo, President of the Republic of Korea, between landing at AAFB and a White House meeting with Mr. Reagan, a visit lasting a total of 42 minutes including a meeting with Secretary Shultz, another record. The preparation for same lasted considerably longer, inasmuch as the Korean culture is very precise as to form and function. We had two advance visits by several embassy staffers, each person having been assigned a specific task pertaining to the 42 minutes. Their entire career, similar, I was to discover later, to that of the Japanese, seemed to depend upon the perfect execution of same. In this instance, the overriding concern seemed to be the height of the chairs for the two interpreters; the Korean interpreter was a high ranking diplomat to be more prominently placed, the Koreans said, than the American professional interpreter. We solved this by offering an elegant antique chair for the Korean's use, putting out a folding and lower chair for our American colleague. I also learned that President Roh did not eat mackerel, strawberries and definitely no kiwi fruit. I was amused, later, when President Roh was due back for a proper visit with President George H.W. Bush, that I was way ahead of his advance team, knowing of his preferences in food. I also observed the subservient role of women in their society and learned that being a woman in charge, as I was, required me to perform a delicate dance.

Before our first visit following the renovation and certainly the first one to be organized and worked by me and my new team, I had spent many hours drawing on my past hotel experience. I outlined my suggestions for preparations and operations of and procedures for visits to the administrative office, the pantry and kitchen, the housekeeping and maintenance and presented it to my staff during a meeting. With some alterations and changes resulting from our subsequent collective experiences, this memo became one of our working tools. The details we would have to contend with were staggering.

They included the preparation of a daily schedule for the visit itself; a request for advance funds so we could pay our bills associated with a mammoth invasion of the premises; installation of extra phones; the preparation of printed maps of the four guest floors, listing in each bedroom the occupant by name and title; name cards for bedroom doors done in calligraphy; stationery supplies for each guest room; the ordering of plants and flowers, arranged on the premises by me; newspapers and magazines appropriate to the specific visit;

and hiring telephone operators to ensure a 24 hour coverage of our phones. This was only a part of it. In the kitchens, headed by Chef, part time staff would be hired; menus reflecting special dietary and cultural restrictions written and submitted to me for approval; food would be ordered; and he and his assistant chef, Greg Uhlein, would begin preparation of breakfast, lunch and dinner for numbers anywhere from 16 to 150 at one seating, often having no inkling as to correct numbers. Flexibility was key, and the learning curve was hard for the first few years.

Meanwhile Jose Fuster would book part time waiters; polish silver; stock up his supplies of coffee, sugar, creams, beverages; and work out table settings. As Jose had been on the Washington scene for 25 years as a freelance butler, he kept his ear to the ground and fed me useful bits of information which he had picked up from friends working in various embassies. Often, before we even met with the foreign advance team to discuss the schedule, I knew that on a certain night the principal visitor would be dining at his embassy, or that he might stay longer due to medical appointments. I sometimes even knew of a visit before the Office of Protocol.

Jemma Rennie, and her ladies prepared bedrooms, to include installing enough hangers in the closets; putting out stationery, pens and pencils; ensuring that all light bulbs, televisions and clock radios were working properly; counting out the correct amounts of amenities for the bathrooms; and making certain all the beautifully monogrammed bed linens matched the overall color scheme of the individual guest rooms. Potpourri was put out everywhere, and from time to time exchanged for fresh scents to fit the particular season. With the housemen doing the heavy cleaning the ladies would dust and polish the first floor as well. Our Facilities Manager checked all systems to ensure a smooth operation of the air condition and heating equipment. Security had their own preparations which entailed endless meetings with and directives from the USSS, the Diplomatic Service of the U.S. Department of State (DS) which protected a foreign minister traveling with his or her president, with USSS Uniformed Police which guarded the perimeters of the White House complex, the Capitol Police if our foreign visitor had appointments in Congress, and the Washington Metropolitan Police Force.

During the advance work we had to rely on full cooperation of embassy personnel, and sometimes that was a problem. The Assistant Chief of Protocol for Visits assigned a visits officer to be the lead for a particular visit. Between us we kept each other informed as to what our particular sources could tell us, and collectively tightened the screws on the more difficult embassy staffers. We did understand, though, that they were often only the conduit for their colleagues back home and that the lack of information was the fault of their presidential staff and often their own president who could not make up his mind.

In my staff meetings preceding a visit I would bring up cultural differences and what to expect from each group. Together we would discuss how to cope with the obvious disregard for "servants" which one finds in Asia and Africa; how my staff would have to "grin and bear it" and remain polite and smiling in the face of, for them, unbelievable rudeness, for our guests, normal behavior: One maid was commanded to wait in the bedroom for a shirt to be washed while the guest proceeded to take it off in front of her. One first lady worked her way through four hairdressers, all of whom left shaking like jelly, while our maid had to clean up all the pieces of clothing, hair brushes, and bottles flung around the room. Other times there would be suggestive invitations to our ladies to spend personal time with an aide, and interestingly they would come from regimes with strict religious rules of law. And Parlor Maid Teresinha Diaz' description of walking into a bedroom and being scared half to death by stark naked security guards spread out on the floor defies description. Brazilian born Teresinha, with her heavy accent getting heavier the more excited she got, had a knack for supplying accompanying sound effects, thus raising her stories and tales to entertainment level. She was our resident comedian.

I drew on my memorable experiences from seven years at the Shoreham Hotel in Washington D.C. telling my staff that the northern Europeans would be easy, the Italians excitable, recalling one particular tour director who in a highly agitated state declared: "I shoot myself, I shoot myself" and, of course, mentioned the French. The Shoreham restaurant employed a beautiful waitress from Jamaica, who charged into our office, tore off her apron, and declared that she was quitting. "But, Angela," said Ruth Hamory, my boss and the international director of sales of the Shoreham Hotel, "what happened to upset you so?"

"I have been insulted," she said sticking her nose in the air and continuing in a high pitched voice, "one of those foreigners, Frenchmen, in your group, pinched my bottom. I have been totally insulted and I shall leave immediately." Mrs. Hamory rose to the occasion magnificently: "Angela, the French more than anybody in the world appreciate a beautiful woman. This man obviously thinks you are gorgeous, and this is just his way of expressing it." So the apron went back on again, and a radiant Angela pranced back to the restaurant.

The East Asians would be different. The Shoreham was completely sold out, so our Vietnamese tour group was housed in the motel section, overlooking Rock Creek Park. One couple with a sixteen year old son were not happy, having requested three beds, instead being offered two king sized beds giving them luxurious space for everyone. A sticky scene followed with the tour director. However, the following morning the tour director and the family were very happy, having worked out the sleeping arrangements to everyone's satisfaction: father slept in one king sized bed; sixteen year old son in the other king sized bed; and mother – mother slept on the luggage rack.

Over the years we would accumulate our own stories, as bizarre as any I could relate from my own past. We would pool our collective experiences starting our hectic day with much laughter, and on the way we discovered how useful the element of uncertainty surrounding these visits was in that it made us immensely resourceful, flexible, and unflappable.

Sam Castleman was the best deputy I could have possibly had at this time. Experienced in the way of protocol, he was a visits officer for a number of years before becoming the chief of protocol for Dallas, Texas. He was plugged in to the mysterious and secretive ways of USSS and other security details. He understood the relationship between all the entities organizing and working a visit. He quickly became knowledgeable in the historic aspects of the complex, and particularly its architecture, a talent which would be invaluable as we would discover many hidden problems behind the walls later on, the renovation and restoration having been more cosmetic than practical. Sam had a strong presence. He was unassuming, hard working, loyal and discreet with plenty of initiative, the perfect partner in the management which would have been a daunting task for me to handle without such competent support. He joined me in July 1988 having been persuaded by Ambassador Roosevelt to return to Washington. I admit, though, that at first when she brought him back I thought that I had failed her. It took a month or so for me to evaluate him, during which I asked Sam to organize and clean up the attic which had not been touched in years, and during which he quietly and efficiently familiarized himself with all maintenance details of the house, before we truly connected. Although at the time we referred to the reason for this as those "damn lilies" I was grateful to them nevertheless.

As part of a gift to the Blair House Restoration Fund by the artist Fleur Cowles a pond had been built in the small courtyard bearing her name, separating the new presidential suite building and two Jackson Place houses used for White House agencies. Boxes planted with water lilies were placed in the pond, obtained through the good offices of the chair of the Garden Committee of the Restoration Fund, Mary Weinmann. Our Facilities Manager at the time, Julian Pike, was charged with the cleaning of this pond, a task he did not relish. Around seven one August evening I went up to check the first floor before going home, when in the Blair Pantry I found Sam, looking hot, harassed, and soaking wet. "Sam, you look like something the cat dragged in; what are you doing?" I asked. "I don't know how to tell you this, but that Julian left the water lilies on the side of the pond and did not put them back in after his cleaning and they are all dead," and he continued furiously to try to revive the drooping and unhappy looking lilies under the tap in the sink. I started laughing, and so did he, and under much merriment we spent the next hours hauling "those damn lilies" from the courtyard, through the Garden Room, into the pantry, trying to fit them into the sinks for some much needed restoration before we placed them in the smaller fountain in the Garden. It was a wet, funny, and bonding experience for Sam and me. The lilies did not fare as well.

The assistant manager when I came on board was transferred to the Ceremonial Office of Protocol in May. She was an elegantly attired and coiffed young woman who never got her hands dirty. She efficiently organized the hospitality suites for the president's foreign visitors at the hotels where they were housed until Blair House reopened. She scheduled my small staff to man these suites under her supervision. I put a stop to this quickly and requested her to hire part timers instead, which, I admit, was not popular with my people, who preferred to dress up and serve orange juice in a hotel suite to scrubbing floors and moving furniture. When Ambassador Roosevelt transferred this woman I was relieved for another reason. I was convinced she was in the wrong job. Before my time when the house had no working elevator, I was told, she <u>forced</u> a maid in advanced pregnancy to carry certain chairs upstairs to the third floor without any assistance being offered.

So, for a period of some months I had no deputy. Also I had no head butler. Jose Fuster was waiting for his security clearance, and would not come on board until mid June. Although parties were organized by the Ceremonial Office of the Protocol Office, and caterers brought in most of the necessary gear, until our kitchens were functional, Ambassador Roosevelt still wanted me to display and, if possible, to use our new gifts of 1500 pieces of Tiffany flatware, and Lenox china and crystal for 150. I spent many an evening counting silver before locking it away in our vault, while silently wailing: "Please may I have my head butler soon – where, oh where is my head butler?"

But I had Jemma Rennie. Mike Coughlin, my guru and mentor, said: "When I see her coming towards me I say to myself that surely the angels must have sent us Mrs. Rennie." She was sworn in one week before I was detailed over from Senator Domenici's office, and I was told that the existing staff, having been a bit laid back until then, suddenly met their match. She had them cleaning and scrubbing, and tidying up so fast they did not know what hit them.

Jemma Rennie, a native of Trinidad Tobago, would become one of my most trusted colleagues. I never had to repeat or remind her of a request. She made a big impression on me immediately. I had been to Blair House on the morning of March 7 to participate in a meeting with Ambassador Roosevelt and to meet the staff. Mrs. Rennie was not present. During the afternoon she called me in my office in the U.S. Senate, most apologetic not having been able to meet me, and explained her dilemma: she was being sworn in at the U.S. Department of State. She was always professional, upbeat, smiling, tireless, and even tempered.

The staff member who had served the longest, interrupted only by the renovation, was Agustinha dos Santos from Brazil. Agustinha was the laundress, but to describe her as such would be totally erroneous.

To care for the linens was the task of an expert. Our linen was exquisite; it came as gifts from everywhere in the world and among the hundreds of tablecloths and napkins, most were hand embroidered, or the lace hand knotted. Our sheets had monograms in many shades, and the blanket covers were particularly silky and beautiful. Its care, through the careful and loving expertise of Agustinha, was second to none. She ran the laundry room with its eight pieces of machinery with expertise and great toughness, and it is a testament to her devotion to her duty that she held the respect of everybody on the staff. She was at times buried in laundry. When visit after visit were on the agenda, Agustinha turned around hundreds of pieces of laundry daily, in addition to looking after the individual pressing and washing needs of our guests. Before and after visits she could get help, but during visits the other ladies had their own duties to attend to. And, Agustinha was a tough old bird too regarding assistance. If you did not do the laundry her way she didn't want you around in the laundry room.

Once when we had a back up of sheets from several visits, over the vehement objections of Agustinha, I insisted we send out the bottom sheets, figuring having some 45 sheets done by a commercial establishment would be a great relief to the volume she had to cope with. Well, little did I know! When the sheets came back, Agustinha detected wrinkles here and there. The sheets went into the washing machine, dryer and under her expert hands through the pressing machine to emerge wrinkle free. I never interfered with her again.

Housemen Frankie Blair and Sean Irby came on board within a year of the reopening. Frankie because of his earlier long career in the White House is mentioned in several books. He worked in the White House kitchen and later on the White House grounds. With his generous heart, big laugh, steady work habits and, despite grave illness which eventually forced him into retirement, our doorman for years, he was known for his smiling face to everyone who passed by Blair House. Sean Irby at first had a checkered career with us, but overcame great odds and contributed considerably to the smooth visits being in charge of the embassy offices and bringing in enormous amounts of luggage. He remains a smiling presence at the house.

Administrative Officer Lynn Keith came to us from the Blair House Restoration Fund, prepared "to scrub floors" to be allowed to remain. She had a background in retail buying, among others for

Camalier & Buckley, and with her inquisitiveness and never-ending curiosity, was a natural to hunt down all the strange and exotic items needed over the years. Lynn could track down the weirdest items. The wife of a Japanese prime minister had set her heart on a birdcage she had seen in a magazine on an airplane. Without much to go on, Lynn found this item in Chicago, and had it shipped in to an amazed and grateful Japanese lady. Lynn was hired to do our accounting and, after an initial resistance to learning the various computer systems, became very proficient and grateful for having become computer literate.

Eventually we would be 13 hired by the Office of Protocol, consisting of the deputy and myself, two kitchen chefs, the head housekeeper and two maids and a laundress; the head butler and assistant/head houseman; two housemen, the administrative officer, and for a while, an office clerk.

Before the renovation U.S. Secret Service had had free access to the house. This stopped when the security was turned over to the Department of State, brilliantly planned and executed by Donald R. Blake, a former metropolitan police officer, who on behalf of the Bureau of Diplomatic Security was entrusted with the safety of the property, and who, during subsequent promotions, never gave up his direct supervision of our security. He created a program to protect the complex 24/7 by the installation of electronic equipment, and having two officers on duty at all times, directed, supervised and controlled by the Head of our Security. Over the years this position was held by few people, and especially Lieutenants Roy Bauman, Paul Rogers, and the current one, Rod Waters, have been outstanding. All of these people integrated themselves into the spirit of the house, understood perfectly the delicate dance we all had to perform to ensure that our foreign guests were contented and had their needs met, while, in the case of security, our rigid rules were enforced. It is a testament to the particular people, mentioned above, that their tact and good sense so often prevailed vis-à-vis the single-minded purpose and disregard for the concern of others by the USSS. The Service, two hours before the arrival of a foreign leader, takes over Blair House and secures it, posting its agents around the perimeter and establishing the command center. Our own security officers from then on are limited to their basement command center, continuing their role of controlling access by personnel and delivery people, and have to perform their duties of protecting the property by picking out trouble spots on the computer screens rather than through personal inspection tours. The agents are also posted inside the guest portion of the house, especially hovering near their protectee, the foreign leader. Don Blake requested early on that the Service appoints a Site Security Agent, with us during visits, who would act as liaison between Blair House security and management, and the lead Secret Service agent for a particular visit.

I needed my Head of Security to sort out the Service during our first visit. An agent holding a Styrofoam cup of coffee stepped out of the elevator onto the first floor when I asked him to remove that abomination at once, and never again to bring paper or Styrofoam cups beyond the basement. I would gain a reputation among the agents after that, which was probably not flattering, but no one ever again brought Styrofoam cups up onto the floors, and I understand this directive became part of the Service's Blair House manual for visits. After all we had our standards, and I intended to enforce them. Mostly, though, the relationship between the Service and the house was excellent, and frequently over the years, I received charming notes from the agents who had "done" the visits, with warm thanks for our cooperation and for our understanding of their particular concerns.

The Blair House Restoration Fund was the private fundraising arm without which the house would have been equipped with standard government furnishings and polyester rather than silk fabrics. In fact, so important was the contribution of this private group that State made available an office for its Executive Director on the premises so that the condition and needs of the house could be monitored on a daily basis in conjunction with State's Associate Curator also housed at Blair House. Over the years the Blair House Restoration Fund did much for the house, and without its Board members and their interest would not have fared well.

So, when George Herbert Walker Bush became President of the United States and was sworn in on a sunny January 20, 1989, he took over a fully operational house, with a well trained and dedicated staff. And would we ever need every skill in the book to deal with the next few years. The show was about to start and the curtain would shortly rise on our next adventures.

ACT II

GEORGE H.W. BUSH
The President

***

JAMES A. BAKER, III
The Secretary of State

LAWRENCE EAGLEBURGER
The Secretary of State

***

JOSEPH V. REED
The Chief of Protocol

JOHN G. WEINMANN
The Chief of Protocol

CHAPTER 3

AMONG THE BUSHES

"America is never wholly herself unless she is engaged in high moral principle.

We as a people have such a purpose today.

It is to make kinder the face of the nation and gentler the face of the world."

George Herbert Walker Bush

"and then, when the children have finished eating, you do as I do at Kennebunkport," Barbara Bush said, her eyes twinkling merrily, looking at me across the uncovered five foot round table, as we ended our tour in the Garden Room, "you just hose down the table."

She was at Blair House in preparation for the traditional stay of the U.S. President-Elect, her husband George H.W. Bush, the few nights preceding his inauguration; they had invited only their immediate family to join them during this special time. As this consisted of their five children, their spouses, and at that time ten grandchildren and two nannies, they quickly filled up the house. Mrs. Bush worried about "my naughty grandchildren" running loose in the newly restored Blair House, and recommended feeding them in the staff dining-room in the basement. But I suggested instead using the new Garden Room. If she would tell me what we could stock up on to keep them amused, we could turn the Garden Room into a play-dining-room as well as movie theatre. It would be far easier to make repairs, I thought, should an accident occur, which it often does with that size small folk around.

The days leading up to the Inauguration were filled with prepara-tory meetings and walk-thrus with the president-elect's advance team and USSS, and Mr. Bush's first cabinet-elect meeting, followed by a reception and dinner with spouses. We were thrilled to do this, and treated it as a gala event. We wanted to show off to our next president, of course, and also give the future cabinet secretaries and their spous-es an opportunity to "inspect" Blair House. Under our policy, they have a right to request the use of the house for meetings and events, while hosting their foreign counterparts, as all events must further American foreign policy objectives, and such an evening gave them a firsthand impression.

Our menu suggestion was approved by the president-elect's office, and by Lucky Roosevelt, still chief of protocol for a few more days. We wanted to dazzle our new bosses with Lobster and Oyster Con-sommé, followed by Beef Wellington, Salad and Cheese, and Swiss Mocha Ice Cream, a favorite of Mr. Bush. We withheld the broccoli and cauliflower which he disliked.

This period, from the election till January 20, 1989, was also the count-down of the Reagan appointees' "lives in the sun," and nerves were definitely on the prickly side. I was between a rock and a hard place all those weeks, dealing with the soon to be former colleagues, who could not quite let go, and the new team.

Ambassador Roosevelt came frequently during the first part of January prior to her leaving office to give me her parting words of advice and to complete some of the unfinished projects initiated by her. We poured over boxes containing curtains stashed away when the complex closed in 1982. "There is no need, Mrs. V, for new mate-rials to be acquired when we have all of this for the lesser rooms," she said, as I staggered behind her loaded down with fabric. As a result of these sessions, the Embassy Office acquired a new look: the green silk damask, used during the Trumans' residence years before, and identi-cal to the Green Room fabric at the White House, appeared adorning the windows of the office and covering the chairs. The staff bedrooms for the Deputy General Manager, the Head Housekeeper and the maids got equipped with sage green linen curtains and bedspreads, while my sleigh bed acquired a hand embroidered bed spread in burnt orange with matching bed board and trunk. No sheer curtain was wasted either.

On January 17, 1989, the Bushes began to move in. First daughter, Doro Bush, arrived. She did not seem like a happy soul, and indeed shortly thereafter broke off her marriage. She would remarry in June 1992. Doro was dark and handsome, with the looks of both parents, and a pleasant person, as was third son, Neil Bush with wife (now ex) Sharon from Colorado with two small children. The following day the rest of the Bush children and their families came: George W. Bush (later Governor of Texas and the 43rd president) with his wife Laura and twins, Jenna and Barbara; Jeb Bush (later Governor of Florida) and his wife with George P., Noelle and Master Jebby, and Marvin Bush and Margaret with little Miss Marshall Pierce. Mrs. Bush had personally inspected and assigned each room, leaving us with a carefully marked floor plan from which we prepared a rooming list. She also had instructed me that absolutely no one was to have room service. "They can all come down and have their meals downstairs. They are not to be waited upon." So, to our consternation, the first morning after everyone had arrived, there was Laura Bush wandering around in a night shirt, with bare feet, smiling sleepily at us, and helping herself to coffee. She was just as relaxed and casual when she returned to Blair House 12 years later. We did hear later that the Texas twins, then seven years old, at the White House after the inauguration, boldly picked up the phone and ordered room service, naturally executed by the obliging White House staff, until their grandmother put a stop to it. I am not surprised. My staff reckoned as how they already at this young age were an enterprising pair, and quickly removed breakable objects from their room.

Mrs. Bush moved down from Naval Observatory Hill, the Vice President's residence, on the 18th January. Mid afternoon she gathered all of the children and grandchildren outside on the risers to cheer on George Bush as he walked across from his vice-presidential office at the White House. I witnessed a charming moment when little Master Jebbie broke loose from the family circle, dashing towards his grandfather, and after a hurried conversation, the soon-to-be leader of the mightiest nation in the world sat down in the middle of Pennsylvania Avenue tending to serious business: that of tying a small boy's shoelaces.

It was a visit of children, of happy noises, laughter and shrieks. Every evening after the young fathers jointly had given baths to the small Bushlets up in No. 43, the little ones were jumping up and down on former President Eisenhower's bed, shrieking with joy. In the daytime, unless they were out of the house, the little ones would roar around our glass top table in the middle of the Garden Room in their go-carts, and paint and draw on long wooden tables. In a corner a Disney movie was showing, and in another a computer was being used by the older children. The Fund's Carter Cunningham organized the playthings, having little kids as well, and thus knowledgeable as to current tastes.

For years I have treasured those moments with the Bush family at Blair House. Although I became an American citizen in 1969, it was not until the presidential primary election of 1980 that I truly liked the individual for whom I voted. In the primary as well as the general election my vote was cast for George Bush, not Ronald Reagan. So seeing him at Blair House, a few times during 1988, but more intensely during those few and hectic days leading up to his inauguration was only a confirmation of why I intuitively had liked him. He was affable, appreciative, low key, and a devoted grandfather. The first night Mrs. Rennie found him wandering around the hallways looking for the grandchildren, wishing to "check up on them." She took him around to each bedroom, and watched him tucking in the children, and checking the temperature, before he quietly tiptoed out.

A precious moment came when Mr. Bush, at the foot of the Blair House stairs, tried gently to coax one of the little girls around the banister and down the stairs. From my position behind the president-elect I silently got the attention of his official photographer, Dave Valdez, who quietly got into position with his camera. The photo of the little granddaughter, Lauren Bush, now a well-known fashion model, appeared in many magazines later. But the most telling photo printed in major magazines around the world about what mattered to this charming man was taken by Dave Valdez, in our Garden, on the morning of the inauguration. An unusually warm day for January, the president-elect had gone out there to read over his inaugural address. There was George Herbert Walker Bush, soon to take on the mantle of the presidency of the United States, sitting in our wrought iron chair studying his inaugural address – and at his feet: a child's toy car. At that time, while his own tie was being cleaned up, he was wearing one of our spare ties. One of the little grandsons, during breakfast, had

had great fun taking aim at "Poppy" with a fork loaded down with scrambled eggs.

He also held a reception and photo-opportunity two days before the inauguration for all known survivors from the San Jacinto squadrons and the Finback patrols from World War II, the VT-51, VF-51 and the 10th Patrol, the people with whom George Bush served overseas, when he was shot down over the Pacific. He was only 19.

Meal times were, as during subsequent inaugural visits, somewhat loosely observed by our visitors who wandered in and out as their schedules permitted. They ate on the run. However, two nights before the inauguration the President-Elect and Mrs. Bush dined alone, as their youngsters were out doing events. We were so pleased. We set the table in the Blair Dining Room, the very place where President Harry S Truman took his meals when residing here. Jose Fuster and I brought out the antique silver candle sticks; the best pieces of the old Blair family china and for the first time actually pulled the folding doors to between the Rear Blair Drawing Room and the Blair Dining Room to ensure them some privacy.

Well, after this evening I have come to the conclusion that the Bushes never had a meal to themselves. I do not think they would know what to do with it, if they had. Especially Mr. Bush was fidgeting, and constantly asking if this one or that one of his children had returned to the house. Soon at least some of their children and aides had joined them, pulling up chairs and partaking in whatever took their fancy on the menu.

During visits the next four years Mrs. Bush entertained the spouse of the President's guest, inviting her to tea or coffee at the White House. I received many comments from my guests when they returned from these outings, such as: "Mrs. Bush sends her regards," or "Mrs. Bush asked me if everything was comfortable and if we were being looked after properly, and I could only say it was wonderful." The spouses told me that Mrs. Bush asked them detailed questions about the house, its comfort, its service, and me. Although I did not know she would be as interested and inquisitive as to what we really were doing, it was, at the inauguration festivities, important to me that she obviously approved of the way I conducted a visit. She was looking at our hospitality table, set up in the Blair Dining Room, from which during the entire day we dispensed beverages and snacks for the hungry, and mentioned how sad it was that her family members were watching their diet so carefully. "Mrs. Bush," I explained, "it really is on purpose I have made the same arrangements for you as I would for a visit. I feel it is important that you and the President-elect see and experience the hospitality of Blair House. It is my hope you may then tell me what you would like to change, to better reflect your own ideas."

At which Barbara Bush looked straight at me and said: "I would not wish to change a thing."

And she never did.

Mrs. Bush frequently accompanied the foreign first lady on a visit to a hospital or a senior center, and dropping off her guest at Blair House afterwards, often stepped inside to bid farewell in our Front Hall.

Thus I saw her often, and was always left with my original impression, that of a handsome lady with a most direct glance, someone very sure of herself and whom you could never fool, and someone who would be loyal to friends and implacably hostile to enemies. She had star quality, this lady. From time to time she popped over unannounced. When the Vienna Boys' Choir was in town her husband's chief of protocol, Joseph Reed, invited them to sing at the house for a select group of his nearest and dearest within the government, and Mrs. Bush came over, to the delight and utter amazement of the Wiener Sänger Knaben, as she did for his tea for Happy Rockefeller, widow of the former Governor of New York and Vice President. Once Mrs. Bush said to me: "You must come over for lunch one day so we can talk about life;" it never happened, of course, but I appreciated the sentiment.

There were, over the ensuing four years, several attempts to "remove" Mrs. V, but the more serious one came a few months after the inauguration. The position as general manager of Blair House was still listed in the so called "Plum Book," the book outlining all the appointed positions in the government. I had been hired as a federal employee that not only gave me a certain job security, but more importantly, gave continuity, and prevented a frequent turn over in management. Ambassador Roosevelt, who had hired me, had personally arranged with the Reagan White House to take the position out of the political arena, where it was placed by the Carters, and make it into a federal one. This decision had not yet reached the "Plum Book." Mike Coughlin, my governmental mentor, on his meanderings around government circles, smelled "a rat" regarding my position, and told Ambassador Roosevelt, knowing she was never one to shy away from a problem, especially not if one of her own decisions, the hiring of me, was being questioned. She phoned Barbara Bush, and got a luncheon appointment with her.

After lunch, Ambassador Roosevelt came straight over to see me, perched herself on the sofa in my office, and related what had taken place. Leading into the question of Blair House, Ambassador Roosevelt asked Mrs. Bush what she thought of it. "Wonderful," Mrs. Bush said. "And how do you like Mrs. Valentiner and the job she is doing?" "Perfect," Mrs. Bush had said. Mrs. Roosevelt persisted: "Are you sure, do you really think she is good?" Mrs. Bush, impatiently, said: "I am telling you, she is perfect for the job."

"Then, Barbara, why is someone trying to remove her from Blair House?"

According to Ambassador Roosevelt, Mrs. Bush called the Director of Presidential Appointments, and asked if he was trying to make changes at Blair House. Apparently this was denied. Mrs. Bush then had said: "I want no changes at Blair House, do you understand? I repeat: I want no changes at Blair House."

I did discover later who had tried to make this change, but as it was probably done to reward a hard working campaign staffer, and not necessarily because I personally had offended anyone, I dismissed it. But it was another warning to keep my nose clean, to be careful, and not to trust anyone. I set strict rules for myself regarding dating and being seen around town, so as not to stir the least amount of gossip.

During the next thirteen years I frequently had to associate with people, who had been close to the seat of power for so long that they had forgotten real generosity of spirit, tolerance and kindness. I expect some got corrupted by power or the perception of same. I learned at home that if you are born on life's sunny side, you have an obligation to be content, and to be generous, but I met more unpleasant and stuck up people in this atmosphere of glamour than I had ever dealt with before, and often found myself at outs with them. I cannot stand pretension, social climbing, nastiness and collegial back stabbing. It was a special privilege working in the Office of Protocol, and being in close proximity to leaders of the world, and through one's work to "represent" the U.S. President, extending his hospitality and build bridges to the world. I felt strongly it behooved all of us to avoid this corruption of the spirit. But it was hard, especially since I was told by Ambassador Roosevelt on more than one occasion when I had tried to economize or put the brakes on:

"Mrs. V, don't forget – you are now playing in the big league."

Alas, so often the big league had feet of clay.

But I maintained an excellent understanding with President and Mrs. Bush and have nothing but the most profound respect for their work, particularly as pertains to the world which has always remained my greatest interest. Frequently during the two Clinton administrations President Bush called on several of our visitors and always had time for the staff which had served his interests so well. Mrs. Bush kept away during the eight Clinton years, and only returned, but with bells on, for her son's inauguration eight years later.

CHAPTER 4

OUT OF AFRICA

"We all pray that Mandela will live."

South African delegation members

"Où est le boeuf?"

Mobutu Sese Seko, President of the Republic of Zaire, hosted a dinner for General Alexander Haig in the Lee Dining Room, during his Official Working Visit to Washington D.C. in June 1989. He took little of the offered dishes. Weeks earlier his own ambassador had chosen veal as the entrée, exclaiming: "the boss will absolutely love it." Well, little did he know!

Jose was in a quandary. "Shall I call the kitchen for a steak for the president?" But I decided not. General Haig had already waited two hours for his dinner. I had apologized for the delays telling him that while I was fully responsible for the food and service I washed my hands of the rest. He had just grinned.

The Zairians had arrived that morning. The embassy had hired a public relations firm to soften the awful image and reputation of this leader through advertisements in all the major newspapers in preparation for this visit. The public relation person had invited the guests for this particular dinner, including Members of Congress and Alexander Haig, former U.S. Secretary of State. This dinner was doomed early on. Mobutu went to a reception and kept his guests waiting for 90 minutes; congressional guests arrived but got called back to vote; no one knew the exact number dining with the president; and downstairs my poor Chef was getting close to throwing a tantrum. Finally at 9:30 pm dinner could start.

And now, the "où est le boeuf" question. I decided that Alexander Haig deserved his dinner now and I would face the beef issue later. But every time Jose bent over the president, presenting to him the seafood dish, the rack of veal, the summer vegetables, the salad, the bread, the cheese, the dessert, and pouring Mobutu's own champagne, pink and of the best brand the world could produce and enjoyed by him and his wife, Mama Bobi, from the early morning hours, President Mobutu asked: "Où est le boeuf," and Alexander Haig, sitting across the table, gave Jose a broad wink.

Blair House was not like a restaurant, more like a caterer where only the food needed for specific functions is prepared, severely limiting our flexibility. However, following this evening, we were never again without beef, chicken and fish in the kitchen, regardless of whether it was on the menu or not. Tonight, though, I felt, considering the menu had been chosen by Zaire's own ambassador that his would be the head on the platter rather than mine. I failed that evening to understand the fundamentals of what guided an absolute despot like Mobutu: the total control he exercised over everyone. Thus no one dared to make any decision, and most certainly should not make any on behalf of the "boss." The Zairian ambassador had been showing off when I had presented him with the menu selection, and pretending he really was in charge. Interestingly enough, when the guests were saying goodbye in the drawing-room, through the front door, brought over from the delegation's hotel, an aide arrived with a tray, complete with steak and French fries. One of the president's people at dinner had paid close attention, and anticipated the later demand.

It was my nightmare visit because of the reputation of the president and his entourage. This visit from Zaire, the former Belgian Congo, in West Africa, our second from that continent, was luckily not indicative of the subsequent utterly charming and colorful African visits. Mobutu had seized power in Zaire in a bloodless coup twenty-five years earlier ending five years of military mutinies, ethnic and other struggles following independence from Belgium. President since 1971, now in his third seven year term, he was considered a staunch ally of the United States with all the attending military and monetary benefits.

The previous fall my Danish friend Anne Merete Petrignani and her husband, the Italian ambassador, had visited Mt. Desert Island in Maine with their prime minister in between official visits in Washington and Ottawa. They arrived at their hotel just after the departure of Mobutu and his entourage, and salacious stories about whoring and thieving were flying around. In addition, Mobutu cleverly traveled with his country's treasury, one way, I suppose, of ensuring no one tried to stage a coup in his absence. The whoring tales scared me. I had visions of facing down his aides on the stoop, barring the entry of the 14th street "ladies of the night" from entering my beautiful house. I had, naively, spoken to the new chief of protocol about it and suggested to house President Mobutu at a hotel instead. Joseph Reed was well traveled in Africa, and knew this particular group. But, I should have known better; in what I had already come to understand was his usual fashion he managed merrily to walk away, without one word to me of encouragement or promise of assistance. I had, surprisingly, more sympathy from Margaret Tutweiler, Assistant Secretary of State for Public Affairs, the official voice of Secretary of State James A. Baker. After being sworn in at the White House, she came over with her brother for a tour. When she heard of my apprehension, and after she and her brother had stopped laughing and teasing me, she told me to come to her if I needed the assistance of the Secretary.

But the Zairians were on their best behavior. President Mobutu had made a diplomatic coup in bringing the warring factions together in war-torn Angola shortly before his visit to Washington, and thus arrived bathed in positive publicity. He also arrived with scores of Gucci bags filled with his country's treasury. The word kleptomania seemed coined for Mobutu; for years he had been "treating the national treasury as his own piggy bank." In his late fifties, on his second wife, Mobutu had about as much charm as a hungry alligator. He was said to have at least fifteen children, three of whom stayed with us. The two nice teenage boys spent the entire time in our Garden Room in front of the TV playing Nintendo games. Their sister was 13 going on 25. The president's wife, Mama Bobi, her sister, her maid, and other personal servants and security of the president stayed with us, all the ministers and advisors, if such existed in his sphere, were at the Vista Hotel. However, all trotted over in the morning to wait around for when they were needed, thus partaking with gusto of all we had to offer. Jose and I, locking up after the first evening, found two quiet gentlemen seated on a sofa. They were waiting, Jose said, after checking with them, to say goodnight to "Papa" before leaving.

Eventually they were dispatched by Mobutu's valet who asked them to return in the morning. I wondered how well they slept that night knowing that they had somehow failed in their duty not being dismissed by the president himself.

Three poor little men were continuously engaged in keeping the president's and Mama Bobi's clothes in order in the third floor pressing room. They did not dare come down to eat if just one piece of clothing needed attention, while the communications man in Room 36 was under orders to remain there for the entire visit. Teresinha asked him to go downstairs for his meals in the Garden Room. Crying, he told her he would be killed if he left the phones for a moment. So, naturally, Teresinha took pity upon him, and brought him his meals on a tray.

The delegation members wore a variation of western clothes with Mao style jackets, worn over beautiful silk shirts, to which, instead of a collar, was attached an ascot. Mama Bobi, and the wives of the ministers, and the maids, wore their pretty and colorful native cotton or silk dresses, with long narrow skirts over which they wore a fitted blouse with puff sleeves. The lower ranking staffers such as security and servants wore their jacket with an attached ascot directly on their body without a shirt, generating a good deal of body odor and consequently much space around them. All the security officers wore alligator boots and expensive watches and carried guns, and all were dead serious, tough, and rather brutal.

I had heard that in an earlier administration, at departure by helicopter from the Washington Memorial to Andrews Air Force Base in Maryland, the Zairian security, one of whom was denied a seat, grabbed the Protocol Officer in charge of the visit and literally threw her off the helicopter to make space. I also heard they added insult to injury complaining about her lack of breasts. I witnessed punishment of one security officer absent from his assigned post in the street, when Mobutu returned from a function. The president clearly noticed. Subsequently, in front of us, his head of security not only gave the poor man a vicious tongue lashing, but whacked him on his neck with a radio causing the poor guy to cry. I was not surprised having heard that even the foreign minister, a former rival of Mobutu's, some years earlier had been thrown in prison, and personally beaten by the president. The minister, a member of the delegation, was small, bow-legged with a pox marked face, jolly and friendly, and sporting a beautiful and charming English speaking wife.

Pink champagne was swilled morning, noon, and night. They requested we include it with soft drinks and coffee, usually offered during meetings, much to the consternation of the American meeting participants. Something much stronger was imbibed by the president every time he left the house and upon his return. This liquid was served by his valet or Mama Bobi out of a heavy briefcase. I know it was heavy as I tried to shift it from our early 19th century rosewood and mahogany piano in the narrow hallway under the Blair staircase. I noticed how it had scratched the surface of the piano, and told the maid guarding it that I would prefer to put it on the floor, as the piano was rather delicate. She almost jumped on me. "No, no, Madame, Mama Bobi has put it here, and it must stay here till she moves it." The president liked Blair House, was often in the Garden and in the drawing rooms with his entourage, and condescendingly nice to me, saying "Ça va bien, Madame" whenever he saw me. Shaking his hand was a disgusting experience. It was pock marked, callused, and very rough and I wondered what it had been used for, when, standing at the sink in the Powder Room, I tried to scrub away the feeling of his hand on mine.

Mobutu was the only visitor who, instead of receiving his guests, would have them wait for him. When everyone was in place in the Lee Drawing Room, his staff focused a spot light on his entrance into the room.

Missing were the trumpets!

He never met anyone outside his own circle without wearing his jaguar hat and carrying his swagger stick, made of ebony and sporting intricate carvings. It broke at Blair House. The agony of the security man guarding it was apparent. He was so grateful being led down to the Maintenance Room containing our collection of Sears, Roebuck tools, a major gift to the Blair House Restoration Fund, where he could glue it together, but my staff was not permitted to handle it.

The president was out of the house for lunch when, from my vantage point outside the Protocol Office, I heard a commotion in the Front Hall, and saw Jose round the corner. "Mrs. V, we have visitors," he said, his eyes bulging, and an odd note in his voice. By this time, having worked with Jose for a year I knew those signs. I immediately got up, walked in his direction and, rounding the corner into the Front Hall, felt like I had been hit in the stomach.

My nightmare had just walked in.

"The floosies, oh my god, the floosies of 14th Street," I thought.

The four women, filling the Front Hall, in tight short leather skirts, were large, ugly, vulgar and common looking, with big teased wild hair, gobs of make-up, and reeking of perfume.

The embassy staffer with them said: "Mrs. Valentiner, these are the daughters of President Mobutu. They have flown down from New York, and need to wait for the president here so he can give them permission to <u>come</u> to Washington."

I avoided Jose's eyes as I welcomed them, and showed them into the drawing room. Soon they had emptied our hospitality table of its pastries, and settled down waiting for their father's permission to be there.

The president thanked us charmingly before his departure, and repeated his gratitude to Secretary Baker who had come over to bid him farewell. I watched the Secretary communicating through an interpreter. His eyes never left the face of President Mobutu, never made the mistake of concentrating on the interpreter – another lesson learned.

Mobutu, in deep trouble, two years later was spending much of his time on a large riverboat, complete with helicopter landing pad, on the Zaire River not far from the capital Kinshasa's international airport, thus, as clever as always, poised for a quick exit should he be forced out. This would come in 1992. Mobutu died in exile September 1997.

What a contrast they had been from the group departing us 12 hours before their arrival.

Arriving from London on Sunday, June 24, 1989 the jolly, laid-back delegation, headed by Prime Minister R.J.L. Hawke of Australia, came for an Official Visit. I recall their apprehension when they realized the beauty and elegance of the house, one of them exclaiming: "Oh no, not another one." "Why do you say that?" I asked. They had not liked their stay in London; they had been accommodated well, but had not enjoyed the food, and had been treated haughtily, and with condescension as some British have a tendency to do with their "colonials."

I knew we had succeeded making our guests feel truly at home when the Prime Minister, Hazel Hawke and the closest ministers and advisors sat down for our four course dinner in the Lee Dining Room where as usual we had laid a beautiful table, with the best silver, candles and flowers – and half of them turned up in shorts.

They were delightful. Bob Hawke, a staunch ally and friend of the United States, was in his third consecutive term as prime minister and leader of the Australian Labor Party. Australia has always been our country's closest ally, participating in all our wars side by side with the American soldiers and Hawke was the instigator and brain proposing the creation of APEC, the Asia Pacific Economic Cooperation forum, forming the basis for cooperative trade in the Asia Pacific area. He was fun, appreciative, charming, irreverent and, as rumored, flirtatious, while Hazel Hawke was rather bland and subdued. I understand that they were later divorced. Both were health conscious, and moderate in their eating and drinking habits. The Prime Minister got in some golf games, and both went to Camp David for an informal lunch with the Bushes. Mrs. Hawke, on their return, said to me: "Mrs. Bush sends her regards," and later that: "Mrs. Bush asked me to tell her if I felt anything should be changed at Blair House, but I cannot think of a single thing."

The prime minister loved sunbathing, so we had bought some stretchers just in case. One late afternoon Prime Minister Hawke asked me to come with him to the Garden. He looked at the sun and wondered if there was enough time to sunbathe? "Mr. Prime Minister," I said, "you have got about two yards of sunshine here, it is about 25 minutes worth. Why don't you go for it?" "Right-oh," he said, disappeared inside, to reappear five minutes later on the top of the staircase, wearing flip flops and clad in the briefest of brief bikinis looking fantastic for a 60 year old. He dashed into the Lee Drawing Room only to emerge a minute later with his half smoked cigar, an ashtray, assorted papers, and grabbing an aide on the way, he asked for hot tea and disappeared into the oppressive heat and humidity in the Garden, as happy as he could be. They departed by 10 pm on the 27th, and President Mobutu of Zaire walked in the next morning at 10:30 am – a different kettle of fish altogether, as indeed our next visitors from the African continent, the Congo, also were.

"I have asked Sean to assist the president's cook to the second floor pantry, Mrs. Valentiner," Chef said: "I am sure you will agree that she will be more comfortable up there." As this statement was accompanied by a speaking glance at me, I immediately shifted my attention to the small, rotund figure next to me who was looking rather put out, and reiterated, in my lousy French, what Russell had said, while I was taking in what Sean had loaded on the luggage cart, and the smell emanating from same. "Go ahead on up, Sean," I said, "I'll be up later."

"Well," Chef said, "it was clear to me that there were stowaways in this food luggage." And so there were. The cook, in the tradition of all who serve the autocrats of this world, was determined to bring proper native food with her so that her president and his lady would not go hungry in foreign parts and blame her. Thus she had carefully packed in several boxes, a suitcase and a kitbag uncooked goat's meat, raw fish, and other delicacies, all of which were without refrigeration during the long journey which brought Denis Sassou-Nguesso, President of the People's Republic of the Congo for a State Visit in mid February 1990. Upon her arrival she had requested to be taken to the kitchen.

I could see maggots making their way out of the boxes and the suitcase on the cart, and while my heart bled for my poor housemen who had to assist in the handling upstairs, I was grateful for my sharp-eyed Chef and his, always, quick and decisive action. He told me he had already, with the little cook's approval, wrapped, very tightly, some of the boxes to put in his freezer with the rest now practically crawling upstairs under its own steam. The stench emanating later from the second floor pantry, located in the Jackson Place Houses across from the Embassy Office, was awful. The little cook, however, was happily preparing all these delicacies for her president for that very evening. Sean, after each cooking session, cleaned the pantry and disinfected it. The doors were kept tightly closed through the entire passage, but the smell still permeated everything.

I was definitely not going to go down in history as the General Manager of the President's Guest House who had been responsible for a million dollar loss to American agriculture. I called the U.S. Department of Agriculture, responsible for all inspections of food on arrival at the country's ports, but glaringly remiss this time. How could they have missed what was in that particular luggage, the maggots already making their way out, and the stench being insupportable?

The Department could only send over an agent in the morning, but extracted a promise from me to contain the trash in as safe a manner as possible. The next day the agent confiscated 75% of the contents of the boxes and the suitcase and all the trash derived from same. The agent, though, had such an exciting moment.

She found a beetle.

This beetle was, according to her, not thought even to live in the Congo. Also, this beetle could bring devastation to agriculture across the entire land. We learned the next day that fortunately the beetle was only a "cousin" of the more destructive one, and therefore, luckily, the house would not have to be fumigated.

Meanwhile how to tell the President of Congo we were confiscating his special foods and the reason for it? We brought in our ammunition, Chief of Protocol Reed, who was rather good at dealing with such delicate matters. At the White House after the Congolese President's official welcome and meeting with President Bush and his Cabinet, Reed simply jumped in the car with the Congolese President and diplomatically prepared him for the confiscation of his foods. President Sassou-Nguesso seemed most amenable. It is specifically spelt out clearly during advance meetings when a president's team sits down with the U.S. participants such as Protocol staff, Blair House management, USSS, White House personnel and other government entities involved in a visit that no food can be brought in to the United States without first having been cleared through U.S. Customs. However, someone always tries; after all, if an autocratic ruler wishes to do something, he writes his own rule, and it is hard for some nations to understand that in the United States even the president is less than the law of the land.

Meanwhile, the cook was upset. Her personal suitcase was confiscated by the Agriculture Department; her kitbag thrown in the dishwasher by Sean. We offered to take her shopping for whatever foods she needed, and we gave her cash for and assisted her in buying a new suitcase.

President and Mrs. Sassou-Nguesso were handsome and elegant, with the president being rather charming and carefree. He presided over a fragmented delegation, with no one in charge, with much quarrel around him, at which he would just laugh, leave them to sort it out, and wander off. He was hard to get down to meetings, keeping his guests kicking their heels for long periods. He kept a group of distinguished journalists, invited for breakfast, waiting for an hour; he cancelled or shifted scheduled meetings around, but kept smiling and laughing, and thanking us. He thoroughly enjoyed my story about the power sofa in the Lee Drawing Room where he hung out during his spare time. His servants hung his portrait in the Library, taking down one of those on loan from the National Gallery of Art to make room, giving our curator fits.

The big story during this visit was the release from prison of Nelson Mandela in South Africa, and speculation as to the future of that country, and by association the effect on the African continent. President Sassou-Nguesso himself was known for his efforts in West African affairs, including the Namibian peace accords. The Congo, a Marxist state, gained its independence from France in 1960, and under Sassou-Nguesso, according to the Washington Post of February 13, 1990, writing a description of his White House State Dinner "is experiencing its own form of glasnost, with increased dialogue with the West, not to mention live satellite transmissions of American television." Sassou-Nguesso was praised for "the move to a free market economy and the growth of Western investment in the small African country."

But all of this was nothing to the impression his wife made on me and others. The Post wrote: "Actually, they were the most chic Marxists seen at the White House in a long time. Marie-Antoinette Sassou-Nguesso, wearing a gold lamé gown and a long blue and gold cape (and diamond necklace and earrings), outshone First Lady Barbara Bush, looking pretty spiffy herself in a hot pink chiffon and sequin number. And instead of his standard combat fatigues, the Congolese president was dapper in black tie."

Madame was stunningly dressed as were her lady-in-waiting and her maid. She managed to cancel most of her meetings to go shopping instead. The cancellations would come out of the blue just before a scheduled event. While Madame would impatiently tap her foot the Secret Service agents who prefer to advance all trips taken by their charges were not happy. I heard she bought no less than five coats at one visit to the mall, made of camelhair, fur, and silk, and somewhat strange for a first lady from a hot and sticky country. I was not surprised to hear on the grapevine that this particular first lady spent a good deal of time, and a vast deal of her country's treasury, in Monaco. She loved our Elizabeth Arden Salon and preferred our hairdresser to her own and asked her to buy lots of the products used. Fortunately by that time I had a good idea of Madame's character, and insisted that the cost of these products be borne by the Congolese in a direct check to the hairdresser, with one of my people supervising the transaction, rather than let the Congolese First Lady get away without paying.

Soon I was to encounter the only visit of my two hundred of which I think I lost control; the midsummer 1990 Official Working Visit of Gnassigbe Eyadema, President of The Republic of Togo.

That first night the phone rang in the Blair Pantry. Jose answered it and immediately launched into French, all the time glancing at me as if he wished me to be in on the conversation. His voice grew steadily shakier, and his eyes looked exactly as they did when he and I, silently, would be sharing, across a crowded room, a funny incident. When he hung up, he turned to me saying, unsteadily, he had to go upstairs to the Embassy Office on a rescue mission. He then collapsed roaring with laughter.

One of the Togolese security guards had given the clothes he wore to another security guard, to be washed and pressed while he locked himself in the bathroom to wait. Hours later, he was cold and wondering where his clothes were, and thus had called the pantry for help. Jose found him cowering and shivering, and totally naked in one of the two bathrooms outside the Embassy Office. As we only equip those bathrooms with paper towels he had had nothing with which to cover himself. Naturally, I wanted to know if he had made it to the nearest telephone naked as a jailbird, or if he had covered himself in paper towels? Jose fetched a dressing gown for him, and found his friend having a nice, leisurely lunch, with no thought of how his naked buddy was faring.

This was but only one of many bizarre incidents over which Jose Fuster would preside during his long tenure as Head Butler of the President's Guest House. He came on board three months after myself, and remained all the years I was there and beyond. He was a tall, powerful looking man with a strong presence. For me, there was comfort in seeing his large frame quietly moving among our guests; and, as he was well known to the old Washington establishment, having served in innumerable households in the twenty-five years preceding his tenure at Blair House, I suspect that my view was shared by many. He entertained me with stories of our guests as they were coming up the Blair front steps, never imparting gossip, but certainly descriptions of beautiful homes, parties he had organized, and children's successes. During my first year I felt that if Jose did not know the guest coming up the front steps, this person probably should not be at Blair House.

A native of Spain, Jose grew up in a large family near Valencia. After his stint in the army he began restaurant training, worked in Switzerland and for over ten years in Firenze where he met his wife. When they arrived in the States they had with them one small son with two more to come later. I know no one who worked as hard, as long hours, and who pushed himself as much as Jose did to ensure his family's security. I consider him a true immigrant success story whereby through hard work and dedication one is able to give one's children good education, provide several homes for the family, and open one's home and purse to relatives and friends down on their luck.

Jose taught me much about his trade, and I learned quickly one of his biggest gripes was seating people tightly together at a table. He illustrated this particular point with an anecdote from his early career in Washington. He was gingerly trying to insert himself with his tray of Cornish Game Hens between Mrs. Nancy Kissinger and the gentleman on her left when Mrs. Kissinger's hand – and she was known for gesticulating a lot – flew up, hit his tray and sent a game hen flying across the table where it landed on the bosom of a very décolleté lady! As a result I was always wary of hosts who absolutely needed to have more guests at the table than was possible.

No one was more generous towards our visitors. Jose would go out of his way for every single guest; he went shopping late at night with Boris, valet to Prime Minister Chernomyrdin of Russia, or Omar, President Mubarak's valet, and out of his own pocket supplied them with their needs: everything imaginable in paper products for the Russian, in eye care for the Egyptian. He always carried a roll of bills, and would gladly extend a loan for however long anyone needed one. He was, in so many respects, truly a grand seigneur. I so came to rely on his presence, and wrote in my diary after he had been absent over Christmas for a few weeks to visit his 90 year old father in Spain: "Jose is back; what a comfort to have his large frame in sight again."

Therefore it was at first a great puzzlement for me that Jose simply could not get along with some of our staff. I thought at first, like they did, that he had a touch of racial bias, but quickly decided it was not so. It was more his incredible stubbornness that once someone let him down he was through with them, and never forgot. Having received his early training in Switzerland, as I myself had, where having the job and keeping it is all the praise one ever receives, he failed to understand that persons of different cultural backgrounds need a different environment in which to perform. He would not encourage or praise, but expected our housemen to do what they had been asked to do, and this without constant supervision. For, as he said, when I begged him to praise more: "Why must I praise when I do not think they have done a good job?" with which statement I could not quarrel. I did understand, having also been trained in Europe where encouragement was somewhat lukewarm, but the paycheck was proof than one met one's obligations. But having worked in America where people relations are considered important enough to have personnel directors guiding same I understood the other approach. Jose was charged with supervision of our housemen, and for years had a cantankerous relationship with both. In all fairness to him I asked myself, and regularly wrote it in my annual appraisal of him, that surely after ten years doing the same tasks one's charges should be able to do them well, in a timely fashion, and without supervision. Jose was not dealt a fair hand, nor was I, in having little choice to terminate employees who did not perform properly, the government being far too generous a master. Fortunately he had as his Assistant Butler Antonio Rodriguez, also a native Spaniard, who not only was hard working and totally reliable, but the only one, beside me, who could line up chairs to perfection!

Of course more times than not peace reigned, and our shared bizarre experiences bonded us all. The Togolese visit will forever be written on our collective minds in capital letters. Some suspicious looking large trunks were brought in with their luggage; I asked Sean to open them. The Togolese had brought in 300 pounds of yams, 200 of okra, bags full of nuts, baskets of eggs, beer, champagne, – and smoked animals.

Never shall I forget Sean going deathly pale under his dark skin, as he stared down at a smoked monkey, lying at the top of the trunk, with its arms raised above its head.

Moving this monkey aside he revealed a giant fruit bat, as well as a lizard longer than his own arm and at least a foot and one half in width. In addition an army of giant cockroaches crawled out.

Later Lynn asked if they were on our access list!

I went in search of the Togolese ambassador.

"Mr. Ambassador," I said, "as you are aware from the letter you were given by the chief of protocol prior to this visit, no food can be brought in to the United States without first having been cleared through U.S. Customs. Unfortunately this rule does not seem to have been imparted to the president's staff," and I explained what we had found, while trying to keep my face completely neutral. I regretted that we had to hold the food in the basement until it was inspected by representatives from the Department of Agriculture. Poor Ambassador Ellom-Kodjo Schuppius was almost in tears as some of the yams had been brought especially for him.

The AG representative agreed that the President of Togo have access to his food during his stay with us but requested it be destroyed once the visit was over. Our chief of protocol went upstairs to see the president about these arrangements. Meanwhile during the visit "you and your staff are responsible for collecting the refuse from this, and keep it safe for our collection after the visit is over," the USDA agent told me.

The smoked monkey, the giant fruit bat and the gigantic lizard were brought not only for the enjoyment of the Togolese president but also his staff. Jose saw the Togolese security personnel suck on the monkey and bat bones, and one security officer simply crushed the bone with the butt of his gun before sucking. Jose jumped out of the way in case the bullets would start flying at him, as the barrel during this maneuver was pointed straight at him.

Having had the food crisis solved amicably it was thus with dismay that shortly after having said goodbye to the Togolese, and closed up the house, helped with clean-up, turned off the lights and getting ready to go home, I was informed by our security that the Togolese ambassador and chief of protocol were at the locked Front Gate wishing to see me. I visited with them in the Lincoln Room, and was advised the president, now in the Willard Hotel starting his two week private tour of the States, wanted his food.

While they each were enjoying a much needed large vodka on

the rocks, provided by Jose, I had to repeat, in French, the confiscation story, which they knew well, and with which the ambassador had been intimately involved. I suspect they were not really keen to be the messengers of the bad news to their president, and therefore were rather hoping I would be. They invited me to come with them to see their president.

I had a much better idea.

Fortunately, Sam was able to locate Ambassador Reed at the White House, and drove with him to the Willard Hotel. I understand, from Chief of Protocol Reed's colorful description of the meeting, that he had found the furious Togo President pacing his room, ready to leave the United States the following morning thus foregoing his trip around the country, and storming out of the room slamming the door behind him.

Ambassador Reed waited. When the president returned, Reed made two moves: 1) he mentioned that only some of the foods had been confiscated and that perhaps it would be a good idea to make a list of what was left with the Togolese; 2) he spoke to the president's "regional" instincts; how important it was to show oneself to the people; how much the Americans had looked forward to his visit in the States and how important it was for future relations between "our two great nations."

Suddenly everything was fine. Beer and champagne were brought out. A great celebration followed.

Prior to the visit I had learned from my French teacher, a native of Togo, in my early morning classes at the Foreign Service Institute, the Togolese food preferences which at least for breakfast were based on their French colonial days: café au lait and breakfast pastries; rarely fruit and almost never eggs. For lunch, their big meal of the day, they liked their meats well cooked, and we found they ate everything in sight and we fed an army during this visit. The personal staff was difficult and would not let Jose assist in serving the president in the Library so I had to have another talk with Ambassador Schuppius. After this it became easier for Jose to gain access, but I learned I was dubbed The Iron Lady.

Upstairs Mrs. Rennie, Teresinha and Chamber Maid Marinete Saias had their hands full with many more visitors in the bedrooms than indicated on the rooming list and few actually slept on the beds.

Teresinha's demonstration and description in her deep voice, rendered less intelligible the more exited she became, of entering one room and not seeing anyone at first, and then being made aware of an eye appearing slowly from behind the bed, attached to a naked body, defies description. The maids also told me that few towels were used; they dried themselves with the bathmat instead. It was increasingly hard for the ladies to get into the rooms to turn down the beds as there were always bodies in them. But, as so many of our guests slept on the floor it became quite obvious that it was, after all, not necessary. Instead we furnished them with lots of blankets and they seemed as happy as they could be.

Soon a totally different group arrived. Frederic Willem de Klerk, State President of the Republic of South Africa, and Mrs. de Klerk came for an Official Working Visit Sunday morning, September 23, 1990. De Klerk was the first South African chief of state officially invited to the United States since the imposition of apartheid 42 years earlier. This was historic. Seven months earlier, on Saturday, February 10, 1990, de Klerk had freed Nelson Mandela from his long imprisonment, thus setting the stage for a new era in South Africa.

This visit was fascinating and euphoric, the group being somewhat overwhelmed not only by the fact they had reentered the world community, but by our hospitality. President de Klerk, in his farewell speech to the staff, told us that he had had occasion to stay in many of the world's official guest houses, and that Blair House "is the very best ever. Only one other comes close to what you do here," which made me interrupt him spontaneously, "May I know which one, Mr. President?" To much laughter from his delegation members and our own distinguished and talented U.S. Ambassador to South Africa, William Swing, he told me Belgium. I could understand that, as among other things, the Belgian cuisine is the best in the world. I was flattered that we actually could come out ahead. Prior to bidding us farewell with such a lovely speech, the President and Mrs. de Klerk had taken leave of the some fifty police, DS and USSS details in the Garden and could not believe the amount of people it took to protect them.

It was a warmhearted visit, rather unexpectedly so given the appalling apartheid regime which these people had participated in. Assistant Butler Smile St. Aubin, a native of Haiti, (later pursuing a distinguished career at the White House) had been particularly apprehensive about this visit. He was surprised to find how nice the de Klerks were, how unassuming and gracious, and exclaimed: "One should not believe everything one hears."

I had occasion, upon showing President and Mrs. de Klerk upstairs, to express my own satisfaction as a private citizen that they were here, actually calling the president "the Gorbachev of South Africa," which he appreciated. I also mentioned the possibility of demonstrations in Lafayette Park against South Africa and apartheid, just to give him a heads up. These demonstrations were aimed partly at his handling of a recent upsurge of black township violence costing over 750 lives. He was not surprised, and had in fact already been told this would happen, but thanked me nonetheless for informing him of this. He also was pretty forthright about the fact that he only had three more years in his term as president in which to accomplish the dismantling of apartheid, as "assuredly I shall not get reelected." Additionally the entire delegation, in my many conversations with everyone, expressed the fervent hope that "Mandela will live," the alternative would, I gathered, have brought chaos.

Sometimes our chief of protocol was a little too eager: Jose was hovering outside the Library where the de Klerks were saying their daily prayers when Ambassador Reed came upstairs. He wanted to show them our Garden, and despite Jose's suggestion to him to wait for a few minutes until the de Klerks could finish their prayers, he barged in, interrupted these two peoples' privacy, and inexorably bore them downstairs into the Garden, making them forego their breakfast as well.

De Klerk was a fourth-generation Afrikaner leader who at the time of his visit was pursuing a path of dramatic political reform, in fact the dismantling of apartheid. He had pledged to abolish racially discriminating legislation and to negotiate a new constitution that would enable the political participation of all ethnic groups. Since assuming office early 1989 he had taken a series of steps to facilitate dialogue with black leaders, including releasing Nelson Mandela and many other political prisoners, removing the ban on antiapartheid groups, repealing several apartheid laws, and proposing the opening of the ruling National Party's membership to all races. He also traveled widely to discuss his domestic efforts, and earlier was in the United

States as an International Visitor Program grantee in the mid seventies and later as his country's minister of Mineral and Energy Affairs.

However, despite the genuine warmth and friendliness towards all of us on the staff, who came in all sizes, cultural backgrounds, nationalities and races, I did not like what had happened on arrival at AAFB. After the official party had disembarked, the U.S. Immigration officials showed up for their usual preliminaries. The immigration officials were African-Americans, so they were directed to enter the plane by the back stairs, while the white South African pilots walked up the front stairs to meet them inside the plane. The dismantling of apartheid might have been a great wish of many, but obviously was still a long way off becoming reality. Mandela himself said "The American people must know that apartheid is still firmly entrenched in this country."

Marike de Klerk considered herself as the "woman beside, not behind" her husband, the President. A mother and grandmother she was heavily involved in fostering the theme that everyone, not just politicians, must become politically involved if the country is to move forward. She wrote her own speeches, worked for women's issues, such as the voting power of women and their importance as the nation's opinion makers. She supported a number of social causes, including hosting social affairs for children suffering from life-threatening diseases, and was a patron of groups concerned with cancer, the aged, and Alzheimer's disease.

Marike de Klerk later was divorced from her husband, and was found some years later brutally murdered in her home in South Africa.

Sam and I had many opportunities of visiting with delegation members, both of us being curious about their life in a country which I considered a milder copy of Hitler's Germany. I was struck by one woman's ignorance of life in the black townships, and her claim of not knowing of the hardships, deprivations, humiliations and brutality the black population had endured. The ordinary Germans also claimed complete ignorance of the deportation to concentration camps of the Jews. We learned how totally separate life was between the races; how you took your life in your hands if as a black person you were out in Pretoria after dark, or as a white person you found yourself in a black township. But repeated many times was how "we all pray that Mandela will live."

President de Klerk, in addition to the all important meeting with President Bush at the White House, held meetings with the Congressional Leadership, and Members of the Cabinet, addressed the National Press Club members, and went to an intimate private dinner party at the Vice President's Residence. The all important issue on his agenda seemed to be the lifting of sanctions against his country, and to establish a personal relationship with President Bush.

In March 1992 over 68% of the white voters in South Africa delivered a stunning victory to de Klerk permitting him to continue his negotiations with the black community leaders on a new constitution. This was described by de Klerk as a decisive turning point in the country's history and a miracle, as it was the first time anywhere in Africa that a white community had voted for a voluntary transition to black majority rule, and in the words of de Klerk, "having closed the book on apartheid."

Robert Gabriel Mugabe, President of The Republic of Zimbabwe, arrived for an Official Working Visit July 23-25, 1991. It is amazing to me that in my notes from this first visit of President Mugabe and his delegation, I characterized them as a "lovely and gentle group of people" considering subsequent atrocities and horrors committed with the sanction and approval of same. He became a stark example of how power corrupts, and absolute power corrupts absolutely. Jim Hoagland of the Washington Post said on August 26, 2001, just a few weeks after I retired from Blair House: "Racism is not for racists alone. It is a handy political and economic tool for the quick, the desperate and the greedy as well as for biological and cultural ideologues. It can become as vicious a diversionary weapon in unprincipled black hands in Africa as it was in white ones in Mississippi. Mugabe now demonstrates this on a daily basis. Zimbabwe's president for two decades, Mugabe has turned his once pleasant and relatively prosperous agricultural nation into an African nightmare. His persecution and brutal dispossession of white farmers – and their black workers – threatens to inflame tensions in South Africa and to shatter the economic stability of the region."

The president enjoyed all kinds of food and had cream of wheat for breakfast as well as his own cornmeal. Being athletic he was an early riser to get in his exercise before breakfast. The delegation members were hearty eaters, and drank gallons of orange juice but with less of a sweet tooth than our other African visitors, and preferred tea to coffee, undoubtedly a remnant from their colonial days. They brought with them another unauthorized load of food stuff, well packed and most of it frozen. I was grateful I could avoid the difficult diplomatic dance involved in informing an authoritarian leader that he cannot import whatever he wants into the United States. As they were going on to London (and the British not caring about these imports) from Washington D.C. we simply held the foods for them till departure instead of having the U.S. Department of Agriculture confiscate it. All was meticulously listed, and accounted for, down to weight and which box contained which food stuffs, very impressive indeed.

Among the foods, they also carried little snack packs of dried minnows and caterpillars.

President Mugabe, in power since his country's independence in 1980, was quiet and had little personality. He was detained for twelve years under the British rule, and played a prominent role in Zimbabwe's liberation struggle.

He returned in May 1995 for another visit, this time having aged considerably, but also newly married to his secretary with whom he had two small children, resulting in much shopping at Sears for sheets, and also stocking up on Cream of Wheat. The visit was considerably busier than the former one, but they were just so unassuming and pleasant. Due to a severe storm they had to turn back from the ceremony at Arlington Cemetery, making their Deputy Chief of Mission remark: "We prayed for rain in Zimbabwe, we just forgot to tell the gods where we wanted it."

Shortly after the above, we welcomed another African leader. In her weekly Washington Post article called Chronicles, Sarah Booth Conroy mentioned my little story regarding my preparations for the State Visit of Abdou Diouf, President of The Republic of Senegal and Mrs. Diouf, September 9-12, 1991. Mrs. Conroy had been on a tour for the Friends of Blair House, organized by the Blair House Restoration Fund, and, on walking through the Primary Suite with a group, I had mentioned how we arranged our six foot long bed for a seven foot tall president. I had in fact been told in no uncertain terms by the Senegalese advance team that "our president cannot sleep in that bed. You must get another one for him." Sarah Booth Conroy wrote about it as follows: "According to highly placed sources, it is not true that the new Friends of Blair House, the presidents guest quarters, are being organized to buy a super-long bed in case the 6 foot 11 Senegalese President Abdou Diouf comes to call again.

Not to make a long story out of it, but Blair House's ever-resourceful staff – without really spending any money – made a bed Diouf could lie on during his visit here two weeks ago.

"Belfair, which set up the great English antique bed for us, told us never to move it, said Benedicte Valentiner, Blair House's general manager. "With the canopy and curtains, it's so complicated to take apart. So I asked my deputy, Sam Castleman, to work with what we have. I suggested a small bench be put at the foot of the bed. Then I went on vacation."

Marinete Saias, the Blair House chambermaid, had a great inspiration – use the coffee table from the women's lounge, just the right size and of matching wood. A hunk of foam rubber brought it up to the height of the mattress. A thin foam mattress pad was stretched over the whole kit and caboodle. Then Saias, whom Valentiner called an "exquisite seamstress," added to the sheets and mattress and blanket cover to bring them to the right length. To finish it all off, a number of decorative pillows were strategically placed. Reportedly, Diouf was "thrilled" that his feet would not dangle off the end of the bed.

"There are no problems, only solutions," said Valentiner, who thought a minute and added, "We say it better in my native Denmark: "Need teaches a naked woman to weave."

CHAPTER 5

OF CHIEFS OF PROTOCOL AND PARTIES

"I cannot bear that the moment has come when I shall have to separate myself from this delicious Cognac."

A Blair House guest

"Goodbye, Mr. Ambassador," I held out my hand, "it's been fun. I wish you well." He took my hand, stood for a moment in thought, then bade me farewell, and departed. I leaned against the wall, too drained to move on.

After his goodbye luncheon, for 57 of his most intimate among the ambassadors, most likely those from whom he had been able to wiggle a medal, on Friday, October 18, 1991, I escorted Joseph Verner Reed, U.S. Chief of Protocol, out of the house via the service entrance on Jackson Place. Due to a demonstration outside his luncheon guests had entered through the White House Conference Center on Jackson Place with which we shared a garden wall. It seemed entirely appropriate that he, who had caused me so much grief, should have to depart his "personal playground" during two years and eight months in this manner. Especially, the preceding five weeks had been extraordinarily tough with a tightly packed schedule, including 23 functions and four labor intensive visits.

Additionally, less than two hours earlier I was in the Blair Pantry, hanging on to Jose for dear life with my hands on his arms, begging him to "keep a lid on it. It will only be a few more hours, Jose, and then he is out of our lives for good. Please, please – for my sake, just stay calm." Jose had charged into the pantry, white around the lips, eyes blazing, exclaiming: "That man, he has done it again." What Reed had done wounded Jose's pride to the core. Ambassador Reed had started changing the table cards around, despite having approved the seating arranged by his Ceremonial Office staff.

Often several of our guests had special dietary requirements: U.S. Senator Joe Lieberman, Jewish by faith was strictly kosher, or U.S. House Speaker Thomas Foley on a strict diet as long as I had known him and bringing his own food in a paper sack handed to Jose on arrival. Jose probably was the only person in the world who could arrange a cut up apple with the accompanying crackers on a plate in such a way that one's mouth would actually drool. Jose always took care instructing the waiter serving these guests as to who would get which plate of food having experienced the excruciating embarrassment of a hapless guest being offered the Speaker's apple and crackers while the angry Speaker pushed away his beef tenderloin, all a result of Ambassador Reed's need to change cards around in the last moment. And today Jose had reached his boiling point, also fueled by an incident he had with the ambassador weeks earlier, which was sufficiently offensive and embarrassing for him to advise Sam and me about. We had agreed to keep quiet knowing that soon the ambassador would be gone for good, but had been careful that Jose and Reed were not left alone together at any time.

I first experienced Joseph Verner Reed during the fall of 1988 when I was asked by Ambassador Roosevelt to show the house to him. I quickly discovered he was not in the least interested in the historic notes or stories, but only wished to appraise its beauty without any help from me. This he did, through two floors, in ten minutes. He seemed impressed and charmed by the beauty and elegance, and with his background, growing up in similar surroundings, certainly understood what he was appraising.

Joseph Verner Reed, at that time approaching his 51st birthday, was United Nations' Undersecretary General. Earlier he was President Reagan's appointee as U.S. Ambassador to Morocco and prior to that for many years a protege of David Rockefeller, and working at the Chase Manhattan Bank. His family and the Bushes were friends.

Fastidious and exacting, he knew precisely what he wanted in set up and service, and also knew to a fault how to extract most use out of anybody and anything. The stories about him were many, and usually very funny. During a visit of U.N. Secretary General Perez de Cuellar, invited on a private visit by President George H.W. Bush as a thank you for his support and assistance during the Desert War, I learned the following: In the U.N. headquarters Ambassador Reed had wangled an office which enabled him, from his desk, to look through his open door down the passage to the Secretary General's offices. Whenever press gathered around in that vicinity, Reed would pop up to participate in the photo-op with the Secretary General, regardless of whether he was invited, or even remotely connected to the event of the day. He was also a sucker for royalty. When he served as U.S. Ambassador to Morocco he was heard to refer to the King as "my King," a really great statement to be made by the representative of a republic. U.S. Ambassador Peter Sebastian and his wife Harvel who served with him there told me "he put a premium on access to his presence!"

He was tall, reed thin, beautifully tailored, and had a habit of shaking his French cuffs out of his jacket while appraising his surroundings as if to see if his actions were being noticed. He rarely passed a mirror without a quick, admiring glance at his elegant person, and never, ever passed by a ready camera. Likewise he had a knack for avoiding trouble of any kind. Often I witnessed his smooth handling of a sticky situation, whether it involved an ambassador, an ambassador's wife who was dazzled by his good looks, and thought that he actually was interested in her, or my own problems which a call from the chief of protocol would have solved in two seconds. He simply turned these problems over to others, and went on his merry way.

He had a great sense of humor, and an ability to focus on whoever talked to him as if that person was his total interest all the while tossing a remark to one ambassador, a finger kiss to another, smiling and laughing, while appraising the room as to whether he held the focus of his audience. Years ago I cut out of the Albuquerque Journal this quote which at long last was matched perfectly to a person: "I wouldn't say he is conceited, it is only that he is convinced that if he hadn't been born, people would have been wondering why."

He was the perfect public relations official. He was called by some the perfect chief of protocol. Life with him was one long theatrical production.

Ambassador Reed did not give parties.

He held events.

He instituted the habit – followed by subsequent chiefs – of inviting newly accredited ambassadors for lunch, bringing them together with interesting members of the arts, government and business community, and always a journalist as this particular chief must effect his publicity therapy and what better way to do so than to include a member of the press? A tea for their spouses usually followed, introducing them to spouses of Members of Congress and the Cabinet. As he had a vast international acquaintance we were privileged to meet many members of the international community and generally from that perspective enjoyed the activities. Undoubtedly he took the burden of much entertaining off the shoulders of Secretary Baker. Frequently his luncheons would be held in the Lee Dining Room, the most historic room in the Lee House.

He was interested in the china and silver used for his parties, and usually mentioned this to his guests, so I typed up a small card, placed to the left of his fork, listing what was on the table that day:

"Decorations:

> Silver Terrines by Paul Store of London, early 19th century; of particular interest for today's luncheon might be the motto on the terrine: FORWARD WITHOUT FEAR;

> Cyclamen in Lowestoft China Bowls, approximately 1780, collected by the Blair Family.

> China and Crystal are made by Lenox and was a gift to the Blair House Restoration Fund, but dessert plates are Sèvres, a wedding gift to the Blairs."

I enjoyed the activity his tenure brought to us. In order to accommodate his wish to entertain the diplomatic corps with frequency, and coping with the Department of State's permanent state of budgetary crunch, I asked our head housekeeper and our maids if they would be willing to assist in butlering for Jose so as to save the cost of having to hire outside help. Jose and I personally trained them for weeks in the servicing of meals, in pantry work, and in cloak room duties. But particularly in the dining-room, Jose in his eagerness to impart to us all his knowledge only succeeded in thoroughly confusing the issue as to how our guests should be served. There are many ways of changing dirty plates for clean ones, and I finally put my foot down and declared: "Here we take the dirty plate from the right, and put down the clean from the left." Food on a tray is presented to the guest on his left side. In Washington D.C. this is known as French service – don't ask me why. But the question of French service cost me a bit of grief:

In the spring of 1988 with my staff I was unpacking the export china after its many years in storage. Ambassador Roosevelt joined me to decide what to do with it. Much would go on display as only few pieces were appropriate for food service. During this discourse she differentiated between various serving styles, and expressed her preference for French service. Her reason, she said, was that ambassadors with their cultural and dietary differences liked to choose what to eat rather than having a pre-plated meal put in front of them. My brain went into top gear: "French service, French service – what is she talking about?" She sensed my discomfort and somewhat accusingly said: "You don't know what French service is, do you, Mrs. V?" I, naturally, vehemently denied not knowing what French service was. After she left, I dived for the phone.

"Anne Merete," I pleaded, "pray tell me at once what the ambassador means by French service?" Anne Merete Petrignani, my friend and wife of Italian ambassador Rinaldo Petrignani, after mulling this over declared that French service was no more than what she and I had grown up with in Denmark. Each course at the dinner table is presented to you on a platter, from the left, and you select the food you wish to eat.

Thus we were able to handle luncheons of up to 14 persons entirely on our own, keeping the cost of an ambassadorial luncheon to the bare minimum. Ambassador Reed was thrilled, and, I believe, grateful. I learned early on to arrange flowers, but in those days with a more than usually stringent budget, instead of ordering some, I often had to be creative and use what was free and at hand: such as the impatiens planted in the Garden. Often Houseman Frankie Blair would dig up a bunch for me which I put into our beautiful export china bowls, and which after the lunch would go back into the Garden again. We became great at recycling – even Chef pitched in and made Rose Petal Ice Cream from roses not needed any more.

Meanwhile Ambassador Reed did not limit his entertainment to the house, but took us on the road asking us to cater refreshments to members of the diplomatic corps for whom he arranged special events: Thus one morning at 5 am, five of us on the staff met to collect our stuff to serve refreshments to the Diplomatic Corps, invited to view a movie at the Air and Space Museum at 8 am; we had to bring in everything. And when the Department of State was dedicating a new building located at the International Center and housing the Office of Foreign Missions, the Diplomatic Corps was invited, as we were: to furnish the refreshments. So our Head Butler, Assistant Butler, Deputy General Manager and I took to the road in Jose's large station wagon, loading it up with folding tables, flowered tablecloths, glasses, trays, napkins, cold drinks and our special breakfast pastries. In the last moment I grabbed two cachepots with flowering begonias – after all we had our standards, and we would jolly well keep up the appearance even if we did have to do so in the driveway of a building.

It did not take long before the ambassador's luncheons had expanded in size, up to 22 persons which was the number we could seat in the Jackson Place Conference Room. We had to hire extra help. So the clever ambassador thought it would be a splendid idea to piggy-back on visits, so that visit "left-overs" could be used for his luncheons which he then often scheduled within two hours of the departure of the President's guests. Soon, naturally, he became impatient having to have his plans interrupted, with something as trivial as a visit, and scheduled the luncheons in the middle of same, and requested that I "move" visit meetings elsewhere in the house so he could hold forth in the Jackson Place end of the complex. As my staff was totally occupied with President Bush's overnight guests, outside help had to be hired to serve the Reed guests, and the cost of the luncheons skyrocketed. They also created a security problem, as adding extra outside waiters meant hiring those who did not have quite the same kind of clearance needed to be at Blair House during a visit. We came close to compromising not only our security standards, but our otherwise excellent relationship with both the Diplomatic Security and the Secret Service.

But, did we make an impression on Ambassador Reed? Of course not, and as for his Ceremonial Office staff, who handled these arrangements for him, they simply did not understand except that "Mrs. V" was being difficult.

Some years later, I had a comfortable chat with Susan Porter Rose, Chief of Staff for Barbara Bush during 12 years, and finally told her some of the more bizarre things we had experienced during Reed's tenure. She exclaimed: "But why did you not tell me. I could have made arrangements. I would have left no footprints." I thanked her, but said: "How could I – he was appointed by President Bush, and further is a family friend. I would have been crucified had I said anything." But I appreciated her sentiments, and told her I thought she had been aware of his more outrageous behavior: hosting functions of his own in the house during the times when Blair House was flying the flag of the President's official visitor.

Susan had walked in for an ambassadorial luncheon through the front door rather than arriving by 700 Jackson Place, and had been surprised seeing the President's foreign visitors milling around. She had seemed uncomfortable when I explained who the visitors were. And I had been convinced she had passed this on to the higher ups. Frequently, on arrival of a foreign visitor, I had had to negate my commitment, made earlier to the advance team as to their potential meeting space, and my embarrassment was acute. That our gallant chief asked me to do so, rather than making the explanation himself, was no surprise, though. I had no confidence in his personal valor at all.

In Washington D.C. the official announcement, expected for a while, that Joseph Verner Reed had resigned his post as U.S. Chief of Protocol was done with much fanfare, nice comments from the White House, and Ambassador Reed even, patronizingly and publicly, commenting on his joy at the appointment of John G. Weinmann to that particular post. There were many parties for him, more medals to be distributed, and many luncheons hosted by him at Blair House, especially during visits.

Some ambassadors were sad to see him leave. As chief of protocol, Reed had worked tirelessly for the Diplomatic Corps, especially looking after the African ambassadors, and gone out of his way to invite ambassadors and their spouses either to his luncheons and receptions, or to expose them to certain American traditions such as baseball, Williamsburg or other museum settings. But much as I had enjoyed the glitter during his tenure, and meeting so many international personalities, I had been so affected by his shallowness and lack of help during certain crises. During one I had even been so desperate

I had invited former chief of protocol Lucky Roosevelt to lunch at the Four Seasons Hotel to ask her advice. After hearing my story she exclaimed: "I shall never forgive Joseph for not helping out."

In order to cut cost State transferred out of Blair House the facilities manager; the consequence of losing this position was no supervision of our systems resulting in a lack of humidity control, devastating for a building with such a notable content. I was so desperate that when Admiral Arthur W. Fort, the Assistant Secretary for Administration, attended a reception and made the mistake of asking me, perfunctorily, "how is it going?" I replied: "Not very well, Admiral."

He was startled, and asked why: "Because of your people, Admiral – we have had no facilities manager here for months; all we have are itinerant people who react to problems instead of preventing them. The result is that our 18th century wallpaper is coming lose from the wall and our floors in the Jackson Place look like Mount Everest is erupting in there." To his credit, within a week, I was meeting in the Lincoln Room with his No. 3, Vince Chaverini, who promised to find a suitable facilities manager soonest. But when I asked that Sam and I be permitted to interview this person, as a certain personality was needed to fit in with the special lifestyle of Blair House, he said that was out of the question. Whereupon I got up, thanked him for his time, and declared there could be no point in continuing this conversation as we had to be able to participate in this selection. He asked me to sit down again and thus Sam and I became involved in the process. Later Admiral Fort made a big gesture towards us turning up with his four key people, spending twenty minutes with us, ending up in the kitchen sampling Chef's chocolate chip cookies. It was not lost on me that he had thus emphasized his firm support of the importance of Blair House and its role to his most influential staffers.

It was of course not only the chief of protocol who entertained, although he had to approve all events. Cabinet Secretaries could request the use of the house for meetings and meals as long as they entertained their counterpart from another country and furthered American foreign policy objectives.

Susan Baker hosted many events during those four years, starting with a lunch for Barbara Bush. "I have heard about your Tiffany china," Mrs. Bush said, referring to the unexpected gift from the Tiffany Co. of a set of china for 100, based on the design in our sofa fabric in the Garden Room, "and I would love to see it – I really do not like my Lenox at the White House." She insisted on going with me to the Blair Pantry. She liked the beautiful Tiffany china, and, to the delight of our staff working there, remained in the pantry to inspect our other pieces of china, especially the donation, years earlier, of the Stetson china, a gift from the estate of John Stetson, son of the "Stetson Hat" inventor, who was U.S. Minister to Poland 1925 to 1929. While there he commissioned Limoges in France, specifically the designer Theodore Haviland, to create a set of china for him. Upon Minister Stetson's death, two thirds of this china was given to Blair House. Cream colored with an intricate gold border it was sufficient to augment our Lenox china, and to mix and match to give some variety to our table settings. However, Jose and I had agreed the 13 remaining dinner plates would only be used as base plates. Mrs. Bush was quite taken with their beautiful designs of birds.

"How are you doing," she asked me, and – "have you met Jennifer yet? I just wonder how you will get along with her." Mrs. Bush's comment to me I took to be a warning to tread lightly.

I had read about George Bush's Jennifer – his aide of many years. Vice President George Bush had presided over the U.S. Senate for eight years, solely to cast his vote in case of a tie, and his office on the Hill had been run by Jennifer Fitzgerald, whom he had now named Deputy Chief of Protocol.

Smallish, pretty and well endowed, with blond hair in an old fashioned bun adorned with a silk scarf matching her Louis Feraud outfits, Jennifer Fitzgerald could not be described as an effective deputy. In her defense it must have been a Herculean task to be deputy to Reed. Her principal object, though, during the four years she served was to escort presidential delegations around the world attending elections, inaugurations, and other high level events. She was, however, very supportive of Blair House, never interfering, and for that I was grateful indeed. She often told me to be careful, as Reed was doing his best to unseat me and her, and was "thrashing us all over town at dinner parties." I took this with a grain of salt, but was nevertheless appreciative of her frankness.

We began a series of dinners hosted by the Secretary of Defense, then Dick Cheney.

The fun part of doing a dinner for Defense was the lack of

budgetary restraints, the Pentagon entertainment budget being enormous; Chef loved planning exquisite menus with no thought of cost. Also the Cheneys enjoyed five course dinners, which was Chef's preference, including a sorbet to cleanse the palate after the first course, often a fish dish. A military quartet in dress uniform stationed in the Blair Front Drawing Room played during arrivals, and the Military Strolling Strings would surprise our guests during dessert. At the Blair Entrance and in the street, a detail of military personnel was stationed to open doors. The evenings were elegant and festive, and we soon developed a stellar reputation in the protocol office of Defense for perfection and reliability. I would maintain an excellent relationship with that office during all my years as general manager.

The Cheneys seemed low-key, were pleasant but impersonal and somewhat remiss in expressing their thanks other than to their own protocol chief – as if we at the house were expendable and had had no role in the success of the evening. Mr. Cheney, an arch conservative, clever, biding his time for bigger and better things 12 years hence, back then too was as smooth as a greased cobra – and now, reflecting on my first impression of him, and on his later role as our country's vice president, I wonder what our one dimensional 43rd President would have done without Dick Cheney.

It was otherwise with Secretary Baker and his wife, Susan, who always showed great appreciation. We saw them often. In the Bush administration, while rarely greeting at Andrews Air Force Base (AAFB) some 35 minutes out of Washington, the Secretary of State went to the Washington Monument where the official visitor landed by helicopter from where they drove together to Blair House. Mr. Baker often remained with our guest for twenty minutes, and undoubtedly used those minutes to get some of the work done for which the foreign visitor had come to America. Meanwhile Mrs. Baker, usually accompanying her husband, with her arms full of flowers for the official guests, spent time in another location in the house with the spouses of the principal guest and the ambassador. This courtesy was followed faithfully by all administrations prior to Bill Clinton's. In the Eisenhower and Kennedy era the President at times personally received his distinguished guests at Union Station when they arrived by train. Following the deconsolidation of the Soviet Union many more countries evolved and the workload greatly increased for our

Secretaries of State. So starting with Bill Clinton, only the chief of protocol would receive on arrival at AAFB. However, in my opinion the courtesy extended by our country in having the Secretary of State personally greet on arrival was very important and set the tone for the negotiations which were to follow, just as I knew how vital the hospitality and warm welcome of Blair House was in furthering our foreign policy objectives.

Equally impressive as her husband, Susan Baker often entertained the wives of the Diplomatic Corps for tea or coffee, took special people on a tour of the house, or gave a small luncheon for a visiting VIP. She came over in the beginning of the first Clinton administration for a tour with her family. She brought me a gift, and told me that she had personally stepped in when Ambassador Reed had done his best to get rid of me. "You did not know this, Mrs. Valentiner, but I made very sure he could do no such thing, and I wanted you to know it." I thanked her warmly, and told her that I knew that my relationship with Reed had been tenuous at best. "I worked very hard for him, Mrs. Baker, and was careful never to make a mistake, thus not giving him any reason for having me fired. But I am grateful to you, as I am to Barbara Bush whom I understand also protected me."

I had an excellent relationship with Secretary Baker who used the house often, and with whom I felt completely at ease. I was careful to gauge his mood on arrival and remain quiet when the situation called for it. But there were times when I could not shut up, and I believe, he liked me the better for it.

In October 1990, as usual our Congress could not get off their duff and finish the budget in time, so the U.S. government shut down for a few days. The Department of State was operating on a continuing resolution meaning that there was no extra funding available, and we could not spend a penny beyond the absolute necessities. This time while the government shut down, however, we had to come to work because Secretary Baker and Secretary Cheney were hosting the annual U.S./Australian Ministerial Meetings on Columbus Day, Monday, October 8, 1990, a federal holiday. In addition, working on a federal holiday, we were by law paid time and a half for each hour worked.

I received Secretary Baker in the Front Hall, and could see immediately he was not happy. In silence I escorted him to the Conference

Room when he turned to me and, glaring at me, said: "I am not going to pay any of you for working today, Mrs. Valentiner." I immediately rose to the challenge: "I sincerely hope, Mr. Secretary, you will pay my staff, who works so hard for you. They do not deserve such treatment," and I glared right back at him. He was distracted then by a staffer, and I slipped into the background, thinking that surely I had overstepped my bounds. At the end of that long day, I escorted Mr. Baker to the Front Door, when he turned to me and said: "Mrs. Valentiner, I am going to pay you and your staff for today," – and he thanked me and took off.

Among the 1800 functions outside of the 200 visits which I presided over during my more than thirteen years at Blair House, I shall not ever forget a specific day with the Bakers. I wrote in my diary on Sunday, December 8, 1991: "I was in the presence of a holy person today."

Sponsored by Susan and Jim Baker, the Prince of Peace Foundation, Escondido, California, held a reception for Mother Teresa, winner of the Nobel Peace Prize for her work among the sick and dying in Calcutta, to give her an award of $1 million. Mrs. Baker had personally arranged everything with me, coming over several times. She collected a notable group of people to witness this event, such as the Secretaries of Transportation and Energy, the Ambassadors of Egypt, India, and the Soviet Union, J. Carter Brown, Director of the National Gallery, whom I had known in Washington D.C. in our younger days, and other notables.

The guests arrived at 4 pm on a Sunday, with Secretary Baker coming in from a golf game at 4:30. A little later, having left his wife and all the guests upstairs in the Garden Room, he went outside with me to wait for Mother Teresa. She was at the Basilica of the National Shrine of the Immaculate Conception witnessing the induction of 27 sisters into the Missionaries of Charity Order which she founded in 1950. So at the appointed time a limousine turned the corner and swung up in front of Blair House.

The driver jumped out to open the door.

The Secretary stepped forward to assist Mother Teresa out of the car.

Nothing happened.

We peeped inside the limousine.

She wasn't there.

Horrified and embarrassed, the driver jumped back into the car, accelerated, and turned the corner on two wheels.

He had forgotten her.

Secretary Baker and I looked at each other. I had a hard time not laughing, but thought better of it. He had just told me that he had played 17 holes of golf and left "the 18th to come in here" and probably was in no mood for a good laugh. The weather was delightful so he elected to remain in the street holding court for passers-by who had the rare treat of being able actually to chat with our busy Secretary of State. I later heard the guests in the Garden Room had grown increasingly restless during this long wait and realized I should have suggested he entertain them with tales of the – soon – nonexistent Soviet Union and the recent Middle East Peace Talks.

Mother Teresa finally arrived 45 minutes later. She was so tiny I had to stoop over her to take her hands which she stretched out to me, while she apologized for being so late. Having been asked to have a plate of food ready for her before entering the ground floor elevator I asked her if I might give her a little something to eat, to which she said no thank you in her charmingly accented English:

"You know, the poor must eat first."

She stayed less than 20 minutes, but left to thunderous applause, with Susan Baker radiant that her careful organization of this notable event had been so successful.

Before Joseph Reed left for New York I wrote John G. Weinmann, the U.S. ambassador to Finland who with his wife, Virginia, had spent two days in and out of the house during the visit of the President of the Republic of Finland and Mrs. Koivisto in May 1991. I was so pleased with his appointment as chief of protocol, and told him how much I looked forward to welcoming him to Blair House as our new boss. John Weinmann had made such an impression on George and Barbara Bush when with six days warning the previous September he had laid on the U.S.-Soviet Summit in Helsinki. Before that he was the George H.W. Bush campaign's Louisiana State Finance chairman, and later a member of his National Finance Committee. His reward after the Bush election was an ambassadorship in Finland. No one, I am certain, could have enjoyed such a posting more than he and his wife, and in the eighteen months I worked with them in the Nation's

Capital their delight in the job was apparent. What was also apparent was the respect for the Protocol Office staffers which they showed.

Later in a letter to me Weinmann quoted Colonel Tarvainen, President Koivisto's military aide, as having said: "I have stayed in many guest houses in all parts of the world and the charm and thoughtful hospitality extended by Mrs. Valentiner and her colleagues is by far the nicest I have ever experienced and it is the most beautiful home I have ever seen".

Our new chief of protocol had a tendency to micro manage. His first great idea was that we give room service to every member of a visit.

That was a really bad idea.

Many delegation members were servants brought to wait upon the principal guests. They were quite as capable of coming downstairs to their meals as they would be excruciatingly capable of taking the fullest advantage of my staff. From time to time spouses of ministers asked for a tray in their room, and we always obliged, so I sort of ignored this suggestion. The question was also raised with the new chief from one guest why she could not lock her door. Nobody could – this was a home.

Following that came the scrutinizing of Chef's menus: the wish, among others, to have ice cream parfait served in tall glasses – which earlier we had nixed as our glasses could not tolerate freezer temperature; the Weinmanns liked to have the meal pre-plated, which was the chic "new" way of serving rather than using French service. That presented us with a problem, overcome because this couple was so sensible. We could pre-plate for small groups, but our dinner plates were not really large enough for Chef to go to town in his decorating apart from the fact that we had no space to put out 84 plates for last minute assembly of the meal. I also had to cope with a certain learning curve: the ambassador and his wife were under the impression that they could drop in having lunch whenever they wished, just as they had been used to at their embassy in Helsinki. We obliged the first time they came, having lovely leftovers in the kitchen. I can still see Ambassador Weinmann looking at me with wide open eyes and a big smile, as he asked for his lunch. However, I was on the phone immediately to Executive Director Clyde Nora in the Protocol Office, who groaned and said: "But I told them it was a different set up." There were other instances but it was all perfectly natural getting used to a different approach to menus. Fortunately the new chief did not walk around Blair House at night checking on our offices as he was wont to do in the Protocol Office where our colleagues would find precisely printed and phrased little notes admonishing them to "keep their desks clean."

As Ambassador Weinmann wanted to emerge himself in the various operations in which he and his staff were involved he arranged for some of us to observe a U.S. Secret Service Training Demonstration early 1992. Dressed casually and warmly as we were expected to participate in several of the exercises including firing weapons we piled into buses sent by the Service and proceeded to Beltsville, Maryland.

Ambassador Weinmann grabbed my hand and dragged me along with him – I believe out of his sense of fun – and we were treated to a demonstration of how a car can avoid bullets – by swerving, speeding, stopping on a dime, turning corners on two wheels. I am proud to say I was not green around the gills, but I came close. I loved seeing the incredible German Shepherds and Belgium Malinois being trained to attack perpetrators or hold them at bay. It was awesome. But I hated firing an automatic.

Ambassador Weinmann, to his credit, also made certain that the many people in the Protocol Office who had served long years were awarded with appropriate acknowledgements. I myself was given one for ten year's service, although at the time I had been in government longer. It was the Meritorious Honor Award "to thank you for the flawless management of Blair House, and for the exacting means by which the house is maintained, and especially on behalf of the innumerable official visitors who were the beneficiaries of your warm hospitality." That he did it at all was admirable. I was so comfortable with this chief of protocol. He was a straight shooter; I always knew exactly where I was as he told me up front. Also he shared my passion for neatness in our drawing and dining rooms and told me he always knew when "Mrs. V was away; the chairs were not properly lined up."

Ambassador Weinmann was whimsical with a delightful sense of humor and very generous. He included my two young Danish nephews in his Protocol picnic in our Garden for all his protocol staff. They were visiting me before setting out across the United States spending five months in a Volkswagen bus and I used their services sometimes to be doormen at events. Joakim and Jakob Valentiner, sons of my younger brother, Gustav, came away from Washington D.C. thinking this was all in a day's work: to hold the door for the President of the United States, being complimented on their Mickey Mouse ties and thanked by him for wanting to meet him; to be introduced to General Colin Powell; to be guests of the Commandant of Washington for the Tattoo on the Mall and at his reception at Fort Myer and get sent home in his car; to have dinner in the gardens at Tudor Place; to get an invitation with free tickets to Williamsburg, and to have a private tour of Mount Vernon escorted by a general's wife.

I met several of our past chiefs of protocol over the years, and especially connected with James W. Symington, former U.S. Congressman (D-MI), well known to me before I came to Blair House. I recall, when, as a young congressman, he entertained, being an excellent guitar player, in the Marquee Lounge at the Shoreham Hotel. Chief of Protocol for President Lyndon Johnson, he says in his book, THE STATELY GAME: "The principal function of efficient protocol is to establish and maintain the context in which meetings between government leaders can occur with a minimum of misunderstanding."

There are, I expect, many definitions of protocol, one of which is that it is form as opposed to substance. It is also a form of mechanical diplomacy, and definitely a strict observance of social conventions. These universally accepted standards of behavior constitute the framework within which negotiations between sovereign nations can take place and the framework within which we in a civil society live and work with each other. Without protocol there would be confusion, disruption, and ruffled feathers. In presidential protocol there is no room for error. Mistakes are not assumed or expected. Therefore the following story is divine:

Jim Symington had just taken office, and his first duty was to escort the Sudanese ambassador to the White House so that he could present his Letter of Accreditation to the President. In those days, Symington told me, there were few protocol officers around to guide his way, so essentially he was on his own. He arrived at the White House with the Sudanese ambassador, not having a clue what route to take, but set out in the general direction of the Oval Office. He stepped out, marching along, with the Sudanese ambassador next to him, and when Symington thought he was just about at the right place he opened a door with great fanfare – and ushered the Sudanese ambassador into one of the White House broom closets!

I wonder if appointed people, such as Ambassador Weinmann, ever anticipate how abruptly their privileged positions are finished. On Bill Clinton's Inaugural Day, January 20, 1993, Ambassador Weinmann, around 11 am, still his country's chief of protocol, and his wife were driven by Gene Lewis, the Protocol Office chauffeur, to the U.S. Capitol to witness the change of power. After the ceremony, however, when they, unsuspecting, went to find their car, they saw Gene drive off with Acting Chief of Protocol Richard Gookin. Mr. Gookin, for years Associate Chief of Protocol, was now in charge until a new chief of protocol was appointed. At all levels of government, the transition was complete.

CHAPTER 6

A PARADE OF KINGS AND QUEENS

"Oh, 'tis a glorious thing, I ween,

To be a regular Royal Queen!

No half-and-half-affair, I mean,

But a right-down regular Royal Queen!"

Sir W. S. Gilbert

Royalty came and went: the Queen of Denmark for a State Visit; Princess Margaret Rose for tea and a tour as did the Queen of Sweden; Queen Noor of Jordan, and the Crown Prince of Denmark lunched while Crown Prince Paulos of Greece popped in from time to time, not to mention his uncle and aunt, the King and Queen of Spain who came for a private visit. Somewhat more exotically, one of the seven wives of the young King of Swaziland had tea. At 23 the King was hard at work meeting his obligation of acquiring a bride from each tribe in his country. His father allegedly had 70 wives and 208 children. Meanwhile, in May 1991, we welcomed Princess Margaret Rose's older sister, Her Majesty Queen Elizabeth II of the United Kingdom of Great Britain and Northern Ireland and His Royal Highness The Prince Philip, Duke of Edinburgh.

As Princess Elizabeth she was a guest of the Trumans and returned as Queen in the seventies for a State Visit with the Fords. The hype was brought to a fever pitch. One Protocol staff member participating in the farewell line-up at the end of the visit hyperventilated from excitement and we had to feed her ice water during the waiting period.

The gifts exchanged between our President and his guest was done at the house between the respective protocol people, and the gifts were then brought over to the White House to be displayed outside the Oval Office. The Queen's gift to President Bush was a copy of King George III's own handwritten document, probably written towards the end of 1782, which resides in the Royal Archives at Windsor Castle and begins with the stirring statement: "America is lost!"

The President and Mrs. Bush gave Her Majesty a Steuben blown crystal bowl, cut and polished to follow the outline of the engraved flowers that formed its rim. Called "Shakespeare's Flowers Bowl" it depicted calligraphic quotations recalling Shakespearean references to flowers in his many works. It was designed by Jane Osborn-Smith and limited to this one example. The Duke of Edinburgh, an accomplished whip, was presented with a hand-colored framed print from the Daily Graphic, an illustrated evening newspaper, of four horses pulling a black and white carriage with ten men in top hats and lounge suits riding on top, called "The Tally Ho Passing Through Broad Street, Newark, May 4, 1878 – The Drive of the Coaching Club from New York to Philadelphia."

I made 64 flower arrangements, using 375 stems of roses; 100 peonies; 130 lilies; adding fillers such as freesia, Queen Anne's lace, phlox, asters, sweet peas, delphiniums, snapdragons, lisianthus, tulips, and godicias. Arranging flowers for the President's visits was my favorite of all tasks. Over the years I saved the U.S. government thousands of dollars in labor costs through my efforts; and working among my beloved flowers was therapy.

But my large bowl of sweet peas placed in the Queen's bedroom was removed as "<u>we</u> have no flowers ever in the bedroom" her dresser said.

Former ambassador, Sir Kenneth Scott, deputy private secretary to the Queen, came twice to America advancing this visit. Years earlier when he was First Secretary at the British Embassy in Washington we played bridge together and I was a guest at his wedding. At two luncheons, one at the British Embassy at Ambassador and Lady Aclands', and at Blair House, respectively, and during two walk-thrus, I had learned the following details incorporated in my schedule for my staff:

"The Queen does not eat shellfish; Prince Philip likes fish for breakfast; they like afternoon tea: Earl Grey with milk (and Chef's tomato and cheese sandwich became her favorite); they like a dry martini; the Queen also likes a two parts Dubonnet and one part Gin mixed with lemon and ice; no teabags at any time. (We would discover she also enjoyed Ginger Beer = Ginger Ale.) Never address The Queen or Prince Philip – wait for them to address you. <u>Never</u> touch them."

The Queen's Page, her personal butler, Nicolas Bray, had to be within calling distance so we furnished the large closet off the Primary Suite Entrance Hall with a table, chair and telephone. Jose was not permitted to wait on the Royals but supported Nicolas during meals. It had been brought home to me – in no uncertain terms – that having no bell rope by the bed was not good form. Princess Margaret Rose, on inspecting the Primary Suite two months earlier, had particularly asked about it, and I had received the same comment from His Grace the Duke of Grafton and his Duchess, with whom I had tea in the Lee Drawing Room before their inspection of the premises on behalf of the Queen, Her Grace being her chief lady-in-waiting.

Our guests had asked to dine in the Library the night following a baseball game in Baltimore with President and Mrs. Bush. Jose and I chose the Stetson china which Mrs. Bush liked so much and our lalicque glass ware, and the old Blair silver, including the candlesticks. I brought up my arrangement of peach and pink roses with peonies some twenty minutes before dinner and was puzzled to find the candlesticks moved to one of the bookshelves. I found Nicolas in the Conference Room finishing off a lavish dinner, and enjoying a glass of brandy. "Nicolas, is there something wrong with using candlelight for Her Majesty – I see you have removed the candlesticks from the dining table?"

"No, no," he said, "there is nothing wrong at all, but <u>We</u> so much prefer using these, just as <u>We</u> do at Balmoral," – and he pointed to the votive candles on the table.

"Right-oh," I said and went to the Blair Pantry, explained the change to Jose, and asked him to bring up five votive candles for the Queen's dinner. I pictured them, after that dinner, slipping their shoes off, the Queen curling up in the armchair, and relaxing just like the rest of us. That image, naturally, did not stick for long. Just as F. Scott Fitzgerald said: "The Very Rich are Different from you and me," these people <u>are</u> different, just in the sort of way members of the British Aristocracy are different, and one should not be fooled by their friendliness and attempt at chatting you up. The barrier, erected by centuries of inbred notions of superiority and privilege, frequently manifests itself in disdain for others.

Her Majesty's delegation was divided into three parts: Her <u>Household</u>, staying with us, headed by The Earl and Countess of Airlie, The Lord Chamberlain and Lady-in-Waiting respectively; Lord Airlie is one of the three great officers of the Queen's Household, responsible for the smooth running of Buckingham Palace and other royal residences, the safekeeping of the Crown Jewels, and the organization of royal weddings. He also serves as the Queen's emissary to the House of Lords.

We celebrated Lord Airlie's birthday, and surprised him with Danish Wienerbrod with one candle at breakfast. U.S. born Lady Airlie was adorable. One morning, dressed in a blue dress with large white polka dots, she found Lady Acland identically dressed, but in black and white. After much laughter, photography and agreement that they had bought their dress in the same shop Lady Airlie went upstairs to change.

The Household included the Master of the Household, a Rear Admiral; her Private Secretary, Sir Robert Fellowes, (married to the sister of Princess Diana); her Deputy Private Secretary, Sir Kenneth Scott; her Press Secretary, Charles Anson, another old acquaintance of mine; and the Medical Officer. They had breakfast in the Garden Room, and participated in a large luncheon party on arrival with special guests from among the White House staff invited by Ambassador Reed when the Queen and the Duke were lunching over there.

Her Majesty's <u>Staff</u>, staying at the house, were the Page; the Superintendent in charge of her security; her two Dressers (bringing in her clothes in upright enormous hanging steamer trunks parked on the third floor outside our pressing room and locked up every night); her Footman and the Duke's Valet. These people needed separate dining facilities, arranged in the Conference Room, but were served the same meal as the Household.

Her Majesty's <u>Officials</u> were a different story. The clerical staff, housed in the Hay Adams Hotel, spent each day in our Embassy Offices. While they also needed to be fed separately, not fitting in with the Queen's Household, and definitely being above her Staff, we arranged meal times for them in the Conference Room after the Staff had eaten.

The Prince Philip, less imposing, shorter and much older looking than expected from his pictures and his press, after arrival wandered around, hands clasped behind him, inspecting the drawing-rooms, albeit in a cursory fashion. I discreetly followed him, just in case he had any questions, and caught him turning off lights in the Lee Drawing Room, muttering: "What a waste." I expect he absolutely had to find something to criticize in America, a phenomenon I am not unfamiliar with during my travels. But I certainly agreed with him, as it was bright sunshine outside. Nevertheless I hurried when he had left the room to put the light back on. I did remember, though, that the Duke of Edinburgh had a keen interest in the environment, and had banned products with aerosol from Buckingham Palace, and possibly smoking as well, an admirable attitude.

There were funny little moments. On arrival, Ken Scott entered just ahead of the Queen and told me: "I am afraid, Benedicte, that your Polish notes went right up to the Queen herself," referring to my lengthy memorandum to him, per his request during one of his advance visits, of our experiences with President Walesa of Poland, as Walesa was expected at Windsor Castle after his American visit, and before the Queen's to the United States. Mrs. John Dugdale, Lady-in-Waiting and wife of the Lord Lieutenant of Shropshire, also on arrival thanked me for my notes on President Walesa, which "had been so helpful – even the Queen said so."

And the Queen, when reminded that it was my notes which had been so helpful in the preparation at Windsor Castle, said to me: "They do eat a lot, don't they?" She also mentioned how much she liked the Walesas.

The Queen was much younger looking than I had expected, and had beautiful and flawless skin. She was dressed charmingly in lovely colors and prints. A few times I was alone with her in the Front Hallway waiting for departure, and marveled at how she seemed to rest in herself, totally detached, but exuding confidence and peace at the same time. I suppose that after so many years of being "on stage" she had found her level of calm. I also wondered how she could separate the person from the institution of the Monarchy, and how anyone so selflessly could have worked so hard in the interest of her country. It was admirable.

Sir Antony Acland, British Ambassador since 1987, and Lady Acland, a former magistrate judge in England – Sir Antony later became the Provost of Eton, the most prestigious among British Public Schools – included me as a guest in the Queen's Garden Party at the British Embassy on Massachusetts Avenue, to which I went in the Queen's motorcade. It took all of five minutes to travel up through Rock Creek Park, with traffic cleared and the sirens at full blast.

One could get used to that. It took me an hour to make it back on my own.

So I arrived with the Queen, walking into the embassy up the magnificent staircase in her wake with her entourage, and then, with most of them, scooted into the Garden where half of Washington's movers and shakers were waiting, some wearing gorgeous and extraordinary hats. I chose to wander off to have strawberries, scones with Devonshire cream, and tea, desperately wishing to get away from the party which at that time was packed in like sardines, in broiling hot sun. I heard later on the grapevine that the Duke of Edinburgh was rather rude to people, which, I expect, was bound to happen. But, worse, he chose to be so to the Director of the Homeless Shelter, visited by the Queen that same morning, and had been overheard saying to her: "Why don't you just leave them in the streets?"

The official arrival at the White House would forever be etched in stone for the Office of Protocol, as to what must <u>never</u> happen. The President and his guest each made remarks from a raised podium. As Her Majesty is fairly short, Ambassador Reed had arranged to have a stool handy, for him to place for her, to give her some extra height during her speech. Lo and behold he forgot, probably being too busy ascertaining if anyone were looking at his own elegant figure. So what the world saw instead of the Queen was a bobbing hat addressing President Bush. Later when she addressed a Joint Session of Congress, a historic first, she opened her remarks with "I do hope you can see me today from where you are?" – and brought down the House.

The weather was sweltering, hot and humid, and although I had learned to drink hot tea in such weather, Reed insisted on serving iced water whenever the Queen and the Prince returned. Prince Philip brusquely refused same and muttered to the Queen: "Hot tea in this weather only" heading for the Blair Dining Room and our hospitality table where, to the delight of the wait staff, the Queen exclaimed: "This is the only place in North America where I can get a bloody good cup of coffee."

The delegation was fun and appreciative. I regaled Lady Airlie and Mrs. Dugdale with some of our stories, and had them in stitches. They said that being with us was like being "in the lap of luxury," that the Royal Yacht BRITANNIA, their next destination, certainly was not like Blair House, and from the staff, who had stuffed themselves on Chef's beef, salmon, crab cakes and veal, washed down with bottles of excellent American wines, we gathered that Buckingham Palace was rather a "cabbage and potatoes" sort of place. But best of all, Sir Robert Fellowes said to me: "I would really like to take you back with me to run Buckingham Palace." I received many thank you letters afterwards from members of the Household.

A large group of people had been invited to bid farewell, to include the Mayor and Chief of Police of Washington D.C. Ambassador Reed who simply could not help himself interfering with the British organizers, was all over the place, and had elicited an exasperated remark to me from Ken Scott the night before: "I seem to have lost control – I wish that man would get out of my hair." Ken, on his return from his embassy's dinner hosted by the Queen, had asked if he could see the arrangements which I, per his specific instructions, had set up for the next day's ceremony in the Conference Room. He was pleased. Certain people were to have an audience with the Queen and The Prince Philip, and receive a small gift. The group was to be held in the Jackson Place Dining and Sitting Rooms, and the Queen and The Prince Philip would receive in the larger Conference Room, handing out the gifts, spread out on the dining table placed in the bay window.

Ken told me Reed had wanted to exclude me and the five staffers whom Ken had asked me to pick out as deserving of a special audience with the Queen, so that he could insert his own acquaintances in our slot. I picked Deputy General Manager Sam Castleman, Executive Chef Russell Cronkhite, Head Butler Jose Fuster, Head Housekeeper Jemma Rennie, and Associate Curator Mary Williams. All of us received gifts. The Queen gave me a brass bracelet inscribed with ER II, and The Prince Philip, while chatting me up as is his job, gave me a signed portrait of them both. Deputy Secretary of State Lawrence

Eagleburger bid farewell on behalf of the U.S. government after Her Majesty had signed our guest book. The Prince Philip showed how very good he could be chatting with every third or fourth person in the line, and zeroing in on our Facilities Manager who was born in Corfu, Greece as was The Prince. Nick was on cloud nine.

Later many stories floated around, and I particularly liked how the Queen actually laughed while being hugged by one of the inhabitants of a rehabilitated South East neighborhood where Barbara Bush had taken her for a "walk about." I also truly appreciated the remarks of the Queen's Ladies-in-Waiting regarding Barbara Bush: "She has star quality – just like Princess Diana." Randy Bumgardner's story was priceless. As Visits Officer he saw Her Majesty off from AAFB. He was standing on the tarmac, the steps were being rolled away from the plane and the door closed, when he spotted a black bag standing by itself, obviously forgotten. He started yelling and waving his arms to draw the attention of the British; the door opened; and Randy flung Her Majesty's Jewel Box up into the plane – he referred to them as "The Crown Jewels." Ambassador Reed, who escorted the Queen on her visit to Florida and Texas, told us that in one hotel in addition to his own luggage he received a black bag labeled THE QUEEN. He reported this, and shortly afterwards two of Her Majesty's staff turned up to claim the bag, totally unconcerned, saying "Should we take off for South America tonight?" eliciting this reply from Ambassador Reed: "Better make it Brazil. There is no extradition with the U.S."

The least fun story I learned later. The Queen, a great admirer of George Washington, went to visit Mount Vernon. Her advance team had made it quite clear to the associate director that Her Majesty would not sit down at any time but walk and stand. However, on purpose the director placed a beautiful chair in a strategic spot and asked her to sit down, and later boasted that now the foundation could auction off this chair for much money as the royal bottom had touched it.

Earlier another queen had visited us. In January, after the official White House announcement I called Karl Christian in Copenhagen. Count Trampe, former Danish Naval officer, and Lord Chamberlain to the King of Denmark, Frederik IX, and later to his widow, Queen Ingrid, had been a presence in my life from my childhood. In fact,

Count Trampe, precisely at the moment when I was 16 was Aide-de-Camp to the Danish CNO. Trampe generously included me whenever the Vice Admiral threw a dinner dance for a visiting foreign naval ship's officers at the beautiful old historic Naval Officers' Club which just happened to be located in the front building of Søkvaesthuset where I lived.

For years I would complain to Karl Christian on the effect he had had on my young love life. "For, you must understand, that you were no help whatsoever after these gorgeous dances," I whined. "There I was, on the arm of a handsome young lieutenant who was going to escort me home (across the courtyard), and there you were, drawing me to the side and saying, "No, you don't," and make me wait so that You could escort me home instead – it was so unfair."

I had forgotten my rancor when I reached him in his office at Amalienborg Castle. I told him how thrilled I was at the announced State Visit of Her Majesty the Queen of Denmark, and what an excellent boost it gave to an attempt at normalcy in Washington D.C. as the first stage of the coalition forces' effort to oust Saddam Hussein from Kuwait was now underway. Denmark's contribution to the coalition forces was rather large, compared to the size of the country and population: the Corvette "Olfert Fischer" was deployed to the Persian Gulf, humanitarian assistance in the form of a medical team was sent to Saudi Arabia, and the Danish Field Hospital was offered for the treatment of wounded. But this time I had something else on my mind.

"What, Karl Christian, can you tell me about Queen Margrethe and Prince Henrik? What are they like on an informal basis, what do they eat and drink, what must I be aware of?" While my friend was hesitant in giving out too much personal stuff, I did learn that they smoked like chimneys, drank a lot of wine, preferably red, and they liked seafood and spicy foods. Also, importantly, the Prince, under no circumstances, should be made to feel he is but number two. I understood it to mean that the Prince being French born, real care needed to be taken that his position as *chef de famille* must not be compromised by the position held by his wife, the Queen, as *chef d'état*.

I had already met with the Queen's advance team and dined with them at the Danish ambassador's residence, but found my talk with Count Trampe far more illuminating. The advance team was headed by the Queen's Lord Chamberlain, General Søren Haslund Christensen, well known to both my brothers, my older one having served in the Army with him, and my younger one having been a great friend of his wife since childhood. But I learned that the Queen liked a boiled four-minute egg, toast and condiments, and the Prince a cold slice of meat, neither smoked nor with garlic, and both would like a brioche with their breakfast.

The Queen went to my school for some years. I saw her there, but we never met until we were both weekend guests at a country estate – ironing our dresses together. Later, from abroad, I had followed her spectacular education at two Danish universities; at Cambridge University, the London School of Economics as well as the Sorbonne; her broad range of interests including archeology, learned at the knee of her maternal grandfather, Gustav (6) Adolf, the King of Sweden; and her artistic endeavors whether in writing, illustrating, painting, drawing, embroidery, or in designing stage settings. She was an extraordinary woman with depth and intelligence and I so looked forward to this visit.

Queen Margrethe was interested in the house, and her lady-in-waiting, an old friend of mine, Anita Van Hauen, was kind enough to advise her that I had personally arranged all the flowers. Her Majesty complimented me on my fantastic color combination which I appreciated coming from so notable an artist. On saying goodbye she mentioned, in a smallish voice, that my being Danish by birth had been the "prikken over i'et" – the dot over the "i" – but that was as much as she could express, hardly opening her mouth to say thank you to the staff. The excuse given that she might be shy I found not acceptable at the age of 50, and after 23 years on the throne and in the public eye. Randy, their Visits Officer, told me that when the Queen and Barbara Bush visited the National Rehabilitation Hospital it was Mrs. Bush who talked to the patients and visited with them, especially hugging the children in wheelchairs. Meanwhile the Queen just waited patiently, but her lady-in-waiting remarked to Randy that "I wish you would hurry up Mrs. Bush and ask her not to hug the children. She is keeping Her Majesty waiting." Doro Bush, the President's daughter, accompanying the party, was horrified, and asked Randy what to do. "Nothing – Mrs. Bush is doing just fine," he said. Randy, a serious collector of autographed pictures, wanted more than anything a signed photograph of Queen Margrethe and upon inquiry through our chief of protocol, the Danish chief had replied: "We only give them to people of a certain rank – otherwise we'd end up giving them to everybody." I cringed hearing this. So when I retired and turned over the reins to Randy, my goodbye gift to him was my own signed photograph of Queen Margrethe and Prince Henrik.

The Queen was so chic with definite style and color sense. She wore gorgeous hats and looked fantastic in all the photos. Her official presence was truly excellent and she was a great success with her intelligence and wit.

The Danish papers reported widely that Secretary Baker was not there to greet her on her arrival. They called it "a slap in the face that he had to send the chief of protocol instead." The same chief of protocol, Ambassador Reed, who always greeted at such arrivals, was much in view during this visit. In fact, perhaps he was a little too excited over the exalted guest, as I saw him commit the ultimate sin: on arrival at Blair House, he took the Queen's arm, swinging her around towards the press stationed some twenty yards away, thus getting his photo-op. Her Majesty looked rather queer coming up the stairs.

Also, the Danish press had clearly forgotten that as the U.S. President and his Secretary of State were tackling the rapidly approaching deadline issued by the United Nations to Saddam Hussein to get out of Kuwait, and the monumental decision when to attack Iraq, Mr. Baker might just have been unavoidably engaged elsewhere. The deployment of the ground forces happened two hours after the State Dinner at the White House in the Queen's honor. I found it was typical, however, that the lesser Danish papers would continue to harp on this. Sadly my former fellow countrymen have a tendency to derision and some envy. Overwhelmingly the population sees the glass as half empty instead of half full, and therefore the negative statements in those articles outweighed the positive fact that the U.S. President, in the middle of an extraordinarily serious time, thought highly enough of Denmark not to postpone this royal visit, but instead took the time to be a charming and attentive host.

During the weeks prior to arrival I worked closely with the Danish Ambassador Peter Dyvig, one of the most generous and charming of the Danish Diplomatic Corps, and known to me for many years. He and his wife, Karen, put Denmark on the map in Washington with their warm hospitality during the many years they represented their country in the United States. This time also they were exceedingly generous in wishing to include me in the Queen's return dinner at the embassy, given in honor of Vice President and Mrs. Quayle. After much thought, I had to regret this wonderful invitation.

My reason was a sad one. I had quietly been advised by my colleague Assistant Chief of Protocol Bill Black that the chief and deputy chief of protocol had been much put out when they saw that I was on the Danish Ambassador's guest list, and had been very emphatic that "Mrs. Valentiner is <u>only</u> staff" and therefore obviously not worthy of going to such an intimate dinner party. The fact that I was one of the more successful Danish Americans they would meet themselves was beside the point. I thought I would avoid future trouble if I did not go. However, when I was invited by President and Mrs. Bush to join their after-dinner guests at 9:30 pm for the entertainment I accepted with the greatest pleasure. The custom of adding around one hundred more guests to a State Dinner by inviting them for coffee and the after-dinner entertainment was a charming one, and included a receiving line in the Blue Room where President Bush greeted me and, passing me on to the Queen, said to me: "Here is your best customer" while Mrs. Bush gave me a hug, both then and later when I left, jumping in the car with Ambassador and Mrs. Dyvig when the Queen returned to Blair House.

The Prince Consort, Henrik, Prince of Denmark, a student of Chinese and Vietnamese, a poet and musician, was a charming French diplomat stationed in London when he met the future Queen. As they had had to leave almost immediately after their arrival for a Danish art exhibition, including Her Majesty's own work, at the National Museum of Women in the Arts, he had not yet been upstairs and later asked me in his heavily French-accented Danish: "Hvor bor jeg?" ("Where do I live?")

Queen Margrethe, prior to the official welcome at the White House, hosted a supper party in the Garden Room following a performance at the Kennedy Center featuring Julie Harris portraying Karen Blixen, the famous Danish authoress and adventurer, in "Lucifer's Child." Ambassador Reed not only included some of his own guests in the Queen's party, but once more committed a faux pas: after seating the Queen at one of the round tables in the Garden Room, he made <u>her</u> get up to greet Julie Harris, when she walked into the room, rather than bringing the actress to the Queen. But apart from this additional flop, the evening went well. Christian Castenskiold from California, a first cousin of the late King Frederik IX, and his wife Cecily, old friends of my parents, were among the guests. Cecily wrote me that she could see where I had been trained – at home by my own mother. Julie Harris wrote me afterwards, as well as the Director of Royal Copenhagen who donated a gorgeous cachepot to the house. I heard from both Ambassador Dyvig and the U.S. ambassador to Denmark Keith Brown as well as Danish Foreign Minister Uffe Ellemann-Jensen. Blair House received no official thank you from anybody at the Danish Court.

I met Maersk Mc-Kinney Møller at the White House, and later gave him a quick tour of Blair House. Maersk Mc-Kinney Møller, the owner and CEO of A.P. Møller, A/S, the largest Danish Shipping Company, was in town to receive an award for peace and trade from the U.S. Secretary of Commerce, Robert A. Mosbacher Sr., for his company's contribution of two freighters to the conflict in the Persian Gulf. Mr. Møller, whose mother was American, was a legend in Denmark, for his contribution at all levels to Danish society, and, I think, for the fact that he and his company remained in Denmark when so many other Danes fled the country to avoid the enormous taxes levied by the government. I recall the often heavy criticism aimed at him for his forward moving ideas because he dared be different. Eight years after this visit, when my husband and I visited Copenhagen, we were passing his office building on the Copenhagen Harbor, and as I was explaining this extraordinary man and his contribution to Adrian, I exclaimed: "perhaps Maersk Møller is no longer alive," when I heard behind me a voice saying: "I assure you he is very much alive." A passerby had overheard me, and wanted to set me straight.

Among the accompanying delegation members I greatly enjoyed the First and Principal Official of the Queen's Household who, speaking no English, was so happy to meet me. Blair House turned out to be pure holiday for him, with no "housekeeping" to worry about. The royal staff marveled at the cleanliness of the house, complaining to me that at the Queen's Castle, the poor housekeeper only had one and one half houseman to do the cleaning, as the Lord Chamberlain would not allow any more for budgetary reasons. My reaction was that they should have had a Lady Chamberlain instead.

Two years earlier I had shown the house to Queen Margrethe's son, Crown Prince Frederik of Denmark. As he was interested in history, I rather enjoyed telling him about the Blair Family, Robert E. Lee and his refusal to command the Union Army, and President Truman and the discussions of the Marshall Plan at Blair House.

What I did not tell the Crown Prince was that years earlier, when his grandparents, King Frederik IX and Queen Ingrid of Denmark, had returned from the White House dinner they invited their escort, the Deputy Chief of Protocol, Clem Conger, to stay for a drink. Conger told me that the King had leaned back in his chair, settling in to a comfortable chat, while slipping off his shoes and wiggling his toes, revealing large holes in the socks.

I had left Denmark for the United States some years before Margrethe II became Queen. Thus her father, King Frederik IX, was "my" King. When in September 1969, with another hundred immigrants, I was sworn in as a U.S. citizen at the Federal Courthouse in Washington D.C. it was bittersweet, not because I was not convinced that my decision to apply for U.S. citizenship was the right one, but contrary to so many other immigrants, I had no real reason for abandoning my own perfectly good, decent country other than my conviction that the United States suited me perfectly. I recall dressing in the Danish colors that day, in a red suit with a white top, and clutching a small Danish flag in my pocket, silently whispering: "Forgive me, King Frederik," as I repeated the oath of U.S. citizenship. Fortunately, my parents were so supportive of my monumental decision to make my life in the United States, and I always suspected my mother of being slightly envious as she adored America.

More Scandinavians came. The Brazilian born Queen Sylvia of Sweden had tea and a tour and I made sure our three Brazilian maids, Agustinha Dos Santos, Marinete Saias, and Teresinha Diaz got to meet her. As expected, Queen Sylvia was very gracious to my ladies thus reinforcing my impression, garnered from afar, of a most down-to-earth lady, stunning looking, and with a great sense of humor. Her lady-in-waiting, a relative of mine, Alice Countess Wachtmeister, I had not seen in years.

A year later I welcomed Queen Margrethe's sister, Her Royal

Highness, Princess Benedikte, and her lady in waiting, Karin af Rosenborg, both of whom I had known in my youth, and gave them tea and a tour of the house; the Princess and my brother Gustav were in dancing class together in Copenhagen.

Mrs. James A. Baker invited Queen Noor of Jordan for lunch. The Queen was always dieting so we worked hard to come up with a delicious diet lunch of Gazpacho Aspic, Broiled Snapper, and Raspberry Sorbet. I remember the Queen as stunningly beautiful with gorgeous reddish golden hair. She had worked tirelessly since her marriage to King Hussein on Jordanian issues, and blessed with intelligence, charm, and a well informed mind, must have been an enormous asset for him.

As King Hussein, on his official visits to Washington, elected to stay at his large property in the area we would not again see Queen Noor. But the charming stories about the King were abundant, and fortunately due to his intense involvement in the Middle East Peace Process during the two Clinton administrations he often came for meetings or meals. Before the restoration he frequently had stayed at Blair House, and was beloved by the staff for his courtesy, appreciation, and obvious enjoyment of our hamburgers eating two or three at a time. He was much admired for other reasons in the Protocol Office. Whenever the King, from his early youth, arrived in Washington, he was received by Protocol in the airport, and his luggage was handled by the late James Payne who for years was charged with the collection and delivery of luggage of all the VIPs. Mr. Payne and the young King developed a special relationship, and I learned later that the King assisted Mr. Payne's son to attend college. I also heard that upon one occasion, during the Reagan presidency, when the King arrived in the airport, he completely ignored the U.S. chief of protocol, in order first to greet his old friend, Mr. Payne, standing some way off, causing Mr. Payne to be chewed out later by an enraged and rather jealous chief. In the more relaxed Clinton Protocol Office, with his first chief of protocol still wet behind the ears as far as international protocol was concerned, the King, for his first appearance in Washington in 1993, was greeted by her

"Hello, King"

and, if my instincts serve me right, he would not have batted an eyelid. His staff was delightful, polite, and efficient, and with him till the end of his life. 30 chiefs of state attended the King's funeral in February 1999, indicative of the influence over 46 years of this diminutive King, whose humanity, tough and strong leadership, and as wise peacemaker had transcended all areas of international societies: whether democratic, theocratic, or autocratic.

My first indication that we might soon experience the most dreaded visit of all – that of Hassan II, King of Morocco, a direct descendant of the prophet Mohammed, came in July 1991 in a message from Matt Smith, the Assistant Chief of Protocol for Visits, who had replaced Bill Black when the latter decided to return to his business in San Diego, California. Bill would be much missed, not only for his warm-heartedness and true kindness to everyone around him, but also for his particular grace, charm, and great presence. His replacement had worked for years deeply immersed in Republican politics, and was abrasive, bold, and rude. But I made the best of it, and I fired off a note to him in response to his message announcing the State Visit of the King of Morocco in September:

"You do know how to hurt a person, don't you? Apart from my sleepless night, the attached, engaging notes out of Mary Edith Wilroy's book on her 15 years as Blair House Manager were enough to ensure a second one."

I included some pages of Mrs. Wilroy's description of King Hassan's first visit to the States in 1963, when, after sailing into New York Harbor on the U.S.S. Constitution, he arrived by train into Union Station in Washington D.C. where President Kennedy greeted him and drove with him to Blair House. Her description of the King's requirements was of great help to me and enabled me to meet with fortitude the thought of scores of lazy servants demanding room service, eating us out of the house, and sleeping wherever there was a free space.

I believe Smith must have shown my memo to Ambassador Reed, a former U.S. ambassador to Morocco. In subsequent advance meetings Reed was vigorous in pointing out the advantages for His Majesty of staying at the spacious Willard Hotel rather than at Blair House where such a large delegation would have to be split up between the house and the Willard. I was fully aware of the diplomatic skills which such a presentation required. As a result the King remained at the

Willard, with Blair House at his disposal for meetings. I also believed that "discretion, on the King's part, was the better part of valor." It was, after all, into King Hassan's bed the chandelier had fallen which caused the complex to be closed for a six year repair and renovation job. He was the last overnight visitor in the old house, and as it turned out he would not again sleep there.

I prepared a regular meeting schedule for the King stretching over three days, including many meetings. The Primary Suite was set up as if the King was going to actually sleep there, and his valet came over from the hotel to arrange his paraphernalia to ensure nothing would be found wanting should the King need the suite. I counted 71 bottles, some of which were made of beautiful gold bedecked glass, laid out in the bathroom; five kinds of hairspray; 3 kinds of American cigarettes; anti tar chewing gum; his own blue flowered monogrammed towels; his Chanel deodorant; embroidered slippers for the royal toes; a three way full length mirror; plexi-glass shelves to hold his monogrammed towels, and – in front – a chair placed on his own carpet. Also as the King loved chocolate, boxes of Godiva chocolates were ready and waiting. I was told that in his suite at the Willard Hotel trays with Godiva chocolates were piled one foot high.

Three times we were notified that King Hassan was on his way, having entered the elevator at the Willard Hotel, only to hear five minutes later that the Royal Mind had changed. Randy, Protocol Visits Officer for this visit, was the conveyor and spectator of this, and I was told later that much of this back and forth had to do with His Majesty's dependency on what the stars were telling him to do. Extremely superstitious, anything that he perceived as a "sign" caused him to change plans in mid stream, including changing his departure date. He traveled with a small granddaughter. In Morocco children are sacred and therefore the King felt that no one would try to harm him with the little girl at his side. The King pushed hard to have the little girl seated at his side at the state dinner. While she did not in the end attend this, she did accompany the King in his car for all other movements. King Hassan had good reasons to be paranoid, having survived several assassination attempts.

The King was late for his official welcome at the South Grounds of the White House, not being an early riser. His royal tea bearers accompanied him and were permitted to make their tea at the White

House and despite the objections of George Bush' staff, were allowed into the Oval Office to serve their special (and delicious) mint tea to their king and his host. What a wonderful spectacle it must have been – the tea bearers in their long white robes and on their feet: today's mule, but with an elegantly curved toe. At the State Dinner the King was similarly but naturally much more richly dressed in a white robe with a tall pointed hood, and on his feet cloth shoes with the pointed and curled toes.

At the finish of dessert, the King suddenly walked out, President Bush so put out he did not escort him to his limousine. While superstition and a dependency on astrology, I expect, guided much of his action, there was also much caprice deriving from the hedonistic lifestyle. I understood it was virtually impossible to pin down the real wishes of His Majesty. Apparently he would give his three confidants: the royal chief of protocol, the consul general to NYC (who was his half brother), and the ambassador to Washington D.C. conflicting ideas of his wishes. All three then separately approached my colleagues as though life or death depended on these requests which took much organization and time. And then the Royal Mind would change; thus a request to close the golf course at Andrews Air Force Base so that the King could play, took two hours of work by the protocol officer, Andrews Air Force Base staff and the U.S. Secret Service to accomplish, only to have the King want something else. Willard Hotel had to replace the carpeting and curtains on his floor, not being able to get rid of the residue of all the incense burning during the visit. Randy described how he could not see His Majesty across his room at twenty feet through the fog of sweet thick incense. I was rather thankful that we had been spared this time regardless of the fact that it cost Blair House – really the U.S. government – $12,000 to be "on call."

King Hassan returned for a similar visit in March 1995 in the first Clinton administration, at which time he really used the house for meetings and asked that I show him the "new" Blair House. I spent half an hour with the King, his ambassador, and the Consul General, and, in excellent English, he explained to me what he remembered, especially his meeting in Jackson Place Conference Room with Alexander Haig, former Secretary of State. I found him, during that half hour in our one-on-one, to be perfectly nice, affable and gracious. It was hard to imagine that he had kept Queen Elizabeth during her State Visit in Morocco waiting outside his palace for hours.

The preparations both times for a day of meetings hosted by King Hassan were detailed in the extreme as the Moroccans were very specific as to the arrangement required in each room the King might grace with his presence. A day early and under the watchful eyes of the Tea Bearers, the Lee Dining Room was arranged as his office by replacing the dining table with the enormous library desk used by President Truman during his residence many years earlier. This desk was placed in front of the fireplace, and set with His Majesty's own monogrammed desk set, ashtray and pencil holder, while in the front were placed two of our armchairs with a small coffee table in between. I was asked to make three arrangements of roses. The Lee Drawing Room was used for his meetings. My inadequate French was helpful in putting a limit on the incense the Tea Bearers could burn throughout the house, and especially in there. The Garden Room was the setting for the signing of a trade agreement between the USA and Morocco, with His Majesty witnessing same. The room was arranged theatre style facing a table at which the signing would take place, and the King's chair was placed in the front on an oriental carpet (swiped from elsewhere in the house) so the royal feet would be properly placed.

The King during his State Visit with President Clinton was focusing on economic development in North Africa, and although cautious as to potential success also here to discuss progress in Israeli-Palestinian relations, the King having worked for peace between Israel and its Arab neighbors for a long time.

The most delightful of all the royals were Juan Carlos, King of Spain, and Queen Sofia who came for a private visit on October 8, 1991 to open the fabulous exhibition at the National Gallery of Art called "CIRCA 1492 Art in the Age of Exploration," kicking off the 500th anniversary for the discovery of the Americas. While the visit of the King and Queen was rather light in terms of functions at the house itself, it was entirely charming as was their second visit early 2000. They arrived mid morning. King Juan Carlos was by far the most down to earth royal we had experienced. Born in exile in Italy he grew up in Switzerland and Portugal. Per request of Generalissimo Francisco Franco he studied in Spain as a young boy, joining the military academies there receiving a commission into each service. Further he studied at Spanish universities and received a thorough education with hands on experience in various ministries in Madrid. He was 21 when he was designated to succeed Franco and 27 when he became King. By all accounts he had created a modern monarchy in Spain and as far as I could see still had his famous common touch.

The King and Queen, so different from our other royals, were relaxed and showing their enjoyment. When the King saw the larger primary bedroom prepared for his use he advised me that his wife had better have this, while he would sleep in the smaller – and very feminine – second bedroom. "You see, she has so many clothes, she needs the space." The Queen wanted to see the whole house, so I took her on a tour, even showing her the hair salon on the third floor which she admired but did not want to use, being in the habit of having her hair done in her own suite. She looked in cupboards and drawers, and asked questions and it was interesting she was so natural. She is the sister of ex-King Konstantine of Greece married to the youngest of the Danish Queen's sisters with whom my younger brother Gustav was in dancing class in his teens, and herself of royal Danish blood. Her great grandfather was a younger son of the Danish King Christian IX; he had been invited to come to Greece as its king.

Per their chief of protocol, Alberto Escudero, the Queen was always late "which comes" he said, "from the Danish Royal Family" – trying to get a rise out of me. Sure enough, prior to going to the National Gallery dinner all the men were waiting in the Blair Drawing Room, being plied with champagne by my staff, waiting for Her Majesty.

The King's aide-de-camps got the sign to "sound the trumpet" from the King who with his hands demonstrated his meaning. The aide ran upstairs only to return totally bewildered.

"Where is the Queen?"

The search party was on – and Jose found her serenely waiting in the limousine. She had pressed the wrong elevator button and had walked out into the basement where Officer Crawford gallantly escorted her to the limousine. They all laughed so much, and the Queen most of all.

Barbara Bush, as she often did with their official guests, came over to pick up Queen Sofia to go to the National Rehabilitation Hospital.

I was naturally on post at the Front Door and enjoyed listening to Mrs. Bush and Queen Sofia chat in the hallway, with Mrs. Bush paying great tribute to Spain's ambassador Jaime de Ojeda, an old friend of mine, who had been stationed in Beijing when George Bush was U.S. envoy there. King Juan Carlos was also present, and it was fun to hear both of them express their admiration for and delight in Blair House, whereupon Mrs. Bush turned to me and said: "and this is the best hotelier in the country."

At 8:30 am on the dot, Thursday, October 10, the royal couple departed. They had been informed, when the invitation was extended, that the President of Costa Rica would be moving in just after they left. I was impressed by the good humor and punctuality they showed in having to vacate their quarters at such an hour. King Juan Carlos came to me to thank me most warmly for my hospitality, and kissed me on both cheeks, asking me to convey his best greetings to "my old friend, the President of Costa Rica" who arrived precisely one hour and five minutes later.

CHAPTER 7

OUR HEMISPHERE –
EL TEATRO LATINO

"Laugh and the world laughs with you."

Ella Wheeler Wilcox

I hung a world map from National Geographic outside our offices and marked each visiting country with a colored tack, each year a different color outlined on a small chart attached to the map, thus indicating where the administration's foreign policy thrust had been directed; simultaneously my staff became quite proficient in geography. In 1990 and 1991, except for Paraguay, Uruguay, and Guatemala, every Central and South American country's president was a guest of President George H.W. Bush. The first of our Latino neighbors to be invited was, in my view, the most important:

"En mi corazon soy Mexicana."

I was escorting Carlos Salinas de Gortari, President of the United Mexican States and Mrs. Salinas to the Primary Suite, when I told them my feelings for their country. President of Mexico less than a year when he arrived in Washington on October 1, 1989, Carlos Salinas could not by any stretch of the imagination have said to be democratically elected, but seemed committed to make Mexico a world power by modernizing the country's politics, economy, and society. In his inaugural speech he proposed:

- To expand democracy by increasing openness of the political system
- To spark economic recovery by lowering inflation, reducing the foreign debt burden, and encouraging foreign trade

- To promote social welfare, guarantee public safety, and reduce narcotics trafficking and consumption

Salinas moved quickly in all these areas. He allowed an unprecedented victory by an opposition party in a gubernatorial election, reached an agreement in principle with creditors on debt relief, and arrested several corrupt and notorious figures, including labor leaders, businessmen, and drug kingpins. Not bad for a leader of a country not known for its democratic ideals.

Sadly, much of the above would be diminished later in the major scandals erupting around himself and his family, with Mr. Salinas fleeing Mexico to settle in Ireland, and his brother, Raoul, languishing in prison.

An economist, Mr. Salinas had received a master's degree in public administration and a Ph.D. in political economy and government policy from Harvard University and spoke fluent English. He, his wife and their delegation members were lively and appreciative, and working hard with a tremendous schedule. Mrs. Salinas' secretary praised us to the sky: "The President and Mrs. Salinas are so happy, euphoric, over the warm welcome of Mr. Bush, of Mr. Baker, and totally overwhelmed by the hospitality which you, Mrs. Valentiner, and your staff have shown them here at Blair House."

Mr. Salinas was small and wiry, a jogger, tennis player, and accomplished horseman. He sported a thick black moustache and a great sense of humor and kept his entourage laughing, particularly after a long and hectic day. Mrs. Salinas was attractive, seemingly warm and caring, with little English. She was also on the go all the time, not wasting a moment. "Everything is so interesting," she said.

Presidents Bush and Salinas already had met, when both were presidents-elect of their respective countries. James A. Baker, in his book THE POLITICS OF DIPLOMACY, notes: "Between them the two presidents-elect created "the Spirit of Houston:" a new partnership that looked forward to common opportunity, not back to an often-troubled past. The subject of a free-trade agreement was not raised. Indeed, at the time Salinas was still publicly opposed to the idea. But the "Spirit of Houston" provided the personal foundation for the revolution in bilateral relations that occurred during the next four years."

I expect the North American Free Trade Agreement, to be known as NAFTA some years hence, was on the agenda during this visit. According to James Baker "from the beginning of the Bush administration, improving our ties with Mexico was part of a broader regional strategy. This included progress toward a peaceful resolution of the conflict in Central America, progress on Latin debt issues, and reform of the Latin American economies themselves."

My warm feelings for Mexico were deep and sincere.

Returning from Iran in 1974, my ex-husband and I lived for two years in the enchanting colonial town of San Miguel de Allende. Enrolled at the Belles Artes for 9 months, five mornings a week, I learned to weave on a big, old Spanish 4-harness loom, taught by a Mexican maestro, Felix Peres who spoke no English, with my Spanish limited, but I learned more from this man about weaving than anyone else could have taught me. "Mire, Señora, mire," and thus I learned the wonderful Mexican patterns, the Greek border, the diamond shape, the various bird designs, especially the swallow, La Golondrina, my signature in my own weaving later on. His classroom was an immense, vaulted room, with murals in the ceiling, painted by famous Mexican artist Jose David Sigueiros. I later met some of the artists who had helped Sigueiros paint this mural, lying on scaffolds up under the ceiling, in the greatest discomfort all day, just to be a part of this endeavor.

I was surprised one day to be asked: "Taler du dansk (do you speak Danish)?" I turned around. "Yes, do you?" and the woman continued in English that her mother was born in Denmark, but she knew little Danish herself. I was intent upon my weaving but, to be polite, I asked: "Where does your mother come from?" "Køge." Køge, just south of Copenhagen was near my family's ancestral home. We both continued weaving, and I thought: "I cannot leave it like this," and asked: "What was your mother's maiden name?"

Afterwards Lisa Smith said she thought I was mad. When she replied: "Valentiner," I stiffened, spun around on the bench, stared at her and spelled out: "V A L E N T I N E R?" "Yes," she said, recoiling slightly. The Valentiner family, although scattered throughout Germany, Denmark, Venezuela, and America, are all one family, and here was a relative in San Miguel de Allende of all places. Lisa Smith's maternal grandfather, Julius Valentiner of Vasebaek Estate was a cousin of my paternal grandfather, and I had often in my childhood seen this handsome man, her beloved grandfather. Lisa and I became close friends, and with one stroke I acquired a large family as she had five children, and now, years later, grandchildren and great grandchildren, many of whom have become dear to me.

Although Mexico's next president, Ernesto Zedillo Ponce de Leon, came three times during the Clinton administrations, these visits paled compared to the excitement of my first from this favorite country.

While President of Honduras and Mrs. Callejas's April 17, 1990 Official Working Visit was low key and nice, it was a poor second to the three day visit of Guillermo Endara Galimany, President of the Republic of Panama, April 29, 1990.

Mr. Endara was about 7 months late to his presidency, as the Noriega regime annulled his election victory in May 1989. Only through American intervention and the removal of strongman General Manuel Noriega would democracy have a chance. I recall vividly the horrifying photos in the newspapers of Noriega's squads beating the newly elected Vice President Billy Ford, the blood dripping down his face from a head wound.

Finally, after several aborted Panamanian coups, harassment of American service personnel, and other atrocities, the United States was handed the reason for getting rid of Noriega: the brutal murder of an unarmed U.S. Marine lieutenant. On December 20, in a secret ceremony at Howard Air Force Base in Panama Mr. Endara and his two Vice Presidents-elect were sworn in, and the surprise American attack on Noriega's regime began. By early January it was over, and Noriega was in U.S. custody.

So, finally, the democratically elected President Endara was at Blair House, jovial, smiling, happy: the president was getting married for the second time shortly after his stay with us. He could not make up his mind whether he loved the United States the most, or our Executive Chef, eating being one of the president's favorite pastimes.

He had one full day in Washington, which included the traditional meeting and luncheon at the White House. Apart from hosting a large reception at the Panamanian Embassy, he spent the rest of the day with us in non-stop meetings: breakfast with the Director of the International Monetary Fund and the President of the World Bank; talks with the Secretaries of Education, Defense, Treasury, Commerce, and the Attorney General, in addition to which Endara managed several interviews with various opinion makers, and in between some hefty snacks prepared by Chef, hence the contest between the president's two loves at the moment: the USA and our Chef.

The president was not the only one holding meetings. Several of his accompanying ministers had their own intense separate agendas.

Between the hours of 1:30 pm and 6 pm 19 separate meetings with five hosts and 47 participants took place at the house.

While the president remained in the Lee Drawing Room, it was more complicated with the four Panamanian officials. Three were assigned to the Jackson Place Conference, Sitting, and Dining Rooms. At overlapping times or because of a size difference we also accommodated a group on the large sofas in the Garden Room. The hard working Panamanian chief of protocol, Jose M. Varela, a Panamanian businessman just doing this job "for fun," was my key to buttonholing the Panamanian ministers hosting the different meetings, while Francisco O. Boyd of their embassy and John W. Rendon doing their public relations were great at directing the correct visitors to the appropriate meetings. If the meeting participants came early, we either held them in the Garden, or in the Blair Dining Room. It was a marvelous afternoon, like a puzzle, with every piece fitting perfectly.

Mr. Endara, following his wedding in Panama, sent me a charming thank you letter: "I was impressed by the professionalism of your staff and, of course, by the culinary talents of your chef."

Early in the Clinton administration, when the next Panamanian president-elect, in Washington D.C. on a private visit, was feted at a reception, I learned that the Panamanians were the most helpful and responsive country with our Haitian and Cuban refugee problems in the early summer of 1994, and that Protocol's efforts with both Panamanian presidents contributed much to these sentiments. "Ah," I thought, "the road to some people's hearts surely passes through the stomach."

Warmth and charm though were nonexistent in the person of Carlos Andres Perez, President of the Republic of Venezuela. The advance for his State Visit on April 25, 1990 reserved the Foreign Minister's Suite for Blanca Perez, similar to our experiences with President Mitterrand of France and his wife who loathed each other and had to be kept apart. Mrs. Perez, however, arrived early, would have none of it and within half an hour had moved into the Second Primary Bedroom. And there she stayed despite the humiliating treatment doled out by her husband who filled his Sitting Room with his staff, partied till the wee hours, making it hard for her to sleep, and impossible to leave her room.

Years later I met a Danish-American couple at the V Day 50th celebration at Fort Myers, VA, who asked me about our guests and their behavior. As Perez in the meantime was thoroughly discredited in his own country, impeached in 1993 for misuse of government funds, I did not feel too bad about further ruining his reputation. The Danes visiting Poland through their hotel room wall heard the most frightful row. A couple was screaming at each other, and it sounded as if the man was slapping the woman around. Deeply concerned they went to the Front Desk manager to investigate and summon assistance. The fighting couple was President and Mrs. Perez of Venezuela.

They brought several daughters with them, one of whom, an employee of the Inter-American Development Bank, an advisor to her father, accompanied both parents to their official events sitting between them in the limousine as the buffer between two warring factions.

Mrs. Perez, a pleasant, ordinary grandmother, and two of her nice grandsons stayed an extra night with us. We pampered and enjoyed them. I heard that Mrs. Perez, married to her husband for 45 years, bearing him six children, was a tireless campaigner in the months preceding her husband's election in December 1988. Her interest was helping children and the physically disadvantaged, and taking an active role in Venezuela's anti-drug education efforts.

My impression of her husband was the opposite. Although a seasoned politician, friendly to the U.S., instituting major economic reforms, reaching out to Latin America and Third World interests and in exile four years in Cuba and Costa Rica during Venezuela's military government starting in 1948, I found him a rather distant person, off-putting with his pock marked face, his impersonal way, and his appalling treatment of his wife. He left a day earlier than she, and had requested that no one from the U.S. government escort him to the airport. However, this little puzzle was quickly solved when I learned from the Visit Officer who is required to see the official visitor off that his mistress and two children were waiting for him at his plane.

Perez was easily one of our more unsavory guests.

The following September we welcomed Rodrigo Borja Cevallos, President of Ecuador since August 1988. Borja was an admirer of Europe's moderate social democrats, particularly Felipe Gonzales, Prime Minister of Spain. He encouraged constructive relations with the United States, but also pursued his campaign promise to reestablish non-aligned status for his country. Among his interests was a pledge "to cut off drug trafficking at the roots."

His amusing Foreign Minister, Diego Cordovez Zegers was a veteran U.N. negotiator serving as Under Secretary General for Special Political Affairs 1981-88, earning high marks for his efforts to mediate the Iran-Iraq war and to secure a settlement on Afghanistan. Despite his vast experience and his stature he still came up short against veteran Press Protocol Officer Mary Masserini, and not the only one to do so. Minister Cordovez insisted on free access for the Ecuadorian press, but Mary would have none of it, as it is "against the policy at Blair House, and press only permitted under very controlled circumstances." Conceding defeat, Minister Cordovez expressed the opinion that "if Ms. Masserini ran the Drug Enforcement Program in Bolivia they would have no more problems."

A dedicated jogger, and excellent tennis player, Borja was invited by President Bush to a game of tennis shortly after his arrival. I saw off a handsome, erect, bouncy president for the game, and received a "limp cloth" at the door a couple of hours later. The tennis game fortunately tied; I am certain our diplomatic President Bush arranged it this way. As the weather was extremely hot and humid, it negated President Borja's advantage of coming from 11,000 feet, but he was soon refreshed after a long nap on the floor of his bedroom.

César Gaviria Trujillo, President of the Republic of Colombia and Mrs. Gaviria arrived late February 1991 for a two day Official Working Visit. Preceding this visit we received eight hundred stems of red roses and carnations in all colors from Colombia as a gift to be used during their president's visit with us. This abundance had arrived the second last day of the Queen of Denmark's visit, on a Thursday, and had to be prepared, watered and placed in a cool spot before they could be arranged for the arrival of the Colombians the following Monday. Despite the generous spirit which prompted such a gift I did not need any more, having many beautiful flowers from the Danish visit to use, and wondered "why, oh why was there no way to preserve these for our less affluent days?"

We had another Colombian visit in October 1998 of President Andres Pastrana, his wife, and their teenage children, Santiago and Laura; I mention them as they were the most polite, attractive, beautifully dressed and well brought up young guests we ever had.

The house was filled by other charming visitors: from Bolivia, and Peru whose "Japanese" president took punctuality to a new level in his Peruvian delegation, and Argentina's president who was accompanied by our American ambassador Terrence Todman born in the former Danish West Indies and speaking fluent Danish after having been our ambassador in Denmark; El Salvador, with its personable, young and energetic President Alfredo F. Christiani who kept his delegation chuckling constantly. And how they all loved Jose! When Jose offered the president a glass of liqueur, produced in the St. Michelle Vinyards in Virginia, and the president asked him what it was, Jose said: "Drinking this, Señor Presidente, is like kissing a seventeen year old Sevillana." While everyone around him laughed uproariously, the president was bereft of speech, but Mrs. Christiani took the glass from him and said: "I shall drink this, and he can kiss ME later."

Equally charming was the visit in April 1991 of Violeta B. De Chamorro, President of the Republic of Nicaragua with her trademark of a warm embrace every time she saw me though the underlying issues of her visit were very serious given the dire economic strains in her country.

She arrived for her State Visit just in time for lunch, and neither she nor her delegation members drew breath during the subsequent 72 hours, gathering in the Library for drinks and snacks at the least provocation, and thoroughly enjoying themselves.

In fact, so much did Christiana Lacayo, the daughter of Chamorro, enjoy herself that she had a nasty fall following the State Dinner. She came out from the Library and walking down the narrow staircase, stopped on the landing, with a glass in her hand. She was looking upwards towards someone outside the Library and not paying attention as she walked out in the air and somersaulted down the stairs. Teresinha, on her way up the stairs caught her, and Jose and I dashed to the rescue with an icepack for her knee and offers of a doctor or hospital visit. She refused although I asked her several times. I had witnessed this fall, and cringed at the potential terrible accident. The staircase is narrow, and the rails holding up the banister are far enough apart that had her leg stuck through these it could have been very serious indeed. Made of stern stuff she remained on the chair for a while, chatting with the delegation gathered around her.

One of the rails cracked under this blow.

Her mother, the president, was widowed in 1978 after the assassination of her newspaper publisher husband Pedro Joaquin Chamorro, revered in Nicaragua as a martyr for free expression. Mrs. Chamorro, as co-owner and publisher of La Prensa, was a vocal critic of press censorship by the former Sandinista regime, of which she was a member for a short while. Attending Catholic schools and college in the United States, she also lived in exile with her husband in Costa Rica for a couple of years. Interestingly enough, her four children were split along pro- and anti-Sandinista lines: one son at that time was ambassador to Taiwan, a daughter a former Sandinista ambassador to Costa Rica, the other daughter, the one who fell, Christiana Lacayo, was chairing the board of the family newspaper, La Prensa, and the youngest son was editor of Barricada, a Sandinista daily.

The farewells in the Blair Dining Room were a gigantic kissing feast, altogether a magnificent, fun, wonderful visit.

Brazil, however, was a different story.

Fernando Collor, President of the Federative Republic of Brazil and the second Mrs. Collor came a few months later for a State Visit, following excruciating and extensive preparations and, on the part of the Brazilians, almost insulting, advising Ambassador Reed that "having their president greeted on arrival and hosted for lunch by Acting Secretary of State Lawrence Eagleburger would not be acceptable," Secretary of State Baker being on the road around the world at that time. At least we were spared such an attitude being the recipients of excellent information as to their working dinners and breakfast, complete with seating charts, table cards and other paraphernalia involved in such arrangements.

The unknown and unpredictable quantity of this visit was the second Mrs. Collor who at 27 was unsophisticated, spoiled, and rather common with an attitude to match. Parlor Maid Teresinha Diaz, assigned to the second floor including the Primary Suite, found herself exclusively at the beck and call of Mrs. Collor. This strained the housekeeping staff considerably, as well as the Pantry when I asked Jose if he could spare Luisa Salvi, our highly trusted and long time part timer, to help out on the second floor.

Poor Teresinha had to deal with this spoilt woman, who, had she been a child, would have benefited from a thorough spanking. She flung off her clothes, dropped them wherever she felt like it, scolded Teresinha and ordered her around. Teresinha told me that in the second bedroom, during her final packing, her jewelry was strewn around so that Teresinha did not dare leave the suite when Mrs. Collor went off for an engagement, for fear they could disappear and she would be held responsible. Mrs. Collor casually told Teresinha that often she would just fling on her clothes with no underwear, including panties, which I could tell. I did not think she would last long in her husband's life, and believe I was correct in that they divorced later.

Mrs. Collor had a rather unattractive face, but beautiful long and thick blond hair. She went through four of our wonderful hairdressers, who all were shaking and sweating during their respective times with her. She only needed to have her side hair fixed with a curling iron, the rest just hung down her back. It did not seem a big deal, except she went into a temper tantrum if the hairdresser did not get it just so, brushed her hair forward, and made the hairdresser start all over again. She made her husband late for the Arlington Cemetery ceremony as she, three times, changed her mind as to whether she would go with him or not.

I did suggest to the embassy that perhaps Mrs. Collor in the future might wish to bring her own maid and hairdresser.

We pressed so many clothes the visit was the most labor intensive ever over the ironing boards. And the Brazilians wanted their clothes pressed now, thank you. The Brazilian ambassador and his wife also stayed with us. Mrs. Moreira who knew Chamber Maid Marinete Saias when she worked for the OAS Secretary General, had called Marinete earlier if she could press her clothes at Blair House. I knew nothing about this, and was appalled at such gross behavior. It would have been easy and appropriate for the ambassador's wife to have all her dresses and suits pressed in her residence and, ready on hangers, brought down from the embassy, a ten minute ride away. Instead the ladies were up till the wee hours pressing clothes, especially on the first night.

I gave them a hand too, and was merrily on a roll downstairs in the laundry room at 1 am pressing shirts when I encountered one that seemed a bit large for the skinny aide-de-camp staying in Room 24. When I found I was actually ironing my own head butler's shirt, it was definitely time to quit for the night.

President Collor de Mello had been a guest for lunch just before taking office a year earlier. He was young and dynamic and his country's first directly elected president in 29 years. Immediately, on becoming president, he took decisive action to deal with Brazil's economic woes, launching a comprehensive economic and administrative reform program. He was 15 years older than his second wife, whom he met when she was 13. President Collor, however, did not endear himself to his own people as later events in Brazil were to show when, faced with corruption charges, he was forced to resign his office in 1992. The only really nice Brazilian in the entire entourage was Lucia Rego, a diplomat assigned to us from the Brazilian Toronto Trade Office. Exceedingly helpful, she was receptive to my request that our three Brazilian ladies: Agustinha Dos Santos, our laundress, Teresinha Diaz and Marinete Saias, our two maids, meet the president of their native country privately. The three of them waited in the Library for President Collor to come by on his way down to bid farewell in the Blair Dining Room. However, he somehow could not find the time.

Fortunately the next Brazilian visit years later was sheer joy. At that time, in April 1995, the ambassadorial couple, the Paulo Tarso Flecha da Limas, were fresh in from their post in London where Mrs. Flecha da Lima particularly had become a close friend of Diana, Princess of Wales. Although their president arrived the day after the Oklahoma City bombing casting a mantel of sorrow over the visit, and particularly the White House portion of it, it was a delightful visit. President Fernando Henrique Cardoso and his wife were elderly, charming, gracious and with a terrific sense of humor. They also showed their appreciation to my staff upstairs and thus we, fortunately, received a very different impression of Brazilians. Generously, Blair

House was given sixteen exquisite tablemats and napkins for use in the Lee Dining Room, embroidered by Ms. Lygia Mattos, Brazil's finest needlework artisan and renowned embroiderer, who by her work was keeping alive traditional needlepoint techniques inherited from Europe and the Brazilian colonial times.

We had precisely one hour and five minutes cleaning up the visit of the King and Queen of Spain before the arrival of Rafael Angel Calderón Fournier, President of the Republic of Costa Rica and his family in October 1991. Because of the narrow window for clean up, bed changing and other preparations we only had time to prepare the Primary Suite and the Library before arrival. While Jose and his crew cleaned up the pantries, reset the Garden Room for the Costa Rican lunch and the hospitality table in the Blair Dining Room, restocking it with Chef's morning bakeries, Mrs. Rennie, Teresinha, and I dashed upstairs to the Primary Suite. While the ladies changed the beds, emptied wastepaper baskets, and changed towels in the bathrooms, I tidied up the Library, straightened newspapers, emptied ashtrays, and put furniture back in place and brought up fresh flower arrangements done the night before.

Sam, also, had his hands full. The Czech and Slovakian advance team for their president's upcoming second visit had to come during this morning. Sam, unconcerned, fitted them in during this exact "open" hour, introducing them to me when he reached the Library, and managed to get them out, happily having finished their tour and discussions, by the time the motorcade rolled up unloading the Costa Ricans.

The Calderóns were an impressive and modern couple. Mexican by birth, Gloria Calderón was the daughter of the former Governor of the State of Morelos, and the granddaughter of a leader of the Mexican revolution. President Calderón's own father was president of his country in the early forties, until forced to flee during Costa Rica's civil war in 1948. Calderón was thus born in Nicaragua during his parents' exile. He was a modern leader with a democratic agenda. Interestingly, and indicative of the attitude of this peaceful and non violent nation, the president traveled with no security personnel at all. We rarely experienced this except for the Europeans. When I had occasion later to visit Costa Rica I was impressed by their commitment to environmental protection which extended to a ban on cutting down any trees in the entire country, thus benefiting the global environment.

The lively Costa Ricans were great fun. Ten of the ministers or high officials brought their wives. Thus Mrs. Calderón was well attended as they went everywhere with her. In addition the four Calderón children, ranging in age from 8 to 18, had different agendas. Mrs. Rennie always remembered this visit as her most favorite.

The youngest Calderón at age 8 had saved up his pocket money for nine months and went off, with much anticipation, to "Toys Are Us," to return with a giant water machine gun, just what I most needed at Blair House. Eyeing this with misgiving, I asked him his intentions. "Oh, I am going to try it out right now," he said. I gave him my most stern general manager look, after which he added: "in the garden of course." However, I told him in no uncertain terms that he had better not take it out of the packaging until back in Costa Rica. "Tu entiendes?"

The crowning moment of Joseph Reed's soon to be ended career in Protocol was that afternoon when he had decided to host a tea for 50 guests of the Council of the Americas, headed by David Rockefeller, with entrance through the Lee House and tea served in the Blair Drawing Rooms. I had been instructed by Reed to move the meetings scheduled by President Bush's official visitor, the President of Costa Rica, to the Jackson Place Houses. Consequently, shortly after President Calderón's arrival he was forced to meet with the Acting Secretary of the Treasury and others in the lesser rooms while President Bush's chief of protocol was entertaining for tea in the drawing-rooms. Ambassador Reed wanted to know when the Costa Rican meetings were finished, so he personally could go down to invite, most graciously and as if he was conferring a major favor on him, the Costa Rican president to Ambassador Reed's tea party in the Costa Rican's own drawing room.

It was downright tacky.

But, generally we enjoyed most of the visitors from south of the border. The spirit of our visitors was infectious even though all the visits were labor intensive with heavy schedules. President Bush and James Baker worked hard to open trade possibilities with Latin America and succeeded to a certain degree.

I have this enduring impression of warmth, charm, friendliness, humor, and great enjoyment of life, and of people with a great wish to embrace the U.S., albeit on their own terms as befit their culture and capabilities, and of course their own political situations at home. Sadly, now into the 21ˢᵗ century the U.S. has succeeded in making itself thoroughly disliked south of the border and it will be a long time before the pendulum will return to its former position.

CHAPTER 8

A CRESCENT OF HOPE AND FEAR

"This is no time to go wobbly, George!"

Margaret Thatcher

"Mr. Shamir is strictly kosher," Sam said, looking worried. "We have to kosher the kitchen before the visit. They said so." He had just discussed preparations for the Official Working Visit of Yitzhak Shamir, Prime Minister of Israel, and his wife, Shulmait Shamir, to Washington in April 1989 with the administrator of the Israeli embassy. We looked at each other. What a challenge!

Executive Chef Russell Cronkhite and Head Butler Jose Fuster joined our discussion, and as would frequently be the case, knew exactly what to do. Chef discussed in great detail the dietary restrictions of the Jewish religion: the separation of dairy and meat products and the plates and cutlery used, and proved quite knowledgeable on the subject, having experienced it all before in his previous hotel career. He suggested that his hot kitchen be used exclusively for the meat preparation for the evening meal, and the cold kitchen and bake shop be set aside for breakfast and luncheon preparations, which would include dairy products. Jose suggested a similar arrangement for the pantries: all breakfast and luncheon china and cutlery to be handled out of the Blair pantry, using the dishwasher there, while evening meals would be cleared away in the Lee pantry, thus never mixing up the china and cutlery.

"But, Mrs. V," Jose said, "they will not accept our Lenox china as it has already been used." "Then I expect we shall have to rent some for one meal, but how about the Tiffany china?" I asked.

The Tiffany Company had created china for 100 that copied the flowered fabric on our large sofas in the Garden Room, now to be inaugurated. A second set of china we would rent. All foods would have to come from kosher markets. And, the embassy demanded, we must have a rabbi on duty during the visit to ensure that proper procedures would be followed.

Rabbi Kawior descended on us ten days before the visit. Although he had emigrated from Poland soon after World War II, he had not yet mastered understandable English. He was a delightful and charming old gentleman, and he and I hit it off immediately; since he spoke Yiddish, he was able to understand my German. I do believe he developed a crush on me. He brought me bagels and breads every day, and insisted on kissing my hand at every opportunity. He also kept repeating how perfect I was for "this house," but as he was hard to understand I may be misquoting him. He closely inspected every pot and pan in the kitchen as well as every piece of Chef's equipment, rejecting much. Chef and Sous Chef Greg Uhlein spent a good amount of time shelving and draping plastic over those items, then sealing the quarantine articles with tape so no one by mistake could use them. Chef also had to buy new utensils to replace the rejected items. With the assistance of Sean and Frankie, Chef and Greg scrubbed the kitchens from top to bottom, with Jose and Smile doing the same in the pantries.

The crowning moment came when Rabbi Kawior, dressed in goggles, turned on a blow-torch with a flame two feet wide. As we watched in astonishment, he collected everything that he had approved for use and torched them. My only comment to Chef was: "Please, please tell me you turned off the gas." I instructed the staff that during the Israeli visit no one could bring their own food to work. Meals would be provided to all the staff on disposable paper plates. We certainly did not wish to undo the koshering by putting a ham sandwich in the refrigerator by mistake.

Throughout this visit either Rabbi Kawior or a second rabbi was on duty, at meal times sitting at a table outside the Garden Room where the meals were being served or, during the preparations, at a table in the kitchen hallway. On the last day, when Chef was exhausted, "I slapped a chicken down on the carving board in the cold kitchen, set aside for the dairy meals. I immediately realized I had made a mistake and snatched the chicken off the carving board. When I looked up I saw Rabbi Klavan watching me." Fortunately the rabbi realized that it was an honest mistake and since only the carving board had been touched by the chicken, this could be scrubbed down, and no harm done. But he did consult his book of Talmudic instructions as to the correct procedure for handling such a situation.

During the first Bush administration we fed, housed, and provided aid and comfort to an Israeli delegation as well as to several Muslim delegations that opposed Israel's domestic and foreign policies. These were among the most important diplomatic missions of the decade, for the dominant issue through that segment of the world for a half-century has been negotiating a truce between Israel and its neighbors, and the United States has been a participant from the first.

President Carter's famous Camp David accord had its beginnings in our Lee Dining Room. And in 1990 as the George H.W. Bush administration worked on the issue, Jack Anderson and Dale Van Atta wrote in the Washington Post: "In the minds of top Bush administration officials, a Palestinian state is no longer a question of 'if,' but 'when.' Officially President Bush and his foreign policy aides are still saying that they oppose the creation of such a state unless Israel is completely happy with the arrangement. But privately, many of Bush's top aides are saying that it's just a matter of time."

The Shamir visit was the beginning of Blair House involvement in ongoing Middle East peace negotiations, at the service level of course. Part of our contribution to that effort was to provide sustenance that conformed to their religious observances. Chef had his hands full with the Israelis. They were heavy eaters, the most gluttonous of all of the delegations that we fed during my thirteen years there. He had to increase his portions continuously.

On his last day, the prime minister asked us to serve lunch for forty guests. He wanted to entertain congressional leaders, and it would be more convenient to have it at the house just before his departure than elsewhere in town. The Israeli embassy would pay for it, thus in effect making us their caterers.

We would never do this again. Expecting Blair House to do what an embassy is supposed to provide could easily become a habit with our guests if we did not put a stop to it. Thus was born our unwritten but fairly consistent rule: that our principal guest was welcome to entertain American business and other guests at the house during their visit but, because it was considered business and not social, the meals would be limited to 22 persons, the most that could fit around our largest table. The U.S. government would pay for this, as it would be in our interest to assist in furthering relations at all levels. However, any social function such as a reception or a meal with guests at several tables must be hosted by the visiting delegation and held at another location. Blair House would never again be used as a caterer.

While the Prime Minister was busy with his meetings, Mrs. Shamir had a full agenda of her own. She called upon me for whatever she needed, whether to arrange a hairdresser appointment for her, to bring her guests up to the Library where she held her meetings or generally to make her feel at home. When her hairdresser had been installed in our hair salon, I swung by the Primary Suite to take Mrs. Shamir up. Then I returned to the Primary Suite Hallway to check on my maids, and on exiting the elevator came face to face with Mrs. Shamir's angry and extremely worried security guard who with blazing eyes yelled at me: "Where is she?"

– and stuck a gun in my stomach.

He was a member of the Israeli Security Force, an organization famed for its toughness, bad manners and arrogance.

I was already fed up with this group and couldn't resist:

"Lost her, did you?"

However, while I did not expect to be shot, he looked ready to do so if necessary, so I relented and took him upstairs to the hair salon.

Shortly before the delegation arrived, Sam noticed that an Egyptian flag, honoring a recent State Visit of President Mubarak, housed in a hotel, was still draped over the Old Executive Office Building directly across from the house. As this might be considered a slap in the face of the Israelis, he prevailed upon the city government to remove it at once. I recall, years later, racing up to the Library to hide our pictorial book on Iraq just before the arrival of the Emir of Kuwait shortly after the invasion of Saddam Hussein and his army into his country. Such was the tiptoeing we had to do.

Contrary to his reputation as a tough leader, rigid in his harsh policies, and as some of us privately said: "a little terrorist," Prime Minister Shamir was appreciative and rather nice. At our farewells, he said: "I shall remember Blair House for its Danish-American hospitality."

Alarmed, I insisted that everything here was American. All I needed was for the Danish part of this little speech to get to higher circles, and my days would be numbered.

The first Muslim visit of the Bush presidency came in June 1989 with the arrival of Mohtrama Benazir Bhutto, Prime Minister of the Islamic Republic of Pakistan, her husband, Asif Ali Zardari and their six-month-old son. Benazir Bhutto was the eldest child of a wealthy family which breathed politics and power. Her father, the country's Prime Minister and first democratically elected leader of Pakistan, assisted President Richard Nixon in opening the doors to China. The beguiling Ms. Bhutto first appeared on the world scene at the age of 18 when she accompanied her father, Zulfikar Ali Bhutto to India for the negotiation of the Simla Accords after the 1971 Indo-Pakistani war. She received B.A. degrees in government from Radcliffe College in 1973, and in political philosophy and economics from Oxford in 1977. After her return to Pakistan, she saw her father discredited by opposition politicians, detained by the martial law regime, tried for political murder, and convicted and executed in 1979. Her book DAUGHTER OF DESTINY describes the agony of waiting for news of her father's brutal execution and of her early adult life in prison, in house arrest and long months in complete isolation, sick and mistreated following her attempt to mobilize public support for his cause. Released in January 1984 she went into exile to seek medical treatment in Europe for an ear infection. In April 1986 she returned to Pakistan as head of her father's Pakistan People's Party. After the air crash which killed her father's murderer, General Zia ul-Haq, ruler of Pakistan for eleven years, mostly under martial law, she ran for office and was named Prime Minister of Pakistan, the first woman to lead a Muslim nation in modern times.

She appeared frail, with impaired hearing in one ear, and was possibly our hardest working visitor. After taking leave of James Baker, who had greeted her on arrival and escorted her to Blair House, her schedule was grueling, following long hours of travel. It included meetings with William Bennett, U.S. Secretary of Education and with her Foreign Minister Yaquib Khan and other advisors, after which she joined a reception in the Garden Room for twenty-five Americans who called her Pinkie. Friends from her Radcliffe days, they included

Kathleen Kennedy Townsend, the older daughter of Robert Kennedy and later Lieutenant Governor of Maryland; Peter W. Galbraith (later U.S. ambassador to Croatia), a former U.S. Senate staffer whom I remembered well; and Marc Siegel, a political consultant. Marc was my advisor on this visit including a heads-up that "Benazir loves peppermint candy ice cream."

Following the reception the prime minister dined in the Lee Dining Room with ten advisors, going over her schedule and speeches, and when she finally came in to have coffee in the Blair Drawing Room, she was tired and grumpy. "Please," Marc asked, "could you bring her some peppermint ice cream? We need her to loosen up and relax." So Jose, with much fanfare, served her the ice cream, with the intended result. She broke up laughing delightedly, and retired happily at 10:30 pm, having had no break since her 5 pm arrival, not even a bathroom break.

Her husband, Asif Ali Zardari, laid-back and irreverent, had a separate agenda. A Muslim, wearing his native dress, he asked Jose to supply him with Scotch upstairs. What a visitor of Islamic faith did when traveling abroad was a very different story it seemed from the piety and dietary restrictions observed in his homeland. When King Ibn al-Saud of Saudi Arabia headed a Saudi Arabian delegation in the early sixties, all the women were housed in the Lee House. They entered the house totally wrapped from head to foot in their native chador. Three hours later they emerged in chic Parisian clothes and started their visit in Washington by happily going shopping Western style.

Mr. Zardari told me he had never met His Royal Highness Prince Bandar Bin Sultan, the Saudi Ambassador, who was en route to call on the Prime Minister, so it was my pleasure to introduce them to each other. I enjoyed listening to their talk in the Front Hall about hawking in Pakistan where Prince Bandar's father had a hunting lodge.

Kent Carnie, my first husband, wanted to specialize in Pakistan because of falconry. Kent was a falconer first and foremost, an army officer second. He joined through ROTC at the University of California at Berkeley and, apart from a brief stint in the Korean War and a longer one in Vietnam, his military career was influenced by the U.S. Army's FAST program (Foreign Area Specialist Training) and he became an expert, not in Pakistan, but in Iran. Having been married to him for eleven years, all of which were spent with falcons and the sport of falconry including the better part of two years in Iran, assisting him in doing raptor research for the Iranian government, I listened happily as the two men discussed "The Sport of Kings."

Benazir Bhutto never paused. Every hour at the house was occupied by meetings: with Barber Conable, President of the World Bank, Carla Hills, U.S. Trade Representative, Michel Camdessus, Director of International Monetary Fund, the Washington Post Board, television interviews with NBC's Today's Show, and with Peter Jennings and Ted Koppel of ABC. In addition to the official welcome in the White House, a meeting with the U.S. President, and his State dinner for her, she lunched at the Department of State and the Pentagon, and addressed a Joint Session of Congress, making what Senator Domenici called "the best speech I have ever heard." She spoke about our most important export: "An idea – the idea of democracy."

Benazir Bhutto and her husband returned to Blair House in April 1995, this time accompanied by her famous mother, the Begum Nusrat Bhutto. After bearing three children Benazir Bhutto was more matronly, her husband was now wearing western dress, and the new dietary restrictions from the Pakistani Embassy were puzzling to say the least, that the prime minister did not eat any flour (thus eliminating breads), and no dairy products (what about the peppermint candy ice cream?) We were puzzled about these drastic changes in her diet. Yet as soon as he walked in the door, Marc Siegel, again my contact, asked me: "Do you have her peppermint candy ice cream ready? She has been bitching about it all the way down from New York!" Ann Stock, White House Social Secretary, asked me what special gesture First Lady Hillary Clinton could make for Prime Minister Bhutto during her visit with her at the White House, to return the generosity extended to Mrs. Clinton during her recent trip to Pakistan. As a result, peppermint candy ice cream was included in the tea menu at the White House. And soon enough the family ordered pizza and hamburgers and obviously had no idea of the peculiar food lists that had arrived in advance of their visit.

The more sophisticated Pakistanis were relatively easy to please, but the servants were primitive and rude to my staff. Bhutto's personal maid was a scruffy-looking, pajama-clad, chain-smoking, older woman, who tried, in Urdu, to boss my maids around, getting their attention by snapping her fingers at them. Some delegation members could not eat together because custom forbade them to mix. Five separate dining areas were required to feed the delegation members. Prime Minister Bhutto dined in the Lee Dining Room with her ministers; her husband preferred to dine quietly with his aide in the Library. When the Pakistani military aide, a general, saw that the prime minister's security were dining in our Garden Room where the delegation buffet was laid out he decided that he could not possibly eat with such inferior people. We set a table in the Jackson Place Dining Room for him, his aide, the chief of protocol and his wife. When the woman discovered that she would have to eat with the two military officers, she had conniptions, and demanded a tray in her room. And the valet and maid came to the delegation buffet only after everyone else had eaten.

Late January 1990 President Ali Abdullah Saleh, President of the Yemen Arab Republic arrived for a State Visit. Although rented dinner jackets were worn by the delegation members at the State Dinner, I was thrilled to see the Yemen President himself in his native clothes, the long white "shirt" over baggy pants, over which he wore a jacket, a scarf, and a belt embroidered with gold to which was attached his enormous jambiya, the curved dagger and scabbard used for decorative purposes but also depicting manliness. Usually weapons are banned at the White House, but since this one was regarded as a native dress accessory, an exception was made.

The Yemen ambassador, Mohsin A. Alaini, was firmly in charge of the schedule and arrangements. A former prime minister and foreign minister, he was his country's longtime ambassador to the U.S. and my contact. While the president and his all-male delegation knew little if any English, they were all smiling and appreciative. The visitors from Yemen were affectionate with each other and often held hands, from the president on down, somehow extending this friendliness to my staff. And they liked to be together; they really, really liked to be together.

The first morning, when Jose brought breakfast upstairs to the Primary Suite for President Saleh, he found eight delegation members already in its drawing room. As soon as he put down the breakfast tray the staffers helped themselves to the president's breakfast, rummaging through it with their fingers and established themselves on the Savon-nerie carpet, happily eating with their fingers. They dipped bread in the honey pot, dripping it all over our elegantly upholstered furniture and the precious carpet. However, wiser by now, the following morning, Jose laid a five-foot round table in the Library next door to accommodate this group more suitably.

I had carefully gone over the Muslim dietary restrictions with Ambassador Alaini and assured him that we were well versed and ready to comply with them. The first night's dinner of Roast Duckling was changed to Lamb Kebab, planned for the next day, as the group had been traveling for seventeen hours, and wanted nothing more than their beds. Therefore dinner was put forward for them, and the duck simply would not be ready in time. We knew that the lamb must be overcooked, and no alcohol served, although "there will be no objection from President Saleh if it is taken by others." It does not matter, "what people do behind closed doors," the ambassador told me. This policy was tested nightly, as Jose delivered a bottle of Scotch to the Foreign Minister's Suite, carried away empty the following morning. The president was fond of tomatoes and boiled potatoes. Every morning Ali, his valet, came to the pantry and prepared the president's power drink in the blender: tomatoes chopped with onions, garlic and hot peppers. His delegation members also loved tomatoes which made me wonder if it was a staple to them, or a luxury. They came with their own coffee, which was strong and prepared individually. The ambassador gave me this coffee recipe: "In a small pot, add 1 heaping teaspoon of extra fine ground coffee for each cup. Add ½ teaspoon sugar for each cup. Add 1 demitasse cup of water for each cup. Bring to a boil, allowing coffee to froth three times. Remove from heat and let sit 1 minute. Pour into demitasse cups."

And there was an added benefit:

"After drinking coffee, grounds should be swirled around edge of cup and inverted over saucer. Grounds drain onto saucer and the future is told from the pattern remaining in cup. Good Luck."

The embassy provided the rooming list well in advance of the visit so we could prepare our folded map showing each floor, all the bedrooms, and the occupant's name and extension number listed in each bedroom. The Yemen embassy superimposed text in Arabic on our typewritten rooming-list so that everyone could understand where they were. At least five more people stayed overnight, using our lush bedspreads bundled up on the floor. When we discovered this the first morning, we exchanged the bedspreads for ordinary white ones, and in addition stocked those particular bedrooms with old blankets, realizing that it would be rather difficult to kick out the "unregistered" guests.

Half an hour before his president was due for the State Dinner, Ali came into the Blair pantry and, to Jose's and my consternation, asked for charcoal. Jose went upstairs with him to find out why. Ali was planning to make a charcoal fire on the bathroom floor. On this fire he would burn incense and then "my president will stand over it, the scent will be absorbed under his robe, and he will smell good for President Bush." Ali had little English, but this was the gist of the operation. I told Ali that "I understand completely, Mr. Ali, but unfortunately," and here I referred to my watch "time is short, and we could not possibly find charcoal at this hour, besides which all shops are already closed. I am so sorry, and if only we had had more time … … …" So we left it at that, silently congratulating ourselves on a near miss. Luckily I escaped the problem of an earlier manager with a delegation from the Arab peninsula who built a fire in the middle of a Persian carpet in the Library to roast goat meat.

A few months later I was showing the advance team for the State Visit of Zine el-Abidine Ben Ali, President of the Republic of Tunisia, through the house. As we entered the Eisenhower Room I pointed out to them the lovely chandelier gracing this room and told them about the collapse of the chandelier in 1982 into the bed of the King of Morocco. They were horrified. "Was the king in the bed," their charming and amusing Charges d'affaires Hedi Gharbi asked. "No, fortunately not," I replied, with a suitably somber expression on my face. "Oh," he said, "what a pity," after which they all roared with laughter.

So I had reason to look forward to this visit May 14-17, 1990. Their dietary restrictions were Muslim, and we were asked to serve no alcohol. The president was so taken with "la cuisine raffiné" that he requested to have Chef brought to him to thank him personally. Chef had prepared for his two luncheons and two dinners among others Red Snapper with a Caper-Lemon Sauce, Paupiettes of Sole and Sole Mousse with Tomato Butter Sauce, Grilled Lamb and Chicken with

Braised Leeks, Asparagus and Carrots accompanied by Orzo with Pine Nuts and Raisins, among other delectable dishes. We became very good at cooking for guests of the Muslim and Jewish faiths, and both our Executive Chefs, Russell Cronkhite and Ian Knox would excel in this specialized cooking. The valet of the Tunisian president got along with Jose like a house afire and brought boxes of sweets into our pantry, to be served with their own tea alongside our refreshments to the president and his guests during meetings. We also kept on hand loads of hard boiled eggs as a snack for the president. We fed an enormous group of people at each meal, even into the night as the Tunisian security had no time before the evening engagements to come to dinner.

For the first time, a country's flag was displayed behind its president during his meetings in the Lee Drawing Room. Also President Ben Ali did not want to sit on the power sofa with his guest of honor but preferred two armchairs for himself and his guest. When meeting with a less exalted person he would sit by himself in the armchair with the guest on an ordinary, and lower, chair on his right.

The house does the laundry for the guests on the premises, and dry cleaning is sent out in the morning to be returned late afternoon. Mrs. Rennie encountered a problem: #35 was missing one undershirt and a pair of socks and "I am so sorry, Mrs. Valentiner, but I made a mistake and I left it in the Foreign Minister's Suite (#32) and when I went in there to retrieve the items, I saw the minister had already closed his suitcase." And then she continued: "I also believe the minister has taken some of our hand towels and how we are to look into his suitcase or even to ask him to open it before us I do not know." I mentally rehearsed the following little speech: "Your Excellency, I have a diplomatic problem of enormous proportions. I want your underwear." Getting to this stage would be rather precarious, so I spoke with the Tunisian Chief of Protocol instead who assured me he was aware of this, and "it will be sorted out in Tunisia." I was not so sure, but retreated, feeling sorry for the unfortunate sock-deprived guest and regretting the loss of the two hand towels with blue monograms. Quite possibly keeping good relations between our two countries were worth that much.

A French protectorate for 74 years, Tunisia became an independent nation and a constitutional republic in 1956. President Ben Ali was serving as Prime Minister when he assumed the presidency in a peaceful transfer of power from former president Habib Bourguiba on November 7, 1987. The less official word was that Zine el Abidine Ben Ali became the second President of Tunisia when he claimed to have a constitutional right as Prime Minister to replace the aged Bourguiba. He had been Prime Minister, the first military officer to hold that post, for all of one month. In April 1989 he ratified his position by popular mandate in a presidential election running unopposed. His main domestic achievements had been to expand human rights and to continue market-oriented economic reforms.

Actually the United States became the first country to recognize Tunisia after its independence from France in 1956. Thus the Tunisian president in his meeting with President Bush would review our friendly bilateral relations and discuss international issues of common interest, including the Middle East peace process. At the request of the United States and other nations, Tunisia had agreed in 1982 to accommodate the headquarters of the Palestine Liberation Organization (PLO), and Tunisia used to be the site of the authorized US-PLO dialogue. The visit also included several meetings with Cabinet secretaries, the media, and the Acting Secretary of State Lawrence Eagleburger.

Our next Middle East visitor was Shaikh Jabir Al-Ahmed Al-Sabah, the Emir of the State of Kuwait, arriving September 28, 1990 for an Official Working Visit lasting all of eight hours. The Emir had been deposed some eight weeks earlier by Iraq's president, Saddam Hussein, and now led his government-in-exile from its headquarters in Ta'if, Saudi Arabia. He cut a sad figure, wasted away to nothing. He spent his time on the small white sofa in the Rear Blair Drawing Room sitting very quietly, sometimes wiping away a tear, waiting to go to the White House for very serious meetings. His entourage with whom we had occasion to speak each had a horror story to relate about the invading Iraqis, and their tears, and ours, were never far away. The Emir also made his case for assistance on Capitol Hill. More meetings followed at Blair House with Secretary of Defense Dick Cheney and Chairman of the Joint Chiefs Colin Powell. He departed from the house on schedule, without acknowledging any of the staff. He would return to Blair House later, happy as a lark, to thank America for restoring his country to him.

When the attack had occurred on August 2 the White House issued a statement condemning the invasion and calling for the immediate withdrawal of Iraqi forces. Later the White House said "The United States is reviewing all its options in response to this Iraqi aggression" and continued that the U.N. Security Council would meet immediately to review the situation.

The U.S. and its allies went to war against Iraq on Wednesday, January 16, 1991, with the objective of chasing them out of Kuwait and back into Iraq. This was accomplished by February 28. Since the previous August 2, President Bush made hundreds of phone calls while Secretary of State Baker logged thousands of miles around the world rounding up international support and building a strong coalition in order to meet the Iraqi aggression against a sovereign nation. In my opinion this was done properly, as behooves a mighty nation, with tact, respect for world opinion, and enormous skill.

When the allied troops left Saddam Hussein attacked the Kurds in the north and the Shiites in the south of his own nation, brutal assaults that took some of the bloom off the victory. Yet it failed to dim the tribute paid to the U.S. fighting troops in the parade along Constitution Avenue in Washington on June 8, 1991. Thousands applauded and cheered them. At last it was back in vogue to be in the military, much maligned since the Vietnam War. Kids from the inner city enthusiastically joined the crowds and hero worship was much in evidence. What a triumph for our President, if only he had been able to harness this pride in country to turn his reelection campaign around.

My irreverent "uncle" Harry Toyberg-Frandzen took note of the unease about America's pullback from Iraq in a verse to me. The retired Danish ambassador, with many years of service in India, Argentina, and Turkey, sent this from his retirement Quinta outside Lisbon:

"All brutes and dumbs I do abhor
with no regard to their color.
No sooner have they lost a push
than all the blame is placed on Bush:
"Oh come, Ye madmen from the East!
Enjoy a courtly Blair House feast
and when knives are licked and teeth well picked
Say: Thank you, Ma'am, to Benedict!""

On the evening, Monday, October 14, 1991, shortly after the arrival of Shaikh Isa Bin Salman Al-Khalifa, Emir of the State of Bahrain, as the final unsavory debate in the U.S. Senate was winding up, it was extraordinary to have the Head of the Emir's household, an older gentleman of small stature but noble proportions, walk into the Protocol Office, beam at me, and say: "We won!" while congratulating me on the Bush administration's "victory" in the confirmation of Clarence Thomas to the Supreme Court. Sadly, as the committee hearings were rebroadcast over and over, the nation heard every salacious moment of the controversy over Thomas' alleged sexual harassment and interest in pornography. I disliked the appointment intensely. I felt that as there is rarely smoke without fire, the nomination should have been withdrawn. Don't we want the best and the brightest on the Supreme Court? And then to add insult to injury, that someone from a Muslim nation identified with this choice – that was insupportable.

The pint-sized Emir was seemingly gentle, and being of frail constitution he always used the elevator to come and go by means of the basement. To ensure that I was present for his arrivals and departures, I ran up and down like a yo-yo. His Highness had been both the secular and religious head of state since Bahrain attained independence from Great Britain in 1971. He dissolved parliament four years later and with his brother had ruled by decree. He was the 10th Khalifa to reign since the family established its rule in 1782. Educated by tutors, he had traveled extensively and spoke good English. A firm supporter of President Bush during the Desert War, the Emir remained a strong ally and defender of the U.S. presence in the Persian Gulf.

The information minister brought me in to talk with the Emir about falconry. I was aware that the Peregrine Fund, the World Center for Birds of Prey in Boise, Idaho, had helped set up a falcon breeding program in Bahrain and had trained its manager, and having known many of those wonderful falconers through my eleven-year marriage to one, we had a lively discussion. The Emir inquired whether I had ever hunted the houbara bustard in the desert, the ultimate quarry in Arab falconry. Twice the size of a falcon and able to blend into the background, it not only has highly developed flying skills, but also at times has been known to remain on the ground defending itself against the falcon, proving a formidable foe. Alas, I had not, but I countered with stories from Caithness, Scotland, and my experience seeing the ghillies with the dogs, the cadgers carrying the peregrine falcons, and the excitement of watching the peregrine falcon circling high above keeping an eye on the dogs on point below. While the Arabs dispatch their falcons straight from the fist at the prey, the American and European falconers send the falcon up in advance, and then loose the dogs to raise the game under the bird. The Arabs consider this practice unsporting, giving the falcon too great an advantage, and the Emir seemed unfamiliar with this form of falconry.

He returned early June 1998, as I was honeymooning in Venice with Adrian Cummins, my Australian husband, and by all accounts so appreciated his treatment that he insisted on giving a large tip to the staff. Randy was called up to the chief of household's room and handed an envelope, and despite pleading that he could not accept any cash whatsoever either for himself or on behalf of the staff, all government employees, he was told that His Highness had specifically directed that this be done. Randy realized the diplomatic insult if he did not accept, and duly expressed his gratitude and appreciation on behalf of everyone. He quickly called the Assistant Chief of Protocol for Visits, brought her the $18,000 to be locked up, and later returned by her to the Bahraini embassy.

I had looked forward greatly to the visit of Suleyman Demirel, Prime Minister of Turkey, in February 1992, and had mentioned my extensive travels in that magnificent country to Ambassador Nuzhet Kandemir with whom I would do several more Turkish visits. My ex husband and I drove through Turkey several times during 1972-1974 en route to Iran for our raptor research. On the first occasion, we had to wait ten days in Istanbul, and what a glorious city in which to wait, for our Carnet de Passage giving us permission to import our car into and out of Iran. We sailed across the Bosporus, and then followed the Black Sea coast to Trabzon before heading inland for the wilds of Eastern Turkey. The country was stunningly beautiful, the people surprisingly gracious, and with so many villages having had guest workers abroad language seemed to be no trouble. I got along with German in the first part of the journey, Kent with Farsi the closer we got to the border of Iran.

Our last journey through Turkey, though, was the most spectacular. With our first wirehaired dachshund, Napoleon, we had spent six months in Iran driving hundreds of miles, camping out, and banding birds of prey in the Mo'or D'aab, (Black Water) on the Caspian Coast, and lured kestrels out of the walls at Persepolis. The work had been grueling and we were dead on our feet. And then, in March 1974 we entered Turkey. We followed the Mediterranean Coast from Syria going from Roman ruin to Greek ruin to Crusader Castle, and saw spring evolving before our eyes. We camped at night, and bathed in the still-frigid Mediterranean. For a month we drove, observed, admired, and our only source of bathwater was the sea. Then we arrived in Pergamum, part of Alexander the Great's vast inheritance from his maternal grandfather. That night we saw just below Pergamum a camp ground and were invited in by the caretaker. Later he came to our van, beckoned for us to follow, and after leading us into a rickety old wooden house and down moldy steps, opened a door for us.

There, in front of us, was the perfect circular Roman bath, lined with turquoise tiles, into which flowed a steady stream of 95 degree water – and into which we literally flowed shortly after. We had arrived at what used to be the most famous healing center of antiquity, Asklepion, which with its library of 200,000 volumes rivaled Alexandria and Antioch in its pursuit of science and literature.

I had just loved Turkey.

Our visitor, the Turkish Prime Minister, was an older gentleman with a background in civil engineering. His country's first Eisenhower Exchange Fellow in the fifties, he spoke excellent English as did his wife, whose interest was women's rights. Their chief of protocol was suave, delightful, and whimsical with a masterful command of English, playing on words, and always with a straight face. In his whimsy he reminded me of our new chief of protocol, Jack Weinmann. Most notable were the two separate agendas by the Demirels, each of them entertaining for dinner, the prime minister in the Lee Dining Room, and his wife in the Jackson Place Conference Room. I also recall with amusement that the second night they walked back into the house after a reception, and, instead of gathering in the drawing-rooms to catch their breath, they wandered down to the Conference Room, sat down and were ready at the table, fork in hand, awaiting their dinner. Jose and his waiters had not yet lit the candles, put out butter and water, and the kitchen was still in the process of preparing the serving trays with their food. But, as always, Jose and his waiters coped beautifully.

My maids upstairs, unfortunately, were not impressed. It was not a "nice" group to serve, they said. Our Turkish guests were rude, demanding, careless, and disrespectful to my staff. I was disappointed that representatives of that beautiful and stunning part of the world did not live up to my memories of their country.

In ensuing years Blair House was intensely involved at a service level in supporting the Middle East Peace Process; many Israeli and Egyptian visits with hundreds of participants from Jordan, Syria, and the Palestine Liberation Authority would come and go, and dozens of other Muslim nations stayed with us. It was fascinating to observe the differences and the similarities between the Israelis and their Muslim adversaries. The dietary restrictions were far stricter in the Jewish faith. Cooking for the Muslim groups was easier as long as we got the meats from halal markets to ensure proper butchering, and avoided pork and shellfish. Basically the two groups maintained a similar diet. While I found the Arab Muslims polite, with beautiful manners that reflected the hospitality and generosity of the desert Arabs, the more orthodox among them, such as the Saudis, seemed disdainful of women. Some would not shake hands, or if they did certainly only with their left, the unclean hand. As for other Muslims, many seemed to have taken on the manners and behavior of their colonialists: British speech and behavior greatly influenced the Pakistanis, and the Tunisians were clearly influenced by their French association.

In succeeding years some of the Israeli delegation members became increasingly boorish, messy and sloppy, arrogantly ignoring the tenets of good behavior. But here too associations played a role, the increasing participation of expatriate Russian Jews influenced both by a high degree of religious orthodoxy and their Russian environment. Dealing with these varied groups of people was a continuous exercise in diplomacy for me, which I accepted as part of making the President's guests comfortable, my own feelings and reactions being beside the point.

CHAPTER 9

ASIA: FRIENDS ACROSS THE PACIFIC

"Dragon in the sky!"

Kiichi Miyazawa

On November 9, 1989, when the Iron Curtain went up and the Berlin Wall came down, I was in the Front Hall, waiting for our resident guest to appear, when I overheard her foreign minister say to the U.S. ambassador: "We might have started something."

And indeed they might have.

Our guest was Corazon Aquino, President of the Republic of the Philippines since 1986. She grew up in a political family and received her bachelor's degree in French and mathematics in the U.S. and later attended law school in Manila, and married Benigno Aquino. Her husband, an outspoken political foe of the dictator, President Marcos, was jailed for eight years. In 1980 after his release from prison for medical reasons he and Mrs. Aquino lived in the United States for three years when he returned to the Philippines to resume leadership of the opposition movement and was assassinated on arrival. Three years later Corazon Aquino successfully helped oust Mr. Marcos, and was elected president.

On the first night of her State Visit she hosted a dinner for Members of Congress. Among eighteen at the table were five U.S. Congressmen and three U.S. Senators, and no effort had been spared on our part to make this a glittering event. In addition to a menu of five courses, served at the Lee Dining Room table laden with our best silver, I had arranged several bowls with yellow roses, the symbol of Corazon Aquino's campaign against President Marcos and his dictatorship.

The conversation flowed; laughter was abundant, until ---- dessert.

The conversation became more subdued, and out of the stillness, from my vantage point out of sight in the Lee Drawing Room, I heard it: the steady drip of water, water which soon became a trickle, then a stream.

It was coming from the ceiling over the open door between the Lee Dining Room and Drawing Room.

For one split second my entire life went before my eyes.

Then I jumped into action, as an equally stunned Jose and his staff of waiters did. While we ran for towels and started mopping up, Sam and Bill Evans, at that time our Head of Security, who had also observed this calamity from the Lee Hallway, ran upstairs. They found, in Room 26, located directly above the dining room, Mrs. Aquino's head of security, fast asleep in the bathtub with the water still running. Turning off the water, they yanked him out of the bathtub, carried him to the bed, where according to Teresinha "he just continued sleeping as if nothing had happened." Meanwhile downstairs, after the first few minutes of stunned silence, President Aquino started laughing. I loved her for it. So under much merriment, and after Jose had dried off the one unfortunate person who was too close to the waterfall to remain entirely dry, dinner continued.

However, after dinner and at leave taking – and I knew what was coming – I had to face five U.S. congressmen and three U.S. senators who were wondering out loud what "all that money on the restoration of Blair House was spent on." They were rather good natured about it, and I was profoundly thankful for the excellent dinner that had made them so mellow.

The next day when I showed President Aquino's daughter around she put me at ease: "In our house (The Malacañan Palace) in Manila we always have buckets in the living room to catch water from the ceilings, so Mother felt very much at home last night."

The president also went to Arlington Cemetery to attend the traditional military ceremony and to lay a wreath at the grave of the Unknown Soldier, a normal part of a State Visit. A frantic embassy official came storming in needing instant help. The embassy had forgotten to order the wreath. Lynn called the White House Floral Director Nancy Clark who, always helpful, sent one of her assistants with a half finished wreath, intended for the National Security Advisor

General Scowcroft who was to use it on the next day, Veteran's Day. In a protocol car, they raced, just ahead of President Aquino and her motorcade, frantically finishing up the wreath on the backseat with the flowers grabbed by the florist on his way out. It was, according to Lynn, "pretty hectic," but they made it, completed wreath in hand, before the motorcade swung into Arlington Cemetery.

Our facilities manager meanwhile checked all the bathtubs and found four which could not handle the overflow due to faulty pipes, and again confirmed that the costly renovation of the complex had indeed been more cosmetic than practical. Over the next few years water disasters would invariably happen either just before or during some important event, or at 3:30 pm on a Friday afternoon. The stoic Blair House staff would become quite adept at handling same. Certainly one would have to do so when during an important dinner upstairs, hosted by the Prime Minister of Japan, the entire basement overflowed with disgusting sewage from the District of Columbia or when water cascaded from the Foreign Minister's suite on the third floor into the second floor Library after midnight.

We had two Japanese visits in 1989 and one in 1992, all of them with different prime ministers. Little did I know then that as long as I remained General Manager, for 13 years and 4 months, no Japanese Prime Minister would ever return for a second visit at Blair House. I was convinced that I had a jinx on that country's prime ministers as they always lost their next election after staying at the house, and certain embassy staffers shared my conviction! Not until I retired did the spell break, with Junichiro Koizumi returning several times under the new management.

Our very first visitor of George H.W. Bush was Noboru Takeshita in February 1989, a marvelous learning curve for my staff. Advance meetings were detailed and exacting, all requests being made in the most excruciatingly polite fashion.

The large Embassy Conference Room and Office were used as office space for embassy personnel and other staff during visits. Telephones per specific requests of the embassy were installed; office equipment was brought in and, as both rooms already nicely appointed also sported two bathrooms and a kitchen, foreign staff was made quite comfortable. We furnished whatever extra pieces of furniture required, but never any of the technical stuff. We learned during this particular visit of the arrangement preferred by the Japanese, and from which they rarely deviated during the many years I was there. Always included were large folding tables pushed together in the middle of the Embassy Office, covered with tablecloth, on which sat 13/20 telephones, all manned by Japanese staffers. Smoking heavily, snacking and drinking coffee, tea and coke for 24 hours, working through our night which was day time in Japan, the Japanese ran the Blair House staff ragged cleaning up after them. The Japanese visits were always heavily staffed with one person assigned per little detail. Five or six people were involved in the organization of the prime minister's meal, and I would have all of them, but at different times, wishing to meet with me to discuss the intricacies of how to place the chairs and especially which particular chairs should be at the table, not to mention specific menus and last minute changes. I realized I had to put a stop to this time consuming and confusing procedure, and I learned to ask for one delegation contact only with proper authority for all Blair House arrangements.

Heavy security traveled with a Japanese prime minister, and they worked incredible hours. A startled Teresinha had been awakened by the security guard on duty peeping into her bedroom in the middle of the night. Telling this story, she gave us her usual performance complete with sound effects, punctuations and shrieks during her description of making certain she was properly "covered" before she left her bedroom to lead him to the elevator going to the embassy offices. Obviously her solicitous behavior did not work as he snuck upstairs again to fall asleep outside my door. His glasses, sadly, were left behind at his duty station, and found by his supervisor the next morning before he himself woke up. We rather worried he would be languishing later in some Japanese equivalent of outer Siberia.

The Japanese were hardworking and focused, at times too much so as experienced by Marinete who found the piece of chocolate, prepared in the kitchen, laid out on our guests' pillows at turn down every night, firmly attached to the seat of the pants of the Japanese aide who, in his eagerness to get to the telephone, had simply sat on it. I found it fascinating in the Front Hall to observe the traffic of these incredible people. Easily sixty of them were moving back and forth, documents clutched in their hands, between the living rooms, the dining room, up and down the Blair staircase which was the conduit to the embassy offices upstairs. Each was totally focused, as he (or rarely she) moved about, incredibly polite to each other, and bending over at the waist in the presence of their prime minister or other higher officials.

The Official Working Visit of Prime Minister Toshiki Kaifu of Japan and his wife at the end of August 1989 was a surprise. It was unusual to have a visit at this time, Congress being in recess and the U.S. President usually vacationing. Also the hot and humid weather does not lend itself to such exertions as official functions, the season really not starting up again until after Labor Day. I was told that Mr. Kaifu, having just become prime minister a few weeks earlier wished to call upon his most important ally before taking his seat in the Diet for its session, as he must not miss just one day. I also learned he was in a shaky position having been appointed to his exalted stage following hard upon a massive political scandal in Japan involving former Prime Minister Ono (in between Takeshita and Kaifu) and geisha girls. Our contacts at the Japanese Embassy joked that at the rate they were changing prime ministers one absolutely had physically to sit in one's seat in the DIET and not stir in order to hold on to it!

The Kaifus were nice, and the prime minister, as reported, sported polka-dot neckties. Foreign Minister Nakayama seemed to keep his own schedule, with several of the delegation members gravitating towards him rather than the prime minister; the two groups had separate meals in separate dining rooms, with Mrs. Kaifu dining upstairs, and the rest of the delegation members in the Garden Room. We were busy with four separate sets of service going, with masseuses coming in at various times for both Prime Minister and Mrs. Kaifu, and the foreign minister. The latter gave us a bit of grief. Late the first evening the minister went upstairs to his suite just above the Library to have a bath before his massage. Teresinha, on late duty, reported that water was leaking heavily out of the Library ceiling on to the 18th century English oval drop-leaf table and on to the Scalamandre satin faille striped fabric on the dining chairs, and our precious Antique Sarouk on the floor. Sam found the foreign minister on the phone, so he resolutely went in to the bathroom to turn off the gushing tab and assessed it was another case of the overflow mechanism inside the bathtub. Meanwhile in the Library our night of hard labor commenced. After patting them as dry as possible, I started blow drying the satin chair covers with a blow dryer and Sean mopped up the water from the carpet, first by hand, then by machine. Teresinha, at my request, went in search of blankets to "upholster" the door leading into the Kaifus suite. She cleverly returned with several down filled covers to prevent the noise generated by us from penetrating into the Kaifus. We expected a waterfall as well the second night, having been asked to pencil in the masseuses again for the Kaifus and the foreign minister, so after they had all retired for the night we covered everything under that particular part of the ceiling with plastic. Sean was up most of that night also, as their luggage, ready outside the doors for their departure in the morning, had to be collected at 1:40 am.

The Japanese are so organized.

Our third Japanese visit was also the last visit at Blair House in George Bush's presidency. On June 30th, 1992 Prime Minister Kiichi Miyazawa arrived for an Official Working Visit. This prime minister would himself be tossed out of office a year later, having to sit through a humiliating no-confidence vote in the Diet and according to tradition bow deeply to the group of people who had just by words and deeds taunted him. But at Blair House, the preceding year, he was made most welcome. President Bush added a trip to Camp David to the prime minister's normal visit schedule as undoubtedly he was a rather special guest for the following reason:

In early January 1992, at a dinner in Tokyo, President Bush threw up into Prime Minister Miyazawa's lap. President and Mrs. Bush had been on a twelve day four nation Asian-Pacific trip, at "normal" Bush speed which meant very hectic, and the President was reported to have had a touch of the flu and being quite fatigued. After a foursome game of tennis with the Emperor of Japan, his son and Bush's ambassador to Japan, the nice Michael Armacost, it became too much for George Bush and he upped his dinner into the lap of his host. Certain images from the dinner at the prime minister's residence cannot easily be erased: the white, slack jawed, rather rigid face of our President being cradled by a distraught host and prime minister, and then later Barbara Bush, in typical superb fashion, picking up the formality of the evening as she gave a speech in her husband's place.

So Prime Minister Miyazawa was here on a special visit, and when time came to write in our guest book, he wrote in his beautiful script a long message, signed it and looked smilingly up at me. "Mr. Prime Minister," I said, looking over his shoulder, "would you translate your message for me, please?"

"<u>Dragon in the sky.</u>"

"But, Mr. Prime Minister, what does it mean?"

"The <u>dragon in the sky</u>," he said, impatiently, looking at me as if I was an imbecile. He prided himself on his English, with good reason, so was a bit annoyed. "You know, a dragon which flies in the sky?" I admit I have never met a dragon, but I persisted. "Does it mean, Prime Minister, that you had a nice stay with us," I probed.

"Oh, yes," he beamed, "<u>otherwise the dragon would have been in the water.</u>"

It might be a mistake but hopefully not an insult to bundle together impressions of our Japanese and Korean visitors, the hatred of one for the other in a historic sense being rather acute, but for us there were enough similarities because of the Eastern quality and mannerism and work ethics that we tended to approach those visits in much the same way, and to prepare somewhat similar menus.

When Roh Tae Woo, the President of the Republic of Korea, his wife, and two children arrived for his first Official Working Visit in October 1989 he was the first foreign visitor to return to Blair House since the renovation, having spent all of 42 minutes with us for a pit stop en route to meeting with President Reagan a year earlier. Well did I remember the excruciating details in preparing for these 42 minutes, especially the debate as to the height of the chairs for the interpreters, but also the president's dietary preferences. I surprised his chief of protocol in our advance meeting this time by stating his president's preferences for veal, fish, chicken, beef and salads, and his dislike of pork, lamb, mackerel, strawberries, and kiwi fruit. He had no idea. But my colleagues at the Ceremonial Division of the Office of Protocol perked up their ears. They were responsible for passing on to the White House Social Office any dietary restrictions connected with the President's foreign visitors for the meal at the White House.

We had many Korean visits during my thirteen years at Blair House and fortunately became adept at this. With the Korean president came scores of security and personal aides, all of whom were immensely convinced of their own importance. I also noticed that the level of difficulty encountered by me and my staff in dealing with this particular staff was in direct proportion to their closeness to the president himself. I noted the same situation with other autocratic regimes however much they may wish to be known as democracies, and became certain it had to do with a fear of their boss, an equally great reluctance to make decisions in his behalf, fearing the loss of their personal status. For instance, the first morning, an upset Jose came to me: he and his staff had been denied access to the Library by the personal Korean staff while the president, Mrs. Roh, and their children were having their breakfast.

I immediately requested a meeting with Ambassador Park Kun Woo, the Chief of Protocol who had been most helpful in all our advance preparation, and who, years later, became his nation's ambassador to the United States. "Mr. Ambassador, we seem to have run into a small problem," and I explained to him what had happened this morning in the Library, and continued:

"I really must insist that my head butler and his assistant be permitted to wait on President and Mrs. Roh in the Library. Your president is a guest in this house and it is our protocol. I am afraid that President Bush will be rather upset when he hears that his own staff at Blair House is not allowed to take care of his distinguished guests."

On purpose I emphasized protocol as the Koreans set great store by form, and it was quite evident Ambassador Park understood my tactics and approved of same. The next morning Jose and his assistant were back again in the Library. But it was no joyride. The president's maitre d'hôtel and several female servants were also present to wait on the four guests. Added to our western breakfast of omelet, fruits and breads, requested in advance, were ten different Korean dishes, prepared in the large second floor kitchen outside the Embassy Offices. Fifty small plates were used for the four people. The maitre d'hôtel insisted on a double set of butter, jam, marmalade and breadbaskets, as his president absolutely was not allowed to move his arm more than a few inches, and thus could not possibly help himself to something from the other side of the 4' table, let alone ask one of his children to pass it to him. In addition the stench from the small pantry directly across from the Library was unbearable. Unbeknownst to us the female servants during the night had installed a crock pot in there, cooking a soup concoction – I guessed Kimche – generating a penetrating odor which lingered for the entire visit. This was the last time anyone ever cooked in that small pantry.

President Roh became President of The Republic of Korea in December 1987 with his country's first direct-vote presidential election in 16 years. His schedule in Washington included meeting and lunch at the White House, breakfast at the house with Katharine Graham of the Washington Post and her editorial board, the traditional Laying of the Wreath at the Grave of the Unknown Soldier at Arlington Cemetery, an address to the National Press Club, a black tie dinner at the Korean Embassy, and a breakfast with Vice President Dan Quayle at Admiral House on Naval Observatory Hill.

The president also went to Capitol Hill to call on our senators and congressmen, resulting in this small story in the Washington Post, October 21, 1989, by Roxanne Roberts:

"And this tidbit from Roll Call, the weekly newspaper that covers the Hill. South Korean President Roh Tae Woo's tour of the Capitol, led by House Speaker Thomas Foley, was reportedly so heavy with security that Capitol police marched six abreast around the House and Senate during his visit this week.

According to next Monday's issue: "When the Korean leader finally departed, tension eased and one Hill police officer said to several others, "Alice is safe. ... Alice is safe."

Was "Alice" a code name for Roh?

No. Actually, it was a little inside police joke. Alice happens to be Foley's canine companion and famous Hill office pet.

Dog is a traditional Korean delicacy."

Roh Tae Woo returned for a State Visit in July 1991.

At Blair House I coined a new phrase then, that of "being salamied," sliced up a little bit at a time, because of the Korean work structure, with each person being assigned one small task on which his life depends. I do not believe the word NO exists in Korean. If I had said no to one person, I would have to start all over again with another working on a slightly different detail of the same event. Sometimes they just wore me down. But during the second visit of this particular president when their maid in Room 21 insisted to do her ironing there and ignoring my ladies who tried to show her up one short flight of stairs to the pressing room, fully equipped for such duties, I hit my limit on patience. I walked in on her as she was actually spraying water and starch around, hitting our precious bed spread. I had brought with me one of the English speaking embassy wives:

"I believe you have been advised to go upstairs for pressing which must not be done in any of our bedrooms. It is quite convenient and very near to here. I would like to say that should you decide to remain here and continue your pressing in this room, I shall personally take the matter to President Roh." Coupled with that speech I glared at her, and as I know I can "kill" with my eyes, I had her galloping up the stairs in two shakes of a lamb's tail.

Despite this small episode our guests from the East remained both fascinating and very exotic for me and my staff, and we always looked forward to these visits.

CHAPTER 10

FROM EUROPE: A CULTURED UNION OF DIFFERENCES

"The hand of friendship extended to us across the ocean."

Richard von Weizsaecker

The European Community's growing power and the deconsolidation of the Soviet Union with new sovereign nations emerging on Europe's flank produced a steady stream of European visitors during the four Bush years. Those visits – from what would later be dubbed Old Europe – were usually easy, with small delegations, and often non controversial, because the Europeans were well able to take care of themselves and only needed us as strategic and trade partners, not as a prop for their governments. My recollections therefore, especially of the Mediterranean countries, are on the lighter side.

The State Visit of Francesco Cossiga, President of the Republic of Italy was anticipated by me with the greatest pleasure, bringing me into close contact with Italy's ambassador to the United States since the Reagan years, Rinaldo Petrignani and his Danish born wife Anne Merete, friends of many years. Once again I was on the phone with Anne Merete, though not this time to work out what was meant by French service at the table, or to learn salacious details about Zaire's President Mobutu in advance of that leader's visit.

She called me to commiserate with me for having to put up with her fellow countrymen:

"You really have my sympathy, Benedicte. You know how frequently we have visitors at Firenze House from the Quirinale (Italy's

Foreign Office), and they are s-o-o-o difficult. You will find they complain a lot and they are so demanding," she groaned. Firenze House, Peggy Guggenheim's former residence, a Venetian look-alike mansion, on beautiful grounds on the edge of Rock Creek Park, was the residence of the Ambassador of Italy. During the Petrignani ten-year tenure it was a center for cultural events. No one was more generous than this couple in "lending" their residence to fundraising events such as the American Cancer Society or the Washington Opera, to name a few, and I contend these two people made as many friends for Italy in their time in Washington as its music and art. And now, although warned I was also rather intrigued and secretly looking forward to whatever the charming Italians might be up to this time, recalling a memorable night in June 1988. U.S. Secretary of State George Shultz was hosting a large dinner for the President of the Council of Ministers (really the Prime Minister) of the Italian Republic and Mrs. De Mita. The Secretary, as host, arrived followed by Prime Minister Ciriaco De Mita and Ambassador Petrignani a few minutes later, but no sign of their ladies. Dinner was scheduled for 8 pm, but this time came and went, as obviously all was not well. The ambassador's aide was several times on the telephone in the Protocol Office, each time emerging looking desperate. The prime minister himself went to the telephone. It was all quite mysterious. Mrs. De Mita, Mrs. Petrignani and Miss De Mita finally arrived, 90 minutes late, and dinner could start.

I was soon the recipient of this little story: Miss De Mita, a while back, had bought a beautiful pink dress in Rome to wear to this gala event, but in the meantime had expanded a bit herself in all the wrong places. The dress no longer fit. So when papa and mama were ready to get into the car taking them to Blair House, it had been thought advisable for Mrs. De Mita to remain behind and sort out her by now hysterical daughter. Mrs. Petrignani summoned her maid to add some material to the seams. But it was still a little too tight so with Antonia De Mita lying on a bed, Mrs. Petrignani draped herself over her holding the seams together, and the maid stitched up the dress right on her.

Really, the dramas surrounding the Italians! Years earlier my first experience with these wonderful people was also dramatic. One particular Italian tour director came into my boss' office at the Shoreham

Hotel in a highly agitated state, probably over some trivial matter, and declared: "I shoot myself – I shoot myself." So I was looking forward immensely to this visit.

The Italians were so sophisticated, and therefore enormously pleased with everything; there were no complaints. They loved the house, they loved the food, they loved everything, and most of all they loved Jose. Jose had spent ten years in Firenze where he met his wife, and where one of his sons were born, so he was fluent in Italian, and as the Italians were certainly not fluent in English, the call of "Giuseppe" could be heard often. Information from the embassy as to likes and dislikes of the president was excellent; he ate no shellfish and pork. I also was advised by Anne Merete that to serve veal was silly, as "it is so much better in Italy," but that they would all enjoy beef medium rare without the usual frills, no birds as chicken was too common, and that the delegation would love crab cakes. And everyone would enjoy chocolate.

"This is truly a home," President Cossiga, a distinguished, scholarly, elderly gentleman said as I was escorting him to a meeting. "In Rome, I go to work every day in a museum, but this – this is a home." When he returned quite late from the White House State Dinner, he walked up the front stairs arm in arm with his chief of staff, singing at the top of his voice: "Home, Sweet Home." The Petrignanis reported to me, at 2 am, how much they all loved their stay. Francesco Cossiga, President of Italy since 1985, was Italy's most senior government official and also a former prime minister, 1979-1980. His duties were "chairing the Supreme Defense Council and heading the Council of Magistrates." I also surmised that he traveled extensively to promote political and commercial ties for his country. During his visit he met frequently with the Italian journalists traveling with him, and was possibly the most informal of all our guests in his approach to members of the "chattering" class, walking into the room in which they had assembled, with open arms, exclaiming: "Amici."

I had been warned too that no matter how many receptions the Italians may take in during an evening, and how many hors d'oeuvres they may nibble on, they still wanted their dinner. So when President Cossiga returned after throwing a lavish reception at Firenze House for Vice President and Mrs. Quayle I was waiting for him at the door, being greeted with: "Please, could we have a little dinner?"

and producing a "little" dinner within ten minutes in the Lee Dining Room. In April 1996 Italy's next president, the jolly and elderly Oscar Luigi Scalfaro, despite having just been offered a lavish State Dinner at the White House, at 1 am asked for – and got – pasta, and a can of soup.

The Cossiga visit was the first of many times when Italy's Foreign Minister, Gianni De Michelis, stayed with us. The first night, just as I thought I could close up for the night with everyone back in from the night's excursions, I was told "the Foreign Minister is still out," at a local disco. As he was protected, on American soil, by an agent of the Diplomatic Security (DS) it would not surprise me if they came to dread these assignments as this minister was a lively one, frequenting discos till the early morning hours. De Michelis was known as the "Dancing Foreign Minister" and among his serious writings regarding political challenges also produced a bestseller surveying Italy's finest discotheques. After this first visit, during which one of my staff waited till 3 am at the Front Door for his return, we changed our tactics, and told his DS agent that from now on he had to return through the Security Command Post entrance in the basement as the Front Door would be secured at a more reasonable hour. De Michelis was swarthy and longhaired, and approaching 300 pounds in weight, a result of a bon vivant attitude which according to legend made him hold his high level brainstorming meetings at a local bar rather than at the Quirinale. He loved food and, I surmise, pretty women, but so do all Italian men. He was something to behold – if indeed he stood still long enough. I expect that time eventually arrived, as in July 1995 he was convicted of corruption charges for having taken kickbacks, and he was sentenced to four years in prison.

Later, on several occasions, Prime Minister Giulio Andreotti and Livia Andreotti stayed with us. She was so quiet and undemanding that I worried how to reach her. I was sadly lacking in Italian, and had been told she only spoke her native tongue, until – at frustration point – I probed: "Parlez-vous français?" – thereby opening a floodgate. Mr. Andreotti who had been prime minister of Italy five times during the 1970s, as well as Foreign Minister, was an experienced Italian politician. He was an author, an intellectual, and much admired by Ambassador Rinaldo Petrignani. The visits of the constantly changing Italian prime ministers continued also in the Clinton administrations:

Romano Prodi in May 1998; Massimo d'Alema in March 1999; Giu-liano Amato in September 2000 – when this frequency had the Italian ambassador call our hospitality "precious."

Of course, we also welcomed, several times, the Prime Ministers of Spain and Portugal, with the former immensely proud that the Head Butler of the American president's guest house was one of their own, but the latter sporting a wife whom it was impossible to please. How-ever, while the Europeans were generally undemanding and traveled with the smallest delegation of any nations including next to no secu-rity, favorites emerged easily, such as Ireland, Greece, and Sweden.

Charles J. Haughey, Prime Minister of Ireland came for an Official Working Visit in February 1990. Ireland at this time held the presi-dency of the European Community, a function which rotates every six months. Thus, included in Haughey's delegation was his close advisor on European affairs, a former Danish diplomat, now attached to the European Union. I had not before met this Dane, but as we had sever-al acquaintances in Denmark in common we spent a stimulating time with each other. I was particularly interested in the consequences of the breaking down of borders to Eastern Europe as we had both, as small children, experienced the German occupation of Denmark for five long years in World War II; thus we shared a mutual concern for the impending united Germany. But, as he said, in diplomatic jargon, "by incorporation into the European Community the hope is that the situation can be neutralized."

Mr. Haughey and his delegation were as easy, as undemanding and unassuming as our jolly Australians the summer before. The prime minister himself was low key, and charming, and on leaving for the dinner at Senator Edward Kennedy's on the second night, admon-ished me "don't forget, now, to put the cat out." He had been prime minister several times, and liked to be addressed by his Gaelic title of Taoiseach (tee-shuk) and was a supporter of the peaceful reunifica-tion of Ireland. He was also a self-made millionaire, owning a Geor-gian mansion near Dublin and a stud farm. He wrote me and my staff a personal thank you letter from Dublin and included this in the note:

"We in Ireland like to think that we are a hospitable people but I can assure you that the hospitality extended by you and the staff of Blair House was in a category of its own."

I had not yet visited the Emerald Isle at the time Mr. Haughey was with us, but would later experience just how true his words were about Irish hospitality.

Constantine Mitsotakis, Prime Minister of Greece and Marika Mitsotakis came for an Official Working Visit on December 11, 1991 to a house decked out for Christmas. The prime minister, leader of the conservative New Democracy party, had a long history and career in Greek politics, and coming from the Island of Crete, had been active in the WWII Cretan resistance and was twice jailed by the Nazis, narrowly escaping execution. He and his family went into exile in Paris during the military coup in 1967, but returned in the early 1970s to go into politics.

They were delightful, the prime minister elderly, tall and very spry, and his wife, crippled by polio, but beaming from ear to ear. She had insisted "to have no fuss made over me," so bravely, on arrival, made her way up the front steps in order to enter Blair House "properly," but at other times agreed it would be "easier" to take the elevator to the basement and walk out the Link Door. She wanted me to show her around and we spent a delightful time together with me regaling her with my personal views of some of our paintings: "Here, Ma'am, is George Washington himself and his white horse, painted by Jane Stuart, the daughter of the prominent portrait painter Gilbert Stuart, and it is, as you can see, quite evident that Miss Stuart did not hold our first president in high esteem." The president was holding on to the horse in such a way that he was shown with the horse's rump by his left shoulder, rather than its head, which is looking around with an expression of madness. "I always have the feeling that his horse was schizophrenic and in a minute the president would be jumping for it!"

It has been a long established custom of several administrations to give recognition to the leaders of the Greek Orthodox faith on their occasional visits to Washington D.C. Usually a cabinet secretary with a specific interest in America's extensive Greek community hosted the events. I had a call from the Personal Assistant to Edward J. Derwinski, Secretary of the Department of Veterans Affairs: "Secretary Derwinski understands that he is permitted to host a function at Blair House as a member of the President's Cabinet?" I confirmed this, emphasizing the necessity that the function assists in furthering American foreign policy objectives, and is actually attended and hosted by the Cabinet member. The Secretary wished to host a luncheon for His All Holiness Dimitrios, Archbishop of Constantinople and Ecumenical Patriarch – the Greek Orthodox Church "Pope" (who died in the fall of 1991). I was delighted and the approval from the chief of protocol was immediately obtained.

This first of several functions over the next ten years for the hierarchy of the Greek Orthodox Church brought me into contact with Father Alexander Karloutsos with whom we worked closely and harmoniously on all arrangements. The luncheons were packed with members of the Greek community, which funded same, and no expense was spared to showcase their hospitality to their church, or their generosity of spirit. Among the guests always were Mr. and Mrs. Michael Jaharis, generous contributors to the Blair House Restoration Fund.

The scenario was similar for all events: we prepared the Primary Suite and one or two other bedrooms so that the Patriarch and some of his accompanying priests could rest prior to the lunch; we prepared especially the Primary Suite with suitable amenities in both bathrooms, juices, soft drinks, non-carbonated waters and for His All Holiness a plate of fresh sliced fruit; guests, served champagne during the reception, were seated in the Garden Room before His All Holiness would be escorted down to the lunch. Another luncheon was in honor of the Archbishop of New York who became His All Holiness the Ecumenical Patriarch Bartholomew I in 1991. His English was wonderful; his sense of humor great; and I recall, when he was still the archbishop, I showed him to the men's room on the first floor. I would have left him there but he would have none of it, but kept chattering through the open door as he was being assisted into his garb. I commented: "You wear more jewelry than a woman, your Grace," to which he chuckled and subsequently had his revenge, having me called in to the Garden Room to speak, without warning, before his luncheon guests and tell them about Blair House. He returned as the Ecumenical Patriarch in the Fall of 1997.

My fondest memory, and the one that lingered with me, was the gentleness exuding from these holy people. They all insisted on kissing me goodbye, and I learnt that the softest beards must be those adorning the faces of these gentle priests. While the Protocol Office would be intimately involved in the Catholic Pope's visits to the United States, Blair House was never on the schedule for those events.

Years later, in my retirement in Santa Fe, New Mexico the Greek Orthodox Church and its gentle priests would again be introduced into my life. Adrian Cummins, my Australian friend of 48 years and husband of 6 ½ years, and an Anglican, wandered into the local small Greek church, to be welcomed with open arms and eventually participating in their vespers on Saturday nights. When Adrian died of a heart attack in 2005 this church held his memorial service, reconfirming my strong belief in the love and caring of this particular group of people.

Another favorite visit of mine were the Swedes, despite my mother's evident boredom with their prime minister. "Han støver" she said on the telephone. She was using the Danish derisive last word on Carl Bildt who was due for an Official Working Visit on February 19, 1992. Støv is dust in Danish, and when used about a personality it means he is boring to the point of inducing sleep in his audience.

However, as I later could relate to her, I found him entirely delightful, and according to the State Department officials, including the Secretary of State, he had been most impressive in the Oval Office, posing thoughtful questions in his meeting with Mr. Bush. I understood two matters were close to his heart. The 1986 Chernobyl nuclear reactor explosion was the worst nuclear disaster in the world, with a big effect on Sweden's agriculture, including the necessity to cull most of its precious reindeer herd in the northern part of the country; nuclear safeguards and disarmament were definitely on the agenda. His second issue, and the prime minister himself told me this, were the Baltic countries.

Prime Minister Carl Bildt was young, energetic, well educated, and came out of a political and military family. He was the first prime minister from the conservative party in 60 years. We had been told he wrote his own speeches on his computer and would use the Library as his study. Anna Bildt who arrived with her baby slung over her left hip was at first a bit stand offish, and was worried about the baby and his care. We had set aside Room 21 across the Library for their two months old son, Nils, and his nanny, but discovered that Mrs. Bildt would have none of it. She slept with the baby in the second primary suite bedroom. The nanny had been supplied by the Swedish embassy at my continuing insistence that "Blair House cannot take on the responsibility of looking after such a young child besides which Mrs. Bildt must be free to participate in all the activities arranged in Washington D.C." Teresinha, who was responsible for bedrooms on the second floor, was supportive of the nanny, relieving her during meal times taking the baby around for some sightseeing. Thus little Master Bildt came away well educated in Blair House history, and totally familiar with all our presidential portraits viewing them from Teresinha's arms.

Mrs. Bildt was thus free to come and go, and while she popped back to the house often to check on her small son, she did enjoy her shopping. One afternoon she was hauling in loads of bags only to go out again. The prime minister when he returned asked for her. "Mrs. Bildt has gone out again," I said and solemnly thanked him "for having assisted in pulling back from the brink of bankruptcy one of our major department stores." He looked stunned, asking: "Is it very bad?" When I nodded, he sighed and grinned. "I thought you would like some news to set you on the right road this afternoon, Mr. Prime Minister," I said, for which he thanked me and laughed out loud. This conversation was in Swedish, and I was rather pleased that I could still conduct a proper conversation in that most lovely of languages, learned by me during my two years in Djursholm Samskola outside Stockholm in 1953-55, when my father was Danish Naval Attache in Sweden and Norway, one of the more happy times in my then young life.

Most importantly for me and laying to rest ghosts from the past was the State Visit in late April 1992 of the President of the Federal Republic of Germany. I looked forward to this visit because the advance work had been excellent, and the advance team members whom I had met over various dinners and luncheons hosted by the German Embassy were the opposite of what I had expected. I dreaded it because of the antipathy of my Danish roots towards anything and anybody German. However, I found that in attitude, demeanor, ideas, and posture the entire delegation was far removed from the stereotype heel clicking German whom I had in my mind, and with whom I had had experience in my early life. Two and one half years earlier all these memories had come rushing back with a vengeance:

It was the morning of November 9, 1989 when the Berlin Wall came down and the path to a reunited Germany started. I had come downstairs when I heard Administrative Officer Lynn Keith call after me: "The Berlin Wall is coming down."

I felt as if I had been hit in the stomach, muttered something and went into my office, my emotions firmly in check. I have always been fairly reserved, and giving way in front of someone who might chatter about Mrs. V at Blair House dissolving into tears was entirely to be avoided. I switched on the television. The images, however, of a people in the grip of the most powerful emotions clawing, hammering and tearing at that despicable symbol soon took care of me too.

I sat at my desk, trying to get a strong grip on myself. President Reagan's famous words directed at President Gorbachev of "Mr. Gorbachev, tear down this wall," had been ringing around the world since he uttered them in Berlin in 1987. President Gorbachev of the Soviet Union, in the words of James Baker "was moving from confrontation to dialogue, to cooperation." The action on this day though was not entirely unexpected, as starting during the summer, the more progressive Hungarian regime has quietly looked the other way as East Germans had begun to slip into Western Europe through the opened up barbed wire fences on the Hungarian/Austrian border.

The consequences would be enormous – a free United Europe again, later the dismantling of the Soviet empire, and the emergence of free nations. For a former Dane, who had started out life under the German occupation of Denmark, then experienced the Cold War era living fairly close to the threatening Soviet Union, this was indeed awesome.

Next morning, during my French class at the Foreign Service Institute, I tried to articulate in my halting French that for a former Dane, with the memory, however misty, of the Nazi five year occupation, the thought of a united Germany was frightening. I had an ally to my feelings in my French teacher, Janine, who as a 16 year old Jewish girl in Lyon had experienced firsthand the invasion of France by the German army, and had to flee. But the American Foreign Service officers in this class would have none of it. They were truly elated and overjoyed and had no fear. They had, of course, never lived under the occupation of others.

And Ruth Hamory, my boss for seven years at the Shoreham Hotel in Washington D.C., born and raised in Berlin, was beside herself. I reached her in Florida.

"We were out shopping," she said, "and Deszö and I stopped for a coffee. The waitress just said: "Did you hear – the Wall came down." I just looked at her – then it sank in – and my tears started flowing. I just could not stop crying. She was so embarrassed and said she did not want to distress me. "Distress me," I said, "I am overjoyed."

Ruth grew up in Berlin, trained there in hotel business and was working at the famous Hotel Adlon when World War II started. Her own story, from the other side, so to speak, is compelling and included being buried alive for 36 hours under a bombed out building, and for months moving from shelter to shelter with an ailing grandmother and mother. Such measures teach you extraordinary skills to survive, and give you a resilience for what life later brings you. She would be the first German whom my parents would invite to their home – twenty years after the war. Other Germans visiting our home came without invitation such as the Gestapo. Ruth became my mentor, my guru, and would teach me more than anyone else what it meant to work within the American business community, so different from the Danish one. She would also become a beloved close friend, and I would call her, with my own mother's consent, "my American mother."

Although the five gruesome years of the German occupation of Denmark are misty memories, I was apprehensive about a united and mighty Germany. Denmark celebrates the official termination of the German occupation on the evening of May 4. Copenhagen on that particular evening for years was like a fairy tale with candlelight glimmering in each window throughout the city to counteract the five years of the occupation, when the entire country, by orders of the Germans, was blacked out at night to prevent the Allied Forces finding their bombing targets, such as the German headquarters at the Shell Building in Copenhagen, and their military installations. On that afternoon, May 4, 1945 when the announcement came over the radio – considered contraband, my mother and her three children were staying at the farm of an old friend of mother's, whose sister was married to my mother's brother Eiler Nielsen. My father, working for the resistance, was still in hiding. The Danish flag was brought out from its hiding place, and raised for the first time in five years. We all cried.

That evening I went with my mother and my aunt over to Rosendal Estate to the Knuth-Winterfeldts. A distinguished Danish diplomat, he was Danish Ambassador to the United States in the early sixties. I spent my first two weeks in this country staying with him in Washington D.C. He went on to become Lord Chamberlain to the Danish King. His younger son, Ditlev, was roommate at Yale with George W. Bush. Rosendal was my father's headquarters, since August 29, 1943, while working in the resistance movement under the name of Stig Jørgensen. Aunt Trudi, Countess Knuth-Winterfeldt, always a grand hostess, had planned for this joyous occasion for a long time; she had secretly made a replica in gold paper of the Royal Danish Crown and placed it in the center of her dining table. I recall she made a toast to His Majesty King Christian X and we all cried again.

Like other navy and army officers my father had entered service with the Danish police after a navy officer, Vice Admiral Vedel, and a small group of sailors, in an act of defiance and to prevent Germany from taking possession, sank the Danish Navy on August 29, 1943, effectually halting the operation of the Danish Armed Forces. By working for the Police my father was able to "legitimately" work in and for the resistance movement. Thus after the dissolution of the Danish police force on September 19, 1944 when more than 2,000 employees of the police were arrested by Gestapo, with many shipped off to concentration camp in Germany, my father went underground, and assumed the resistance movement's responsibility for receipt of weapons dropped by the Allied Forces in Southern Sealand and on Møn. For the next eight or so months until the occupation came to an end my brother Claus, 8 years old, was shadowed every day en route to and from his school by a member of the HIPO (Hilfspolizei) in civilian clothes, who hoped that Claus would lead him to our father; he even continued his surveillance when the school temporarily moved to another location. But Claus did have an even greater emotional experience: he was missing our father so much and begged our mother to be allowed to see him. She gave in, and carefully instructed him how he had to remember that Dad was no longer Commander Jørgen Valentiner, but was now called Engineer Stig Jørgensen; if he did not remember this he would be sent back to her immediately without seeing Dad.

Claus, happy and excited, disembarked the train in Ringsted, was received by our father's cousin, Knud Kaalund, and when asked who is your father, naturally said: Jørgen Valentiner. It was a very sad and teary brother who returned to us in Copenhagen who had not been allowed to see his father.

Gustav and I were also members of the resistance movement. My mother hid monies in our little ski suits when we traveled into the country to meet my father in one of his hiding places. The monies were used for board and lodging for the people my father had stationed along the coastlines to report on German naval movements. As my mother casually remarked, it was not likely the Gestapo would suspect a young blond mother traveling with little kids. I do remember clearly the bombings by the British going after German installations in Copenhagen. Heavy, deep throated sirens sounded the alarm, warning of pending bombing attacks. Families would have perhaps fifteen minutes to get into a shelter. My mother, I expect, being super organized and totally calm under pressure, would have ready a bag complete with blankets, toys and nourishment for such occasions. The cellar, under our apartment house, was a pretty rough place, nothing really but a storage place with cement ledges along the wall on which we, twenty at any one time, sat. The only light would be from candles. A different sounding siren would tell us when the danger was over.

But a poignant and clear memory, which for many years influenced heavily my sentiments towards Germany, was when Gestapo came for my mother.

I was in my playroom adjacent to the drawing-room when two men entered, and my mother, quick as a flash, pushed me behind the door and closed it. But I saw them and I remember. To this date I have goose bumps when I see the German uniform with the long boots, the cap with the slightly curbed cover, and still, sometimes, can imagine the clicking of the heels. Mother was questioned at Gestapo headquarters as to my father's whereabouts and doings, but was released the same day. Many years later she told me that, while there, she had witnessed a Dane jumping to his death, flying past her window. Later she learned he was one of the Danish resistance movement's leaders who took this gallant way out rather than betray his comrades during torture.

Gestapo had actually come to interrogate my mother earlier.

Mother had gone down to the neighbors just below us. She returned to our apartment and, strangely, found the front door locked. She had left it with the latch off, so was standing there wondering why she had locked herself out, when it opened, and she found herself with a gun in her stomach. I am not surprised that she actually told the German soldier off, and got away with it. I always believed she was equal to anything, and that there was no one I would rather be around in an emergency than her. Standing there "debating" with the German, she had in her hand a rolled up measuring tape, her errand to the neighbors involving some measuring, and, she told me, she knew she would be alright because her hand did not shake as she unrolled it slowly, rolled it up slowly, and unrolled it slowly during the questioning. It was her test on herself. She also kept hidden in our apartment the Melchior family until they could escape to Sweden – Aunt Vippe was one of mother's close friends.

During one of the war winters which seemed colder than subsequent ones, probably because the country was heavily rationed with fuel, going out to my grandparents for one overnight we ended up staying four months because all three of us children got sick. While the boys caught every second ailment, I caught every childhood disease known, except for scarlet fever and mumps. The latter came years later. For four months my grandparents ran a hospital for three small children. However, the overwhelming experience that, small though I was, I shall never forget, was what happened to Gustav, the youngest sibling, at that time eighteen months old:

In August 1944, there was a general strike in Denmark. Everything broke down, nothing moved. My father was underground. One evening, my mother was busy with Claus and me in one end of our long apartment, having left Gustav in the bedroom sitting on his little chamber pot, when Claus, having wandered off, suddenly screamed: "Mummy, Mummy, Gustav is dead." She found her baby, trapped against the wall in the narrow passage where a bridge table, stored against the wall, had fallen on his throat. For four hours my mother gave Gustav CPR. The neighbor, hearing our screams and shouts, came up to help, and for the first time ever Claus was able to unlock and open our heavy front door, his fear having given him unexpected strength. The neighbor ran into the streets in the forlorn hope of finding a vehicle that could take Gustav to the hospital, – and miraculously found one. For six weeks he was strapped to a bed so as to remain immobile, my mother at his side, and no indication as to what would be in store for him.

Gustav was our beloved baby brother. We were convinced that he was dead, and were so grief stricken, that Grandmother took Claus and me out to the hospital. We stood in the street as he was not allowed to have visitors, as he was held up in the window so we could see with our own eyes that he was alive. When he came home he was fundamentally changed, crying easily, and clinging to my mother who could not leave him alone for a moment. He was like an empty shell and my mother feared brain damage. Claus and I made sure he was physically with us during our activities even if mentally he was elsewhere. Then, one day, six months after his near death, as he was sitting curled up in a wing chair, out of the blue, he heaved a big sigh, crawled out of the chair, and joined us in our games. He would become deaf in one ear as a result of this, and also during his teen years developed an uncontrollable temper brought on when he was exhausted physically.

My mother when talking about us, her children, and her attitude and love for us, often mentioned that Gustav was special, because "he was born to me twice." Gustav, charming, fun, talented, became an architect, married, had two great sons, got divorced, and spent the rest of his life searching for and experimenting with lifestyles, and in the end, in 2004, shot himself, fulfilling my mother's prophesy that he would commit suicide. He was 61.

Germany's president, Freiherr Richard von Weizsaecker, in his second five year term, and his wife, Marianne, turned out to be — remarkable. It did not hurt of course that their appreciation for our hospitality had them say over and over again that "there is no other guesthouse like Blair House in the world." They were handsome and well educated, and although the president's position was largely ceremonial and non partisan, he had worked tirelessly to unify his nation and speaking out on issues often hidden away from the public consciousness in his country. The president was one of the first people to shame his nation into facing up to its past, such as their parents' and grandparents' role played in the genocide of its citizens of Jewish faith, and finally introducing the subject of Hitler, concentration camps, and the holocaust into the nation's classrooms. He was, I believe, what the Germans would call "ein Mensch," a man of great humanity. We spoke Danish as his father Ernst von Weizsaecker had been stationed at the German embassy in Copenhagen, and he was schooled in the Danish system.

While we had set aside the Foreign Minister's Suite for Hans Dietrich Genscher, we knew that he preferred to stay with the rest of the delegation at the Watergate which had been his "home away from home" in Washington D.C. during all his years as Germany's foreign minister. I was rather relieved. He had a reputation of bringing with him truckloads of telecommunications equipment which would have been hard for us to accommodate. In retrospect it was disappointing as this would be his last visit to our country as foreign minister, resigning the post two weeks later. But he came over twice, and thoroughly enjoyed the suite which we had prepared and stocked with all amenities. His wife loved it, and both regretted – they told me – not having moved in.

Often, piggybacking on such a prestigious event as a State Visit, cultural events showcasing the country are planned to coincide with same. The Stuttgart Ballet was engaged by the John F. Kennedy Center for the Performing Arts, marking the opening of the German Cultural Festival "A Tribute to Germany," kicked off by its president. I attended its performance of "The Sleeping Beauty" as his guest. The president addressed a Joint Session of Congress during his State Visit and began thus:

"May I, to start with, refer to the Sleeping Beauty, by which of course I do not mean this august assembly after exposure to a few sentences of mine, but the classical ballet which will be presented tonight as part of my invitation to the Kennedy Center for the Performing Arts. What is the significance, so I have been asked repeatedly, of showing this ballet tonight?"

I will not venture to re-narrate that age-old German fairytale, but let me try to give you a parable: you might, if you like, attribute the active role in the story, that of the Prince, to America. For the sleeping beauty I leave a role for your imagination to pick, but here is my offer for this morning:

The Sleeping Beauty is "life, liberty and the pursuit of happiness" for all mankind, kissed awake by the Prince. ---------- And he finished in this manner: "In the words of an outstanding American statesman, West Germany has been throughout a long period "an economy in search of a political purpose." This is no longer so. Today we are free and united. We are one of the driving forces of the European Union. And we belong to the Atlantic community in all its aspects.

This development began with a gift: The hand of friendship extended to us across the Ocean and followed by others in Europe. ------------"

In the Clinton Administration we had two short visits by the German Chancellor Gerhard Schrøder, cigar smoker and red wine drinker, with arrival at 3 am, and departure 16 hours later. Interestingly, and somewhat revolutionary for post war Germany, the process had begun in that country to reconsider the historically tough question of whether Germany should participate in conflicts outside their border. I expect that to obtain a European identity the country would have to consider any regional conflict as its own. Kosovo was such a conflict, and discussion during the Schrøder visit in March 1999 were centered around such issues as NATO peacekeeping in Kosovo, the influence on Germany of such a conflict, and indeed Germany's own participation in same. Sadly, as horrors were unfolding in Bosnia, Europe stood by. Later, the first visit from Holland had me stunned. The collective attitude of the ministers was that "there has always been trouble in the Balkans. It is no good getting involved."

It would be Bill Clinton who would take this on.

CHAPTER 11

THE DECONSOLIDATION OF AN INCOMPLETE GIANT

"Please, Sir, may I have some more?"

Charles Dickens' Oliver Twist

A new world was emerging after the fall of the Berlin Wall in November 1989 and the break-up of the Soviet Union two years later. The United States and its allies had a vested interest in welcoming the former members of the Soviet Union and its Bloc countries into the arms of the free world. Thus following this deconsolidation President Bush invited the new leaders to Washington and Blair House. Those with nuclear capabilities had intense talks with U.S. officials; all went up to Congress with their hand stretched out for aid; some addressed a joint session. Each group had its own distinct characteristics, despite being forced into a union long ago with identical schooling, language and ideology. They were, however, similar in looking tired and grey, being dressed in ill fitting clothes, smoking like chimneys and having healthy appetites.

Arriving February 19, 1990 our first visitor was Vaclav Havel, President of the Czechoslovak Socialist Republic, his country's most prominent living playwright, long time dissident, and opposition voice and negotiator with the Communist regime. His enormous popular support catapulted him into the political limelight and, though a reluctant politician, the presidency. Born in 1936 into a wealthy family he was denied access to university due to his "class origins." Working as a theater stagehand, and attending the Academy of Arts, he became a writer and producer for a Prague theater, and also attended the U.S. premiere of his play The Memorandum here in 1968. Supporting the Prague spring reforms in 1968 and opposing the Soviet-led invasion he became active in the dissident community and consequently a target of continual police harassment, interrogations, and detentions. His longest prison sentence was a four-year term during 1979-83; his most recent was from January to May 1989. Overnight he became his country's president following its "Velvet Revolution" and planning for its first free election in a generation

He addressed a Joint Session of Congress on February 21, 1990 and began in this manner:

"My advisors have advised me, on this important occasion, to speak in Czech. I don't know why. Perhaps they wanted you to enjoy the sweet sounds of my mother tongue. The last time they arrested me, on October 27 of last year, I didn't know whether it was for two days or two years. Exactly one month later, when the rock musician Michael Kocab told me that I would probably be proposed as a presidential candidate, I thought it was one of his usual jokes. On the 10th of December 1989, when my actor friend Jiri Bartoska, in the name of the Civic Forum, nominated me as a candidate for the office of President of the Republic, I thought it was out of the question that the parliament we had inherited from the previous regime would elect me.

Twelve days later, when I was unanimously elected president of my country, I had no idea that in two months I would be speaking in front of this famous and powerful assembly, and that what I say would be heard by millions of people who have never heard of me and that hundreds of politicians and political scientists would study every word I say. When they arrested me on October 27, I was living in a country ruled by the most conservative Communist government in Europe, and our society slumbered beneath the pall of a totalitarian system. Today, less than four months later, I am speaking to you as the representative of a country that has set out on the road to democracy, a country where there is complete freedom of speech, which is getting ready for free elections, and which wants to create a prosperous market economy and its own foreign policy.

It is all very strange indeed."

Lally Weymouth, daughter of Katharine Graham of The Washington Post, wrote the day before Havel arrived in Washington: "After two months on the job, Vaclav Havel still isn't quite sure how a president is supposed to act." In Prague she had questioned him about his future plans negotiating the withdrawal of Soviet troops from his country, or the possibility of actually signing a pact with Moscow. The new president had said: "I don't know what I can tell to newspapers and what shouldn't be told. I am an inexperienced president."

He was also openmouthed when I ushered him in to the lush, colorful, elegant Primary Suite.

His wife was made of sterner stuff. Olga Havlova seemed to dislike public life, was impatient with protocol, and was said to be a most unwilling first lady. Married over thirty years, standing by Vaclav Havel through all his arrests and imprisonments, she had been active in distributing his writings throughout Europe. A thin, unsmiling woman with silver grey hair, dressed mostly in black and wearing boots, she was rarely, like the delegation, without a cigarette in her hand.

They were all modest in their requirements despite our attempts to spoil them with our good food and willingness to serve. Extremely busy with individual meetings, they disliked all forms of discipline. They resented having USSS agents following them around as it reminded them of their recent past. Interestingly, every time Mrs. Havlova left the house, she turned to me, seeing her off at the Front Door, and informed me where she was going. The Secret Service agent on post in the Front Hall commented: "How thoughtful she is to tell you where she is off to, isn't she?"

But I knew better. In their eyes, I was the equivalent of the communist spy – the babushka – stationed by the authorities on each floor of their building, with whom they used to sign in and out. I had no illusions as to what I represented, at the Front Door, to this group.

However, I was the best informed as to everyone's movements!

The National Democratic Institute for International Affairs was entrusted with most advance work preceding this visit, President Havel having no confidence in the loyalty of his embassy staff appointed by the communist regime. Assisted by his good Washington friends, especially Dr. Madeleine Albright, Professor at Georgetown University, Czech by birth, later U.S. Representative to the United Nations, and our country's Secretary of State, he installed his own support staff of volunteers at Blair House. The newly appointed Czechoslovakian ambassador, Rita Klimova, who had translated the works of Vaclav

Havel and Jiri Dienstbier, his Foreign Minister, and smuggled them to the United States, explained to me why the embassy personnel was supplanted for this visit. I personally observed how the few embassy people present tried to sabotage this visit.

Deputy Prime Minister Vladimir Dlouhy only got his luggage the night before departure. Forgotten and locked in the Czechoslovakian plane, parked at Andrews Air Force Base, with the full knowledge of the embassy people, none of them lifted a finger, despite our entreaties, to collect it.

Such behavior made us very angry.

Showing up at the White House for the official welcome and subsequent meeting with the President of the United States in less than proper order was not an option. Arthur Adler's, a Men's Haberdashery in Washington, was called for assistance. Seven minutes before departure for the White House event, their Mr. Pratt, with the assistance of Sam and Jose, was in the Lincoln Room stripping Mr. Dlouhy to the waist and trying shirts on him. Within five minutes the Deputy Prime Minister of Czechoslovakia emerged a "new" man, properly attired for the big day.

Mr. Havel was a delight, one of the gentlest visitors ever. On departure he was beaming his gratitude and appreciation at all of us, and in addition I received a hug and a kiss. Indicative of his warmth and love, part of Havel's signature in our guestbook was his trademark drawing, in red ink, of a large heart.

Unbeknownst to me his Foreign Minister, Jiri Dienstbier, had signed our guestbook. I was not pleased, as our precious guestbook traditionally only contained the signatures of Chiefs of State or Heads of Government. In retrospect, though, I am most appreciative as I frequently would reflect on Dienstbier's words: "To remember: Everything is otherwise," which was an apt description of life behind the scene at Blair House.

President Havel and Mrs. Havlova and many in his delegation returned for a State Visit on October 21, 1991, with a new name for their country: The Czech and Slovak Federal Republic. They were less exuberant than 18 months earlier. At the White House dinner Mr. Havel said: "The era of enthusiasm, unity and joy at freedom regained is long behind us. The present time is a kind of everyday work." Reality had caught up with them. Here to drum up business for their country, to ease trade barriers and lay the groundwork for entry into NATO and the European Community they were subdued and serious. A year later the country would be on its way to divide into the Czech and the Slovak Republics.

This second visit, though, showed one big and happy difference: no one any longer turned to me at the Front Door to tell me where they were going. This time, I was ignored at the door, as they came and went, free at last; I knew nothing, and very happy about it I was too.

Minister of Finance Vaclav Klaus also returned and advised me he had arranged several interviews with journalists, putting me between a rock and a hard place. Interviews except with the principal guest were not permitted under our new press policy. Mr. Klaus, the future President of the Czech Republic, was to be photographed and interviewed on camera by Forbes Magazine. Ambassador Klimova whom I suspected of some bias against Mr. Klaus, a rival to Foreign Minister Dienstbier, decided this could only take place outside in Lafayette Square. Mr. Klaus was amenable especially as I allowed the continuation, off camera, of the interview with Steve Forbes in the Truman Study.

Prime Minister Tadeusz Mazowiecki, the first freely elected prime minister of the Republic of Poland, came for an Official Visit in March 1990. He was reputed as the most popular and trustworthy politician in Poland. Holding office since August 1989, he was a Catholic intellectual, with strong ties to church leaders and a close friend of Pope John Paul II, dating from when the latter was Archbishop of Krakow. Founder of one of Poland's only publications then open to independent writing, he was an author, a student and labor activist and close advisor to the labor union's leader, Lech Walesa.

The prime minister had little personality, even less humor, and no English. He spoke some French and was fluent in German, which he seemed disinclined to use, so I only tried it once. I could well imagine his dislike of speaking German. I was certain that having Poland's borders secured once and for all given his country's sad history as a football between European powers must have been high on his agenda.

The Polish delegation seemed comfortable around their prime minister, always an indication of a good leader. The relationship with their embassy personnel was interesting; the latter had been appointed by the former Polish communist government. Chris Hill (later well known for his efforts regarding North Korea), the Polish Desk Officer of State, explained that a compromise had been worked out between the old timers – the communists – and the present government – the elected ones. However, despite this cordiality, shortly before the Polish Prime Minister's meeting with U.S. Secretary of Defense Dick Cheney, the Polish Military Attache was shown out of the meeting room. Obviously there were limits.

I asked delegation members about conditions in Poland during the transition from communism. The official interpreter now earned $80.00 per month in addition to a travel supplement. While here he bought a $35.00 hair remover for his wife representing a sizeable chunk of his monthly salary. His suit, Polish made, had cost him $7.00 which, when he bought it, was half his monthly salary under the communist rule. At that time his living expenses such as rent and phone were very low, and now "everything is much more expensive even though I earn so much more." The Polish doctor's birthday present to his wife was, he said, an item of luxury – a large roll of aluminum foil.

I wanted to spoil these people with great variety in their diet, as though, through our food, we could somehow alleviate what they and their nation had endured during the communist rule. This particular group would be remembered as one of exceptional large food consumption for a small number of people.

One person drank 30 oz. of orange juice in one sitting. Fresh fruit, always available at breakfast and during the day on our hospitality table, had to be replenished constantly. Jose compared their food portion sizes to "the Himalayas – Mount Everest – Mont Blanc."

One night the prime minister and his ministers were due to dine at 6 pm in the Lee Dining Room before leaving for a reception at 7:20 pm. The prime minister was an hour late; no one wanted to start without him. So after a quick cup of Duck Consomme, followed by a Loin of Veal, only two mouthfuls of which were consumed, the prime minister declared it was time to go.

One minister at the table obviously did not want to go, clinging to his plate of veal loin, shoveling the food into his mouth, until he was firmly but irrevocably retrieved by a colleague, the minister whimpering: "It is SO good, it is SO good."

A year after the Polish prime minister's visit I welcomed their president and national hero, winner of the Nobel Peace Prize in 1983, Lech Walesa and Danuta Walesa. The president gained international prominence for his part in the creation of the Solidarity independent trade union movement in August 1980. He chaired the Solidarity delegation to the Roundtable Talks during the early spring of 1989 with representatives of the communist regime, leading to the first Solidarity government. An electrician by trade in the Lenin shipyard in Gdansk he joined his first strike in 1970 and was arrested, and played a major part in subsequent union-led work stoppages and strikes against the communist regime. His wife, the mother of his eight children, actually collected his Nobel Prize in Norway on his behalf, as Walesa was afraid he could not return home.

They were modest and so appreciative. I wrote extensive notes about their visit as requested by my old friend, Sir Kenneth Scott, Deputy Secretary to Queen Elizabeth II during the British advance team visit preparing for the Queen's State Visit mid May 1991 as after his State Visit to Washington D.C. Walesa was due at Windsor Castle as guest of the Queen and The Prince Philip. Sir Kenneth came for the Queen's second advance visit a few days after our Polish visit and was most eager to know "all the Polish details" to assist him in his own preparations in England. These are excerpts of my notes written as a memorandum, addressed to Ken Scott, dated March 28, 1991:

"President and Mrs. Walesa are modest and unassuming, she to the point of being extremely shy and almost afraid to express the least wish, the president somewhat the same except he was on a "mission" which demanded overcoming such feelings. They were always on time. They are incredibly energetic, and were on the go from morning to night, and ended up rather exhausted, especially the president (I believe he is diabetic).

They had no special requests as to our service, were pleased with whatever we served them, but through staff we learned that they would enjoy always having fresh fruit and nuts in their suite. Both drank several glasses of orange juice in a sitting, the president would ask for coffee at times but rarely touch it, and Danuta Walesa drank tea often (we mix Earl Grey and others). They and the delegation had healthy appetites, for instance, a breakfast of ham, sausage, bacon, ranch potatoes, and eggs plus assorted breakfast pastries, rolls, mountains of toast, and <u>tons</u> of sliced fresh fruits, i.e. pineapple, three kinds of melon, raspberries and strawberries, kiwi, oranges and grapefruit, and gallons of orange juice, disappeared quickly. Everyone in the delegation waited for the president and all marched in together for breakfast (no room service we were told), sitting down immediately, so that my staff plated from the buffet and brought plates to the table. The president would have wine with dinner, she would sip hers only. Delegation drinks everything. Our collective impression was that everyone in the group ate for three (including the president) and we planned for this knowing the hardships they have endured and face daily. (The Blair House kitchen calculated three large portions per meal per person, then doubled the amounts – and everything was consumed.)

President had forgotten toothpaste, shampoo etc. which we furnish on request. She did not need hairdresser as she had a companion with her to assist.

The president's Director of the Cabinet and Personal Assistant is Mieczyslaw Wachowski (was his driver when he headed Solidarity,) and I suggest going to him for answers. The Chief of Protocol Switkowski is pleasant, but tends to go to pieces when things get hectic. In an advance meeting you will find him somewhat posturing and long-winded. The Foreign Minister Krzysztof Skubiszewski is delightful and well-educated, with manners of the old school. He is Harvard educated and had lectured in the Universities of Geneva and London, and done research work at Columbia U.

Some speak English, one or two German, otherwise it is all Polish."

It had not exactly been a smooth beginning at Blair House.

Secretary Baker, escorting President Walesa, had scheduled a meeting with him and his foreign minister in the Lee Drawing Room immediately following arrival. Chief of Protocol Joseph Reed, though well informed as to the planned meeting, nevertheless decided to take Walesa on a sightseeing trip through the house, while Secretary Baker was slowly stewing in the Lee Drawing Room waiting – and waiting – and looking daggers at me. And Jose was not so pleased with me either:

He had set the table for sixteen in the Lee Dining Room for President Walesa's dinner. Informed by the embassy an hour before arrival that only ten would dine I had asked Jose to reduce the table. Five minutes before arrival the embassy people had increased the guest list to sixteen. Jose gallantly refused to tell me "I told you so." He didn't have to – I knew what he was thinking. But why finish there: the final straw to that rather comical evening came when the Polish interpreter in Room 24 asked me to come up to his room. He took me into the bathroom and showed me a lady's bra hanging in his shower – "and it is not mine, I assure you." A rather red faced chambermaid was asked to dispose of the bras, and after making profound apologies, I fled.

A short while later another country freed from the Soviet Union came to call.

Punsalmaagiyn Orchirbat, President of the Mongolian People's Republic and his wife, Mrs. S. Tsevelmaa arrived in January 1991 for an Official Working Visit – another extraordinary experience for us.

Watching and studying them I imagined them, centuries ago, on fast horses, fiercely engaged in battles, following Genghis Khan on his quest across Central Asia. Or they could have wandered across the Bering Strait down through Alaska and Canada into the Western States and settled in New Mexico, my home state, where I visualized them in one of our nineteen Pueblos, wearing a headdress, taking part in an ancient ritual. It was a toss-up.

President Orchirbat came to review four years of friendly bilateral relations with the United States, and to discuss issues of common interest, including the situation in the Persian Gulf, ongoing during the visit. The Mongolian People's Republic is a large country almost the size of Arizona, New Mexico, Texas, and Louisiana combined with no more than two million people, squeezed between Russia and China. It was a communist state until July 1990 when a democratic government was elected, with President Orchirbat its first democratically elected chief of state, and the first communist country in Asia to commit itself to reform as noted by James Baker in his book. Our government recognized Mongolia early 1987, our embassy was established in Ulaanbaatar 18 months later, and in the summer of 1990 Mr. Baker was the first U.S. Secretary of State to make a visit there. He notes in his book the extraordinary and colorful hospitality of his Mongolian hosts, as well as the lack of communication with the outer world. In 1998 Secretary of State Madeleine Albright also visited Mongolia and met with another democratically elected Mongolian president. She returned to the States with admiration for this small country which so quickly had rid itself of former communist market controls and introduced private investment laws, sweeping away preconceived ideas that modernizing an economy cannot be done simultaneously with offering free elections and political reform.

I heard that because Orchirbat's free time was limited, the president's preferred pastime was sleeping because he believed he worked best when well rested. Surely he was the first person in such an exalted position to admit to such a favorite pastime.

Ten days earlier the wife of the U.S. ambassador to Mongolia called to offer her assistance, not too much being publicly known as to habits and dietary restrictions in Mongolia. Grateful for any suggestion, having meager knowledge to impart to my staff, I added her information to the visit schedule and function sheet distributed prior to the visit.

Mongolians are nomadic living on what they herd such as sheep, cattle and camels which translates into meat and dairy products, with emphasis on fatty meats. The guest of honor is usually served the fattiest piece, sometimes pure fat. Mrs. Lake, perfectly seriously, assured me that "the Mongolians do not particularly care for camel meat." How disappointing! In my head danced the delicious picture of our Chef lassoing a camel on Pennsylvania Avenue. But at least that was one less worry for me although I was certain Chef would have loved to try his hand at camel burgers.

Mrs. Lake had never seen chicken in Mongolia, and told me "they grow few vegetables, but eat mushrooms, potatoes, tomatoes, cucumbers, some onions and cabbage for flavor. They start each meal with a potato salad covered in cold cuts, and their meats are served dry without sauce. They eat no seafood. They like wild strawberries, and heavy breads. The food is not spicy, and they have a sweet tooth, and love chocolate and candy." They had no problem in the drinking department, liking vodka, beer, some wine, juices, coffee and tea with "lots and lots" of milk although she was unsure as to the temperature of the milk "Blue" she said, "is the favorite color, and when used in flowers and tablecloths is a sign of welcome."

Mrs. Lake got five stars.

Chef naturally put his own spin on this and I applauded him for adding fried chicken to the luncheon menu the last day as "this is a typical American dish and perhaps they will enjoy it," just as Jose added Coca Cola to the served drinks. We served a heavy soup at lunch and dinner with our beef, lamb or duck entrees, and sweet chocolaty desserts. At lunch on the buffet we added the ingredients of how to make an American sandwich, and with some assistance from our staff, the Mongolians wrapped themselves happily around this, for them, strange fare. We augmented our breakfast sausages, ham and bacon with a variety of cheeses and yoghurt, and while we did not expect them to eat our usual selection of freshly cut fruits, we put it out anyway.

I had several advance meetings, including one with the Mongolian ambassador, to be followed by their deputy chief of protocol, and the presidential head of security, all with an interpreter. They were so polite that I had to read between the lines to discover what they really wanted. Little English was spoken by the delegation members.

Although by probing either in German, French or Spanish I was usually able to assist my guests, I shall always regret that I did not start Russian classes in 1990. Everyone from the former Soviet Union and its satellite countries spoke Russian, and when I reflect on the vast number of visitors from the area, and the classroom training I could have had, I could kick myself. However, instead I opted to improve my Spanish and French at the Foreign Service Institute.

And I shall always remember the Mongolians. On departure the president was enthusiastic and deeply appreciative. Saying goodbye to me he shook my hand vigorously, not wishing to let go, while I was screaming inside from the pain of his grip. He burst a blood vessel in my hand.

And what a contrast the Ukrainians turned out to be: the most akin to my notion of a KGB driven and dominated group!

Antonina Mikhaylovich Kravchuk accompanied her husband, the President of Ukraine, arriving on May 5, 1992 for an Official Working Visit. Three hours late, they went straight from AAFB to open their new embassy, and therefore on arrival wanted none of us but instead scooted upstairs to bed right away.

Mrs. Kravchuk was a dour woman with no reaction to anything being offered, suggested, or asked, as I did: "Madame, is everything to your liking? Madame, would you like a hairdresser? Madame, do you need the maid to press your clothes? Madame, are you comfortable here?" Susan Baker had the same reaction as I did, and quite gave up trying to pry a conversation out of her. As for Secretary Baker sitting next to Mrs. Kravchuk during the luncheon he and Mrs. Baker gave in their honor at State, he said: "She was impossible to get a word out of, so I just ignored her and enjoyed my lunch in peace."

She never said thank you or even goodbye on departure. I can best describe her bland personality as vanilla ice cream on a white wall – and that would be an insult to the ice cream.

I wondered how she could be effective as an assistant professor of political economics at a Ukrainian university, and holding a Ph.D. in economic sciences, as surely some form of communication skills were required to guide a student body along the way. Alternating between three suits which looked like they were left over from World War II, she said no to everything we offered, and for me typified the worst of a communistic attitude, with its awful systematic breaking down of values, manners, consideration for others, and common politeness. This attitude was evident in the Ukrainian Visit advance team, which invariably from those countries consisted of former KGB agents. Coarse, unfriendly, and derisive, they were incredibly rude especially to our Secret Service agents, who, to their credit, kept their collective temper under control.

Leonid Makarovich Kravchuk, on the other hand, was quite jolly, and here on an important visit which in addition to the usual meetings and luncheons at the White House and the Department of State, included going up to Camp David for a further meeting with President Bush. According to James Baker the overriding issue was control of nuclear weapons, and Ukraine's reluctance to give up their stockpile to Russia. The START agreement between the United States and the Soviet Union had been signed a year earlier, but this now had to be renegotiated between the now independent states with nuclear capabilities: Russia, Ukraine, Kazakhstan, and Belarus. Baker did say in his book that it was an immensely successful visit with certain treaty signings as well, and President Kravchuk was credited with taking a strong public stand against Russia in defense of his country's independence.

In contrast to Mrs. Ukraine, Mrs. Kazakhstan, on arrival mid afternoon, made it clear what she wanted the minute she walked into Blair House:

"American Perm," she said, and touched her hair to make sure I understood her.

Our faithful hairdresser arrived armed with equipment. But how to interpret Sara Nazarbayeva's request that it be "a vertical perm?" We decided she wanted a soft one, the opposite of what was, to stick to her metaphor, "a horizontal" one – somewhat on the frizzy side. Later she appeared: washed, curled, dyed, and permed to the hilt, and was so happy about it she had another hairdo before departure. Mrs. Kazakhstan was certainly ready to experience everything, and to enjoy herself thoroughly.

The Official Working Visit of Nursultan Abishevich Nazarbayev, President of the Republic of Kazakhstan, came two weeks after that of the Ukrainians, and was delightfully different. The first of several visits from that Central Asian country, with the same president, it was labor intensive due to a heavy schedule, but unusually exotic and surprising.

Kazakhstan was the second largest republic in the Soviet Union, and its president at that time one of Central Asia's most highly regarded politicians. He was generally looked upon as a staunch advocate of market economics and had hired several western academics to assist him in reforming his country's economy. After his first year as president he was reelected, a few months before visiting Washington, in his country's first popular presidential election.

I expect the most important issue, for which this president had been invited for talks to the White House, was nuclear weapons, crucial to ratification of the 1991 Strategic Arms Reduction Treaty (START). James Baker writes in his book: "Once the Kazakh president arrived in Washington at mid afternoon on Monday, May 18, I spent an hour with him at Blair House, and then we breakfasted for an hour the next day in an effort to finish off the agreement, which we did in time for President Bush and Nazarbayev to announce it Tuesday afternoon. The START Protocol was done, and we would sign it that weekend in Lisbon, where all the states involved were meeting for the conference on assistance to the former Soviet Union. I breathed a sigh of relief….." I have no doubt Chef's delicious breakfast of poached eggs on crisp potato cakes with salsa, served in our Lee Dining Room, contributed to this. One should never underestimate the power of food. But the road to this had taken many turns and twists, and I particularly enjoyed this description of Baker's visit in Kazakhstan nine months earlier when at the end of a long day and dinner, Nazarbayev asked Baker if he had ever had an "eastern" style sauna, and Baker wrote:

"So soon enough, our interpreter, Peter Afanasenko, Bob Strauss (U.S. Ambassador) and I had stripped down and were sitting with Nazarbayev and our vodka in the presidential banya – a Russian sauna that was large and comfortable, even by Western standards. Ron Mazer and the rest of my security detail posted itself outside, along with Dennis Ross, who had begged off, citing a cold. Nazarbayev told us about Kazakh customs and history, Peter tried to interpret through the steam, and Strauss and I relaxed, leaving geo-strategic worries far behind. After about twenty minutes, Nazarbayev picked up a large bundle of eucalyptus branches and beat me on the back and legs in order to open the pores and increase the therapeutic value of the heat. Upon seeing this, Strauss said he'd had enough and stepped out.

"Damn!" he jokingly told my security detail outside. "Get me the President of the United States on the phone. His Secretary of State is buck naked and he's being beaten by the President of Kazakhstan."

Kazakhstan had not yet established an embassy in Washington D.C., so several private U.S. firms were vying for the privilege of funding the president's trip to the United States, undoubtedly with dollar signs dancing in their heads, Kazakhstan sitting on enormous, untapped natural resources such as oil, natural gas, coal, and iron ore. The first advance person turned up with two Russian speaking employees of the Texas Timber Company, engaged to underwrite the AT&T communications arrangements for the visit. Later James Giffen's Mercater Group in New York got in on the act, to the point of actually manning the Embassy Office during the visit's normal working hours. They were very helpful, speaking Russian, and handling the many incoming messages. James Giffen, the U.S. business consultant of the Kazakh President, made himself very much at home during this and subsequent visits. Another group involving itself intimately with the Kazakhs was Chevron Corporation, even managing to move their dinner for the Kazakh president from a local hotel to Blair

House, after my several U.S. bosses advised me of its importance for American business. I was happy to oblige even though the onus was thrown on our shoulders. During the Chevron dinner, their mutual historic agreement to a $20 billion oil development, the largest ever between a private company and a sovereign nation, was signed in our Conference Room. The companies represented at the dinner table the following evening were still more of our industrial giants: Archer Daniels Midland; Atlantic Richfield; once again Chevron; Enron; Fluor; Kerr-McGee; Newmont Mining and to provide some leaven: a Citizens Democracy Corps' representative as well as Ambassador Weinmann, U.S. chief of protocol since six months.

The advance work had been anything but routine. The first advance person was a handsome, big "mountain" man with a large moustache, a great deal of charm and a fierce glint in his eye. Trying to find some common language, not liking to work through an interpreter of the Texas Timber Company I probed: "Sprechen Sie Deutch?" "Njet, njet," he said. I tried again: "Habla espanol?" "Njet, njet." "Parlez vous français?" – and we were off to a rollicking start, both speaking French rather badly. We discussed among other things the Muslim dietary restrictions and preferences of his president. Naturally I assured my new found friend that we were familiar with that particular diet, adding: "nous considérons bien que vous ne buvez pas d'alcool – and we know, you do not drink alcohol" to which, shocked to the core, he replied: "vous vous trompez, Madame, ce n'est pas comme ça du tout – you are wrong, Madame, it is not at all like that."

Sure enough, they happily drank anything, and just prior to departure, the Kazakh president invited everyone, his own delegation, the entire Blair House staff, U.S. Secret Service, and Secretary Baker with whom he had just signed a treaty between our two countries, to gather in the Garden Room for the farewells. President Nazarbayev insisted on treating us to his country's delicacies: fatty sausages and other meats, and a large quantity of vodka and brandy brought by his staff. I put my entire staff on notice that it was worth their jobs if they did not pretend to drink and eat.

But my most extraordinary experience with this particular world came on Friday, June 26, 1992 at 5 pm when leaving Blair House I took off in a north easterly direction walking through Lafayette Square towards

16th Street, turning north past the Hay Adams Hotel and St. John's Church, and up to 1125 16th Street NW. I turned in at the wide open gate and entered the Russian embassy residence, until recently best described as a fortress, guarded by security, dogs, cameras, and with no access unless one's visit had been carefully prearranged, rechecked, and pre-approved by Moscow. This night no one stopped me; no one asked me my name; I was met with a big smile by an aide and invited to walk up the stairs. Tonight just like at any other ambassadorial residence, the front door of the residence was thrown open to a gala event, its windows were lit up, and a genuine welcome was extended to its guests.

I had goose bumps. This was historic.

Ambassador Vladimir Lukin had invited to a gala reception everyone involved in Boris Yeltsin's visit, and rolled out the red carpet for us. The recently restored ballroom, gilded and mirrored to the hilt, was sparkling, Russian delicacies were served, and vodka flowed to smooth the way.

One week earlier we had bid farewell to Boris Yeltsin, after his State Visit and Summit with President Bush. President Yeltsin's thank-you speech to the staff was pure poetry. Then he turned to me, saying to my staff: "As for your boss here" and he proceeded to describe me by using his hands: he closed one in a fist, "On the one hand she is firm and tough" then, opening the hand, and with the other stroking it, he said: "on the other hand she is soft and gentle."

Needless to say my staff loved it, as did I. Then I got a bear hug from Boris Yeltsin.

Since the Iron Curtain was lifted and the Berlin Wall came down, in the Soviet Union, President Mikhail Gorbachev had tried to bring his country into a free-market democracy. After the 1991 botched summer coup in the Soviet Union, the emergence of Russia's new hero, Boris Yeltsin, and the communist party beginning to unravel it was not long before there was nothing to be president of any longer. Gorbachev had little time left, resigning at Christmas 1991 – and thereby dissolving the Soviet Union.

Boris Yeltsin was big, masculine, charming, exuberant, and in far better shape than expected. Naina Yeltsin was quietly interested in everything, and both were smiling and obviously appreciative of our attentions. On arrival I showed them upstairs, not only into the Primary Suite, but also the Library after the president asked me: "Where is my study?" He wandered on, with Mrs. Yeltsin and me on his heels, while I tried to get a handle on numbers and time for their first night's dinner, having gathered that such decisions were made at this particular level. I promised him an American feast, and he wanted to know: "Will I have finished eating by midnight?" All of this conversation took place as we wandered, the Yeltsins inspecting everything. Seeing our American newspapers laid out in the Eisenhower Room, the president sat down to see how his name appeared in "English script," while I told them, through an interpreter of course, the story of the chandelier which was the reason for the closing of Blair House in 1982 and its subsequent $14 million renovation.

At the point of my story when the chandelier fell into the bed of the King of Morocco, President Yeltsin, who despite being engrossed in the English spelling of his name, shot out of his seat, with surprise and an incredulous grin on his face. I was glad to discover I had not been boring him.

The objectives and results of the historic summit between President Bush and President Yeltsin were summed up in a Washington Post June 18, 1992 editorial:

"That Russia is now a striving democracy made the Bush-Yeltsin Summit the first meeting ever of an American president with a democratically elected Kremlin leader. It mattered. It's not just that Presidents Bush and Yeltsin determined to reduce strategic nuclear warheads – now at the combined level of 22,000 – beyond the 15,000 of the unratified START treaty to 7,000 over the next 11 years. Mr. Yeltsin agreed to give up all of Russia's most menacing weapons – land-based intercontinental ballistic missiles suitable for a first strike. ... Mr. Bush won this unprecedented bow to American strategic superiority – and this promise of exclusive American relief from a first strike threat – on grounds that Washington needs more power for its continuing global responsibilities, while Moscow no longer has a global role or foe. Mr. Yeltsin accepted the new dispensation on the basis that for Russia parity was at once unnecessary and expensive. "We cannot afford it," he confessed. He will fare better if he gets the economic support dictated by the surpassing American and Western interest in nourishing democracy in Russia. There is a bargain waiting to be closed. Mr. Yeltsin has made a historic gamble to join the world democratic order. He is doing more than anyone had imagined, not least in becoming a guarantor of American nuclear superiority and security. It is the West's turn."

For the black tie State Dinner, Boris Yeltsin dressed in a business suit, but that, according to my inside reports, was the only thing not festive that night. He was exuberant, and wanting to dance in the middle of the dinner, took a swing on the floor with the lady next to him and declared this was "the best day of my life."

In addition to the standard State Visit package his packed schedule included several signings of treaties and other agreements, among others on arms reduction; a speech to a Joint Session of Congress; a boating trip on the Severn River in Maryland at Annapolis with President Bush; and breakfast with Vice President Quayle.

The advance team for this visit of the first President of the Russian Federation was led by their chief of protocol, a handsome older man with a great appetite for orange juice and an equally great reluctance to agree to anything the Americans wanted, saying "Njet" more times than could be counted. He reverted to Russian whenever he was going to be nasty, although perfectly at home in English, which he used with me walking around the house, begging me for "more beds, more beds, Mrs. Valentiner." They had a problem. They admitted to having no money for hotels, and did not want their security to sleep at the embassy. Please, please could they have roll away beds?

How could I not help? We fitted in seven more beds for this visit, and particularly Room 36 turned into a dormitory for 12 security guards with the four beds being occupied all the time, and the bathroom in a constant state of disarray. Fitting people into the house was so important to this group that I was asked to accommodate their high ranking people in the lesser single rooms, leaving the more elegant and larger ones for those who could share with someone else. We even provided blankets and pillows for the Embassy Office staff, figuring that the sofas up there were just too tempting, and we might as well protect our fabrics. Our kitchen provided large and sustaining meals, and discovered that in terms of quantities eaten, the Russians were more than a match for the Poles, as they most certainly were in terms of what they had to drink. Wine and champagne were sparingly taken, but more than made up for in vodka, gin, and scotch, to include the four gins and tonic consumed for dinner the first night by our principal guest himself. The total alcohol consumption of the 13 guests dining in the Lee Dining Room the first night, including Boris and Naina Yeltsin, were 25 gins and tonic and two bottles each of champagne, white and red wine. The 39 delegation members dining in the Garden Room were more modestly whetting their whistles with five bottles of white wine, four of red wine, eight glasses of cognac and four of scotch. Much of the alcohol consumed was brought in by the Russians. And Jose and I so enjoyed Assistant Butler Antonio Rodriguez spending a lot of time searching for a black Russian – when he had actually been asked to serve a "Black Russian" – a mixture of coffee liqueur and vodka!

The delegation members were not considerate of each other. Chef put out grilled shrimp on the first night's buffet, and one person filled his plate with the shrimp to bursting point regardless of the delegation members waiting behind him for their turn. He could not have cared less. I expect that standing in line all his life, or seeing his mother do so, for a bit of bread or a jug of milk, and having had to shuffle and push and fight for everything that we in this country took for granted, he could not be entirely to blame for getting "it" while he had a chance.

They were poor, they were badly dressed except those who were in power and well traveled, and I gathered it was a trying time for all of them. Tensions between Russia and Ukraine had developed over President Kravchuk's insistence that part of the Black Sea Fleet belonged to Ukraine. Interestingly enough, one of President Yeltsin's security guards told me the following: When the two former Soviet Union mates settled the question of the division of the Black Sea Fleet, his own brother was on a naval ship in Chile. Because his brother was Russian he was left behind in Chile to fend for himself, as the – now – Ukrainian naval ship sailed away.

Many events furthering U.S.-Soviet relations had taken place at Blair House leading up to this historic visit. Two years earlier, in the spring of 1990, four luncheons, three meetings, and a tour of the house took place during a period of three weeks as part of the Protocol Office's preparations for the State Visit of President Gorbachev, who sadly did not stay at Blair House. Six months after that we had a dinner honoring Yevgeny M. Primakov, member of the Presidential Council, Union of Soviet Socialist Republics, attended by John H. Sununu, the Chief of Staff for President Bush, Andrew H. Card, Jr., Assistant to the President, Robert Gates, Assistant to the President and Condoleezza Rice, Special Assistant to the President.

Mr. Baker, six months prior to the Yeltsin visit, hosted one of the more prestigious luncheons which I have ever been involved in, the guests being the foreign ministers and other high officials from the 54 countries participating in Secretary Baker's Coordinating Conference on Assistance to the Republics of the former Soviet Union. He wrote in his book that he wanted to use this conference "to jump-start assistance efforts in three ways. First I wanted to send a very clear signal of support to the Russians, Ukrainians, and others that the entire world wanted their experiments with democracy, free markets, and independence to succeed. But I also wanted to add a touch of drama that would break through typical media coverage of such a diplomatic event. I wanted to create a story line that might be transmitted by CNN and other international media to help instill hope in those in need in the former Soviet Union, while also galvanizing a public consensus (and private efforts) in the United States. At my request, Rick Armitage (of the Department of Defense) who had taken command of our assistance efforts to the former Soviet Union, put together what we called "Operation Provide Hope"– a plan to fly fifty-four sorties of food and medicine in one week to all of the new independent states, including an initial twelve sorties of giant C-5 transport aircraft out of Rhein-Main Air Base in Frankfurt."

Baker wrote how he personally "shook down" the Director of the Office of Management and Budget for $645 million, and how his deputy, Larry Eagleburger and others on his team "found, cajoled, borrowed and begged a wide variety of assistance from other government programs." It was quite a feat, and at Blair House we played a small part, that of ensuring these hard working ministers the "fuel" with which they could do all these good things. So Chef prepared a buffet aimed at honoring the dietary restrictions among so many of religious and cultural backgrounds:

Grilled Swordfish and Shrimp
with Tomatillos and Roasted Peppers

Medallions of Beef Sirloin with Red Chile Sauce

Southwest Style Rice and Vegetable Medley

Salad of Jicama, Chicory
and Bibb a la Vinaigrette
Avocado, Grapefruit and Melon

Assorted American Cheeses

Key Lime Buttermilk Tart
Mocha Pecan Cheese Cake
Fresh Strawberry Shortcake

Llano Estacado 1989 Texas Chardonnay
Robert Mondavi 1987 Cabernet Sauvignon

Many of the foreign ministers had stayed at Blair House with their leaders and were so happy to see us again, especially Jose who had left no stone unturned during their earlier visits to ensure their comfort.

I was talking with Sweden's Foreign Minister, Margaretha av Ugglas, discussing the upcoming visit of her prime minister and his new baby, when I turned away right into President Bush, making a surprise visit to greet the foreign ministers. His chief of staff, Samuel Skinner, former Secretary of Transportation, was accompanying him.

Some months earlier Mr. Skinner had hosted a dinner party in the Conference Room in honor of foreign transportation ministers. I remembered it well. I had put the oval Blair mirror, beautifully edged in silver grape leaves, in the middle of the long table and on it placed a silver rickshaw, found by Jose and myself in our silver vault. Jose had worked for days polishing it up until it was positively glowing. I had been so certain these ministers might enjoy looking at an example of one of the earlier forms of transportation. How wrong I was – no one noticed.

After President Bush had visited with the foreign ministers for twenty minutes Mr. Skinner asked me to "get the President out of there." I was not going to touch that one with a ten foot pole. "That is your job, Mr. Secretary" and Skinner, rather sternly but with such a twinkle in his eyes replied: "I hereby delegate you to do it."

Being a firm believer that discretion is the better part of valor, however, I suggested the chief of protocol were to do so. Consequently Skinner and I tried to gang up on Jack Weinmann – who just grinned.

Samuel Skinner was relieved of his job as White House Chief of Staff that summer, and President Bush asked James Baker to give up the Department of State and return to the White House, I expect, to tighten up its operation and supervise his campaign for reelection. One morning we were called by the White House that "someone" would be coming over to meet with "someone else," and could we please take care of it in the most discreet fashion. I assured the person that we would be very discreet, but in order for these persons to gain access I would have to know exactly who was coming. Mr. Skinner came by 700 Jackson Place to avoid the press, while Mr. Baker conspicuously drove up at the front entrance. I escorted a nervous Skinner to the Truman Study, and took Baker to him. After the Secretary had departed, I left Skinner alone for fifteen minutes, having heard the rumors and therefore having a good idea of what had just happened. I wanted him to have enough time to collect himself. I was aching for him.

I was very sad when James Baker had to give up his post as Secretary of State to move back to the White House and run George H.W. Bush reelection campaign. I expect he was sad too, but suppose one heeds the call of one's president, especially as their political fortunes had been so interwoven. I missed him, as I liked him so much, and always had gotten along perfectly with him. I also admired tremendously his work as our country's secretary of state. He was the best in recent memory. Fortunately, sometimes news of him was heard on the grapevine.

The Blair House staff being so small we augmented with extra help in the pantry and the kitchen, and thus were up on the latest rumors in town brought in by our roving part-timers. Don Trelstad, navy cook at the Vice President's residence and often working at the White House Mess, let slip this little story: James Baker had wandered into the White House Mess kitchen asking if he could have a rare hamburger and kept asking how <u>rare</u> it could be done.

Don got a bit impatient with him, and after assuring him for the third time he could do it very rare indeed, finally said: "Well, Sir, as soon as I have cut off its horns and wiped its arse, I'll bring it in to you" – at which James Baker cracked up and roared with laughter.

However, not only were big changes in the wind abroad, but certainly this election cycle brought about it own. We were way ahead although we did not yet know it: some of us had actually met Governor Bill Clinton of Arkansas, campaigning for the Democratic presidential nomination when he came for a half hour meeting with Boris Yeltsin.

I recall perfectly this day, the first time I met Bill Clinton. He was larger than expected, and rather red in his face which I thought might have been nervousness prior to his meeting with Yeltsin. I greeted him at the door and introduced myself as the general manager of Blair House, omitting to tell him my name, as I felt it was of no importance. But this would not do. He asked me my name immediately which showed rather a nice touch. I showed him and the eight staffers accompanying him into the Lincoln Room and asked if I might offer him some coffee. "Yes, please, do you have decaf by any chance," he asked, to which I replied: "But of course, Governor – this is Blair House." He laughed, and I like to think he remembered later the friendly welcome afforded him at his future guest house.

We would remain on the best of terms with the Clinton people during the next eight years.

In the ensuing months President Bush was on the campaign trail. I was very sad at the time that a president I had always admired and personally liked had so drastically failed. I thought he was not well during the last eighteen months of his presidency, seeming somewhat sluggish and non-peppy and later learned this was confirmed as a thyroid problem and I now understood better the lack of exuberance, energy, and enthusiasm during his last campaign.

At a reception after the election three hundred sad and shocked looking people jammed into the Garden Room for speeches, reminiscences, and thanks, when the staff of the National Security Council bid farewell to their president, George Bush, and director, Brent Scowcroft. Then the President and Mrs. Bush left for Camp David.

Jose put two bottles of Robert Mondavi Fume Blanc in a cooler in their car, and the President left carrying a handful of biscuits with ham and turkey, which made me exclaim: "Is this the best we can do for you, Mr. President, by way of a Blair House Care Package? Could we not give you, at least, a napkin?"

And Barbara Bush, true to form, said: "I hope nobody photographs him outside."

The last time President and Mrs. Bush came to Blair House during his presidency was on January 14, 1993 when his cabinet secretaries honored them at a farewell dinner. It was the end of an era.

When he arrived, James Baker thanked me for all I had done for him. I told him what an honor it had been for me to be on his team, and, as he turned away, said: "As an immigrant it has been very important to me what you did, and Mr. Secretary, you never missed a beat," at which he turned around, came back, and gave me a big kiss.

Shortly after this, President Bush came up to me as I stood on post in the Front Hall, saying as he shook my hand and gave me a hug: "If I do not get a chance later to say it, I want to thank you for all you have done for me.

You have been superb, absolutely superb; – everybody has said so."

My father, Jørgen Valentiner, born 1907.

My mother, Elga Valentiner, born 1910.

Their children, Claus, Benedicte and Gustav, whom they called
THE LIONS.

I must have been very naughty – with time out in our summer cabin.

The only time I sat for a formal portrait at the age of 16.

Lt. Col. S. Kent Carnie, USA, and I were married in Washington D.C. November 1969; Danish Ambassador Torben Rønne hosted the reception at his residence. During our eleven year marriage we lived in Texas, Iran, Spain, Mexico and New Mexico.

In 1998 in Edinburgh, Scotland my brothers gave me away in marriage to Commodore Adrian R. Cummins, Ao, RAN, Rtd., my friend of 42 years. I wore a lace and silk dress which belonged to my late mother. This was the last time the three of us were together; Gustav (on the left) committed suicide six years later.

The Blair complex at 1651 Pennsylvania Avenue N.W. consists of four historic buildings situated diagonally across from the White House. (Courtesy Mandel Ngan/AFP/Scanpix)

In March 1988 my boss on the Hill, U.S. Senator Pete V. Domenici (R-N.M.) detailed me to Blair House per special request of Chief of Protocol Lucky Roosevelt; at the same time I continued my work for him while my State top security clearance was being processed.

In the Blair Pantry: Marinete dos Saias, Chamber Maid and superb seamstress; Jemma Rennie, Head Housekeeper; myself; and Parlor Maid Teresinha Diaz – what would I have done without my ladies!

My trusted Head Butler, Jose Fuster, with whom I shared many adventures – and a rollicking sense of humor.

Executive Chef for ten years, Russell Cronkhite and I pose in the Garden Room on Valentine's Day; the Chief of Protocol was host for the embassy ceremonial secretaries.

On April 25, 1988 President and Mrs. Reagan reopens the greatly expanded and restored Blair House, and meet for the first time its new General Manager – me.

A warm goodbye to Barbara and George Bush; they were great supporters of us all during their four years in the White House.

Not everyone ends up in the arms of President Boris Yeltsin of Russia ...

... or hobnob with President George H. W. Bush and his guest, Queen Margrethe of Denmark, in the White House.

Famous and heroic Vaclav Havel visited us three times: as President of Czechoslovakia, then of the Czech and Slovakian Republic, and finally of the Czech Republic. Here I am giving him the Blair House book during his first visit. Randy Bumgardner, at that time a Protocol Visits Officer, and later my Deputy for eight years, is shown also.

Secretary of State Jim Baker, whom I admired and always respected, often came over.

To Benedict Valentine
with appreciation for your
service to our country —

Bill Clinton

President Bill Clinton made me a democrat.

President Harry S Truman began creating the Marshall Plan in the Lee Dining Room when it was his Cabinet Room during his more than three years in residence; here Mr. Clinton lunches with King Hussein of Jordan and Prime Minister Rabin of Israel following their historic agreement in July 1995 to end the 46-year state of war between Jordan and Israel. They all signed the photo for me.

The Clintons were so hospitable. Adrian and I are their guests at one of their Christmas parties in the White House —

— and one year when Adrian was in Australia, I was escorted by my brother, Claus.

While Hillary Clinton is waiting for her guests I am pointing out some of our beautiful antiques in the Lee Drawing Room.

England's Prime Minister Tony Blair visited us twice, and was liked so much by all of us.

The Koreans preferred group photos in the Garden; here we are with President Kim Young-Sam and his wife in July 1995.

Spain's King and Queen stayed with us twice and are bidding farewell to my staff here; Lieutenant Rodrick Waters, our Head of Security, is seen in the back.

Adrian and I are guests of Secretary of State Madeleine Albright in the Diplomatic Reception Rooms at State; all the Clinton people were incredibly generous.

Nelson Mandela charmed everyone and is here in the Jackson Place Sitting Room with his wife, Graça Machel, and lucky me.

We also entertained "ordinary" people; here I am with Douglas Fairbanks Jr., famous film star and heartthrob many decades ago, attending the 50th anniversary celebration of Harry S Truman's presidency. Mr. Fairbanks reckoned that even if he did not know who this Mr. Blair was "he sure had a hell of a house!"

Egypt's President Hosni Mubarak came nine times during the two Clinton administrations; the ultimate moderate Arab leader of his time, he was the one called in to sit at the table during the Middle East Peace negotiations.

We had a fascinating visit by China's President Jiang Zemin and his wife, our first Chinese guests in eleven years; here we have just been discussing the power of languages, the president speaking excellent English, learned, he told me, from the American missionaries who made him recite the Gettysburg Address!

Randy Bumgardner, my wonderful deputy, and I are posing for a Christmas photo in the Garden Room. Randy is presently General Manager of Blair House.

I am allotted two minutes to say goodbye to Secretary of State Colin Powell and must talk fast to effect the appointment of Randy Bumgardner as my successor.

July 3, 2001

Benedicte Valentiner
Blair House
1651 Pennsylvania Avenue, N.W.
Washington, D.C. 20503

Dear Benedicte:

Thank you for writing to inform me of your
retirement and for your very kind words. As you
leave your position as general manager of the
Blair House, I want to thank you for your
outstanding service during my Administration and
throughout your remarkable career.

Since its establishment as the President's guest
house, the Blair House has played a significant
role in many historic events, and you can be
proud of all you have done to ensure that it
remains in keeping with its grand heritage.
Thanks in no small measure to your hard work and
careful attention, countless foreign dignitaries
and other guests of the President have had a
comfortable and meaningful experience during
their visits. I know that the skill, energy,
elegance, and kindness with which you fulfilled
your demanding responsibilities will be deeply
missed by the staff and guests of the Blair
House -- but I also know that you have left it
in excellent shape for many years to come.

As you begin a new chapter in your life, Hillary
and I extend our best wishes to you and Adrian
for much happiness in the years ahead.

Sincerely,

Bill Clinton

A letter of appreciation for my service to the Nation from President Bill Clinton.

ACT III

WILLIAM J. CLINTON
The President

***

WARREN M. CHRISTOPHER
The Secretary of State

MADELEINE ALBRIGHT
The Secretary of State

***

MOLLY RAISER
The Chief of Protocol

MARY MEL FRENCH
The Chief of Protocol

CHAPTER 12

THE ARRIVAL OF THE CLINTONS

"There is nothing wrong with America that cannot be cured by what is right with America … by your vote you have forced the Spring."

William Jefferson Clinton

Bill Clinton's victory over President George H.W. Bush in the 1992 presidential election sent shock waves through Washington. For the first time in twelve years, not only would the reins of the national administration be turned over to a Democrat, but a generational shift in government was also taking place. The city was apprehensive and excited at the same time. Although at Blair House we consciously avoided discussing politics, most staff members were probably Democrats. And although I had not voted for Clinton and had a deep loyalty to President Bush, I was undisturbed and confident. I was a civil servant, which afforded me considerable protection although I was aware that others might covet my job. I was also aware that I would have to prove my worth to the incoming president, and that the main chance came during the pre-inauguration visits. While old-timers were whispering that as Clinton came from a backwater state he and his people might not know how to conduct themselves I had a different perspective. In reading about Clinton and watching him on television, I was impressed not only with the depth of his knowledge and his common touch, but with a quality that Reagan and Bush lacked: his humanity.

Soon after the election, however, it looked as though I might not get my chance with the young victor prior to Inauguration Week.

President-elect Clinton did not wish to use taxpayers' money by coming to Blair House, preferring to stay at a hotel while in Washington during the transition. I also heard talk that the Clintons intended to fly on commercial airlines. Getting stuck in airports is a waste of time when one should be making haste to learn how to govern a country. I did not think these goofy notions would last. The Bush people should have talked them out of these impractical plans, but it appeared that the Bushies were unable to rise above sore-loser politics. I'm not sure whether the Clintons ever flew commercial, but the hotel idea was dropped after one attempt. The bill for Clinton's stay at the Hay Adams Hotel just across Lafayette Park must have been a jolt. So on December 8, 1992, we welcomed Governor Clinton for a one-night visit, which turned out to be our only chance to host the president-elect prior to the traditional pre-inauguration stay at the house.

A president-elect has the right to request the use of Blair House, subject to approval of the President, whenever he is in Washington for transition work in addition to his traditional stay at Blair House in the few days leading up to the Inauguration.

During the transition period Jimmy Carter had visited the house five times for a total of nine nights; Ronald Reagan twice for a total of nine nights; and George H.W. Bush once for two nights. And immediately following the inaugural ceremony on Capitol Hill, Blair House traditionally feeds the diplomatic corps for luncheon after which the ambassadors view the inaugural parade from risers set up in front of the house. This luncheon, for up to 500 people, by long-standing custom takes place two to three hours after the president-elect and his entourage end their pre-inaugural stay.

I was ready to experience an interesting era of one party taking power from a defeated rival, a defeated incumbent at that, and one of my first glimpses of the human element of that transition was startling.

During the transition period, the 2 ½ months between the general election and the inauguration of a new president, the old and the new teams interact to ensure a smooth transfer of power. That's how it's supposed to work, but it seemed a bad omen that I was completely left out of the process as far as Blair House was concerned. When a representative of the Clinton Transitional Team asked the Protocol's Executive Director, a Foreign Service officer, what it would cost for the Clinton party to stay at the house, for example, I could have provided complete records of previous transition costs. Curiously, the Executive Director never consulted me, but instead went to the career civil servant who administered the Secretary of State's representational funds. (These funds are used when the Secretary of State holds working luncheons and dinners in connection with his duties.) As funds for neither the Clinton visit nor the inaugural diplomatic lunch came out of the State Department, but was paid for by the Inaugural Committee, the smell of petty politics was in the air, and as for the State Department administrator, I suspected her of having an animosity towards Blair House.

Once, questioning the abundant buffet meals we served to our guests, she had suggested to me that "sandwiches were good enough for the President's foreign visitors." This time she had told the Executive Director that Blair House "was not to hire any extra help as the Clinton visit would be small and short" and that the inaugural luncheon for the diplomatic corps could not exceed 250 people.

Meanwhile I was kept out of the loop as the Protocol's Executive Director gave erroneous information to the Clinton advance people, and made arbitrary decisions as to my requirements during the Clinton team's visits. I didn't like the way the arrangements were being made and was distressed because the Executive Director and I had always gotten along well.

So I mustered my ammunition; I called my boss, Chief of Protocol Jack Weinmann. We had developed an excellent relationship. He trusted me, and I always found him totally supportive and a good listener. I had talked with him as early as August about possible post-election-pre-inaugural activities at Blair House were Bill Clinton to win. I had also prepared for Weinmann, in that eventuality, a list of visits of former presidents-elect and the resulting costs to Blair House.

Weinmann quickly linked me up with the Clinton team, including the Clinton contact person for the Inaugural Day diplomatic luncheon. In addition, and I can still hear him on the phone, he said: "Mrs. V, I told them you personally would cook the lunch for the ambassadors!"

When the Clinton team met with me any lingering doubt about what they might be like began to dissolve. It was my privilege to deal with the nicest group of people I had as yet come across. One of these was Brooke Shearer, wife of the future Deputy Secretary of State Strobe Talbott. Ms. Shearer was in line to head up the White House Fellows and later became Deputy Assistant Secretary of Commerce. Meanwhile Chef called the Governor's Mansion in Arkansas. The mansion's cook told him that while the governor would eat healthy foods, particularly soups, as his wife preferred, he would enjoy more "hearty fare." Already having heard about Bill Clinton's taste for hamburgers, we had expected as much. We also learned that he was allergic to chocolate, and that flowers should not be left in his bedroom.

Governor Clinton and his team came on December 8, 1992 for 27 hectic hours, and my staff and I and the extra waiters we had hired (despite the cockeyed instructions from State) were kept hopping at all hours. Not yet out of the campaign mode, one young staffer turned up with Governor Clinton's suit on a hanger, planning the change in our cloakroom before a scheduled event. My representations to her that a perfectly beautiful and convenient primary suite was waiting for him upstairs were to no avail. She finally admitted that he had to change in the cloakroom, since otherwise "we lose him." And she probably never forgave me, although I claimed total innocence in what happened next. Clinton's staff meeting in the Conference Room was just breaking up. At the end of the corridor I saw Jose leading the governor into the elevator, which swallowed them up. The staffer turned to me to question where he was going. I guessed Governor Clinton had asked Jose where his room was, and Jose, not knowing of the plan for the cloakroom quick-change, very properly took him upstairs and installed him in the Primary Suite. No wonder the staffer was so anxious about getting the President-elect changed and out. Upon seeing our wonderful king-size tester bed, he decided to take a little nap and was two hours late for his scheduled event.

This "small and short" visit filled the house. Hillary Clinton was among the party, as was U.S. Senator Al Gore, to whom I assigned the Foreign Minister's Suite. My first impression of the vice president-elect, among Senate staffers privately known as "Prince Al," was of a pompous, stiff, not particularly jovial person, an impression I revised quickly as I got to know him better. Al Gore was generous and charming, with a keen sense of humor and could be delightful. I love this story: During a State Dinner, Mrs. Gore's old mother fell asleep at the table. Al Gore and Mel French devised a way of getting her away without creating a fuss: they each took her under an arm and pretended they were just escorting her out without carrying her. Out in the cross hall of the White House they sat her down between them, and simultaneously looked down and discovered that she had no shoes on. Mr. Gore suggested to Mel French that she had better retrieve them. Mel French reckoned as how she was the Chief of Protocol and did not have to crawl under a table. To which Gore said that as he was the Vice President he outranked her. But Mel French had the trump card in this one: "She is YOUR mother-in-law" – and after that they found a WH staffer to do the deed.

Many aides whom I had seen on television during the campaign were there: George Stephanopoulos, Bruce Lindsey, Capricia Marshall, Susan Thomases, and Dee Dee Myers among others, while still more were on the access list and came and went during the visit. They were less manicured than staffers of earlier presidents. They gave the impression that their healthy looks were the result of exercise rather than massages and diets, and they drank boiled water often and snacked on plain bagels. As scheduled meals became completely unscheduled, as people came and went, grazing on our buffet, and kept us going at all hours, the necessity of our extra wait staff became very clear.

That one-day visit was our only live contact with the Clintons until their inaugural stay in January 1993. Here's how Hillary Rodham Clinton described it in her book LIVING HISTORY:

"During inaugural week, our families and personal staff stayed with us in Blair House, the traditional guest residence for visiting heads of state and presidents-elect. Blair House and its professional staff run by Benedicte Valentiner, known to all as Mrs. V, and her deputy, Randy Bumgardner (actually Sam Castleman at the time, BV) made us feel welcome in the quietly elegant mansion that became an oasis during a hectic week. Blair House is famous for being able to accommodate any special need. Our crew was tame compared to certain visiting heads of state who demanded that their guards be nude to ensure they carried no weapons, or imported their own cooks to prepare everything from goat to snake."

And George Stephanopoulos, advisor to Bill Clinton during his campaign and his first administration, commented on the stay in his book ALL TOO HUMAN:

"We had arrived in Washington on Sunday of inaugural week and gone straight to Blair House, the president's guest house. A handsome hostess with silvery blond hair (silvery blond hair! – I suspect that as George Stephanopoulos was but a kid himself, I probably looked to him like his mother) and a continental accent greeted me at the door and offered me tea as if I were one of the guests they were used to – royalty, a head of state – not just one of the staff. Only a handful of us were invited to stay with the Clintons at Blair House. As the butler ushered me up to the second floor, I pocketed the gilded card that carried my name, spelled correctly, in an elegant calligrapher's script. Closing the door, I lay back on the feather bed and luxuriated in the feeling of being one of the chosen."

The party arrived at Blair House Sunday, January 17, 1993 at 7 pm after a long bus ride from Monticello. They had begun their journey to the White House by the same route President-elect Thomas Jefferson took to his inauguration 192 years earlier. Before arriving they attended a concert at the Lincoln Center, and marched across Memorial Bridge to ring a replica of the Liberty Bell and to watch fireworks. Forty upbeat, excited, and chilled people, including the Clintons, dined on our scrumptious buffet in the Garden Room.

Mrs. Clinton's parents were also staying with us, her father beaming from ear to ear in his wheelchair. Chelsea Clinton and her friends took over the fourth floor and had their own program including a picnic prepared by our kitchen. Their favorite foods such as pizza, hamburgers, chicken fingers, potato chips, cheese dips, tacos and, of course, ice cream with hot fudge, milkshakes, chocolate desserts and peanut butter and jelly were available at all times. And our future President grazed on these delicacies as well. While we only saw Chelsea Clinton sporadically over the following eight years, we heard reports regularly from many sources of her development into an outstanding young woman. Her reputation as a considerate and kind friend and her scholastic prowess were known all over Washington. It's a measure of their character that the Clintons, in contrast to presidential families before and after them, raised an exemplary kid. And I often wondered why those who brutally criticized the Clintons so conveniently overlooked that fact.

The President-elect was a night owl, which impacted the rest of us. Our Library was set up with podium, mike, and prompter screen for him to rehearse his inaugural address. Stephanopoulos and others monitored these rehearsals, and I especially remember Tommy Caplan, a novelist and writer from Baltimore and a Georgetown University chum of Bill Clinton's.

Tommy Caplan wrote a memo (which was among the papers gathered up by my staff after the visit) outlining his suggestions for the inaugural address. He cited President Kennedy's address as the most resonant in our time, and said that now as in the Kennedy era our nation must "reimagine itself. Human beings die, but the ideas which animate them – and which they animate – are eternal." I was particularly struck with this point: "America's interests and security, as well as our principles, demand that we continue our historic engagement with, not begin to retreat from, the community of nations." (When I reread this three-page memo to Clinton in the fall of 2003, I was struck by how the George W. Bush administration had rejected those principles.)

Jose, at 2 am on Inaugural Day, found Bill Clinton fast asleep in an armchair in the Blair House Library, clutching his inaugural address.

At 7 am on inaugural morning General Brent Scowcroft, President Bush's National Security Advisor, came to give an official briefing to the President-elect. General Scowcroft brought with him instructions in case of nuclear attack.

After Clinton's inauguration, Richard Gookin, a career foreign service officer, and acting chief of protocol, managed protocol affairs for the first few months. Thus, with no Clinton chief of protocol in place, and in the wake of the Clinton party's happy pre-inauguration visits at Blair House, the White House called me often for advice on protocol matters and menu selections.

The Clinton people, it was said, found the White House permanent staff stuffy; the White House staff found the Clinton people brash. The Clinton people didn't help by responding to annoying advice from the White House staff with the remark, "Well, that's not how it's done at Blair House." I imagine the solemn White House permanent staffers were chagrined at being compared to their country cousins across the street; and the Clinton forces were annoyed by the condescending tone of the White House staff. As the White House staff saw it, they were permanent fixtures, while the President and his people were but short-time occupants. And the White House staff had just bid a sad farewell to a family that had been around for twelve years, only to be saddled with "a bunch of kids who didn't know anything."

Kelly Craighead, who did advance work for the Clinton visits, confirmed that the White House staff gave them a tense welcome. "We had such a downer getting over there after the inauguration, Mrs. V." For one thing, the Chief Usher had physically intervened when Capricia Marshall, Mrs. Clinton's personal assistant, began to lean on an antique chair. After this, relations between the Clintonites and the White House staff became greatly strained. While I sympathized with Chief Usher Gary Walters' concern for the White House's historic furnishings, a gentle admonition would have been better than physical restraint. At Blair House we were used to dealing flexibly with many different cultures, for us Clinton Culture was just one more. Everyone got the impression that at least for a while the new White House occupants wished they were back with us.

The Clinton staff of Baby Boomers didn't have the discipline of the previous administrations of Reagan and Bush. Our permanent White House sources told us about the lack of formality, of the difficulties the new staffers had of getting out of the Motel Six campaign mode. High-ranking visitors had to step gingerly around the Styrofoam food boxes strewn through the offices; most shocking of all, a U.S. general was dismissed by a young female staffer who declared, "I do not talk to the military." The transition from campaigning to the seat of power always takes time for any new administration; the winners only gradually come to realize the enormity of having won, and that they have to settle down and start delivering on their promises. It took the Clinton people a while to show the discipline that governing requires.

And though the Clintonites eventually donned the mantle of discipline our young President never really grasped the virtue of punctuality. Frequently during the next eight years I had to pretend nothing out of the ordinary was happening, while in the Front Hall our visiting foreign president was drumming his fingers and looking at his watch, waiting for the call to cross over to the White House for a State Dinner. Of all the State Dinners during the Clinton years to which I had to send off our guests, not once was our President on time. Lucky Roosevelt had told me: "Mrs. V, the only time your guest has no say in the matter is when he or she goes to the White House; <u>never</u> keep our President waiting." But now the situation was quite the reverse. When Bill Clinton was first elected, and the term "to be on Clinton time" was first floated, I should have taken greater notice. A year later, I was amused to read the following:

In Illinois an employee who for nine years had never showed up for work on time filed suit against his former employers after being fired, claiming job discrimination against the "temporally handicapped" – and won. In a stunning decision by Judge Purvis Waffler of the North Central Circuit, as reported by the Washington Post in January 1994, the Judge wrote: "In the Declaration of Independence itself – the very cornerstone of intellectual freedom in this society – the Founding Fathers guaranteed their countrymen life, liberty and the pursuit of happiness. <u>But at no time did the Founding Fathers ever stipulate that anybody seeking life, liberty or the pursuit of happiness had to be on time to receive it.</u>" So what could we all do about our President?

But I forgave him his tardiness. Bill Clinton made a Democrat out of me.

President Bill Clinton's two administrations were my happiest years at Blair House. The country-club set of earlier administrations, mostly white, middle-aged males and wealthy white women of the "trust-baby" kind, were gone. I liked most of the Clinton people so much.

The Clintons were about inclusion. It mattered not what color, creed, race, or religion one was, or where one was born; we all mattered. I felt it acutely myself. I speak with an accent; my manners and style differ from those of other Americans. I have a Scandinavian style of undecorated directness. I brought an alternate perspective and attitude to the group, and found it was welcomed, and often embraced. It hardly mattered whether you had been on the campaign trail with the President or had worked for former presidents. In the latter case, the experience was considered valuable.

A few months into this new administration, I was flabbergasted when the White House Deputy of Presidential Personnel (a truly powerful though not widely-known position in our federal government) asked me to meet with one of their candidates for chief of protocol. I gulped and asked why they wanted me to evaluate the very person to whom I would report. The deputy was perfectly sanguine about this. She reckoned as how I had been around for a while and would know if their candidate had the necessary qualities. Thus over a three-hour visit at Blair House I got to know Fred DuVal, who would become not chief of protocol, but the deputy chief of protocol, and the direct supervisor of Blair House before he would move on to become deputy director of the White House Office of Intergovernmental Affairs.

I cannot stress enough what a joy it was to work with such intelligent people, especially during the first Clinton term. The chief of protocol, her deputy, her executive director and the assistant chief for visits had more brains among them than had been seen or would be seen again in that office.

I admit the Protocol Office was not as structured as in Lucky Roosevelt's days. However, it became a warmer, happier, and more human place to work, where even the smallest accomplishments were recognized.

With the coming of the Clinton era, Protocol staffers were privileged to take part in colorful and exciting programs and functions of the Protocol Office with a degree and frequency of involvement previously unknown. Suddenly staff members who had done the crud work to see to it that every last advance preparation had been made for a State Visit found themselves on the South Lawn of the White House ushering guests to their assigned places and getting a front-row look at the colorful welcome ceremony, complete with trooping the colors, gun salutes and welcoming speeches. More frequently they would be assigned upstairs, in the State Department's beautiful Diplomatic Reception Rooms, to assist diplomatic visitors attending a function with our Secretary of State. One of the rewards for this assistance was to get a close-up look at some marvelous clothing. The African delegations were especially gorgeous, the men clad in fabulous robes, caftans and sashes and the women wearing tight long skirts, fitted jackets with puff sleeves and regal headdresses, all made of stunning materials. Most fun of all was to escort a new ambassador to the White House for his meeting and accreditation with the President.

It was great to be included, and this spirit of inclusion represented what the Clintons were all about. In their recognition of my services at Blair House, I felt the warmth and generous spirit that they radiated.

Every year during Christmas month, when the White House was festooned with legendary holiday decorations, the Clintonites invited my staff to take a special tour, outside normal visiting hours. Some of the more experienced protocol staffers were asked to assist at the annual White House reception for the Diplomatic Corps, when the Clintons privately received each ambassador and spouse for a chat and photo opportunity. It was pretty heady stuff for some of us in Protocol to arrive in evening clothes as any other guest, and after some light duties (checking in the ambassadors) we were free to mingle in the East and State Rooms, partaking of refreshments and helping to make the ambassadors feel at home.

I readily justified my presence on one occasion. The British ambassador, Sir Christopher Meyer and Lady Meyer were distraught. They were far back in the queue winding its way from the East Room, through the Green Room and the Blue Room into the Clintons in the Red Room, but they had to catch a plane for London, and would have to leave "without seeing the President and we are very unhappy about this."

"Come with me," I said, mentally crossing my fingers, and walked them across the Grand Foyer and stopped just short of the entrance to the Red Room. I stood for a moment till I could catch the eye of one of the deputies of the Social Office who, after her initial shock at seeing me there, came out, and after having had the situation explained to her, went back in to consult with the Social Secretary. A few seconds afterwards the Clintons received the Meyers with open arms – and they made their plane to London.

My first impression of the Clintons never changed. I found Bill Clinton warm-hearted, fun and friendly, with a great sense of humor, and able to focus completely on the situation at hand. In contrast to his predecessors, he frequently used the house for special events, loved its history and intimacy, and never failed to express these sentiments with charming informality: "I just love this house," he sometimes said, standing in the doorway before paying attention to his guests. Once he wandered into the Blair Pantry during a reception, where, to the delight of Jose's staff, he conducted a quick caucus with his Vice President and advisors at one end, while our waiters continued their tasks at the other. I expect his spontaneity drove his staff, the U.S. Secret Service and White House personnel up the wall, since they had little idea of what he might be up to next.

At one cabinet meeting and lunch in 1994 we encountered a rather typical and funny Clinton incident when he and the Vice-President returned for the afternoon session from their own diet lunch of veggie burgers in the Oval Office. He asked me what we had offered his cabinet for lunch and when he heard the menu of Tortilla Soup, Grilled Marinated Chicken and Pineapple Salad, and Bitter Chocolate, Blood Orange, Raspberry, and Sour Cherry Sherbets he and Al Gore looked at each other and said "YES, PLEASE" – and roared with laughter, with the President teasing Al Gore about his choice of veggie burgers for their White House lunch. The President loved our Tortilla Soup and ate two helpings.

Hillary Clinton was more formal, much more disciplined, and could be tough to be around. I recall when a White House senior staff meeting was held in the Lee Dining Room, with heavyweights like David Gergen, Harold Ickes, Mac McLarty, George Stephanopoulos and Maggie Williams in attendance, and I overheard some of them catch hell from Mrs. Clinton for tardiness. But she was as fond of Blair House as her husband, and her personal staff was a delight. As she became beset with faultfinders and attackers, my admiration for her grew. Previous first ladies had been on the receiving end of various complaints, but Hillary Clinton got it for everything: for her looks; for her hair style; for changing her hair style; for wearing a hat during the inaugural parade; for her evening clothes; for changing the menus in the White House; for being involved up front in policy matters; but mostly, I believe, because she so vocally wanted to contribute to and continue her mission of ensuring social justice in this country. She was perceived as a threat, I believe, because she was far cleverer and brighter than most of the people who made hateful comments about her. While I expect many men were scared to death of her and her keen intelligence, I often wondered why some women expressed such hostility to her. Did they ever stop to think that women with Mrs. Clinton's brand of foresight and activism had won all of us the vote and various other basic rights of equality under the law? It was women like Mrs. Clinton who had paved the road that we females could now travel, who opened up opportunities far beyond those of motherhood and glorified housekeeper.

Hillary Clinton is an extraordinarily gifted woman who does not hide her talents, who dares to be different, a modern woman, the equal of any man, and therefore she had to be punished. How could we suppose that such a woman, an equal partner of her husband for 17 years, a woman who had "brought home the bacon," would or should suddenly disappear from view? We would not have expected it had the spouse been the First Husband, would we? And would we have talked about naked ambition had a first husband given a helping hand with health issues? Of course not, we would have said how nice it was that he could assist his busy wife.

I like to think that Barbara Bush was as staunch an advocate of equality between the sexes as was Hillary Clinton, but having come out of a very different environment and an older generation had chosen to exert her talents as a private advisor to her husband while looking after the home front. I well remember the student uproar when Wellesley College announced Barbara Bush would speak at the June 1990 Commencement. Some Wellesley students were outraged, as they perceived Mrs. Bush as a mere appendage to her husband. I was overjoyed at how Barbara Bush brought down the house with her closing words: "So I offer you today a new legend: The winner of the hoop race (referring to a Wellesley tradition) will be the first to realize her dream ... not society's dream ... her own personal dream. And who knows? Somewhere out in this audience may even be someone who will one day follow in my footsteps, and preside over the White House as the President's spouse. I wish him well."

When Mrs. Clinton came to the White House one aspect of the Bush legacy was under intense discussion.

It began in the last year of George and Barbara Bush: a State Dinner they gave for the President of Germany in April 1992. It was too "safe and comfortable" in the view of Anne Willan. "It's a shame," she said in an interview in the Washington Post. "The White House should be displaying the best of modern America, not 50-year old French cuisine. It is high time they got into salads." I know Anne from the 1960s, when she was food editor of the Washington Star. In those days she tried out her recipes on 18 of us who shared summer digs at Rehoboth Beach in Delaware. Founder of La Varenne Cooking School in Burgundy, France and author of over forty cookbooks, Anne knows her stuff.

The menu to which Anne referred was undoubtedly good fare, but safe and predictable: Supreme of Maine lobster with cucumber mousse and caviar sauce; saddle of veal with wild mushrooms, asparagus and carrots; spring salad; and pineapple champagne sorbet cake with guava sauce. In other words, fish, meat, salad and dessert and the use of masses of butter and cream.

In 1993, with a new administration in place, a group of American chefs exhorted Mrs. Clinton to end the long reign of foreign-born and/or foreign-trained executive chefs in the White House kitchen. They called for an era of American cuisine.

And Hillary Clinton listened. Walter Scheib was lured away from the Greenbrier Resort in West Virginia to create a White House cuisine that was innovative, healthy and delicious, and American to boot.

Although the White House had not yet configured its approach to foreign visits, Kim Young-Sam, President of the Republic of South Korea, staying at Blair House, was provided with a formal White House dinner in November 1993, Clinton's first for a foreign guest, and in effect a State Dinner. The guests comprised a cross-section of people in politics, the arts, the church and business. The menu was the result of consultation with distinguished chefs around the country, who were probably thrilled to be consulted. It was built around beef, the favorite food of the Korean president, and must have been scrumptious. Phyllis C. Richman of the Washington Post wrote the day after: "It offered enough fruits and vegetables to fulfill almost a day's worth under the new USDA dietary guidelines. It was seasonal, with acorn squash, litchis and clementines, and fashionable, from the tarragon tomato vinaigrette with the appetizer, to the ginger flavoring in the dessert. From the appetizer – shellfish mousse with pistachios made with only two quarts of cream for nearly 140 people, to the dessert, ginger almond ice cream made with 2 percent milk, it was an elegant promotion for the Clinton's health initiative."

"When I hired Chef Scheib," Mrs. Clinton wrote in her book, AN INVITATION TO THE WHITE HOUSE, "I asked him to make the food at the White House as good as that served in the best American restaurants. His recipes take their inspiration from regional American cuisine, and take advantage of the unprecedented variety of produce and products available year-round. The new White House cuisine showcases the best and freshest ingredients, combined in unusual and exciting ways, enhanced with light sauces, not overpowered by butter and cream. It is food that is lower in fat without sacrificing flavor." In addition, French service was eliminated, and all food was served on individual plates, American style. All the wine served was American as well.

The Clintons kept the incumbent White House Pastry Chef, Roland Mesnier. The legendary Mesnier concocted his desserts completely independent of the executive chef, and he continued to plan and prepare his elaborate, tasty, and distinctive treats. I was able to sample one of them when my boss, Chief of Protocol Mel French, invited me to go with her to a luncheon celebrating the Smithsonian's exhibition on the Vikings. I was among ninety Scandinavian guests in the White House State Room, including the King and Queen of Norway, the Crown Princess of Sweden, the Prime Minister of Finland, and the younger son of the Queen of Denmark. Dessert was sorbets served in chocolate replicas of Viking ships. M. Roland never repeated himself, and always surprised everyone including his bosses.

Mrs. Clinton's antagonists did not let the changes occur without showing their claws. But Scheib stayed, and lasted through the first George W. Bush term, although he was handed his walking papers in 2005. (Scheib says the parting was amicable.)

The Clintons faced constant sniping from disgruntled Republicans in newspapers and on TV talk shows about their entertaining: they did not do enough of it; they did not have State Dinners (a criticism based on rigid guidelines as to what comprised a "State Dinner"); they did not put on a grand enough show for foreign visitors invited for lunch or dinner; there was too little ceremony. In fact the Clintons had twice as many events and three times as many guests in their first year as the Reagans or Bushes had in any year and I expect the talk at the table to have been very substantial.

The Reagan and Bush administrations offered a series of standard packages to the official foreign visitor. A State Visit, honoring a chief of state such as a monarch or president and an Official Visit, honoring a head of government such as a prime minister, would include the following:

A morning welcoming ceremony on the White House South Lawn with a 21-gun salute for the chief of state, a 19-gun salute for a head of government; a lengthy meeting with the President; a State Dinner at the White House to which 14 members of the official foreign delegation were included in the 130 guests; after-dinner entertainment by famous American performers; several limousines with drivers, Secret Service protection for the duration of the visit; a luncheon hosted by the Secretary of State held at the Benjamin Franklin Room in the Diplomatic Reception Rooms at State; interpreters, and three nights' accommodation at Blair House.

Both chiefs of state and heads of government frequently were invited for an Official Working Visit, which included a meeting and luncheon with the President at the White House, several limousines with drivers, Secret Service protection for the duration of the visit; interpreters; and a two-night stay at Blair House. And a Visit included a limousine with driver, Secret Service protection, and a handshake and short meeting with the President but no accommodation. The Reagan and Bush administrations rigidly adhered to these packages. The Clinton White House would adopt most of them but allow great flexibility to accommodate individual requests.

The Clinton method of entertaining was different, that is true, but that they were inhospitable was ludicrous. Later, they instituted much larger dinners than ever before handled at the White House, putting up an enormous tent on the South Lawn for 700 guests, instead of the usual 130 in the State Room, where half the guests, high level staffers, had often dined before. They democratized the White House and, I say, bully for them. They were so creative, full of ideas, dining in various places in the White House, and with great attention to all details, as they showcased the best in American cuisine, as well as in the arts and crafts through their revolving exhibitions. (One element of this creativity displeased me: Mrs. Clinton took a liking to our set of Lenox base plates, made for Blair House, and insisted on borrowing them for far too many of her large dinners.)

History will record that it was the Clintons who banned smoking in all federal buildings. (The ban is still in force.) I was not surprised, however, when Capricia called to exempt Blair House from the ban. Mrs. Clinton knew full well that, much as we might want to, there was no way we could prevent our nicotine-addicted foreign visitors from lighting up. Such a ban would effectively mean a great shortage of visitors at the house.

The Clinton people had a profound influence on me over the course of their eight-year stay. I saw an unprecedented generosity of spirit; I saw an embrace of people from all walks of life; I saw a respect for all people in all circumstances; I saw that across the board warm hearts as well as brilliant minds were at work, and I loved it. In December 1994 I wrote Bill Black in San Diego who served in the first two years of President George H. W. Bush's administration as Assistant Chief of Protocol for Visits, inviting him to come by when he was next in Washington. I added: "And in case you are reluctant because of all the Clintonites please don't be – they are extraordinarily inclusive – we Republicans could learn much about this very endearing and human trait, which has made my life in Protocol most enjoyable."

Despite the changes that President Clinton triggered in my political beliefs, I remained a registered Republican until December 2007. Why? Because in my home state of New Mexico, I recall with great affection the party I trusted over thirty years ago when my political beliefs were first formed, and because I cherished the memory of the Republican Party as an honorable, fiscally-responsible, socially-progressive political organization. However, in December 2007 I switched; Hillary Clinton needed my vote in the primary, and I wanted so desperately to support her run for our presidency.

CHAPTER 13

THE MIDDLE EAST: TILTING AT WINDMILLS

"... it is time to put an end to decades of confrontation and conflict -----"

Excerpt from the Declaration of Principles
on Interim-Self-Government Arrangement

One month into the Clinton presidency we still had no visits – the justification for our existence – as Mr. Clinton wished to concentrate on domestic challenges. The British prime minister stayed at his own embassy and the Japanese, given our strained relationship at that time, did not want to be the first to stay with us.

However, foreign affairs frequently sneak up on our presidents. Soon we were into the most elaborate security preparations for the President of Egypt arriving on April 3, 1993.

Hosni Mubarak on earlier visits had declined the two nights offered at Blair House, not wishing to have to change accommodations midstream. This time, however, the U.S. Secret Service was taking no chances as threats against Mubarak were the highest in the world. A major player in the Middle East Peace Process and our ally in the Gulf War, Mubarak was seen as too cozy with the West by radical Muslims and had become their prime target; flyers distributed in Cairo and on this continent called for his assassination. The Service needed the house to properly protect him, and President Clinton invited Mubarak to stay with us for his entire stay. The Service assigned their most senior people to this visit; the boss, SAIC (Special Agent In Charge) of their DPD section (Diplomatic Protection Division) Buck Tannis was Detail Leader; Jonathan Miller was Lead Agent in charge of the 29 car motorcade with Mubarak's limousine unmarked by the usual U.S. and Egyptian flags. Half the cars were manned by armed agents. 17 USSS Uniformed Police were stationed on our side of Pennsylvania Avenue in addition to scores in Lafayette Park and in front of the White House along with Metropolitan Police and Mounted Police. Sharpshooters around the clock were stationed on neighboring rooftops, agents posted at intersections during motorcades, and fake motorcades at times moved on parallel streets to the president's motorcade. Our Front Door was locked, with visitors announced by telephone.

It was like a Clint Eastwood movie, only this was for real.

When President Mubarak returned six and one half months later, his protection intensified and Pennsylvania Avenue was closed to traffic for five days by the erection of large boulders at either end, a great imposition on Washingtonians who lost an important route to downtown. (In Egypt that August while sitting in his car, Mr. Mubarak was wounded by a potential assassin.)

A bizarre situation occurred when an Egyptian security officer leisurely jogging in our vicinity was stopped by the Uniformed Police who did not appreciate that he carried a loaded gun but no identification. Belligerently, the Egyptian reached for his gun; the officer reached for his baton; and our Head of Security, Lieutenant Waters, stepped in to sort it out.

President of Egypt since the assassination of President Anwar Sadat 12 years earlier, Mubarak, 65, established diplomatic relations with Israel in 1982. He continuously had to balance a western-oriented educated minority pursuing modernization and a conservative majority guided by traditional values and ways of life. His country's Air Force Commander in Chief when he became Anwar Sadat's vice president in 1975, Mubarak graduated from both of Egypt's Military and Air Academies, and was a fighter pilot training in the former Soviet Union. With a master's degree in sociology Suzie Mubarak was an energetic advocate for improved opportunities and education for women and children in Egypt; of Egyptian and Welsh parents, she was 14 years younger than her husband and only 17 when they married. I noticed how deeply they cared for each other and had a loving and close relationship with their two sons.

President Mubarak, our most frequent Middle Eastern visitor, came nine times as Mr. Clinton's guest. His arrival on a Saturday after lunch and departure 4-6 days later was followed with few variations. On arrival he settled down in the Lee Drawing Room with his ministers and his ambassador of seven years, the affable and effective Ahmed Maher El Sayed, (later his foreign minister), enjoying coffee, tea sandwiches and cakes, before going upstairs to his private quarters, not to appear again till the next morning. Mrs. Mubarak accompanied him a few times; their older son Alaa, a banker, and his wife came twice with their two babies. But it was nearly always Gamal, his younger son, who was at his dad's side.

Jose crossed himself and rendered thanks when he saw the name of Omar, the valet, on the rooming-list, knowing the instructions as to the president's wishes would be both correct and timely. When another valet, indecisive and afraid to ask his master directly what he wanted, accompanied Mubarak, Jose was cross. Gamal Mubarak, at that time a banker in London, made an excellent substitute for the impossible valet, but was only applied to in the direst circumstances. The president was modest in his wishes, though, enjoying grilled cheese as well as tuna salad sandwiches. We supplied honey in sealed jars and bottles left corked – for safety reasons. The president enjoyed our Vermont Feta Cheese so much he brought 16 pounds back with him. On his night off our generous Jose took Omar shopping for the delegation; once, more than 200 bottles of cheap hair shampoo, eye and ear drops were bought. And on Omar's afternoon off Jose put him on the metro; at a certain station he was met by Jose's wife, who took him shopping for our "wonderful American bed linens."

President Mubarak was jovial and humorous, the butt being Sean who usually attended the television crews in Jackson Place. When the president walked in for the first of his three television interviews, he looked at Sean's tummy: "Have you had any breakfast yet?" and after the interview, he patted Sean's tummy and asked him if he had had any lunch yet. He learned Sean's name and mercilessly teased him, asking him what he had for lunch, and how big his portion was. At a later visit Mubarak ignored the greeting and outstretched hand of Steven Hurst of CNN, and instead walked over to Sean: "How are you, my friend. I have been looking all over for you." This banter continued during the years.

While television interviews at the house were made possible as a convenience to our busy guests, the Secret Service never permitted President Mubarak to do them elsewhere. He held several during each visit, all in the Jackson Place Houses.

He was attended by his foreign minister, economic minister, spokesman, press secretary, and ambassador. With the delegation members listening around the rooms, his security agents and the Secret Service agents placed in strategic position inside and outside, and our own security officer posted at the 700 Jackson Place entrance door, not to forget the television crew stationed behind the cameras and lights, the space was packed.

This "moderate" dictator was surrounded by military and loyal friends. His National Security Advisor Osama El-Baz and his Chief of Staff General Aziz came every time; his personal aide, General Sofi, came frequently. Once, he and Chief of Protocol Bakir, straight from Paris, brought me greetings from the French Chief of Protocol who had referred to me as a "lady who knows exactly what is going on and never misses a thing."

The Egyptians were fun, closely inspecting everybody wearing a skirt and showing legs. Their security complained about our lack of exotic television channels. They were rather rude to the maids upstairs, inclined to snap their fingers at our ladies, – a class thing, as well as the unavoidable gender discrimination; their deputy chief of protocol snapped his fingers at me as well – and I just ignored him. Fortunately during these repeat visits our staff and the Egyptians got well acquainted, and increasingly would greet each other by name and with pleasure. The visits were labor intensive inasmuch as President Mubarak, especially during the first few visits, rarely left the house. They kept our kitchen hopping, drank enormous amounts of coffee and tea, and snacked incessantly. A staggering statistics from one visit: during five days 67 cases of soft drinks – 1608 bottles – were consumed, while the pantry help washed up constantly.

The Blair Drawing Rooms were packed with staff, while the president held meetings in the Lee Drawing Room. One six-day July visit, with excessive heat outside and heavy smoking inside, was unbearable – hot, stinky, and smelly. Our air conditioning system was not up to such abuse, and Foreign Minister Amr Moussa complained about the heat. I could only reply that "it does not help that you all smoke like chimneys."

Over the years little changed in the Egyptian visits, basically the same staffers came every time except for new security personnel which brought its own challenges; I found Houseman Frankie Blair on post at the Front Door – standing up. He had been told to remove the chairs to "make more room for our president." As Frankie, per my request, moved the chairs back I explained that for six visits President Mubarak had been able to walk past the chairs in the greatest of comfort and I was certain he could do so again. Upstairs Teresinha was barred from and the new guys wanted keys to the Primary Suite. "Why suddenly now after six successful visits does your president need a key?" General Aziz sorted them out.

One Mubarak visit kept being extended. Mrs. Mubarak was checked into the hospital for tests and an operation; Gamal flew in from London to remain in Washington during his mother's recuperation. President Clinton invited the president to remain at Blair House for as long as he wished in order to be near his wife. Meanwhile in the kitchen our parsimonious Chef only ordered enough food at a time to take care of 24 hours. Jose similarly lived from day to day regarding wait staff, and I tried to shift schedules so each staff member could have half a day off.

President Mubarak became the unavoidable catalyst for everyone involved in the Middle East Peace Process; although he had fought against Israel, he also inherited from his predecessor, Anwar Sadat, a country increasingly friendly towards the West and the beneficiary of enormous sums of money from the United States – not too popular with his neighbors or with Muslim extremists; Egypt for years was suspended from the Arab League. Mubarak, the ultimate moderate Arab leader of his time, had a foot firmly in each of the competing worlds; he was the one called in to sit at the table.

Bill Clinton worked tirelessly trying to effect an acceptable outcome. Scores of intense discussions were held at Blair House, and during the Mubarak visits we were hopping. The American Jewish and Arab Community leaders came. King Hussein of Jordan frequently stopped by, as did the various prime ministers of Israel. The Saudi ambassador and Members of Congress and the press popped in and out as well as Mr. Clinton's Middle East negotiators. It was a fascinating time.

In Israel Yitzhak Rabin had succeeded Yitzhak Shamir as prime minister in the summer of 1992 – like day following night. Shamir, leader of the conservative Likud party and a product of the Jewish ghetto and the Holocaust, was convinced that the whole world was against the Jews; this manifested itself in the wish to deal with the Palestinian conflict without American involvement and a belief in Israeli statehood as the only means by which people of Jewish faith could have any roots. Rabin, leader of the Labor party, and the first Israeli-born prime minister believed that Israel had made enough friends and coalitions in the world to compromise and find mutually acceptable solutions instead of unilateral ones.

Within nine months of Mr. Rabin taking office the secret talks between Israel and the PLO, the Oslo Accord, had culminated in Norway in August 1993 with a declaration of principles. The Washington Post on September 22, 1993 summarized the agreement: mutual recognition, and Israeli withdrawal from Gaza and Jericho, the first agreement ever between Israeli and Palestinian leaders. And reporting the meeting at the White House under the headlines: "Israel and PLO Sign Peace Pact" Tom Shales wrote: "It all came down to a handshake – then the President took a small step back and spread his arms, almost messianically, almost but not quite touching Rabin and Arafat, and this was the cue. Rabin and Arafat shook hands and all the eyes in the world seemed to be on them as those two hands shook."

A year later, Prime Minister Rabin, Foreign Minister Peres, and PLO Chairman Yasir Arafat were awarded the Nobel Peace Prize.

The Rabins had dined at Blair House during the Reagan administration, but their first overnight visit came in November 1993. Leah Rabin was such fun and interested in everything. She wanted the Primary Suite very hot, with the fireplaces going, and extra heating elements in the bathrooms. We also readied a tray in the suite with Black Label and Soda for him and Campari for her.

They had a scheduled 45 minutes visit to the Holocaust Museum, and I asked if I could come too.

I returned one hour later, drained to the core. I had walked in there, in the wake of the Rabins and 30 other descendants and survivors of the Holocaust, and wondered if anyone was as overpowered as I was, or whether this was such an integral part of their own history and therefore more familiar, and no longer scary. My early childhood was filled with the stories of courageous Danes, including my mother, risking their lives to hide the Danish Jews and help them flee to Sweden, referred to by both President Clinton and Vice President Gore when the museum opened the previous April.

But nothing had prepared me for the walk across a bridge under which was a pile of shoes, worn, burnt and of all sizes – the only remnants after their owners had been gassed and burnt; for the walls plastered by photos of the Lithuanian villagers throughout decades, until suddenly, after September 1941, there were no more. The Nazis shot 3,500 inhabitants in two days. I walked by the cattle cars which transported the Jews to the concentration camps and the gas chambers – it seemed surrealistic, except it wasn't. And I stood before the world map, listing individuals in other countries who so bravely had done their best to save the lives of Jews. I read it slowly, and noted that Denmark was the only nation named, thus encompassing all Danes for having assisted the Danes of Jewish faith. Five names were singled out – and I was stunned to see my father's first cousin, Gerda Valentiner, listed; she had a safe house in Copenhagen, and afterwards was made an honorary citizen of the State of Israel.

This was the nicest of many Israeli visits, led by an extraordinary individual, an old warrior, a distinguished military man, and former ambassador to the U.S. Mr. Rabin became his country's first native-born prime minister in 1974, later its Defense Minister and returned as its prime minister in 1992, and now pragmatic peace maker. Yitzhak and Leah Rabin must have been very successful in influencing their delegation and embassy staff; they were all so easy and unassuming. They requested little, including laundry and dry-cleaning; their nation had no servants; they "did for themselves." They returned for a quick visit in March 1994.

At the White House on Monday, July 25, 1994, witnessed by President Clinton, King Hussein and Prime Minister Rabin shook hands over an agreement to end the 46-year state of war between Jordan and Israel and to work together for peace in the Middle East.

President Clinton walked King Hussein and Prime Minister Rabin across to Blair House to celebrate this monumental event. They lunched, each with four close advisors, in the Lee Dining Room. The U.S. participants were Vice President Al Gore, Secretary of State

Warren Christopher, National Security Advisor Anthony Lake, and David Satterfield of the NSC.

The White House advance team had debated how to seat the group so as to give equal importance to the two principal guests. I loved working with the Clinton staffers; they never minded suggestions; this time they followed mine: placing President Clinton at the end of the table, with King Hussein on his right and Mr. Rabin on his left. "This way, not only can there be no ruffled feathers as the President is between the two VIPs, but when seated at the head of the table he does not have to crane his neck addressing his guests, and the two guests have an equal chance of talking with each other across the table. Besides which," I added, "the photo opportunity will be superb from the Lee Drawing Room double door."

An additional 75 participants in this momentous agreement enjoyed a buffet lunch in the Garden Room.

In the Lee Dining Room the atmosphere of relief was strong; the smiles approached grins, with the Israeli Ely Rubenstein issuing a flow of small talk which had them all roaring with laughter. After President Clinton saw off his guests in the Front Hall he thanked me profusely: "It has been so special after all the work we have been doing this morning at the White House, to come over here to Blair House to relax."

Three months later on the Israeli-Jordanian border the treaty was signed, thus formally ending the over forty year state of war and beginning a broad partnership of neighbors.

Our next participation in the Middle East Peace Process came on Sunday, February 12, 1995: Blair House was the stage of a last minute, logistically mind boggling, "shuttle" diplomacy between the Israelis, the Jordanians, and the PLO with Secretary of State Warren Christopher moving between the participants. President Clinton arrived directly from church services, and used the prestige of his office on this day, as he did for the following five years, to effect a positive outcome.

The Blair House Declaration, following this unprecedented meeting of the Foreign Ministers of Israel, Egypt, Jordan, and a leading representative of the Palestine Liberation Authority, with involvement of President Clinton and Vice President Gore, agreed that there can be no real peace in the region without security and stability, and reaffirmed the importance of fostering economic development and investment, and a general agreement on the need to build bridges between peoples, to overcome barriers to understanding, and to share information and expertise to deal with common problems. Most importantly, the parties pledged to work to ensure that there can be no turning back in the Arab-Israeli peace process.

That was the official story.

Earlier I had danced a tightrope dance. The day before, I spent four hours, off and on the phone, with White House aides who insisted on changing everything already agreed upon during five different advance meetings and walk-thrus on the Friday. On the Sunday further requests for changes continued. I dealt with some sixty people each with an opinion or two from the White House Presidential Scheduler; Presidential Advance; Presidential Press and WHCA, the White House Communications Office; National Security Council personnel; not to mention Vice President Gore's staffers; the U.S. Secret Service; and the Office of the Secretary of State; the Near East Bureau; and the Public Affairs Office of the State Department; with the individual Desk Officers each looking out for his or her country's interest: Israel, Egypt, Jordan and the PLO, not to forget my own colleagues in the Protocol Office; each country delegation was assigned a Visits Officer. More than one hundred persons from these groups spent that Sunday at Blair House and this number drastically increased the minute the President joined the meetings; his accompanying staff always included his medical doctor and his military aide with the Black Bag, giving the President instant access to the Nuclear Button. The entire complex was buzzing.

Being Ramadan our Muslim visitors were not permitted to eat during the day so we placed trays of sandwiches and cookies for the Americans and Israelis behind a screen in the Jackson Place Dining Room, and I enjoyed seeing our distinguished and rather distant Secretary of State hiding behind a door munching on chocolate cookies.

By September 1995 the White House was planning the historic signing of the Israel-Palestinian Agreement when Israel pledged to turn over land to the Palestine Liberation Authority. Chief of Protocol Molly Raiser had instructed me that "Secretary Christopher wishes to use Blair House for his meetings and functions with the thirteen foreign ministers attending this important event." However, as soon as I heard that President Mubarak and King Hussein were invited to be the prime witnesses my antenna went up. I called my boss. "Ambassador, I am certain the Secret Service will not permit Mr. Mubarak to stay in a hotel," and I proceeded to give her the background of his first visit a few months before she was appointed. But she was adamant: the National Security Council had decreed that only the Secretary of State could use the house at this time.

I remained skeptical, and so certain was I in my assumption that I directed Mrs. Rennie to prepare all bedrooms and alerted the others; I dug out the schedule and events during the last Mubarak visit to use as a guideline; I prepared my order for flowers; – and I waited.

On Monday afternoon, before the important event the following Thursday, I received the call: "Mrs. V, guess what: President Mubarak has been invited to stay at Blair House and is arriving at 8:40 am on Wednesday. Do the best you can." Naturally the thought "I told you so" never occurred to me! Within ten minutes my staff was packed together in my office, pen and paper in hand.

It never was a surprise to me how fast this diverse, multi cultural and multi lingual staff could rise to the occasion. My people frequently, because of those very differences, squabbled, and were at each other's throats, but never when the chips were down. "Chef, do the best you can – here are the meal numbers from the last visit. I shall inform you of times later. Count on breakfast on arrival, but make it light. They have traveled all night." And Chef left to write menus, order in his food, and line up his extra part-timers. "Jose: here are the numbers from last time. Get help in and if you need someone to give a hand tomorrow ask one of your waiters to come in. Again, set up for a light breakfast. If they don't want it, the tables are ready for lunch." "Mrs. Rennie: let us congratulate ourselves that we prepared for this." "Lieutenant Waters, could you keep Secret Service and Diplomatic Security out of my hair, do you think, and deal with them alone?" And I went down the list. We were totally winging it with no information at all except time of arrival.

The bilateral meetings at the White House started early on Thursday, September 28. President Clinton met each party at staggered times, beginning with Chairman Arafat, followed by Prime Minister Rabin, President Mubarak and King Hussein. Then President Clinton met with all of them together in the Oval Office, followed by a giant press conference in the East Room, also involving the Foreign Ministers of Russia, Spain, and Norway (Russia was the unavoidable party; Spain hosted the Madrid Peace Conference in October 1991; Oslo was the site for the secret negotiations between Israel and the PLO.)

Later in the day President Clinton and the four principals hosted a reception at the Corcoran Gallery for Jewish and Arab Community Leaders. At Blair House everyone involved had popped in for meetings, meals, or tea with the Egyptian president. King Hussein, that grand and gracious King, came for breakfast; Chairman Arafat, scruffy and unprepossessing, came for a meeting; I actually was rather excited about meeting someone who was referred to as "the little terrorist." Following the Corcoran Gallery reception we were surprised by Israel's prime minister and foreign minister coming up the stairs, invited by President Mubarak to come back with him.

It was the last time I would see Yitzhak Rabin. Coming up the front steps he looked up, saw me at the door, and burst into a great smile. I received a hug, and a little chat about his wife. Later in the Blair Drawing Room my deputy, Randy Bumgardner, asked Foreign Minister Peres to autograph his new book, which the minister did with great gusto and fanfare, making Mr. Rabin laugh. Randy exclaimed: "I have never heard you laugh before, Mr. Prime Minister," to which the prime minister, in that deep, gruff voice, replied: "I do not have much to laugh about."

I could not accept this. Prime Minister Rabin, the soldier, warrior, statesman, had put heart and soul into moving beyond boundaries set by decades of hatred and mistrust, even shaking hands with his old enemy at the White House two years earlier. I hoped he had some sense of accomplishment despite the cynicism which I expect everyone living in that particular region were born with.

Saturday, November 4, 1995 was a day, which for me, to paraphrase President Franklin D. Roosevelt 54 years earlier "will live in infamy forever." I was listening to the radio when the announcement came of the assassination of Yitzhak Rabin at a huge peace rally in Tel Aviv by a Jewish anti-peace extremist. My tears flowed, uncontrollable in their vigor, and my grief for the faltering Peace Process in that troubled region, which, finally, had seemed to be moving ahead, was profound. And etched on my mind, forever, is the expression on the face of Leah Rabin and those of her husband's closest aides, known to me, shown on television during his funeral.

Within five weeks of Rabin's tragic death, Acting Prime Minister Shimon Peres, former foreign minister and architect of the Oslo Accord, came for an intensely emotional visit. Everyone was in shock. Their security was even tighter, and only after my meeting with their new head of security did my staff gain access to the Primary Suite.

Peres addressed a Joint Session of Congress. His intonations, voice, the pauses he made in his speech contributed to emotional moments. In between short sentences conveying sentiments and statements regarding the Peace Process, he interspersed: "And Rabin is no more – And Yitzhak has gone – My senior partner is gone – And he, the captain, is no more – The singer, not the song, was killed." He also, unintentionally, according to his speechwriter Ambassador Yehuda Avner, impressed upon Congress the role of the United States, forced upon us and inescapable, as the leader of the free world. He said: "Yitzhak and I were always firm believers in the greatness of America, in the ethic and generosity inherent in your history, in your people. For us, the United States of America is a commitment to values before an expression of might."

Mr. Peres warmly thanked the United States for the unprecedented show of support and strength for Israel in the U.S. delegation attending the funeral of Prime Minister Rabin. The visit was intense, with no breaks, and with an undemanding principal guest who ate and drank sparingly. Only the last evening did he turn to me: "Now I need a Scotch – and please make it a double" – and when it came he gulped it down.

At departure Mr. Peres took my hands in his and gravely thanked me. "Mr. Prime Minister, could I ask for the most tremendous favor?" He stiffened. "And what is that?" "Would you please bring from the Blair House staff our love and greetings to Mrs. Rabin. I did write her from all of us, but it is much more meaningful if our sentiments are brought personally by you." He visibly relaxed, and assured me he would do so gladly. I saw Leah Rabin at a book signing in Washington D.C. a few years later, just a short time before her death from lung cancer, and was struck by her frailty.

The Rabin visits were in complete contrast to all others from

Israel. Increasingly the visitors became unpleasant as the arrogance, boorishness, rudeness, sloppiness and lack of manners increased on the part of most of the Israelis having access to the house. After the Peres visit I sent a memo to my chief of protocol:

"In addition to us having to feed the entire embassy staff breakfast, lunch, and dinner, and in between what amounted to a feeding frenzy of snacks, they augmented their incredibly sloppy bathroom culture with circumventing ashtrays and dropping the smoldering ashes into wastepaper baskets, and generally continuing their practice of piling up their dirty glasses and cups on any surface in the Embassy Office, obviously finding the few steps to the trays provided for same far too exhausting. They then had the gall to chew out my staff for not cleaning up after them!

While the prime minister checked out before 4 pm, some delegation members and most embassy staff stayed on (till wheels up later), with some embassy personnel having a tryst in Room 26, and one demanding shampoo and as bold as brass taking over Room 25, having a long hot shower and leaving a trail of dirty towels all over the just cleaned and spotless bathroom. Jose tells me that he put out all the left-over finger sandwiches half an hour before embassy staff departure, and was shocked to see them shoveling and pushing each other to get at the table. This in no way applies to Prime Minister Peres and his delegation, but only to the embassy staff."

In May 1996 leader of the Israeli Likud party, Binyamin Netanyahu, narrowly defeated Mr. Peres as the Israelis, following several terrorist bombings, chose security over peace. Prime Minister Netanyahu took a hard line approach, increasing the potential for violence in the region, as the Palestinians saw their dream of land for peace fade.

Educated in American high school and universities, and with a business background in Boston, Bibi Netanyahu, celebrated among conservative Americans, was bright, intelligent, and a skilled politician using the American system to his advantage, impressing everyone with his perfect American accent, his oratorical style and telegenic performances. He played our Congress like a violin. He also, according to my confidential source, "engages in classic bullying" and was described as "shameless and dangerous." He played a key role in bringing on the Second Intifada, and was, I believe, more than anyone responsible for the collapse of the Oslo Peace Accords as his government pushed ahead with settlements on the West Bank.

I listened to remarks addressed to Netanyahu by members of the American-Jewish organizations and our more confrontational opinion makers: "Well done, Bibi, well done – congratulations." A large segment of American Jews had worked ceaselessly and openly for his victory, without regard to expense and effort, taking out countless newspaper ads, demonstrating before the White House and in other places, and holding concerts, rallies and writing newspaper articles voicing their orthodox view of Israel. I was seething, watching their jubilation, their smirking and joy, and thinking to myself: "It was your words and public support which helped influence a young radical to murder Rabin. You "held" the gun that killed him."

Words indeed have consequences.

Netanyahu, arrogant and overbearing, rarely was gracious during the staff goodbyes, which he obviously found too irksome, never putting down his briefcase when signing the guestbook, or looking any of us in the eye. His wife was pushy and bitchy. One particular incident stands out. Mrs. Rennie and I had checked on her and her comfort no less than three times during the first morning before her lunch with Mrs. Clinton. Mrs. Clinton's personal assistant, Capricia Marshall called me that Sara Netanyahu was cold, and why had we not made her comfortable? I learned later my sentiments regarding this woman were shared by a large number of Americans involved in the Peace Process.

The Netanyahus returned several times, usually at 2 am. They traveled with their two small unsmiling boys and a nanny. And Mrs. Netanyahu always accompanied her husband; even to the 1998 Peace Conference at Wye Plantation when the White House had specifically asked that no spouses attend. I learned that as the prime minister had been twice married before and known to have a roving eye, she was not going to let him out of her sight. So there she was – like a leech. The Eisenhower Room was assigned as a playroom until one little boy climbed our antique screen with the nanny paying no attention. This seemed odd as his mother held an advanced degree in child psychology; had a reputation as a neat freak; forced everyone to wash hands before touching the children; and did not allow them to play on the floor.

A 48 hour Middle East Summit September 30, 1996 came out of the blue. Progress toward implementing the Oslo agreement had come to a virtual halt since Netanyahu's victory, and became especially cantankerous when the Israelis opened a tunnel close to the sacred place in Jerusalem known to Jews as the Temple Mount and to Arabs as Haram al-Sharif.

The Israelis, the Jordanians, the Egyptians, and the Palestine Liberation Organization met with the United States delegation members, using the entire complex for holding rooms, office space, and separate meals. Emotions among the participants such as exhaustion, resignation, patience, and annoyance were the order of the day – or night rather. During the intense round the clock negotiations Mrs. Rennie was concerned that "there is a man in the Primary bed." That was just carrying it too far, I thought, so I tiptoed up to see who the offending party was – none other than U.S. Ambassador to Israel Martin Indyk, who was, naturally, left in peace. His exhaustion was understandable. While the PLO delegates were difficult, I noticed several times our U.S. participants furious and exasperated with the Israelis; and with both parties when they dug themselves into mutually exclusive diplomatic positions. A few weeks later the all important Wye, Maryland summit took place, with President Clinton presiding, and King Hussein gallantly breaking off his cancer treatments to lend a helping hand. One remark from these meetings stands out:

King Hussein to Prime Minister Netanyahu: "Arrogance gets you nowhere. Wisdom and vision will. Your predecessor paid for same with his life." The King followed up with a scathing public letter five months later criticizing the harsh policies and attitudes of Netanyahu. Even President Mubarak said to Charlie Rose in his television interview at Blair House in March 1997: "Netanyahu ought to resign." We were not quite free of him yet, though; he, his wife, the two boys and an entire delegation came end of September 1998 for a pit stop of 6 hours, and managed to mess up much of the house in the process.

Other Middle East visitors provided some change. Predominantly Muslim Turkey had elected its first woman prime minister, Tansu Ciller, described as a modern, highly educated and clever woman; I was truly looking forward to her visit.

And what a disappointment she was!

Dressed in identically cut suits made of different materials and colors changed after each meeting, this sexy babe, the Prime Minister of Turkey, certainly made an impression on her mostly male visitors from the U.S. Cabinet, World Bank and International Monetary Fund. At the house she was demanding, imperious and inconsiderate of her staffers who were scared to death of her, and thus extended their dissatisfaction to my staff.

But all of our small frustrations paled when their chief of protocol made the most startling pronouncement. Late Friday afternoon I had just congratulated myself that soon she would be out for the evening; then another light schedule Saturday morning; and then – Hasta la Vista, Baby! He said sheepishly: "President Clinton today invited my prime minister to remain at Blair House through the weekend, so we shall be leaving you Monday instead of tomorrow morning." After catching my breath I called Chief of Protocol Molly Raiser who made a gallant effort to reach Mr. Clinton in order to verify the truth of this. She could not reach him, and thus: "Mrs. V, I have to make a judgment call and approve this. I really do not wish to make a liar out of the prime minister." But, she continued, "Do the minimum that you can get away with."

My staff, disliking this particular delegation, was in tears – and Mrs. Rennie, normally the sunniest tempered individual, became quite agitated: "I now know that we shall all go to Heaven, for surely we are being punished on Earth."

I had more reasons to be disgusted: aides had gone with the prime minister's college age son to Nordstroms to buy a suit; Marinete was ordered to alter the pants in the waist and to shorten them, but under no circumstances to cut into the fabric; young son accompanied his parents to a big dinner that night; Sunday Marinete was ordered to reverse the process, and on Monday the suit was returned to Nordstroms. Ambassador Raiser later asked our President about his alleged invitation to Tansu Ciller to remain at Blair House. He definitely did not think, she told me, he had invited Ciller to stay on, but did remember that she felt she "was being pushed out" of the house, and that he might have tried to smooth over this. Well, after those four days it was quite plain that this particular prime minister arranged life according to her wishes – at all times.

Soon another spoilt ruler arrived, but at least one with gracious manners. His Royal Highness Abdullah Bin Abdulaziz Al-Saud, Crown Prince, Deputy Prime Minister and Commander of the National Guard – and effective ruler – of Saudi Arabia arrived September 23, 1998. In 1989 the State Visit of King Fahd Bin Abdulaziz Al-Saud, the Crown Prince's half brother, was cancelled a few days before arrival, but my notes were still helpful. Their diet consisted of lamb, chicken, beef, rice, vegetables especially cucumber, lettuce, tomatoes, green peppers, eggplant and fruits; yoghurt, honey, nuts and absolutely no alcoholic beverages served.

I was spared one aspect though: in 1989 the U.S. chief of protocol informed me that the King could not be photographed shaking hands with a woman; my deputy, Sam Castleman, should be in the doorway on arrivals and departures. I had inquired at the time if perhaps I had better stay at home – imagining a lovely couple of days of leisure – but the ambassador would have none of that. "Just stay out of public view" and – "all female employees must be modestly dressed with long sleeves and showing little leg."

However, this time, with the King's half brother in charge, things had eased up a bit. I was permitted to greet on arrival and advised during the excellent advance staff work that the Saudis "understand the role of women in your society, and that women will be looking after all the bedrooms." I reminded my staff to be discreet, flexible, and understanding of the cultural differences.

The instructions from the embassy were clear: The Lee Drawing Room was chosen as His Royal Highness's "throne room." Our power sofa was replaced by two armchairs, behind which was placed the Saudi flag. One of our mirrors was replaced with a portrait of the Saudi King. The regular sofa table remained, and the two armchairs were separated by a square table borrowed from the Foreign Minister's suite; no oval shapes were permitted. Mixed nuts, Kleenex boxes, incense bowls were scattered through the room, and the dining room chairs were used for the King's visitors.

Two 35" televisions were supplied by the embassy for the Primary Suite, and two 61" sets for the Embassy Offices, as well as a leather barber chair (ours not being elegant enough.) The royal valet brought the Crown Prince's own towels, sheets, blankets, and extensive amenities such as gilded Kleenex boxes, and we borrowed a full length free standing mirror from the White House. The instructions included the temperature in the bedroom; the head of the bed raised by 3 inches; the mattress on the firm side. While I was asked to do extra flowers, the Saudis still had delivered enormous, expensive and, in my opinion, rather ostentatious flower arrangements, suitable only for our Library. The Saudis, and other Arab leaders enjoy ostentation, and I was not surprised when former Secretary of State Henry Kissinger mentioned to me the late Egyptian President Anwar Sadat's derisive comments about the "Blair Palace" – our charming but in their eyes ridiculously small guesthouse.

The valet requested a bed outside the Crown Prince's bedroom; Moroccan by birth, he was fluent in Spanish and French, helpful in the extreme, so he and Jose were soon joined at the hip.

His Royal Highness dined at midnight. His medical team from Canada and New Zealand explained that due to excessive heat in Riyadh the Saudis work short hours, eat at 4 pm, sleep till midnight when they have their family meal, and then dose off again around 5 am. It was to be our privilege to experience those hours at Blair House.

The Saudi ambassador, His Royal Highness Prince Bandar bin Sultan bin Abd al-Aziz Al Saud had been in Washington so long that officially he was the Dean of the Diplomatic Corps, though noticeably absent from such duties, earning him the nickname of "the Invisible Ambassador." He was, however, as helpful as I, having known him for years, expected. He would provide the midnight meal while our kitchens prepare the afternoon meal for the delegation served around 4 pm, with an omelet sent up to His Royal Highness.

I watched from afar when at 1 am the first night His Royal Highness and his ministers, all princes, dined. Fingers digged into the common food bowls, were licked between each journey, and after the Crown Prince left to go upstairs for the night, the Saudi security took over, happily digging their fingers into what had been stirred up a few minutes earlier by royal fingers. Three waves of security took turns at the leftovers before Jose could clean up at 3 am.

While the princes stayed at the Hay Adams Hotel, with only the Crown Prince and his household staff at Blair House, the entire delegation spent the day with us. Dressed in their native garb complete with keffiyeh and agal, they were polite, immaculately groomed, portly, manicured, with the softest hands and weak and pudgy faces – as if they had never faced real adversity and therefore had built no character into their features. They were the most pampered, by tradition and right, of all our visitors. Speaking only his native tongue of Arabic the Crown Prince was fairly typical, I was told, of most of the senior Saudi princes in that he received only a traditional, informal education with little travel. He lived the traditional existence of the royal princes: he was privileged beyond imagination. I also learned he commanded considerable knowledge about regional affairs, and like all Arabs was not pleased with the failure of the U.S. to apply pressure on Israel to further the Middle East Peace Process. He was said to be very sensitive to protocol.

Clearly he was not comfortable in our western setting, and definitely totally put out during our farewells. Prince Bandar had approved this ceremony. Therefore we were stunned when, after stiff and silent farewells by the Crown Prince, shaking hands with the staff but increasingly becoming red in the face, he sat down to sign the guestbook. He froze in front of it, suddenly stood up, threw the pen down, and stomped out of the house. I expect that the humiliation of having come face to face with mere servants and – heaven forbid – have to shake their hands, was too, too much. Fortunately Prince Bandar, always quick on his feet, assured us all was well, grabbed our guestbook, and promised to have it signed before the Crown Prince took off from AAFB.

In Jordan, Abdullah Bin Al Hussein, King of Jordan since his father's death early 1999, ruled with his beautiful, smart, and forward looking Palestinian born Queen Rania. In May that year the King came with his family to introduce himself to the U.S., and to stress the continuity of his father's foreign policy as well as asking American business to invest in his needy country. Having a British mother Abdullah was trained at Sandhurst Military Academy in England, and was commander of Jordan's Special Forces until his elevation to the throne. The King is very like his father in his politeness and the kindness he exudes and blessed with the common touch. When he saw our chefs grilling meats in the Garden for his staff's lunch he asked if he could join them, and consumed four hamburgers – later telling our chief of protocol they were wonderful. His father also had loved the Blair hamburgers.

His visit coincided with the Israeli elections and an interesting moment came when the King was handed a cell phone by his chief of protocol who just said: "Mr. Barak" and my staff overheard the King congratulating Mr. Barak on his election as Prime Minister of Israel, and assuring him that "we will stand by you through thick and thin." I missed this visit as I was in Nantucket with my husband of one year, but was so keen on the election in Israel that I followed the returns carefully, and – almost – "danced on the table" when Ehud Barak's victory over Mr. Netanyahu was announced. I was later told that in Washington during our administration's similar celebration Chief of Protocol Mary Mel French and the Assistant Secretary of State for the Near East Martin Indyk were congratulating each other and discussing that no one could have been happier than they were – when they suddenly stopped, looked at each other, and both exclaimed: "Except for Mrs. V at Blair House."

Prime Minister Ehud Barak came during the summer of 1999 for six nights; such a glorious difference from Netanyahu – a total delight, immensely polite and appreciative. As some in his delegation had been on staff with Yitzhak Rabin it was a personal and charming experience for us. However, improved though the general atmosphere was, I did find that there is something in the Israeli culture which has left behind certain mechanical courtesies such as the way one eats, behaves in the bathroom, tidies up after oneself. I put it down to the earlier lifestyle of living precariously and therefore with no time for life's niceties. But by the same token I think it is time they all acquire some polish, and learn to smell the roses.

The election of Ehud Barak, deeply committed to the peace process, certainly presented, per Henry Kissinger: "an unprecedented opportunity for Middle East peace." This visit, July 14-20, 1999, was long, and intensely packed with events, especially many extra ones with President and Mrs. Clinton including a night at Camp David and a large dinner at the White House.

The Peace Process continued. While Israel had traded peace for land since its conception I expected, with Mr. Barak's election, a more diplomatic and less belligerent approach as prior to his first visit at Blair House Barak had met with Palestinian leader Yasir Arafat on the border of Israel and the Gaza Strip for the first time. Ehud Barak was the most decorated soldier in the history of the Israeli army with an impressive list of exploits to his name as a commando leader. These included the liquidation in Beirut of the PLO members believed responsible for the death of the Israeli athletes during the 1972 Olympic Games in Munich. He also was a musician with a predilection for Beethoven, and rumored to be President Clinton's equal in cerebral powers. There was such hope for the future of the Middle East when his coming to power overlapped with Bill Clinton's.

Now Israel also had a real chance of peace with Syria and settling the issue of the Golan Heights occupied by Israel since the 1967 war. Thus, at Blair House during December 1999 when large holiday receptions had been planned and two visits from the Ukraine and Kazakhstan respectively were expected, and our Executive Chef Ian Knox had worked feverishly to prepare and fill his freezers, President Clinton announced to the world that important peace negotiations between Israel and Syria would shortly take place in Washington: the main players were Israel's prime minister Ehud Barak, and Syria's Foreign Minister Farouk Charaa. I was not surprised when told to exchange our holiday receptions for 1600 people invited to five different parties over four days for the one hundred participants of these negotiations over 48 intense hours. I only hoped the Israelis and Syrians would enjoy our two thousand empanadas and wontons.

However, only procedural matters were on the agenda with the goal of reaching a core agreement on issues regarding borders, water and Lebanon to be discussed in follow up meetings at Sheppardstown, W. Virginia after the New Year. However, these talks constituted the highest level contact ever between Israel and Syria.

As usual our preparations for these two days were detailed in the extreme with every room made available and the principals and delegations spread all over the house. Beverage and bakery service in the Garden Room for the Israelis and Americans was ongoing, while the Syrians preferred to have available in their rooms Iftar foods such as dried fruits and nuts, and fruit juices of orange, date, and tamarind.

The dietary restrictions of Muslims and Jews, called Halal and Kosher respectively, are not very different. Basically neither can eat pork and shellfish. The Kosher rule is to keep dairy separate from meat products so we served dairy for breakfast; dairy with a neutral meal such as fish or chicken at lunch, and avoided it at night. Ian Knox used to cook for King Hussein at his private home outside Washington, where he learned the wonderful Middle East cuisine. He made breast of chicken stuffed with fresh spinach, roasted vegetables with pesto dressing and grilled fish for lunch for both groups; and served lamb loin and beef for dinner, the latter well done with some bones left on the meat so it could be identified, and although marinated left semi dry. It was definitely an art to adhere to our guests' dietary restrictions and still be able to show off our culinary talents. Always during Israeli visits we asked the embassy to provide some frozen Kosher meals and their own microwave oven in which to heat it up should someone be strictly Kosher. We also put out on the buffet tables, in addition to our regular dinner ware, paper plates, Styrofoam cups, and plastic cutlery in its original individual wrappings for those Israelis who preferred not to eat on dishes which had perhaps not been cleaned in accordance with strict orthodox teaching. I always maintained that it was NEVER due to Blair House if the negotiations did not go well.

Prime Minister Barak returned for a 20 hour visit in April 2000 to attempt to revive his plans for a comprehensive Middle East peace settlement as the Syrian Peace Talks, begun so well at Blair House at Christmas time, were temporarily on hold after Syrian President Hafez Assad had declined the Israeli terms for returning most, but not all, of the Golan Heights. At this particular time President Assad did not have much time left. He died a few months later.

All the pieces came together with the July 2000 event known as Camp David, the Middle East Summit between the Israelis and the Palestinians, instigated and presided over by President Clinton trying to forge a final settlement of their 52 years old conflict. It was a perfect setting where, in 1978, President Jimmy Carter successfully brokered a peace accord between Israel and Egypt (which actually had been started in our own Lee Dining Room.) However, this time, despite two weeks of intense talks, and under a complete news black-out preventing outside political influence to sideline the talks, they could reach no agreement. It was tragic. This was the best chance ever to lay the groundwork for stability in the area. I understand that it was Arafat, Chairman of the Palestinian Authority, who blew it, despite the Israelis offering the most extensive concessions ever. Arafat was described later by Dennis Ross as "a Chicago Ward boss who personalized everything – with him no change was possible." Both leaders were weakened at home, though, Barak having had two of his government coalition partners walk out on him due to his willingness to negotiate with the Palestinians, and barely surviving a vote of no confidence in Knesset. Arafat faced a restless people who wanted all or nothing. And President Clinton, with only five months left in office, stood to lose much as well, having betted the prestige of his presidency for seven years of hard work on a suitable outcome.

The White House provided the Mess personnel as a back up to the existing Camp David Navy personnel, but with no clue as to Jewish and Muslim dietary restrictions or food preparations, Ian Knox was asked by Protocol to go up and sort them out, while we at the house got to do all the laundry from Camp David; the White House does not do laundry. And laundry they had. For the two weeks the Israelis, Palestinians, and Americans were up there, we received up to 22 bags of their clothing every second or third day; one Israeli negotiator sent down nine suits to be dry-cleaned. Of interest were the names of the individual cabins at Camp David marked on the laundry bags: Dogwood, Hawthorne, Rose Bud, Walnut, Sycamore, Redwood, and Birch.

Continuing deadly violence in the region set off by a visit of General Ariel Sharon to Haram al-Sharif / Temple Mound brought on yet another summit in October 2000, this time in Sharm el-Sheikh in Egypt. And I wondered how they could expect to agree on anything when one party at least, Yasir Arafat, not only walked away from the Camp David deal, but was suspected of actually stoking the current violence, choosing instead of becoming a statesman ruling over his own country to revert to that of a terrorist exploiting another diplomatic stalemate for a short-term advantage.

Early January 2001 Arafat was back in Washington regarding yet another American compromise plan for peace in the Middle East, but could not be swayed, or did not understand that this might well be the last best chance in many years for a settlement.

A few days before the end of his presidency, Mr. Clinton wrote a letter to the Palestinian and Israeli, bidding farewell and admonishing each to continue pushing for a comprehensive peace. "... ....Nothing you have accomplished has been accomplished through violence, and nothing will be... ...." This was an extraordinary gesture by the President who for the preceding eight years had spent countless hours on the issue. I was so sad; that all this effort by the most talented President yet essentially had been in vain. Little would be accomplished by the incoming administration.

CHAPTER 14

ALLIES FROM THE EAST

"They do not get easier with time, but we get smarter."

Mrs. V

The Pakistani ambassador's wife was worried. Could we prepare the proper halal Muslim diet for her prime minister and his family? I assured her of our expertise, but did she prefer a particular halal market? I now had an ally in Mrs. Khokhar and got some dietary heads-up: they did not like sweet vegetables such as yams; they loved chocolate in desserts; and while berries would be a treat, the different kinds should not be mixed with each other. And the prime minister loved mushroom soup.

Prime Minister Mian Muhammad Nawaz Sharif, his wife, their 21 year old son and 17 year old daughter, his brother, his brother's wife, and their two children arrived December 1, 1998 and soon filled the house, in more ways than one. Traditionally in the Muslim world the larger the woman the more fertile she is perceived to be. While the 21 year old son was large, the 17 year old daughter was enormous, and likely to increase at an alarming rate based on what she consumed at meals which included pizza and hamburgers.

Prime Minister Sharif, conservatively dressed in his native brown long shirt, was quiet and appreciative. Pakistan's prime minister numerous times, he had been asked to form a government after Benazir Bhutto, on grounds of corruption, was fired, a charge which would also be leveled at Sharif some years later, forcing him into exile. An experienced politician he skillfully used his country's religious fundamentalists and the Islamic law – sharia – to consolidate power in his own hands; he suspended civil rights in parts of his country thus systematically dismantling the frail democracy in Pakistan, and he was suspected of supporting the Taliban.

The visit was serious and important. The prime minister asked the U.S. president for improved relations, economic and military, with his country, and Mr. Clinton in turn asked him for certain commitments: no testing and deploying of nuclear weapons; better cooperation on apprehending Osama bin Laden, and using his influence on Afghanistan to break the Taliban power base there. Thomas W. Lippman wrote in the Washington Post December 3, 1998:

"Clinton said he could not satisfy Pakistani appeals for U.S. intervention to help resolve the decades-old conflict between Pakistan and India over Kashmir, the border region that represents the most volatile flashpoint in South Asia. "I've enjoyed my opportunities to work with the parties in the Middle East and Northern Ireland," the President said, "but it only works when both parties wish the United States to be involved. Otherwise we can't be effective." India, which insists Kashmir is an integral part of India, has rejected outside mediation."

We were to have another – short – visit by this particular prime minister.

After an endless week culminating in a tough visit a few hours earlier, I had just returned home Saturday July 3, 1999 around noon when my phone rang. Chief of Protocol Mel French – away on a long weekend – needed Blair House the next day, July 4, to be available for President Clinton to meet with Prime Minister Sharif for a few hours.

So much for our Independence Day celebrations!

And could I gather up enough staff to feed forty Pakistanis and who knows how many Americans on the biggest weekend of the year? My staff had disbursed already; the butlers, in a foul mood from fatigue when I bid them goodbye, were now on the road to the beach.

The next eight hours are best forgotten. Suffice it to say that I managed to round up most of my staff and that Chef got to the Muslim market just before it closed for the holiday. I could only prevail upon two of our part timers to help on the 4th July, but Luisa Salvi and Pietro Tundo worked their tails off serving forty some people, assisted by our own ladies.

But as always, you just get on with it, and given the bizarre situation we all found ourselves in, we got into a rollicking mood. At Blair House on the 4th July, after throwing together whichever flowers from the recent visit were still alive, I managed a quick meeting with my staff; a walk-through with the White House staff; U.S. Secret Service came by, followed by the Pakistani embassy staff; as did our President's valet. While hoping he would lend a hand seeing how frantic we were, I had learned over the years to expect nothing whatsoever from the White House personal staff. They ONLY serve the President. But the West Wing staffers from the National Security Council were great. Discussing the day's program which included feeding the Pakistanis at 11:30 am and the President's meeting with the prime minister at 1 pm in the Lee Drawing Room, I asked why the prime minister had to come at this particular time? "He is being taken to the woodshed by the President over his country's support of guerilla activities across the seize-fire line in the Kashmir." "Oh," I said, "in that case would you like him to sit on a lower chair than Mr. Clinton's?"

The four hour meeting had several cool down periods, and President Clinton also called Prime Minister Vajpayee of India from the Lincoln Room. I asked the President if he was satisfied with the outcome of his meeting, to which he replied that he most definitely was.

And, the Blair House staff can say that they spent the last 4th July of the millennium with the President of the United States.

President Clinton, in his book MY LIFE wrote this about that memorable day: "Prime Minister Sharif called and asked if he could come to Washington on July 4 to discuss the dangerous standoff with India that had begun several weeks earlier when Pakistani forces under the command of General Pervez Musharraf crossed the Line of Control, which had been the recognized and generally observed boundary between India and Pakistan in Kashmir since 1972. Sharif was concerned that the situation Pakistan had created was getting out of control, and he hoped to use my good offices not only to resolve the crisis but also to help mediate with the Indians on the question of Kashmir itself. – Regardless, he had gotten himself into a bind with no easy way out. – I told Sharif – if he wanted me to spend America's Independence Day with him, he had to come to the United States knowing two things: first, he had to agree to withdraw his troops back across the Line of Control; and second, I would not agree to intervene in the Kashmir dispute, especially under circumstances that appeared to reward Pakistan's wrongful incursion. -----

On July 4, we met at Blair House. ------ Once more, Sharif urged me to intervene in Kashmir, and again I explained that without India's consent it would be counterproductive, but that I would urge Vajpayee to resume the bilateral dialogue if the Pakistani troops withdrew. He agreed ------.

After the meeting I thought perhaps Sharif had come in order to use pressure from the U.S. to provide himself cover for ordering his military to defuse the conflict. I knew he was on shaky ground at home, and I hoped he would survive, because I needed his cooperation in the fight against terrorism. Pakistan was one of the few countries with close ties to the Taliban in Afghanistan. Before our July 4 meeting, I had asked Sharif on three occasions for help in apprehending Osama bin Laden ---- We had intelligence reports that al Qaeda was planning attacks on U.S. officials and facilities in various places around the world and perhaps in the U.S. as well. We had been successful in breaking up cells and arresting a number of al Qaeda members, but unless bin Laden and his top lieutenants were apprehended or killed, the threat would remain. On July 4, I told Sharif that unless he did more to help I would have to announce that Pakistan was in effect supporting terrorism in Afghanistan."

Three months later Nawaz Sharif was removed from office by the Pakistan military forces on charges of treason and placed under house arrest. Two months later he was sent into exile, granted a pardon but forfeiting financial assets and property, forbidden to return to Pakistan for ten years and ever again to seek public office. His confiscated estate in Pakistan was opened by the military for tours to journalists. As reported in Washington Post November 8, 1999 Sharif had built himself a 22 room mansion complete with all modern conveniences, a testimony to charges of massive corruption and swindling schemes.

Army Chief of Staff, General Pervez Musharraf, became president. As our law dictated, following a military coup in a country, all U.S. aid gets suspended. The U.S. Senate Republicans chose this moment, when Pakistan, possessing nuclear weapons, was in the grip of turmoil, to defeat Clinton's Comprehensive Test Ban Treaty, thereby shattering what had been at the center of global efforts to curb the spread of nuclear weapons. Washington Post Editorial, October 14,

1999 said: "It will resonate far beyond America's shores, and long after any political benefit here has worn off. It sets back incalculably an effort that stretches back decades to lessen the threat of nuclear war by barring any explosions of nuclear weapons."

Prime Minister Musharraf of Pakistan and Prime Minister Vajpayee of India both attended the United Nations General Assembly in September 2000. While Musharraf was questioned frequently by the press about his sanctioned guerrilla insurgency in Kashmir, and his plans for restoring democracy to his country, Atal Bihari Vajpayee enjoyed considerable goodwill on his Official Visit in Washington D.C., when he addressed a Joint Session of Congress and made his way around town. Several times elected prime minister the bachelor minister was a poet, a former student activist and journalist, a gourmet cook and aficionado of classical music, thus intellectually and culturally the opposite of the most recent leaders of Pakistan.

While Pakistan, since years, had deliberately gone after U.S. investments, particularly military aid, and the U.S. had been pleased to establish military bases in Pakistan and thus in South Asia, relations between India and the U.S. had never been particularly good, except perhaps briefly during the Kennedy administration. India took the U.S.-Pakistani relationship as a slap in the face and turned to the Soviet Union which was ready, able and willing to give them all the military hardware they wanted. This alignment of India with the Soviet Union, countering China's influence, further soured our relationship.

India, after partition in 1948 and independence from Britain, had wanted no ties to the world and started a policy of non-alignment with other nations and hostility to a free market economy with devastating impact on its own economy. The Indians seemed to equate colonialism with capitalism and kept their distance. But following the collapse of the Soviet Union in 1990 India needed to make up to the United States, the only super power remaining in the world. The United States had for years been somewhat ambivalent about India, seeing no particular reason for engagement. For the U.S., India had no strategic value, no economic advantage, and no cultural ties with large immigrant populations which in the American psyche had catapulted the small country of Ireland to the forefront over the years. All that changed when India acquired nuclear capabilities. While Mr.

Clinton had approached India wanting to mend this shaky relationship, the goodwill had been seriously damaged 2 ½ years earlier when India conducted nuclear tests, resulting in wide ranging sanctions. However, the U.S. still encouraged India to sign the Nuclear Test Ban Treaty and called for restraint in missile and nuclear testing, so a door was kept open and a dialogue continued.

In addition President Clinton, as the first U.S. president in 22 years had gone on a visit to India a few months before Vajpayee's visit, and had been received with open arms. His speech before the parliament in Delhi was described as superb, and even those members who never missed a chance to criticize the United States had been enthusiastic. In Washington D.C. the Clintons went all out to welcome Vajpayee during their dinner for 700 on the south lawn. Surely this bonding between two great nations in an atmosphere of such goodwill and friendship somewhat helped in pushing aside for a while the threat of a potential nuclear conflict between India and Pakistan, and the ongoing troubles in Kashmir.

I was disappointed in this visit which was rather slow and not at all exotic as expected. Every second summer in my childhood, my father's close friend, the Danish ambassador to India, Harry Toyberg-Frandzen, whose daughter, Elisabeth, is my oldest friend, and his family borrowed our apartment in Copenhagen for home leave while we were in the country. When we returned we found extraordinary gifts waiting for us: perfume bottles, silver ankle bracelets, hand painted boxes and books; saris and carpets; add to that a feast over the years of sumptuous movies and great novels set in India, painting a totally different picture of the continent.

Prime Minister Vajpayee seemed frail, moved slowly, and suffering from osteoarthritis had to avoid our front steps. I greeted him curbside and escorted him in through the link door and upstairs in the elevator. The instructions from the embassy in preparing his bathroom had been specific: a stool to use in the shower; a hand held shower, and the embassy insisted on bringing their own bucket so he could rinse off himself. We borrowed a special toilet seat from the White House Medical Unit, to enable him to sit down and get up unassisted. We also were asked to provide water for his bedside at all times, one pitcher chilled and one at bedroom temperature.

AP International had reported various ailments which caused

the prime minister to delay his visit to the U.S. by two days such as a knee problem, and rumors had circulated that he had prostate cancer, vehemently denied by his government. However, our experienced housekeeping staff reported on the extraordinary chemical smell in his bathroom.

He had few appointments at the house and was out frequently on his official engagements. Accompanied by President Clinton, he dedicated a statue of Mahatma Gandhi near his embassy. This process had taken 13 year involving the federal government which owns the site; the Congress which authorized the Indian government to create a park on the site; the Commission of Fine Arts which approved the design and inscriptions on the statue, and the commissioning of the statue created by an artist in Calcutta. This statue certainly was symbolic for America, inasmuch as Ghandi, whose non violent but civil disobedience movement had united India against colonial rule, had provided the inspiration for Martin Luther King who spread the non violent civil rights movement here.

When the prime minister was out one day, an unidentified man, not on any access list, tried to enter his bedroom. Immediately apprehended by the Indian Security on duty, he was turned over to Secret Service, who found the intruder unarmed and there "to speak to the prime minister." The Service admitted to a security lapse, and our own Blair House security, confined to their command post during visits, went into high alert sessions to figure out how it could have happened. The Indian press had a field day, using this as an opportunity to take a swipe at our otherwise meticulous USSS and describing this incident as sloppiness.

While we also welcomed Sheikh Hasina Wazed, Prime Minister of the People's Republic of Bangladesh, and Australia's Prime Minister, Paul Keating, who told me that after the Washington visit he was going to see the Queen at Balmoral in Scotland to tell her "that Australia really does not want her anymore!" yet another ally from the East provided comic relief in a particular Official Working Visit from the Philippines in July 2000. What a contrast to President, General Fidel Ramos and President Corazon Aquino who preceded this common little man, Joseph Estrada, elected president in the Spring of 1998! I muddled through as best I could; my first task was to unscramble the embassy rooming list. People were assigned to our sewing room, linen closets and several people to each single room. And one afternoon when both the president and his finance minister held meetings in the house, there was no advance notice, consequently no preplanning, no pre set-up, and a constantly changing access list. We just rolled up our sleeves and went at it, spreading forty meeting participants over eight different sitting rooms; Jose and his staff were kept hopping serving refreshments, adding chairs, and taking them out again, and Randy and I were hoping we took the appropriate meeting participants to the right meeting room. One meeting, hosted by President Estrada himself, however, grated to a sudden halt.

Down the staircase leading to the Jackson Place Hallway and into the open Conference Room drifted the sound of gun shots. His security sprinted up the stairs, guns drawn, towards the source of the sound which came from the general direction of the Embassy Office.

There, to their chagrin, they found one of their own having such fun – popping the bubbles on bubble wrap!

This particular Philippine president and his family were rather unsavory, having picked up the worst of our exports: crudeness, brashness, and drinking-out-of-bottles sort of culture. He was later forced to step down and face corruption charges having allegedly accepted millions of pesos in bribes from gambling syndicates running an illegal numbers game. Rumors were also floating around of deal cutting at night, circumventing the public process; a lavish lifestyle, carousing and keeping several mistresses; he was said to have eleven children by six women. One could wonder how such a man ever got elected, but a former actor, he was admired and loved by the poor of his country who respected where he had got to. He lasted two years.

Nowhere among the world's continents are the contrasts as sharp between our visitors than among our "Allies From The East." I was endlessly entertained. The Pakistanis, Indians, and Bengalis, Hindu and Muslims alike, are all products of British colonialism, with the resulting language, mannerism, civil service, and cast differences. The Philippines have taken on the worst characteristics of their earlier American masters, and the Australians – our close ally – will almost always provide a delightful antidote to everyone else. The Koreans and Japanese could not be further from all of the others in behavior, looks, culture, languages, and in their interrelationships. Women were still subservient to men, evident in the almost dismissive way they were treated by their bosses.

The Koreans ate enormous meals, with two security officers eating 16 strawberry yoghurts in one sitting. I wonder where that went, as Koreans, like the Japanese, are slim people as opposed to our visitors from Pakistan, India and Bangladesh.

During one Korean visit new security officers seemed particularly difficult: when they complained of "too many press people too close to Blair House" I explained about freedom of the press and access, thinking: "Hello there, this is a democracy;" they constantly ran after Jose for the least reason, even waking him up three times in the night. The grandfather clock outside the Conference Room which chimed softly and beautifully was considered "too noisy."

Kim Young-Sam and Mrs. Kim, (Son Myong-sun), arrived Sunday, November 21, 1993 for a three night stay. To all intents and purposes this was a proper State Visit, but as it was Mr. Clinton's first from Korea his National Security Council had not yet figured out what to call it. However, it was our fourth Korean visit, and I wrote to my staff "they do not get easier with time, but we get smarter. Thus, expect masses of staff; five persons dealing with one issue; very difficult security and personal servants who will slice you up if you allow it. Be firm and consistent."

The Kims used heavy make-up before appearing in public so needed extra lamps, and lots of face and hand towels for makeup removal. Both were heavy users of our hair salon for massages and hair-dos.

This visit was easier than earlier ones. President Kim presided over a civilian government, so the military presence was smaller and security less obtrusive. In addition the Koreans are organized, detail oriented, and there are few changes in the last moment. By the same token many persons are assigned to cover one event, each person being responsible for a small detail, so every single item is scrutinized ad nauseam. I remember one Korean chief of protocol after our advance meeting suggesting we all break up in individual groups as to our specialty, and how deflated he looked when I had to tell him that his staff of twenty would have to deal with just three of us.

President Kim who spent most of his career in political opposition, switched to the dominant party to become his country's first civilian president in more than three decades. His agenda was ambitious, including political and economic reforms, and widespread anti-corruption probes. The top agenda for his visit with President Clinton was described by Ruth Marcus and R. Jeffrey Smith November 24, 1993, in the Washington Post: "The United States and South Korea agreed yesterday to adjust their strategy for persuading North Korea to drop its development of a nuclear weapon and open nuclear facilities to international inspectors. The change, while subtle, is part of what some officials are calling a last-ditch diplomatic appeal to North Korea before the United States seeks punishing economic sanctions against the country."

President Kim returned for another State Visit in July 1995. I worked closely on this visit with Ambassador Park Kun Woo, Korea's ambassador who was chief of protocol during our very first Korean visit years earlier. About ten days prior to his president's arrival Ambassador Park had held a press conference discussing the recent North Korean threat to "scrap" the armistice that ended the Korean War, a dangerous proposition. Park also emphasized the symbolic importance of this state visit, the president being the first civilian president of Korea, and mentioned the joint dedication of the two leaders, Clinton and Kim, of the Korean War Veterans' memorial on the Mall. But even more important, as noted in an interview at Blair House, conducted by Jim Hoagland of the Washington Post, was the Clinton Administration's deal with North Korea of immediate shipments of U.S. heavy fuel oil and two nuclear reactors ten years hence in return for an immediate freeze on all nuclear development and their weapons program, (they were suspected of having one or two atomic bombs already in place.) We all know today that the North Koreans lied through their teeth, but at the time even the South Korean president reckoned this a good deal. Back then it was also expected that the North Korean regime would implode quickly due to their disastrous economy.

One of the first acts of preparation for a visit is a meeting between our chief of protocol and the country's ambassador when the chief of protocol presents the ambassador with a letter, clearly detailing what the United States government will do for a foreign leader while here. Also included is a statement that gratuities to U.S. government employees are forbidden under the law. That did not deter some nations, following their own customs, to try to hand me an envelope stuffed full of dollar bills. I became adept at standing with my hands on my back so that I did not even have to touch this, and at declining it. This worked most of the time, except with this group back in 1993. The chief of staff of President Kim was almost in tears. His president would be offended if we did not take the monies, he said, and he seemed horrified at the thought of having to hand back the cash. I felt cornered. To divert the issue I suggested his president might wish to make a donation to a worthy organization instead? "Oh, wonderful," the chief of protocol said. "Would you have a suggestion?" Perhaps President Kim might make a small donation to the Blair House Restoration Fund earmarking it for an Exercise Room? The chief left me beaming and totally satisfied as President Kim was heavily into exercise. Five days later I received, from Ambassador Han Seung-Soo, a beautiful thank you letter on behalf of President Kim for "your gracious hospitality," and a check for $3,000 made out to the Blair House Restoration Fund.

In advance of President Kim's next visit in July 1995 I had asked if perhaps he, having provided the gift of the seed money, would like to inaugurate our Exercise Room? Surprisingly this event was written into his schedule for twenty minutes before dinner on his first night. We invited Lloyd Hand, former Chief of Protocol for President Lyndon B. Johnson, and current Treasurer of the Blair House Restoration Fund, to represent the Fund; we popped the champagne, and wrapped the exercise equipment in red/white/blue ribbons as well as decorated the pair of scissors to be used for cutting the ribbon. All was ready when President and Mrs. Kim and some thirty others of their entourage made their way upstairs. President Kim was beaming as I handed him the scissors – and then caused a moment of diplomatic panic when he asked: "what about my wife – she is going to cut also?" With only one pair of scissors at hand I recovered my diplomatic footing: "Mr. President, perhaps you could cut half way through the ribbon, and Mrs. Kim the other half?" Under much merriment they divided the task thus, earning me a rare compliment from Lloyd Hand who figured: "You are a diplomat, Mrs. Valentiner." The President of Korea was photographed happily and energetically trying out our stationary bike.

During the Asian economic crisis Korea elected Kim Dae-Jung, the Mandela of the East, as president just five months before his first State Visit to the White House in June 1998. He rode in triumph to Congress to address a joint session, and to reminisce about his long stay in America in the 1980s during a time of military rule and corruption in Korea when as an outspoken and bold dissident he was imprisoned, and later exiled. He came with a particular message: a message regarding his northern neighbors, his "relatives" to the north, and his conviction that stretched out hands in the shape of aid and smart decisions such as an easing of sanctions were far more politically astute than threats. He called this his Sunshine policy. Despite exuding moral authority and integrity and character, and standing as a synonym for unbelievable courage, our authorities remained skeptical of his proposals regarding North Korea. Also hoping for American investments in his beleaguered economy, he fared better in this regard.

President Kim and his wife entered and departed through our Link door. He walked badly and propelled himself forward by shuffling his feet; he could not lift them sufficiently to negotiate the front steps. His limited mobility was a result of a deliberate attempt on his life during his presidential campaign: his car had been rammed, his leg badly damaged, and he was denied treatment by the authorities. His wife, Lee Hee-ho, also had a compelling story, told in her memoirs, MY LOVE, MY COUNTRY, which she gave me and which is the story of their "living hell" under Korea's dictators, and of the particular strength and determination of the families of political prisoners and the impossible odds they had to overcome to prevail. Mrs. Lee was well known in America, having been awarded honorary degrees from three universities, and was a recipient of many awards, among them the 1984 Human Rights Award.

This remarkable couple came twice more. President Kim won the 2000 Nobel Peace Prize for his Sunshine policy, 27 years after he had been taken to sea, bound and blindfolded with his feet tied to a heavy weight, moments away from being thrown overboard by agents of his government, resenting his attempt to bring democracy to Korea.

Both were quiet and distant during the first visit, which, however, deserted them on departure. Having bid farewell in our usual ceremony, I escorted them down in the elevator, and before walking out in front where his motorcade waited, I thanked him for the charming presents he had given to be distributed among the staff. He looked at me, smiled broadly – the first smile I had seen on his face – and said: "You are beautiful," and took off.

The Koreans were always extremely polite, gracious, and with as exquisite manners as the Japanese. The men wore western suits, but the ladies, for official functions, would wear their <u>hanbok</u>, a two-piece long dress, in beautiful colors. They were generous, showering us with gifts, usually scarves and ties. In addition the Korean ambassador would give a party at the embassy afterwards for everyone who had been involved. It was at times embarrassing to receive their gifts inasmuch as in their tradition gift giving is a means of obtaining favors and accepting a gift carries the responsibility of reciprocity. But I always considered the Koreans far too sophisticated to expect us to reciprocate, which, of course, was neither legal, nor in accordance with our own American traditions. When Randy Bumgardner became my deputy, he and I underwrote a large purchase of mugs depicting a drawing of Blair House, which our own staff could buy at cost, but, more importantly, which Randy and I used to give foreign staff members who had been particularly outstanding and helpful. We also had lapel pins made with the Blair House logo for the same purpose the cost of which was borne by the two of us.

During many of these visits one particular Korean security guard, later the Deputy Director of Korean presidential security, Choi Jong-wook, was part of the detail – always to our great delight. During one visit, in November 1993, he came, with an interpreter, to tell me that his second son had just been born in Seoul, and had, by telephone, been named by him "Blair." Such an honor for us; from then on, we sent back presents to our little namesake on the other side of the world, and from time to time received photos of a handsome, laughing little boy named Blair.

In the meantime I continued my jinx on our important ally: Japan. Every prime minister only managed one visit at Blair House before he lost his office during my tenure. I modestly mentioned my extraordinary power over their leader to a friend at the Japanese Embassy, who reckoned that I was absolutely right and "I am so glad to know that it is your fault that they change so often!"

Though relations, in February 1994, between the United States and Japan were at an all time low with many unresolved trade issues, Prime Minister Morihiro Hosokawa of Japan in a speech at Georgetown University revealed a delightful sense of humor during a visit which was anything but delightful for him:

"I have been very comfortable during my brief stay in Washington, but I have two difficulties. I expected one, a little rain on my parade from the honest difference of opinion our countries have on trade. But what I didn't expect was that my parade would be snowed on and ice-bound."

Just two months later this prime minister was forced to resign his office, accused of lying to his parliament about a large stock purchase eight years earlier.

Symbolically, during his visit, Washington was iced over and the government closed due to the weather. Under such conditions all non-essential government staff may remain at home. At Blair House, however, just before and during a visit nobody is non-essential, so we moved in the night before, including our faithful part time waiters and some of the cooks, who realized that they might not get home again for a few days. We accommodated them as well as we could. I was asked by the White House Social Office if I "would look over the menu to be served at President Clinton's luncheon in honor of the Japanese Prime Minister to ensure it would be acceptable." So I checked a perfectly beautiful menu of Clear Crayfish Soup with Pacific Northwest Mushrooms and Beet Raviolis, followed by Roasted Black Angus Sirloin with gorgeous condiments, and was pleased to approve.

The string of Japanese prime ministers continued during the Clinton administrations: Tomiichi Murayama came in January 1995 and while visit was somewhat symbolic of the 50th anniversary year of the end of World War II, I think his excitement at meeting, as the first foreign leader, the newly elected Speaker of the House of Representatives, Newt Gingrich, was a bit misplaced. One particular visit stands out: Ryutaro Hashimoto and his wife and family came for an Official Working Visit towards the end of April 1997. They were smiling, appreciative and so down to earth with a beaming prime minister bouncing up the stairs. He had much to beam and bounce about. Until the day before his arrival the Japanese embassy residence in Lima, Peru had been occupied by the Shining Path Party terrorists, and their ambassador and his dinner guests held hostage for a number of days, until Peruvian forces successfully liberated them. In preparation for the management of this crisis during their Washington visit the Japanese had asked us to set aside one of our embassy offices to be used as a command center for the prime minister.

In between the usual meetings and conferences including a number of our cabinet secretaries, the prime minister had "glued" to his hip his new grandson, born to his daughter and son-in-law studying at Columbia University in New York City. They were such a happy family. The prime minister was a macho master of kendo sword fighting; he was also handsome, and sported elegant suits and a cigarette holder. He was due to return for an Official Visit in July 1998, the equivalent of a State Visit for a Head of Government, but alas, my hex on the Japanese prime minister was still in full force, and ten days earlier he lost his election. The same happened to Prime Minister Keizo Obuchi. I was bad news on the incumbency of the Japanese prime ministers.

The Obuchis came early May 1999 for an Official Visit. Chef was relieved he did not have to figure out how to serve sea urchins as Mrs. Obuchi does not eat them, and Jose happy to be told the prime minister would enjoy beer, whisky, and red wine. The prime minister was said to be gaining popularity in Japan as he was perceived, according to our Ambassador, as having "decency." He had also worked hard to ease economic and diplomatic frictions with Washington. As was customary, President Clinton and Prime Minister Obuchi exchanged gifts. An intense period had preceded this moment involving Dr. Thomas Elias, Director of the National Arboretum. Prime Minister Obuchi, being an aficionado of bonsai, had presented President Clinton with two bonsai and a viewing stone during a Clinton visit in Japan. Dr. Elias suggested to the White House that President Clinton might consider giving to Mr. Obuchi an American Bonsai and viewing stone. I can only imagine the meetings, calls, letters, and hard work to organize this, and I salute Dr. Elias for his persistence. Dr. Elias asked if I would like to borrow some for the prime minister's stay. Thus guests were greeted by two perfect bonsai at the entrance and still more inside the house.

Prime Minister Obuchi suffered a major stroke during the Spring of 2000, and Mr. Yoshiro Mori was appointed as his successor after a long and distinguished career in government. He came for a short visit in May 2000 and will be remembered as the only Japanese prime minister who actually made us laugh. At goodbyes, he told us: "20 years ago I stayed here as a member of the delegation; I was upstairs in one of the smaller rooms, and when I put my suitcase on a chair, I broke it. So like your George Washington and the cherry tree, I couldn't tell a lie, but confessed."

Indicative of the respect which I earned from both Korea and Japan during my many years of service to their official visitors, at my retirement, I was honored by a private dinner with their ambassador and his wife at the respective residences. During the Japanese dinner they realized that I was born in Denmark. The ambassador abruptly got up from the table, ran out of the room, to return with a faded photograph of the old Emperor Hirohito of Japan (the father of Emperor Akihito), and Queen Margrethe II of Denmark at a banquet in Japan. Behind the two principals the ambassador is standing, acting as interpreter of what the Queen, speaking French, is saying to her host – and all of them are laughing uproariously. The Emperor had just commented to the Queen that he was certain she would prefer many more women to occupy positions of power in the world, to which the Danish Queen had replied: "Not at all – the women would be at each other's throats in such a situation."

There can be no doubt as to the importance of Japan to the U.S. as a trusted and respected friend and strong ally with trade and other economic ties, and as a military base. Japan is part of the G-8, the Treasury Ministers and Bank Governors of the industrialized nations. But, equally important for the nation of Japan, steeped in a culture of ceremony, would be a lavish ceremonial visit to celebrate this friendship, and thus President and Mrs. Clinton invited, with relations back on track again, in June 1994 the Emperor and Empress of Japan for the Clintons' very first state visit.

Five weeks earlier we had begun the preparations. The Japanese instructions were precise: the Lord Chamberlain of the Imperial Household assigned the Sitting Room of the Primary Suite to be used as Empress Michiko's Dressing Room as she needed room for several attendants to get her into her ceremonial dress before the State Dinner; the Eisenhower Room as Their Majesties' private dining room; the Library as their sitting room; and the Lee Dining Room as their official dining room where they entertained guests.

Details as to who would have access to the Primary Suite and how the personal attendant would handle the pressing of the imperial wardrobe were discussed, with the Chamberlain surprisingly amenable to my suggestions and my strong insistence that my staff must have access to the Primary Suite. I explained that having a notable museum quality collection on the premises only my staff was entrusted with the moving of any of the objects. I assured him that no one from our staff would enter when Their Majesties were there, and at no time without proper supervision from the Imperial Staff. It undoubtedly helped that we had just gone through an excellent meeting downstairs with the U.S. Chief of Protocol, the Executive Director of the National Security Council, White House staff, and everyone else who was to be intimately involved in the logistics of this important and symbolic visit. Breaking up the slight stiffness of everyone, as the Protocol Visits Officer assigned to Their Majesties, Chris Hathaway, went over the schedule and pointed out that "Their Majesties then return to Blair House for a bite" – I heard myself saying during a lull at the table: "We don't serve bites at Blair House." After the roars of laughter had died down, Chris elegantly continued: "After a lavish lunch at Blair House ...," and the Lord Chamberlain could not stop smiling. Certainly the warmth and appreciation of our attitude and services continued through the entire visit, and was charmingly demonstrated by the Empress herself. She noticed everything.

Jose and I placed a table from the Library in the middle of the Eisenhower Room to give the imperial couple a clear view across to the Old Executive Office Building. This was on purpose. When the White House hosts a state visit, the City of Washington D.C. goes all out. The U.S., the foreign visitor's, and the District of Columbia's flags are flying everywhere, including a giant version of the U.S. and the foreign one hanging side by side on the wall of the Old Executive Office Building. The Imperial Couple could not get over this view during their meals. I arranged three different flower arrangements to go on the mantel piece, and to give it a different look each day I had collected 6 pairs of Staffordshire birds from various bedroom, to compliment the flowers with birds of the same color. Her Majesty noticed, and remarked to Jose: "Yellow last night; blue today?" and burst out laughing at Jose's reply: "One changes clothes; one set during evening, one during day."

One morning Jose was visibly shaken. He had just served Their Imperial Majesties their breakfast. "Mrs. V, I had just left the room, when I was called back by their attendant. When I came in the Empress got up from her chair, walked out in the middle of the room, and" – here Jose bowed deep to me – "did this. She said "I apologize, Jose-san, for spilling water on the table. My hand shakes."" "These people cannot be for real," I thought. I was stunned by this display of incredible courtesy and appreciation shown to him and other members of my staff by this remarkable couple from Japan – who sometimes seemed to be two big excuses for their very existence. The Empress knew us by name very quickly. And one particular incident showed how thoughtful and gracious they both were. They were waiting to be joined by former Vice President Walter F. Mondale, our Ambassador to Japan, and his wife before going to the White House for the State Dinner. Their ambassador had asked our "resident photographer" Lynn Keith to take some pictures of them in the Lee Drawing Room. Our curator Mary Williams decided to go with her, in the role of film bearer – and, I expect, to have a closer look at this extraordinary couple, when they asked Mary to sit down and engaged her in conversation. The Mondales arrived all too soon interrupting this little interlude.

Emperor Akihito, the 125th emperor in an unbroken line of rulers, and heading the world's oldest reigning family, probably has less power, actually none, than any other chief of state as a result of the post-World War II Japanese constitution which specifically prohibits the emperor from assuming powers related to government. His role is that of strict symbolism to advance national unity, and by all accounts he has done it superbly. He also has managed to cultivate an image of a modern monarch, and at least when he travels seemed to be approachable, affable, and genuinely interested in his surroundings. During his schooling after the war, one of his tutors was an American Quaker credited with exposing him to Western philosophy and literature, and encouraging him to express his own views and wishes rather than deferring to his retainers. A marine biologist and author, he was the first emperor to marry a commoner and to raise his children at home himself and sending them to universities abroad. Protocol Gifts Officer, Connie Dierman, had the delightful surprise to be informed that the Imperial Couple wished to receive their gift from President Clinton personally from her hands, rather than having the exchange done protocol to protocol. So Connie spent fifteen minutes alone with them in the Conference Room where they admired, asked questions, and engaged her in small talk while looking at the magnificent eagle sculpture, created for them, by Allan Houser, Native American artist and resident of my own state of New Mexico.

While visiting America, in addition to the official welcome at the White House in the morning, the state dinner, and the laying of a wreath at the Grave of the Unknown Soldier, they focused on a closer look at American history: they visited the Martin Luther King Center in Atlanta; Jefferson's Monticello, and studied Abraham Lincoln's Gettysburg Address then displayed in Los Angeles; they reached out to young Americans by visiting young disabled artists in their gallery and a school where the children were immersed in Japanese math and science lessons. They went to Freer Gallery to see its superb collection of Japanese art, had a luncheon at the National Academy of Science, tea at the Library of Congress, a performance at the Kennedy Center and even a Cardinals baseball game in St. Louis. This was a hard working couple. I read that despite their symbolic positions in Japan they tend to official duties some 300 days a year.

Their Majesties had arrived in the late morning of Sunday, June 12, and had asked for a small luncheon to be served in our Lee Dining Room for seven people, hosting the U.S. Chief of Protocol Molly Raiser, Japan's ambassador to the United States Takakazu Kuriyama and his wife, and our own ambassador to Japan, former Vice President Fritz Mondale and his wife, Joan. As we had just been given tablemats and napkins from the estate of Nell Hodgson Woodruff, sent by Martha Hodgson Ellis of Atlanta, Georgia it was such a treat for me later, when I thanked her, to tell her who had inaugurated her exquisite gift.

Suddenly, during dessert, Her Majesty abruptly left the dining room, and I saw her walking into the Garden, searching for something.

I hurried after her.

"Your Majesty, may I be of assistance, perhaps?"

"Yes, please," she turned to me, "I am looking for the silver birch."

I had no clue what she was referring to, but probed: "Did the tree grow in this garden, perhaps, when Your Majesties stayed here in 1960?" (when then Crown Prince Akihito and his bride of 17 months, Princess Michiko, were the guests of President and Mrs. Eisenhower.)

"Yes," and she continued, "it was so beautiful, like silver in the moonlight. We could see it from our bedroom window. When we left my husband took seeds from that tree, and planted them in our garden in Tokyo, where our son now lives." I loved this little story, but had to admit to her that in the renovation of the complex, everything had been removed from the Garden, and the tree lost.

This story was so romantic I passed it on to Ambassador Raiser, who passed it on to Mrs. Clinton who told it to a journalist of the Washington Post thus sharing it with the world. And shortly before this lovely visit was over, I walked into the Lincoln Room to say good-bye to one of the chamberlains, Haruhiko Chizawa. I had an ulterior motive. "Your Excellency," I said, after the usual preliminaries of expressing my good wishes for a safe journey home, "you will have heard of Her Majesty's story of the silver birch tree?" He nodded.

"Would it be possible, perhaps, one day, to have seedlings from that tree returned to us so that we might again grow the silver tree at Blair House?" I had no indication that he took me seriously, but in usual polite Japanese fashion he indicated my request had been noted. At least I had made the effort.

Precisely seven weeks later Mr. Chizawa called me from Tokyo. After the initial greeting, he asked if the trees had yet turned their color on Sky Line Drive in Virginia, discussed the weather for a few minutes, and then came to the point: The Emperor had given permission to grant my request, and now the Head Gardner of the Imperial Household was hard at work figuring out how best to get us a tree.

My casual remark had indeed sparked an interest.

It took three years, before three little naked "sticks" arrived with much conversation and correspondence between Mr. Chizawa and me, heavy involvement by the U.S. embassy staff in Tokyo, and personal involvement by the Emperor who suggested producing layers off the original tree rather than growing a tree from seeds. In the press release issued upon the shipping of the three little saplings by the Imperial Court, it was mentioned that "seeds may not produce genuine species as there are many other birch trees in the Akasaka Imperial Grounds" therefore producing the layers instead. In Washington I could not have managed my end of "Operation Tree" without the expertise and hard work of Roy Peddicord, the Chief Horticultural-ist of the General Services Administration. He not only guided me through this process, but collected the trees at Dulles Airport in October 1997, organized a quick but required check by the U.S. Department of Agriculture, and found a home for the little "sticks" with Dr. Elias of the National Arboretum, who graciously agreed to house and nurse them through their first winter until one of them could be planted at Blair House, keeping the other two at the Arboretum as insurance.

On April 21, 1998, in the Fleur Cowles Courtyard with much ceremony and attended by an illustrious crowd, including former U.S. Senator and Ambassador to Japan, Mike Mansfield, the ribbon was cut by Japanese Ambassador Kunihiko Saito, and the European Weeping Birch "Betula pendula Roth" had its homecoming to Blair House. The sapling planted in our courtyard was marked: Layer taken from the tree layer of the seed-grown tree (the Blair House seed), making it the "grandtree" of the original Blair House tree. A charming article by the late Sarah Booth Conroy was written in the Washington Post.

I consider this one of my legacies to Blair House. And I have held the Japanese in warm affection since then, having personally experienced their unfailing politeness and courtesy, and that they keep their promises.

CHAPTER 15

THE WINDS OF CHANGE

"It has come to this!"

The Washington Post

The calm weeks of August, our time for maintenance and staff vacations, were over; Labor Day weekend behind us. With a shorter than normal congressional recess the Clintons' vacation had been shortened, bringing them back before the air conditioning ducts in their bedroom could be replaced and other maintenance performed. So, could they stay at Blair House for a short week, perhaps?

Sam Castleman, until the preceding April my Deputy, was detailed to be our White House contact. He was five months into his one year contract with the White House as an Usher, brought over by Mrs. Clinton to give her an outside assessment of how "things" could be improved. I thought at the time Sam was exceedingly brave to accept. The White House had been run for years by Gary Walters, the Chief Usher; I had wondered how he would receive Sam, but as no one was more deliberate, diplomatic, and disarming than Sam all apparently went well.

As funds expended had to come out of the Clintons' pockets, supplies would come to us through the White House but we would prepare all meals. Service staff, including Buddy Carter, who was Houseman at Blair House when I became General Manager, came from the private quarters of the White House, and my staff would take turns to look after them upstairs. With flextime we had little extra expense accumulating. So, with the full approval of the chief of protocol, the Clintons moved in, surely the easiest and most appreciative guests ever. They left in the morning for work and met at night over dinner in the Library. They seemed so happy in truly private quarters without the possibility of running into tour groups, meeting participants, staffers, or members of the press. Only once did we have a mishap. Randy was waiting for the President to come back from his morning run. However, the Front Door was locked down, and, with the Clintons in residence, only the Secret Service could open it. No agent was in sight when there was a loud banging on the door. And a shocked Randy overheard the Secret Service agent, running to open the door for an annoyed President, try to blame us for not being ready.

The Clintons liked to do for themselves, so we stocked the small pantry outside the Library with plain bagels, chips and salsa, veggies, fruits, juices, tea and decaf. Jose set up a dining table in the Library as they obviously preferred to treat the second floor as their "home away from home" and not come down for dinner. The three of them dined together, on healthy meals prepared in our kitchen, and had lively conversations as far as I could tell. Chelsea slept in the second bedroom in the Primary Suite, and did her homework either there or in the Eisenhower Room where we had added some table space for her, and the few staffers on duty.

Their visit was not without a major drama, though; the Washington Post reported on Monday, September 12, 1994: "A small airplane flew over the White House fence early this morning and crashed on the grounds. ---- President Clinton and his family were staying across the street in Blair House last night."

President and Mrs. Clinton were comfortably sleeping in our Primary Suite when they were notified; it sure beat having to be dragged to safety by the Secret Service had they been at the White House.

They were incredibly lucky.

As were the Secret Service, and all others who should have detected the small airplane as it flew into prohibited airspace.

But still, it must have been like a holiday for them to stay with us, aptly expressed by the President in our guestbook: "Once again we have enjoyed our stay – while the White House is being worked on and on this day while a small plane was crashing into the south side of it! Thank You."

But change was marching on. Two months later the question of the White House's vulnerability raised its ugly head again when a crazy guy with an assault weapon peppered its north front with bullets. Already then rumors began as to the permanent closing of Pennsylvania Avenue.

While security at Blair House was always tight given its proximity to the White House and its high level guests, I had not felt threatened or particularly restricted in any way. All of that changed when, on April 19, 1995, a truck bomb exploded outside the federal building in Oklahoma City, killing scores of federal employees and their children. Our lives in the nation changed drastically. The perpetrators, young Americans, alienated from the system, were quickly apprehended. They had listened to anti government sentiments espoused by others and wanted to "send a message." President Clinton admonished the nation that "words have consequences," and I took this opportunity to remind my staff, especially the gossipy ones, how true those words were.

The tightening of security around us was drastic. Pennsylvania Avenue overnight was closed to traffic by giant boulders. The ongoing debate that cutting off traffic past the White House diminishes the values of our democracy was an issue in the 2000 presidential campaign with the Republicans boasting that their candidate would not be afraid to restore traffic to the avenue. I was warned by a Republican friend not to debate the issue. He had heard that should the Republicans win the White House, they would absolutely open up the avenue, and I could only harm myself by discussing it.

Of course, the avenue was never opened up again and still looks like a fortress.

The Clinton chief of protocol frequently met with Secret Service agents, trying to solve this difficult issue for us. During visits they controlled the access, but during events not involving the Service there was less understanding of vehicle access to our portion of the avenue. It took some education of the Service, and was done well by the two Clinton chiefs of protocol, neither of whom ever shied from or walked away from any problems involving us.

The west end occupants of the avenue, Blair House and the Renwick Gallery, met with the Director of the National Park Service, responsible for the beautification of the area around the White House. The director was adamant about installing, right in front of our Lee entrance, enormous cement tubs with foliage to prevent a hit and run car bomb attack. I was equally adamant about finding an alternative location so as to permit proper vehicle access to the house. The patronizing director bragged about his close friendship with Leon Panetta, Mr. Clinton's chief of staff, and indicated it did not really matter what I wanted for Blair House as he would have Mr. Panetta's backing. "Well," I said, "I also know Mr. Panetta, and I do not think he is going to be pleased when he drives up in front of Blair House and has to step into one of your flower pots." We came to a mutually agreeable compromise.

Bizarre episodes kept happening: the Uniformed Police and our Security had a fright when a furtive looking character carrying a parcel under his arm suddenly jumped over our wrought iron fence. Immediately apprehended and thrown to the ground by a number of security officers, he was only released when he had explained that he was delivering a parcel to our kitchen. Randy dedicated the following to our Chef:

> "Once upon a time, at a palace guarded by high walls and armed security, a man looking like a terrorist screeched up to the front gate. The bearded man leaped from his car with a parcel under his arm. He appeared apprehensive as he looked east and then west, peering along the south wall of the palace. Suddenly man and parcel leaped the iron fence and ran for the palace door. Alarmed sentries and palace guards emerged from everywhere to apprehend the package and the man. The royal chef witnessed the scene with horror. Realizing the severity of the situation the royal chef sprinted closer to the scene to offer assistance. His royal chef career flashed before his eyes. You see, the would-be terrorist was a misguided delivery man. The package was that night's dinner – a nearly assassinated salmon."

We even had ghosts. Our officers had encountered weird situations during their nightly inspections especially in the Lee House and several asked to be transferred out. Once, after midnight, in Room 38 containing Mr. Blair's bed on which President Abraham Lincoln had often snoozed, Lt. Waters, guided by his flashlight, was moving towards a lamp when it turned on by itself, and he saw the shape of a person in front of him. The lamp turned off as he retreated. On days with no wind or draft our Garden Room doors rattled. Of course not everyone believed our ghost stories; in the Blair Dining Room, touring with friends of Mrs. Clinton, Randy relayed some of them, and was huffily dismissed by one lady. At that precise moment a candle fell from the chandelier, causing dead silence in the room. The woman turned white as a sheet and said no more during the rest of the tour. One of the funnier incidents came at Christmas one year: the Chief of Protocol had hung a battery operated motion sensitive Christmas wreath in the shape of the head of Santa Claus on the Protocol Office door. Someone forgot to tell that to our officer on duty at night who, on being greeted with a jolly "Merry Christmas," came very close to shooting out the door. We on the permanent staff never "saw" our ghosts, nor did any of our guests. I considered them friendly and appreciative of our care of their house.

But we were not otherwise protected. I was out of town on a mini vacation, when on the 11 o'clock news, I saw the house veiled behind a thick cloud of black smoke. After I scraped myself off the ceiling I learned that an empty and parked tour bus had caught fire outside the Conference Room, resulting in a couple of cracked windows, some scorched window frames, and the loss of two elm trees – and that Randy had failed to call me as he had not wanted to "disturb" me on my weekend away.

We implemented new policies following a couple of suspicious disappearances of three valuable items in our collection. I asked our security to routinely search all staff bags before departure. As expected some of our more vocal and complaining staff members took strong exception. However, when Randy and I took the lead and patiently waited our turn with open bags, everyone calmed down and got used to it.

Several bomb scares necessitating evacuation of Blair House became routine, as did our near perfect staff evacuation drills. During a fire in our laundry room our security force brought in the fire brigade to deliver what has been dubbed a textbook case of what to do. We were under extra security alert whenever a demonstration took place in the neighborhood such as the "Million Man March" in October 1995 called by Louis Farrakhan, the national representative of the Nation of Islam and every time the G-7 (or G-8) met at Blair House.

We were to play a small part in the administration's security concerns. In the fall of 1995 Ambassador Raiser advised me that the level of threats directed at the National Security Advisor was so high that President Clinton had ordered Secret Service protection around the clock for him. The Service had requested he find a more secure place to stay than his apartment. Could we, secretly, accommodate him at Blair House when we had no visits? He would need no service, just a room, and no cost. So for some months, during which time we had few visits, Anthony Lake was accommodated in our foreign minister's suite. We filled the refrigerator with soft drinks and waters; put out coffee and tea ready to be brewed; and sometimes left a small tray of finger sandwiches, cookies and fruit for him. He seemed rather overwhelmed at being accommodated at Blair House and asked "would you mind if I use your washing machine now and then, and could you show me where it is" and was happy when I told him just to put his laundry on his bed in the morning, and that we would gladly take care of it. At times I had to write him a note as "we have an advance visit from Israel (or Angola) and you might wish to move your things out of the way," and occasionally, with plenty of warning, he had to move out for three days during a visit. For several months he either stayed permanently with us under the above conditions, or would come for a few days at a time. In my memos to the few on staff who needed to know, he was Our Guest, and never referred to by name.

A further tightening of security came in July 1998 when a gunman burst into the U.S. Capitol, searching for U.S. Congressman Tom DeLay, and killed two Capitol policemen, and a few weeks later when our embassies in Nairobi and Dar es Salaam were bombed by terrorists. The bodies were brought back from Africa to AAFB on August 13 accompanied by Secretary of State Madeleine Albright. Naturally President and Mrs. Clinton were on hand, comforting the grieving families as they met with them privately before the official tributes. Several of us from Protocol were on hand too on this desperately sad day. Our President retaliated with American air strikes on paramilitary training camps in Afghanistan and in Sudan within eight days.

As the year 2000 approached a special Y2K White House office was set up next to our Jackson Place Houses. The world's governments and businesses cooperated over many months to address the issue of changing electronic systems and computers from 1900 to

2000 and leaders around the world threw in massive amounts of funding, executive prestige and expertise into minimizing major disruptions of service, such as energy break-downs which could make us all vulnerable. At Blair House all cabinet secretaries, and heads of FEMA, CIA, Nuclear Regulatory Commission, OMB, Federal Reserve Board, OPM, Science Technology, USTR, Drug Control Policy, Joint Chiefs of Staff, and high officials from the White House and Vice President's office came for an all morning meeting one Saturday in September 1999 going through every imaginable scenario should all systems break down. We organized emergency supplies and prayed that our generator would keep our systems running. Some of us were expected to be on duty New Year's Eve. Having a gorgeous evening planned at friends' house ten minutes away I packed a suitcase, and my cell phone, and was ready to dash down to Blair House. Nothing happened, no glitch, no problem and everyone could breathe a sigh of relief.

A funny e-mail, meant in great seriousness, had come from Dee Lilly of the Ceremonial Staff at Protocol:

"... here's a heads-up from Debi Schiff, Assistant Chief of Protocol for Ceremonials: Secretary Albright has scheduled a dinner for members of the American Muslim Community on January 4, 2000 in the Diplomatic Reception Rooms. But if we run into any Y2K problems it would be moved to Blair House." and I replied: " I do want to remind you that if the 8th floor has Y2K problems, SO DO WE!!! However, thanks for the compliment."

State had its own problems, all reported publicly. A classified laptop computer containing thousands of pages of top secret information disappeared from an INR secure area. Another 16 went AWOL. Earlier an unidentified man in a tweed coat had strolled into Secretary Albright's outer office and removed documents in full view of staff working there. A planted device on the department's seventh floor was revealed and a Russian diplomat was caught listening from outside the building, consequently expelled. The disappearance of the classified laptop was so serious, and Madeleine Albright not told about it for two months that she blew her stack, suspended the deputy of the Bureau of Intelligence, disciplined six of its members, and caused the bureau boss, Roy Stapleton, to retire. It was all very upsetting, going all the way to a hearing on Capitol Hill. In May 2000 all streets around the department were closed off to daily traffic.

And in October 2000 massive bombs detonated by a small skiff going alongside the U.S. Destroyer COLE, anchored in Yemeni harbor, killed 17 crew members. My Australian navy husband, with five sea commands and five wars under his belt, commented on the mistake of anchoring up <u>inside</u> the harbor of a questionable ally.

The bank meetings mid April 2000 brought with it giant demonstrations against "global poverty" at the World Bank and International Monetary Fund a little further up Pennsylvania Avenue. These meetings were preceded by an all day meeting of each country's Treasury Minister, his Deputy, and National Bank Governor, and for years those had taken place at Blair House. This time the threats of massive demonstrations had tightened security so we were advised to come in the night before, as by 3 am on the day of the meeting the White House area was cordoned off.

Our law enforcement community had been on their toes for months. Washington D.C. Chief of Police Ramsey was determined that a repeat of the massive destructions by demonstrators in Seattle a few years before would not happen on his watch. To his credit and the meticulous planning undertaken months before including special riot training and superb coordination between the U.S. Secret Service, their Uniform Police Detail, Park Police, Metropolitan Police, and U.S. Marshals it was relatively peaceful, with only scattered violence and passive demonstrations. The buses housing those arrested parked near us. It was later reported that some arrests had been made just to get people off the streets and not for breaking the law.

But I wondered how the employees of the World Bank and the International Monetary Fund felt being singled out in this manner. The World Bank fights against poverty; the IMF fights against financial mismanagement. Many of the Bank's employees have devoted their working lives to further the aspirations and ideals of people of the World. Both organizations are filled with experts on the basics: the building of roads, electric power, clean water, AIDS related diseases, education, and many of them have spent times among the sick and the poor trying to help. I read suggestions that "the demonstrators would benefit from working in a poor country for a few years, seeing what it's like and how difficult it is to make progress." I also reflected on the amount of money it cost to entertain the leaders of the financial world, at Blair House for instance, and the difference only half of that money every time could have made to a particular village.

During the Clinton era everything seemed to change; the old guard as represented by President Richard M. Nixon and Jacqueline Kennedy were dying; the Cold War was over; the world was veering in a new direction, less secure and infinitely more violent, and in the November 1994 election the Republicans gained the majority of the House of Representatives and elected Newt Gingrich of Georgia their Speaker. The Democrats lost a total of 60 Senate and House seats. Speaker Gingrich threw down the gauntlet: President Clinton would be very, very dumb to try to stand in the way of his (Gingrich's) conservative agenda. He called the Clintons "counterculture McGovernicks" and their White House staffers "left wing elitists" and said that with Senator Bob Dole, Leader of the U.S. Senate, controlling executive appointments, and the U.S. House of Representatives the appropriations, Republicans would control the government.

The watershed for me and my political beliefs came in 1995.

Congress seems to be genetically unable to pass a complete budget by October 1, when the fiscal year starts. Only few departments such as Defense gets funded up front, the rest of the agencies operate under a Continuing Resolution, the length of which varies till everyone agrees on a budget. Blair House usually found itself in a financial squeeze every fall. During the fall of 1995 everyone gambled; the Republicans would not budge; nor would President Clinton. Meanwhile the federal employee became the ball tossed between the two warring factions.

Only when I transferred my government service from the legislative to the executive branch did I realize what a bad person I was. Accusations were hurled at the federal employee by Congress: we were lazy, self serving, useless, a drain on resources, and should be consigned to oblivion. These sentiments were mostly directed at those of us who lived in the Nation's Capital. Those living stateside were not tainted. They were neighbors and friends, while I and the rest of the federal work force in the D.C. area were the contemptible bureaucrats. Never mind that all of us in the federal workforce put our lives on the line precisely due to our association with the Federal Government. The bombing of the Federal Building in Oklahoma City is a prime example. U.S. government employees were held hostage in Tehran; were assassinated by terrorist bombs in Nairobi and Dar es Salaam and on the USS Cole; assorted kidnappings or assassinations in various cities around the world targeted American diplomats.

My personal moment of truth came when the government shut down, in the fall of 1995, as a result of the budget fight between President Clinton and the Speaker of the House, architect of "Contract with America" and self proclaimed emperor of the anti government forces, Republican Newt Gingrich.

I stepped off the Republican Party bandwagon. I could no longer support a party which I had worked for, and been loyal to, in view of this stupidity and the increasing self serving and limited viewpoint. It was very hard for me to come to this moment: I was brought up in Denmark to believe in fiscal conservatism and social justice, and the moderate brand of republicanism in this country, the Rockefeller and Mark Hatfield brand, suited me perfectly. My republican friends in the New Mexico State Legislature were compassionate, fair-minded, fiscally conservative people; some were ardent environmentalists. Now, however, the GOP was increasingly spouting an ideology which had nothing to do with the common good of the country, consistently siding with the wealthiest and stripping away environmental protection. Everything seemed to be politicized in the meanest possible way, with no room for compromise, let alone civility and courtesy. This time the venom, the derision and the snickering was directed at us, the federal employees, by Newt and Co.: Dick Armey, Congressman from Texas and Majority Leader of Newt's House, and Tom DeLay, also a Texas legislator, who decreed that Members of Congress must continue to be paid their salaries, while hundred thousand federal employees were being furloughed without pay, and consequently struggled to meet their mortgages and other bills. My salary in the U.S. Senate came from the Federal Government, as did that of my former boss, Senator Domenici, as well as the considerable sums of money expended annually on his many offices and various other perks and privileges, thus making him as much as me a recipient of public monies. We even were under the same pension system. Members of Congress have free parking at the office, in the D.C. area airports; use of U.S. embassy staffers during jaunts abroad who on their return have the gall to question why the Department of State is needed. During the 1995 Christmas shut down of the government the U.S. Congress proceeded with 25 separate congressional and 18 staff delegation trips abroad, all expecting services ranging from transportation, facilitation through customs and airports, sightseeing and shopping trips by embassy personnel who were being denied their paycheck as long as the government was shut down, an outrageous use of power.

During the three week government shut down including Christmas and New Year people all over the country suddenly woke up to the fact that federal employees played a heavy role in their daily happiness:

Where were the Social Security checks and the Meals on Wheels; service at the Veterans Hospital where a beloved relative was housed? Why did all work suddenly stop on the Interstate Highway so necessary to their daily commute? Why could the children not go camping in the National Parks or attend Head Start or other federally funded educational activities? The Environmental Protection Agency had to shut down toxic waste cleanups at 32 sites across America. Workplace safety activities were shut down. And on and on it went. In Washington D.C. the beloved Smithsonian, the Washington Memorial, other museums accessible free of charge were closed to the public. And, horrors, even the White House tours were no longer.

At Blair House, only essential personnel were on duty. I kept one maid and one houseman plus security, and spent my days writing my annual report. The first shut down lasted four days, after which there was broad agreement between the President and Congress to keep government functioning by extending the continuing resolution till December 15 when hopefully a permanent agreement could be reached. This did not happen, beginning the three week government shut down over Christmas. Randy and I took turns at the house as did the maids and housemen.

It was alleged that Newt Gingrich felt slighted "being made to sit in the back of the plane" when he flew with the President on Air Force One to Israel for the funeral of slain Prime Minister Yitzhak Rabin a few months earlier. Wanting to embarrass the President, he was said to have sent him a much tougher budget than expected, thus resulting in a veto and a shut-down of government which back-fired big time. The President held the high ground. In addition the White House staff, with photographs, could prove that the President had sat down with Gingrich and other congressional leaders on the plane, something Newt Gingrich claimed did not happen. Our national cartoonists had a field day. Words such as cry baby, pique, tantrums, flew around; and the nation laughed, while some Republicans muttered that "Newt needs to go home and take a nap."

The Clinton Administration was also rather lukewarm about the size of government; Vice President Al Gore was directing all federal offices to cut staff through his Reinventing Government program, and Protocol was ordered to cut seven positions. Done without firing anyone, without rancor, without nastiness, with retirements and shifting around of people it was a testament to their sensitivity.

I have no doubt that when the Democrats had the majority they also rode roughshod, but the rancor, nastiness, meanness and exclusion of those not of your own ilk, was never worse than it was with the Republicans in control; there was never less consideration for the common good in the nation, and it started with Newt Gingrich as Speaker of the U.S. Congress and continued with George W. Bush and Dick Cheney in the White House.

All of this rancor and nastiness came full circle during the Clinton impeachment proceedings.

From my Diary January 23, 1999:

"They are winding down the process of the question and answer period on the Hill – I am almost numb by now. The Republicans are demanding the right to witnesses – the White House furiously fighting it. What more do the Republicans need to know after the 6,000 pages of material already available? Kenneth Starr raised his sanctimonious head today again, when the "managers" – the executioners from Congress – turned to him for help in being permitted to interview Monica Lewinsky. Is this the way he gets his own jollies?

The President has behaved like a teenager with his testosterone in high gear, thinking with his penis instead of his brain and in general in a reckless manner. He has behaved despicably, and I expect will pay dearly for same for the rest of his life. I cannot even begin to imagine the emotions of Hillary Clinton and Chelsea for being put through this public humiliation. Their behavior has been dignified and exemplary in all of this, and I expect Hillary Clinton will come out swinging – whether going for a Senate seat, or some other high office. Should she make it to the Senate she will make mince meal of the more righteous ones.

But I do believe that Bill Clinton has been more venomously attacked than other presidents; after all who was this audacious guy who challenged our purebred New England scion of the Bush family; who had the gall to run for president, coming from a rather insignificant backward state, from a less than exalted background, pulling himself up by his bootstraps and by a scrappy, hardworking mother – what an insult! In addition he questioned the Vietnam War, and did his best to dodge same, not being privileged through his family and connections to choose easy duty at home. To cap these insults he came up with new ideas, used his enormous intelligence to pull sufficient voters towards the middle, and adopted many of the better ideas of the Republican Party as his own and for that he had to suffer. This crime: sex in the office – lying about it! I am guessing two thirds of the Senators and Congressmen quietly crossed themselves when the news first broke a year ago, and muttered: "there, but for the grace of God go I!

It is all too base, and not worthy of our great Congress."

And nothing Mr. Clinton did came close to the utter disdain for propriety, decency and honor that Members of Congress showed when they released the Starr report on the Internet, under the so convenient disguise of "the people's right to know." It was venomous and vindictive; this sexual McCarthyism of the impeachment would have been unthinkable in an earlier age. As the headline in the December 28, 1998 Washington Post said: "It has come to this."

Rereading this mid 2011 I am struck by how the same atmosphere of nasty disdain has surfaced towards the administration of President Obama, as Republican legislators give him zero cooperation in helping to solve the country's many problems. Mr. Obama's crime, however, is not sex in the office or having beaten George H.W. Bush, but being African-American.

It was poetic justice that Newt Gingrich had to step down as Speaker and resign his congressional seat. I heard on the radio: "Every revolution devours its own, this one just had its main course." I read that when he told his first wife he wanted a divorce he was visiting her in the hospital where she was recuperating from an operation. Charming; just a real nice guy! And to show his general popularity, he managed to be the first ex-Speaker to need a full-time security detail assigned to him due to persistent threats during his tenure.

Then Speaker-elect Congressman Bob Livingston (R-La) confessed to extra marital affairs and resigned on the same day Congress approved two articles of impeachment of President Clinton, for obstruction and lying about his dalliances. A few months later Mr. Livingston with his wife was co-hosting a CARE reception at Blair House. A heavy set white middle aged male was fawning over him, calling him Congressman, extolling his virtues, telling him how much he missed him at the helm. When he saw our photo of the Clintons dancing close together at their second inauguration, he exclaimed in the most contemptuous manner: "Give me a break" and I was fit to be tied. I went up to him and sweetly said: "Isn't that a lovely photo of the Clintons. We love them dearly here at Blair House and they have been so supportive and helpful to all of us! And may I offer you some hemlock – uh, wine, perhaps?"

On February 12, 1999 the President was acquitted of both articles of impeachment.

I have always been convinced that behind every powerful male leader in the world lurks a woman, or two, or three. You have to have fire in the belly to campaign for any kind of office, and if that fire is a bit lower down, so be it. For a national office you need a river of testosterone flowing around your body – it goes with the territory. It also is none of my business, and certainly the safety and security of my country do not depend on my leaders' sexual appetites or lack thereof. Watergate, in the seventies, was entirely different. It was a constitutional crisis, meriting an impeachment, with a president, Richard Nixon, who deliberately misled and undermined his Department of Justice, his FBI and CIA and maintained a secret, privately financed investigative unit in the White House engaging in covert and illegal activities, a far cry from what Bill Clinton had done.

For me, a constituent, the most important is that I am not lied to or misled as to matters of national security and so, as I write this (before Barack Obama became president,) I wonder how long it will take for our nation to treat George W. Bush in the same manner and bring impeachment charges against him whose lying and misleading the country into a devastating war, a staggering national debt, and an impossible international situation are far greater crimes than lying about having sex in the Oval Office.

At dinner parties during this time there would always be someone maliciously wanting to tell a dirty Bill story. I usually jumped in: "while I am still a registered Republican I do like the Clintons so much; they have been so supportive of Blair House," and nipped the story in the bud. But one, I hate to admit, had me in stitches, told me by Anne Merete Petrignani. Her maid and the maid's girlfriends were furious with Bill Clinton as their husbands, and other males in the Latino community, were putting great pressure on their wives to improve their sexual performances and be more like Monica.

World opinion was that what a leader does with his equipment south of the navel in private had no bearing on his national office, unless national security was at stake, which even a Kenneth Starr and Tom DeLay would have a hard time proving in the case of Bill Clinton, though I daresay they tried their best.

Shortly after the impeachment process, we had a visit of President Mubarak. Following a press conference at the White House, his Information Minister told me: "Mr. Clinton will go down in history as the most intelligent and excellent president. He is amazing; he does not miss a beat and can answer with depth many questions consecutively, and remember all; he has done much for the U.S. and the World. Very sad that here one pays such attention to private lives. In Egypt and other places abroad generally, only if your private life impacts on your public one and endangers security, are there consequences."

Not one of the leaders staying at Blair House during this awful period had any but the most glowing words for our President and for his leadership in world affairs. None of them could begin to comprehend why the Republicans had been able to make it such a big issue, considering the shaky grounds most of them themselves stood on, and certainly did not understand the frenzy in the newspapers about what elsewhere in the world is a private matter. I still have a hard time understanding the degree of intolerance and small mindedness which exists here of all places; that we must do all we can to destroy, despite endangering our prestige in the world and the respect which our ideals have always generated.

David Broder in the Washington Post, January 14, 2001 wrote about Bill Clinton: "By almost every measurable standard, he leaves the nation stronger than he found it in 1993 – its finances, its crime rates, its environment and its economy all improved." But like others, Broder also talked about squandered opportunities, immaturity, lack of prudence, and a certain deviousness, though I for one think that is part and parcel of being a politician, and <u>that</u> Bill Clinton is, the ultimate politician combining that particular shrewdness with an extraordinary mind, capability to assimilate information and formulate policy, campaign, and his superior ability to connect with an audience. At first he surprised me with his excellent grip on foreign policy; as a consummate politician he could translate this into an understanding of foreign leaders' viewpoints, as they were politicians too.

Bill Clinton has been described as a uniquely American character, seemingly thriving on adversity, always prevailing, and emerging battered and bruised, but somehow stronger and for many of us more endearing; he certainly presided over and contributed to extraordinary events. I had high hopes of his life after the presidency, and I have not been disappointed.

CHAPTER 16

A TALE OF THREE VISITS: STRUCTURE, CHAOS, AND DISASTER

STRUCTURE

Eight years had passed since the Chinese government's killing of hundreds of their own citizens in Tienanmen Square with the world watching in horror. Despite signs of harsh measures taken to repress all political dissent, China was able successfully to pursue economic reform, with sanctions against it being lifted, and its most-favored nation trade status being renewed by the U.S. Congress. The complex U.S.-China relationship had to be pursued and nurtured. In late October 1997 President Clinton invited Jiang Zemin, President of the People's Republic of China and Madame Wang Yeping to come to Washington on a State Visit.

The Chinese were organized; they were structured; they were detail oriented. The preparations for this visit were the minutest and time consuming of any, but – when the visit started there were no changes, no deviation from the schedule, and it went like clockwork. During five weeks prior to the visit eight separate walk-thrus took place with different groups, all with their own specific agendas. We met 107 Chinese embassy people during these encounters.

Chief of Protocol Mel French chaired the all important advance meeting on September 22 including the Executive Director of the National Security Council, the White House Social Secretary; the Desk Officer of the Department of State; the U.S. Secret Service; the

Protocol Office Press person; and the Protocol Visits Officer who out-lined the daily visit schedule to the Chinese with corrections, ques-tions and comments from all participants. The White House had devoted much thought to arranging a spectacular State Dinner for their guests (including borrowing our 100 base plates again), and enticing the National Symphony Orchestra to play for the Chinese President. The Social Secretary explained how the official morning welcoming ceremony on the White House South Lawn would be moved to Fort Myers across the river as the South Lawn would already be prepared with a large pavilion to house the greatly expanded dinner party. The National Symphony would give the concert in the East Room.

The Chinese would have none of it.

Their Deputy Chief of Protocol made it quite clear that the Chi-nese President expected the identical State Visit accorded the last state visitor from China 11 years earlier. But the Social Secretary continued to wax eloquently on how festive and enchanting the planned evening would be: "The Irish president recently enjoyed these arrangements so much," to which the Chinese Deputy snapped:

"The Irish are Irish, and the Chinese are Chinese!"

Prior to our walk-thrus I was faxed a list of the items the Chinese wanted to discuss – and this agenda was strictly adhered to. Their ambassador's cook and valet came to meet our Chef and Head Butler respectively. Chef had a heated discussion about the cooking arrange-ments, the cook stating he could not possibly cook on the electric stove in the second floor visit's kitchen, and Chef not wanting him in his kitchen during his own meal preparations. With the help of the only interpreter present, Chef solved that problem by asking the Chi-nese to do his preparation work of chopping, slicing, deboning, quar-tering and filleting upstairs, and the cooking itself in Chef's kitchen on his gas stove, using a limited space. Chef promised to have any equipment he might need ready for him upstairs including trolleys to transport the food. During the visit itself our kitchen personnel had a wonderful time with the Chinese cook, assisting him and studying his methods, and he in turn watched and had a go at the American way of cooking.

Jose and the valet, without an interpreter, sorted out their lan-guage problem in their own unique way. "I gave him paper and pencil, Mrs. V, and asked him to draw me pictures." So the valet proceeded to draw requirements for his president: sewing gear, vase with flowers, ruler, tape dispenser, paperclips, slippers, shoehorn, shaving soap in can, comb, plastic dish for hand washing in bathroom, refrigerator, spoon for medicine, tray with glass, a bed with a board to make it firmer, and on and on. Further, for the delegation rooms he drew a toothbrush, toothpaste, comb, shaving cream and after-shave, soap, and slippers. He wanted several electric kettles available as the Chinese drink all their water boiled, in addition to a thermos with hot water or tea in each bedroom, and no flowers in the Primary Suite itself. While we provided all of these items as a courtesy, Ambassador French told me it was otherwise in Beijing. When President Clinton went to China on a State Visit his delegation was billed for every extra item used in their guestrooms.

Fluent in English, Li Jianping was our embassy contact during this visit. In the tradition of the suspicious Chinese, while stationed in Washington with his wife, his young child was left behind in Beijing with the grandparents. He was perfectly sanguine about not seeing his child for some years; that was their way. I thanked him frequently for his extraordinary help to me and my operation and suggested he deserved a promotion. "I am not worthy," he said.

Ambassador Li Zhaoxing asked for an extra bed in the primary bedroom for Madame Wang who was rather sickly and always slept in the room with her husband, the president; he was very solicitous of her and liked to keep an eye on her during the night. In the daytime she was always with an aide. Chef's bed, which rather fitted everything else in the room, was moved down and they were content. And Chef was pleased; this way he had to go home every night and sleep in his own bed.

The Chinese wanted to translate how every piece of equipment in the house worked: how to use the shower and bathtub in the Primary Suite, the elevator, the in-house telephone, and the televisions and VCRs. We were requested not only to furnish the list of TV channels but also "to remove those which could corrupt the Chinese." I presumed they meant sexually explicit channels rather than our regular news channels. Actually Blair House cannot receive any pornographic channels (much to the chagrin of the Egyptian security.)

Prior to the visit Ambassador Li invited a number of us from the White House and State to the embassy for lunch, an interesting experience as their buffet contained dishes which we, at Chinese restaurants in this country, had never tasted before, just as we had not been exposed to Chinese habits of talking while eating and picking teeth. The Chinese Embassy is located in the former Windsor Park Hotel, which was partly owned by Bernie Bralove, owner of the Shoreham Hotel across Rock Creek Park. During my seven years there in the sixties many of our international groups were housed at the Windsor Park where my boss and I had an office. It was fun to go down memory lane.

President Jiang asked me to tell him the history of Blair House. I also pointed out the twelve late 17th century Chinese lacquered Coromandel wood screens, restored by Charles R. Gracie & Sons, Inc. in New York during the six year hiatus, by which we were standing during our conversation. The design on the front of the individual panels is complimented by the text on the backside celebrating Mrs. Chin Kao's 80th Birthday. In beautiful artwork her life is described, her role extolled as daughter, sister, pupil, wife, mother, grandmother, and community participant, done in exquisite drawings. Gracie's kindly provided a complete translation of the text, written in the fall of the year of Ting-Mao (1687), Kang His, by Li-Kuang-Di, surely the most beautiful and extraordinary birthday card ever.

President Jiang confirmed my interpretation, but, as others in his group, seemed to have little interest in what had been crafted so beautifully in his own country long ago. China's Cultural Revolution seemed to have erased all pride in their cultural history; it was as if no one knew of their past; as if no one cared. Blair House is filled with 18th and 19th century Chinese export: porcelain, rugs, furniture, and screens, as well as our gorgeous Lee Drawing Room wallpaper, but no one reacted to it. It was a sobering experience. It was a relief then that our resident Buddha, a c.1750 seated figure of Kuan Yin!an which resides in the Lee Drawing Room, did elicit a reaction. I found the wives of President Jiang's foreign minister and ambassador, looking at the Buddha in its cabinet niche. One of them commented:

"Buddha does not like to be so close to the floor."

"I am so sorry," I said. "Would Buddha be comfortable on top of the cabinet?" "Yes, please."

"Would Buddha like some flowers?"

"Oh, yes," was the reply, "but sparingly."

I moved the lamp, as well as the other decorative pieces on top of the cabinet, and placed Buddha there, with two small cloisonné vases, each holding a perfect Ociana rose, for company. The ladies were happy and satisfied that we had not offended Buddha.

And, when China's Prime Minister Zhu Rongji arrived 18 months later, Buddha, of course, was ready and waiting, on the pink marble, in his perfect little flower garden.

I discovered how much English President Jiang actually understood as he translated our conversation for his wife. My compliment lead us to a talk about the importance of languages and how they build bridges among people, and what a shame it was that all children could not automatically have a second language early on. We spoke German for a while, and he probed a bit in French, and then told me about his middle school where he learned English from the missionaries. "And do you know how I learnt?" he asked. "My teacher made me recite the Gettysburg Address."

"Well, Mr. President, then I must show you the most historic room in the Blair House," and I brought him to the Lincoln Room, told him about Abraham Lincoln and his frequent visits there with the Blair family, and left him happily being photographed under the portrait of our famous president while reciting the Gettysburg Address.

Jiang Zemin was overscheduled. We had to be in total control of the logistics to make it work. One afternoon starting at 4:40 pm he was scheduled to meet with our Secretary of Defense; at 5 pm with Senator Dianne Feinstein of California; at 5:10 pm with 40 Senators and Congressmen; at 5:20 pm with the World Bank President; at 5:40 pm with Senator Mitch McConnell and his wife; at 5:50 pm with former Senator Bob Dole; at 6 pm with 60 members of the Chinese-American community. Each meeting, which ran late with such little time for each group, included press with cameras entering the meeting room, my staff bringing in refreshments, and cleaning up before the next meeting started. The two large meetings were in the Jackson Place end of the house; the others in the Lee House. It was a tight-rope dance for me inasmuch as Secretary of Defense Bill Cohen, who in the last moment had requested a meeting, was late, and Senator McConnell and his wife were way too early, and the Chinese Chief of Protocol suddenly decided that his president was tired, could not walk down to Jackson Place, so "why don't we bring up the 40 senators and congressmen to the Blair House dining-room?" I bluntly refused, eloquently supported by the Minister Counselor. We plied the waiting senators and congressmen with refreshments, and Senator and Mrs. McConnell were moved from chair to chair, and finally installed happily in the Truman Study till their ten minutes, delayed by two hours, came around.

The next day, my too-honest Jose told me that during those two hours he had watched me "age 10 years."

18 months later I welcomed Prime Minister Zhu Rongji, and his wife Lao An, both multilingual as were their two children who both had studied in the United States.

The Prime Minister was here to finalize China's entry into the World Trade Organization. Negotiations were not going well. The Prime Minister made an unexpected visit to the White House the night before his official welcome to meet with President Clinton and to try to iron out their differences. I expect that the two main issues in our ongoing relations with China will always be human rights and the future of Taiwan, and I see no way those will ever go anywhere. However, the issues at hand were the export of American cars, and general Chinese imports into this country. When Zhu departed Washington he came away with little, but after charming his way through New York, Chicago and Cambridge, Mass., meeting with American business leaders, he was able to have President Clinton agree to resume the WTO talks.

Zhu Rongji, Premier of China since one year, was approved by 98% of the delegates to the National People's Congress, and appeared to have a mandate to press ahead with streamlining the Chinese bureaucracy and strengthening their economic reform. He was said to be a stern task master, cutting "frivolous" government expenses, downsizing and restructuring government bureaucracy and reshaping the banking sector along Western lines of operation. Already as mayor of Shanghai 1988-91 he was the leader of Shanghai's renaissance. Some said he was the best thing that had happened to China, being bold and decisive and being intolerant of corruption. It seemed expeditious for our government not to weaken this most promising Chinese leader to emerge from its unyielding regime. He seemed an extraordinarily clever politician and proved every bit as savvy politically and giving as good as he got, as President Clinton did during their joint and very long press conference at the White House. It was said "he played the U.S. like a violin." I was not surprised. After all, at the house during his numerous interviews and meetings I observed his fantastic public relations performance for China. Jim Lehrer of PBS came to interview him, and none of his questions had had to be pre-approved as they were with President Jiang.

Like the earlier Chinese visit it was structured with a grueling schedule, teaming with people moving constantly like ants on an ant-hill, but everyone so nice, polite, appreciative and with a terrific sense of humor, especially their thoroughly charming, expansive, and witty prime minister. He hugely enjoyed that I called him MR. CHINA.

CHAOS

"The King will decide," Ambassador Jaidi casually said.

My heart sank. I was well aware that one of the reasons we had avoided housing the late King Hassan of Morocco was Ambassador Abdeslam Jaidi's honesty as to the required accommodations which gave our chief of protocol a reason for persuading them to go to the Willard Hotel as Blair House could not accommodate this size group. This time, however, Ambassador Jaidi, the old King's half brother, and Consul General in New York City since years, was much more circumspect; he would not tell me who was coming except for the King, his sister and her two children. As to the rest: it was anyone's guess, and mine was that he was going to pull a fast one on me.

And so he did.

My experience with the Moroccans was limited, but my deputy Randy Bumgardner, during his years as a Visits Officer, had done a State Visit of King Mohammad's father, King Hassan, during the Bush administration. Thus when King Hassan was invited by President Clinton for a State Visit in March 1995 Randy was able to advise the Protocol Office on the do's and don'ts, and of what to expect. Before both visits it was decided, with much and strong input from the chiefs of protocol, Ambassador Reed in the Bush administration, and Ambassador Raiser in the Clinton Administration that "His Majesty will be so much more comfortable at a hotel where he can get all the space he needs for his very large staff etc. etc." so King Hassan had rented half of the Willard Hotel, but was offered Blair House for his meetings.

However, this time the Willard Hotel was off the hook; we were to house the entire visit.

I do not hesitate to describe the four-day State Visit of His Majesty Mohammed VI, The King of Morocco June 19-22, 2000 as The Visit From Hell.

In a memo to Ambassador Mel French later I made two recommendations:

- "that His Majesty for future visits is offered Blair House only for his meetings, and that he is accommodated with his entourage in a hotel;
- that Blair House is not the proper environment for a visitor who brings his enormous private staff, expecting conditions in the home country to be completely duplicated, and whose cultural differences put such a strain on our resources and the contents of the house."

In his thirties, King Mohammed VI, King of Morocco since July 1999, was known as "the King of the Poor" for his big heart and his big vision for Morocco. Upon his succession he dismissed his father's Interior Minister, typifying the inevitable generational shift. I learned that the young King wanted to make Morocco's system more representational, politically and economically, to its people, putting emphasis on finding schools and jobs for the 70% of his population who were under 30 years old. Further he declared women equal to men and that the Koran, which he as a direct descendant of Mohammed was empowered to interpret, said as much.

All of this was certainly commendable. I would like to add that in addition to our collective long list of negative observations, our staff also had charming experiences. Mrs. Rennie mentioned how warm and down-to-earth Her Royal Highness had been, and how she always had a friendly smile whenever she came into contact with my staff. Similarly our Executive Chef Ian Knox mentioned that the cooks were congenial, receptive and light hearted, and due to the linguistic skills of some of our part-timers, an understanding and team work were reached.

That in no way diminished the frustration at the lack of information and the secrecy, surrounding everything we asked about, and everyone with whom we were in contact prior to the visit, who was guided by the mantra: "The King will decide." Ambassador Jaidi, advancing the visit, evoked this mantra constantly.

The King's father, King Hassan, had elected to stay at hotels, as we could not accommodate the enormous personal staff with which he traveled. I expect, this time, because Jaidi knew our rule about one bed/one person, we were not given a rooming list, but only told about the Princess and her children, and that "His Majesty will decide who will stay here when he arrives." Thus he avoided mentioning the dozens of extra people who ended up sleeping on floors, sofas, and doubling up in beds. Soon the third and fourth floors were filled to capacity with staff sleeping in the hallway and as Mrs. Rennie described them: "..... running around barefoot in a breathless state." Embassy staff members, despite their own homes in D.C., also took showers and were seen to sleep on the floors curled up in the bedspreads and cushions. Luggage was stacked everywhere having been brought in by a couple of 23' moving trucks and three vans. Over 100 Moroccan vehicles had to be cleared for access to Pennsylvania Avenue.

The Prince, at 13, was a ham who clearly relished being the nephew of a king. He was also undisciplined; he splattered paint with a paint ball gun on the walls of three bathrooms, as well as in the Curio Room used for women's and children's meals, and sprayed water indiscriminately everywhere else. We were not able to make any inroads with the people supervising him or with anyone who could curtail the equally atrocious general staff. I expect my only course would have been to go to the King himself, as Jaidi was no help, but that thought made me cringe. Additionally, the Moroccans, when my staff was not present, moved furniture around, and in the process bumped walls and scraped furniture and doors. Bubble gum was stuck in carpets, and they spit out their fruit seeds and pits directly on our floors and carpets. We found cigarette burns on silk fabric, cigarette stubs in sinks, and ashes indiscriminately dropped everywhere.

Tabitha Bullock, our Administrative Assistant, helping Mrs. Rennie upstairs, encountered one of the Moroccan women, who quite rudely told her: "You need to be in your office typing. You have no business being upstairs." This woman also chastised her for not speaking French. And, Tabitha said: "I couldn't believe it; I actually saw two men passionately kissing each other."

The Hair Salon was heavily used. The 15 year old daughter of the Princess required special hair treatment after she self-bleached her hair prior to boarding the plane in Morocco. It had turned blond en route, giving His Majesty a royal fit. The young girl was not permitted to go to the White House for the arrival ceremony, or be seen in public until her hair had an acceptable color for a Moroccan girl. Our faithful hair stylist, Kelly Funk, was called in and was not dismissed until King Mohammed personally gave his approval. Kelly had a ball. It was not every day he got to hobnob with a king and dye the hair of a princess.

Down in the kitchen Ian Knox went through his own hell. The private cooks of His Majesty would not cook in the second floor kitchen, mostly due, they claimed, to the proximity of the Primary Suite, and the lack of gas ranges, and thus established themselves, just like that, in ours. Of course we could get no information ahead of time of food requirements other than some few items, so on arrival, the Moroccan cooks insisted on getting their own supplies, and Ian sent them off accompanied by our assistant chef. They grossly underestimated their requirements and consequently raided our larders, creating a logistics nightmare for Ian who had carefully planned his menus. Ian mentioned that the head cook was a cousin of the King, and was there to ensure he was not "harmed." It was shocking to see her legs and feet, swollen, malformed, sick looking. For some it was obviously not a privilege to be the cousin of a king.

The Moroccan kitchen crew was extremely messy; they burned our pots; they did not lift a finger to assist in the clean up. Along with them in their luggage came a large amount of uninvited visitors, with no diplomatic visas, in the shape of 1-2" long royal cockroaches. Fortunately George Wilks, our Facilities Manager, had a number of insect traps. The remaining cockroaches were flushed down the drains during the convenient flooding of the basement by torrential rains during the last night of the visit. The flooding incidentally occurred at 12:15 am just as the royal baggage was being collected in the basement for departure later that day. By 4 am all baggage was loaded unto three 23' moving trucks and all flood water had receded.

His Majesty's meals, served in the Primary Suite, the major one by midnight, required the service of fifteen personal attendants, each carrying several plates of different morsels to tempt the Royal palate. They used our entire set of Theodore Haviland Limoges china (some 125 plates of varying sizes) per meal and broke some. The enormous amounts of food prepared for the King went mostly untouched and was thrown out afterwards. Jose and his pantry staff had never experienced such extravagance and waste before and their clean-up was staggering, as no help was offered by the fifteen attendants. At most one other person would share a meal with the King.

Despite our Garden Room being prepared for delegation meals Her Royal Highness' children and their two friends were served their meals by my staff in the Curio Room on the third floor, reached by elevator to the third floor Jackson Place, and up and down two staircases. The Princess' staff also used it; fifteen of whom would take most of their meals there, following the children's meals. We could not entice them to eat in the Garden Room.

The private attendants and security were useless and bone lazy, and preferred to eat in our Embassy Office. They brought in Thai, Chinese, and Indian foods to augment our cooking just in case His Majesty expressed a desire. The staff was thoroughly prepared for the King's culinary pleasures. The messes created on our furniture, carpets, and chairs were substantial. No attempt was made to assist in the cleaning up.

And surprise, surprise: two tiny dogs were traveling with the group: His Majesty's Teacup Yorkshire Terrier and a two months old German Pincher, belonging to Her Royal Highness. I walked into the Garden Room the first morning and saw on the floor what looked like a dirty rag; then it moved and turned into a big hairy rat which, fortunately before I could whack it on the head, was identified as the King's dog, Godzilla. The Yorkie, sometimes wearing an elegant knitted overcoat, was allowed to wander around the Garden Room with no attention paid to it where it did its "business" despite suggestions to walk it in the Garden. I was so incensed that the attendant paid no attention to its piddling on our Serape in the hallway that I handed her a paper towel: "nettoyez, s'il vous plaît," stunning the woman who had never had to clean up before. Both dogs were hanging out on silk chairs outside the Primary Suite, and frequently left on sofas in the Garden Room. According to our ladies, they both mostly went to the bathroom on certain carpets upstairs two of which had to be sent out for some deep cleaning later. The staff was not the least discomforted. Special meals of chicken, beef broth, and mashed vegetables for the royal pooches were prepared in our kitchen. However, the effect of these requests on Ian is best left to the imagination.

Secret Service was requested by Moroccan security not to be on post outside His Majesty's suite during the night, and not to be on the first floor either. Of course USSS ignored these demands. Several Moroccan Security attempted to get into the White House for the State Dinner despite being told only one agent could escort the King. Soon this agent was found wandering around the State Floor brandishing his weapon.

During Randy's and my walk-thru with Ambassador Jaidi he was forthcoming on certain requirements for the Primary Suite: "His Majesty cannot sleep with any light showing." Randy and Sean covered the window blinds with tar paper; taped these blinds to each side of the windows; and pulled the curtains tightly together, where they remained for the duration of the visit. The embassy delivered special dark curtains to be hung on moveable rods outside the bedroom doors during the night. Even the clock radio and telephone, showing tiny lights, were taken out. The Moroccans brought in a special television which was unplugged during night so as not to show the "on" light. As His Majesty, being a direct descendant of Mohammed, cannot sleep on a mattress used by someone else one was custom made to fit our 18th century bed. And His Majesty "can only sleep in a frigid temperature," Jaidi told us, so two free standing air conditioners were bought and installed to use the fire place chimney as the vent. All extra cost was born by the Moroccans.

"And," Jaidi said, "all furniture has to be removed in order to make room for the King's clothes racks." We were in the second bedroom of the Primary Suite. I agreed except for the 18th century bed which never gets moved. And naturally, on arrival when the Maitre d'Hotel saw the excellent closet space already available, he asked for all the furniture to be moved back again.

Jaidi asked us to partition the fourth floor with a screen so that the guests (their lazy staff) would not be disturbed by my people some of whom had their bedrooms there. The Exercise Room was changed around to accommodate His Majesty's Stairmaster and other equipment.

King Mohammed was certainly a totally different creature from his entirely royal and despotic father. He seemed to dislike the obsequious way in which he was greeted by his entourage: they grabbed hold of a piece of his clothing and kissed it. Although I understand that yanking away one's arm denote humility in the eyes of his people, I saw the distaste in his face when he did so, and wondered if this might be one of the customs he is doing away with at home. I was secretly hoping that his cleaning out would include 75% of the lazy good-for-nothing servants surrounding him. He was certainly most gracious saying farewell, posing for pictures outside, joking around with the staff, and taking time with us. It was a ghastly visit.

DISASTER

Despite my excruciating preparations, organization, hands-on involvement, and my staff's hard work, frequently before and during events we had little control over happenings, and could only react. The following, although not typical, was rather indicative of what might occur "behind the scenes at Blair House," but, because we on the staff took such pride in the way in which we seemed effortlessly to deliver our service, and only rarely had been known to inconvenience our guests, our visitors had no idea of the dramas being enacted off stage. This tale happened just prior to the visit of Chile's new president, Eduardo Frei, on Monday, June 27, 1994, scheduled for an arrival at 10:20 am:

5:30 am - (4 hours and 50 minutes before the arrival)

Early that Monday the police, while transporting a convicted felon in shackles and handcuffs, managed to "mislay" the prisoner in the vicinity of Blair House. Our Security was asked to keep an eye out for him, and located him lurking in the moat surrounding two sides of the building.

6:30 am - (3 hours and 50 minutes before the arrival)

Just as Randy arrived the smoke detector in the Security Command Center went off; the location was the Lee Pantry. Randy and one of our officers found the pantry thick with steam. Officer Jacquet Thompson bravely turned off the burst hot water valve, burnt himself in the process, and had to go to the emergency room. The hot water had already made its way into the Lee Dining Room, where, per special request of the Chilean Ambassador, the table had been laid for his president's lunch. As my staff began to arrive they went upstairs to tackle the clean-up.

<u>7:15 am</u> - (3 hours and 5 minutes before the arrival)

On my arrival I inspected the damage in the Lee Dining Room. Randy was on hands and knees trying to pat the large Persian carpet dry with towels, and other staff members were busy on the curtains. I suggested moving the lunch to the Jackson Place, and using a blow-dryer on the fabrics. This was a frequent participant in our regularly scheduled Friday afternoon water dramas when we first started up at Blair House when, for a while, water either would trickle in through the walls, or appear in other unlikely places. From our curator we had learnt to gently pat the excess water off a sofa or curtain, after which we dried the fabric with the hairdryer. That way no residue stain occurs. Then I went downstairs to my flower pantry to take out of the refrigerators the arrangements I had made two days earlier which, after spraying and watering, I would then distribute throughout the house, a task which normally takes over an hour.

However, here was my own personal disaster. Due to a faulty wire in the large walk-in refrigerator, many of these flower arrangements had died over the weekend. While I frantically tried to rearrange, and rethink how I could at least have some decent arrangements in the Primary Suite, and the drawing rooms, Randy walked in to tell me that the Chilean president would now arrive half an hour early, bringing the arrival to 9:50 am.

<u>8:30 am</u> - (1 hour and 20 minutes before arrival)

As I was wondering how my staff, usually very busy before an arrival, was coping with the extra clean up, my fingers flew among the flowers – some in the separate refrigerators had survived, and it was a matter of consolidating and rearranging. Then Randy returned bringing tidings of more calamities: Marinete had discovered water to be dripping from the ceiling in Room 21. The inaccessible fan coil unit in the Curio Room, directly above, during the weekend, had leaked so much water that the entire carpet and floor were soaked. Again Randy had to pull the staff away from their own hectic visit preparations so that the furniture could be moved, the carpet rolled up, and the floor cleaned.

<u>9:15 am</u> - (35 minutes before arrival)

I was dashing around with a luggage cart on which I had placed my flower arrangements, organized by floor. As I exited the elevator on the third floor and rounded a corner looking down the hallway, I realized that in the haste of moving the water soaked carpet out and mopping up, my staff had forgotten to put back in the Curio Room the furniture still stashed out in the hallway.

In half an hour the Chilean Foreign Minister would have to climb over it to get into his suite.

I hollered at the top of my voice for Randy.

He came galloping up the stairs with the speed of summer lightning and very much out of breath. He took one look at the furniture in the hallway, looked at me, and both of us collapsed in roars of laughter which made us almost non functional for a couple of minutes. However, time was a luxury we did not have, so while he moved the furniture back into the Curio Room, I finished my flower distribution.

<u>9:35 am</u> - (15 minutes to arrival)

After returning the luggage cart to my flower pantry, I flew up to my bedroom on the third floor in the Jackson Place House, to spend seven minutes changing my clothes. Flying down the stairs I heard a commotion on Pennsylvania Avenue, yelling, shouting, and blowing of whistles, far fiercer than was normal when the police cleared the street of traffic before the arrival of a foreign dignitary's motorcade.

And no wonder: as we could hear the sirens of the Chilean president's motorcade coming up 17th Street, a garbage truck had stopped in front of Blair House, and proceeded to unload its unsavory contents right in front of our entrance.

The USSS Uniformed Police went ballistic.

The thoroughly flustered garbage collectors had just scooped up the last of the garbage and started to drive off by the time the motorcade rounded the corner and drew up in front of Blair House.

<u>9:50 am</u> - (arrival)

Heaving a deep breath, Randy and I stepped forward to welcome the President of Chile and Mrs. Frei.

CHAPTER 17

FROM AFRICA: A MAN FOR ALL SEASONS – AND HIS NEIGHBORS

"We have seen the end of discrimination ------"

Frederik W. de Klerk

The announcement that Nelson Mandela would shortly be the official guest of President and Mrs. Clinton was met with buzz, excitement and great interest. The visit itself was electric; the air filled with joy, curiosity, awe; no one familiar with his extraordinary and tragic story could escape this.

His farewell ceremony inside Blair House rivaled the Queen of England's in the amount of people attending, though far surpassed hers in smiles, happiness, and awe of being in his vicinity.

Two months earlier South African ambassador Harry Schwarz came to see me. He was among those rare, white South Africans who, as an outspoken opponent of Apartheid, had served on the legal team defending prominent ANC (African National Council) officials including Nelson Mandela. I learned the president wished to be called Mr. Mandela; was a tea totaller, drinking water and fruit juices, and fond of fresh fruits; preferred white meat to red, but no pork; Ambassador Schwarz was very specific that Nabisco Cream of Wheat or alternative grits be supplied for breakfast, and concerned that Mr. Mandela, during his many events, "might not be able to eat." I reassured him. Also because of his long imprisonment, Mr. Mandela had weakened eyes; no flash camera should be used around him; he would gladly bid farewell to everyone, but preferred not to shake hands.

Mr. Mandela arrived October 4, 1994 half an hour before his 11 am official welcome at the White House. Despite his statement to me that "I do not like elevators – I got stuck in one twice after getting out of prison" his U.S. Secret Service agent, with him since his arrival in the United States, had noticed his bad knee, and persuaded him to use the elevator, assuring him of its modernity. I rode up with him, and could see he was not comfortable. No wonder that he might suffer from claustrophobia. Imprisoned by his government several times, Nelson Mandela, in 1964, was sent to Robben Island Prison for life; after 26 years in a tiny cell he was released by President de Klerk in 1990.

Five months earlier President Frederik W. de Klerk had conceded defeat to Nelson Mandela in South Africa's historic all-race elections as reported in the Washington Post, May 3, 1994:

"---We have a new and dynamic constitution; we have the assurance that there will be no domination of any South Africans by any others; we have seen the end of discrimination; we have equality before the law; minority rights have been secured; individual rights and all these other rights are guaranteed by a charter of fundamental rights and by a strong and effective constitutional court; and during the past week we have held our first universal franchise election. ... Mr. Mandela has walked a long road and now stands at the top of the hill. A traveler would sit down and admire the view. But a man of destiny knows that beyond this hill lies another and another. The journey is never complete. As he contemplates the next hill I hold out my hand in friendship and cooperation."

Despite his appalling treatment in his own country, our guest seemed a gracious, generous, gentle, and wise man. His diverse staff represented the multifaceted South African population. At a meeting Mr. Mandela had everyone in whoops complaining about the women in his cabinet and on his staff "who are always telling me what to do and bossing me around." Tall and handsome with snow white hair, and a dazzling smile he was interested in everything and inclusive of everyone. He was also tough.

On the third of this four-day visit Haiti's deposed President Jean-Bertrand Aristide was late for his meeting. Mr. Mandela admonished him: "You are half an hour late; I do not have time for you now, so you must come back tomorrow" after which he marched Aristide outside for two seconds worth of press time, and took off. I appreciated this action and commented on it to his chief of staff who just grinned, brushed his hands together, and replied: "Don't mess with us." Aristide was late again the next day.

The Clinton administration had encouraged this meeting because of Mr. Mandela's success in bridging racial and class divisions, good lessons for Haiti's president. A few weeks earlier former President Jimmy Carter had negotiated an agreement that the military rulers of Haiti would go into exile. 20,000 U.S. troops currently were occupying the island nation. General Colin Powell, the Chief of the Joint Chiefs, was sent with Mr. Carter (as I heard on the grapevine) "to keep an eye" on the former president's tendency to be a loose cannon with his own ideas as to what the U.S. government ought to do in such situations. I was somewhat amused later to learn that being late was not unusual for Aristide. On the day when the U.S. government was ready to fly him back to Haiti to properly install him as president, he was over three hours late keeping Secretary of State Warren Christopher waiting for him at AAFB. One would have thought that he could at least have been on time on this particular day, but then Mr. Aristide did not strike me as being particularly thoughtful.

Aristide's successor President René Préval came in March 1996. While praised by the Clinton White House, which seemed to appreciate this president's directness and clear answers contrary to his strange predecessor, Préval did not fare as well among the Republican Members of Congress. They had had no high opinion of Aristide, had objected to the administration's use of American troops to restore him to power a year earlier, and condemned the killings which had continued after the restoration of (so-called) democracy. These particular visitors left rather unsavory reminders of themselves. In the hallway by the staircase, I was discussing our schedule with Jose and Randy, when I stopped in mid sentence, my eyes riveted on a large pink object neatly placed on the side of one of the steps. They burst out laughing at my expression of incredulity. "Mrs. V, it is at least the ninth place we have found chewing gum, a small legacy of the Haitian visit." They had discovered gum under chairs, under tables, on mantelpieces, and had had a devil of a time removing it especially the pieces ground into our carpets.

Mr. Mandela never lost his grace and kindness as he embarked on his grueling schedule around town. He addressed a joint session of Congress and towards the end of his mesmerizing speech said: "I do firmly believe that the people of this country who have done so much to write the history of the world have the vision, the wisdom and the daring to strive so that what is good shines over the cities and the villages of that world enveloping man and land. Once you set out on this road, no one will need to be encouraged to follow. Surely the order of the day is: Forward, march. ... Shall we not awaken to the challenge of our times and bend every effort to achieve so magnificent a result?"

At the Shoreham Hotel Mandela received the $100,000 Africa Prize for Leadership, sponsored by the Hunger Project and attended by President Clinton; this was reported in the Washington Post October 6, 1994: ""Clinton said he'd awakened yesterday morning before dawn, thinking of Mandela. "And I asked God to free me of all the petty resentments and negative thoughts." It occurred to him at that moment, he said, turning to Mandela, that "neither I nor anyone I have ever known has faced the spiritual crises that you must have faced over and over," and that Mandela had gotten through hard times by reaching "deeper and deeper within yourself.""

The White House moved the State Dinner to the East Room to accommodate a larger group. Blair House participated: our precious 100 Lenox gold and lattice work base plates with the Grand Seal of the United States which Mrs. Clinton had taken a fancy to, put in a command performance. I disliked lending out our china, but had no choice.

Ambassador George E. Moose, U.S. Assistant Secretary of State for African Affairs, bid farewell on behalf of the Secretary of State. I invited him and his colleagues from State to have dinner in the Garden Room when Mr. Mandela, faster than expected, finished his farewells to my staff and moved into the Blair Drawing Room to see the official American delegation. I hurried to the Garden Room, and suggested "you might like to join Mr. Mandela in the drawing room." The speed with which their little party broke up was astounding, all rising from their chairs simultaneously as if released by springs. Ambassador Moose just made it into the Front Drawing Room when Mr. Mandela entered, and thus was able to bid an official and very proper farewell. I also had occasion to introduce my houseguest, one of my oldest friends, Danish diplomat Lisbeth Oxholm. Mr. Mandela was beaming. "How is Denmark?" he asked. Denmark always was outspoken against Apartheid.

At the Front Door, he took my hands in his once more, held them tightly, looked into my eyes, and exclaimed:

"Such a beautiful house. You are the house" and departed.

During the next few years we welcomed others from the African continent such as the delightful Presidents Rawlings of Ghana and Soglo of Benin; we also experienced the Angolan President Santos and his unsavory wife among others. But in October 1999 President of the Federal Republic of Nigeria Olusegun Obasanjo and Mrs. Stella Obasanjo came for an Official Working Visit, six months after becoming president. I dreaded this visit, though I certainly understood the foreign policy importance of supporting budding democracies in Africa, especially Nigeria which was the most populous on the continent, with great oil reserves. Even though their last election seemed to offer a faint hope for the future they were known to be appallingly corrupt. This particular president, a former military officer and Chief of Staff of the Nigerian Armed Forces, was praised for having voluntarily relinquished power to a democratically elected government after his first term as president in the late seventies, and had proven himself to be a skilful politician acting as advisor, and sometimes opponent resulting in a prison term, to those who succeeded him. A friend described him as "the best of the lot." Obasanjo had emerged as a skilled negotiator in Africa on issues affecting among others Angola, the Sudanese government and insurgents, and was the founder of the African Leadership Forum involved in training future leaders to deal with Africa's socioeconomic problems. He was definitely a player on the international field in African issues. I learned he discussed with President Clinton building a strong Nigerian military for peacekeeping in Africa, and that he spent much time here seeking debt relief and investments in his oil-rich nation.

Heavy and fleshy at 62 years of age, the owner of a chicken farm and an agricultural consulting firm, he was a British-trained military engineer with an honorary doctorate degree from Howard University in Washington. He had also published several works. His ties to the United States included a friendship with former President Jimmy Carter and Ambassador Andrew Young. He and his wife had five children, but he was said to have numerous children with other women.

Stella, his wife, was difficult and demanding upstairs, hard to please and never smiled. I found it disconcerting greeting both of them warmly and receiving in turn a limp, damp handshake. They would not look me in the eye, but at least I knew that was considered impolite in their society. Stella Obasanjo hosted a lunch for representatives of Africare, Catholic Relief Service, Children's Defense Fund, and a variety of institutions involved with children. The embassy sent over a cook to work alongside our chef and prepare some of their native dishes. We received specific instructions as to the serving of pounded yam with an assorted meat stew; and a breakfast menu of boiled yam, sautéed liver, vegetables and fried eggs. They liked fried plantains, very well done and dark, and drank tea. We were told to make our food healthy and low fat and that as the Nigerians live a communal life everyone would eat together. I learned that this First Lady was no different from others in Africa in that she would ensure government funds would flow freely her way by taking on issues regarding children, but that, interestingly, this president, as opposed to others, had taken drastic measures to curb his wife's extravagances and high rolling, abolishing the official Office of the First Lady, denying her use of government transportation abroad, and generally curbing her tendency to self-enrichment.

Scores of Nigerians residing in the Washington D.C. area descended upon us within five minutes of this arrival, and made themselves thoroughly at home, participating in meals and some staying overnight. We were overwhelmed by the constant schedule changes and non prescheduled events. Confusion reigned supreme. Never have we fed as many without knowing who really needed to be there. This became such a problem that their chief of protocol and chief of security, to whom I turned for help, decided only they could approve the access of this community.

And approve they did.

Everybody who wanted to be there was invited in.

Two little girls already in pajamas arrived at 1 am. We fed 135 at one meal, a first for us, and 90 was an average figure.

The president held non-stop meetings, and ran as much as two hours late, making my job a thankless one trying to keep the high ranking guests happy while waiting for their meeting. Jose brought them beverages, finger sandwiches and newspapers, and I checked constantly on them at least giving them the feeling that someone cared. The president also met with PBS's Jim Lehrer; with Wall Street Journal and Washington Post, Exxon, Mobil, Merrill Lynch and Chevron representatives; World Bank president, – everyone came.

Obasanjo also hosted a lunch for Andrew Young, former U.N. Representative and Mayor of Atlanta; Robert Rubin, former Secretary of the Treasury and others. The president having non-stop meetings in the Lee Drawing Room adjacent to their dining-room, we had them wait elsewhere until lunch was served.

To my horror, when his last meeting broke up, Obasanjo led his ministers into the Lee Dining Room telling Jose he could start the service, forgetting his impending lunch party.

What to do? We called our NSC contact; he rang the cell of Obansanjo's military aide, seated at the table; the aide told the president who left the dining-room filled with his own ministers already well into the lunch, and a few minutes later returned with his distinguished guests. Bedlam ensued as the president pointed his finger at several of his ministers who obediently jumped up and took off, still in the process of chewing. The president then made his American guests sit down. Jose, deeply embarrassed, scrambled to remove the dirty dishes; to bring clean cutlery and napkins; and proceed to serve yet another group.

Afterwards, when offering our apologies, Robert Rubin said that "only Blair House staff could have coped with this so well."

After the farewells and guestbook signing, the president asked if his embassy staff was present. He then took on a very mean attitude, explaining that he had learned that Americans applying for visas to Nigeria were told to wait three weeks. He declared that he wanted visas issued in 48 hours and if this wasn't done he wanted a report sent directly to his home telling him who was not complying with this order. "Such a person will not be continued in service." All of this, however justified, was relayed in a loud voice in front of the entire group, to the acute embarrassment of both the Nigerians and the Americans. Upon the completion of this salvo he departed without another word.

In the spring of 1999, new presidential elections were held in South Africa, and Mr. Mandela's successor was Thabo Mbeki, a frequent visitor at Blair House as South Africa's Prime Minister working with Vice President Al Gore on the U.S.-South Africa Commission. He came for a State Visit in May 2000. Described as a "well-educated, socially conservative communist" President Mbeki, like Mr. Mandela, had also been imprisoned for working to rid his country of Apartheid; he was an intellectual and was said to be the author of South Africa's new constitution.

Mostly I was struck by his alleged stubbornness as regards the question of HIV causing AIDS and his refusal to distribute anti-retroviral medicines, and the subsequent tragic exacerbation of this cruel disease in his own country. At a luncheon with Washington Post editors and writers he and others in his official party defended his association with fringe scientists who denied that the human immunodeficiency virus causes AIDS, and their government's decision to withhold the drug, AZT, which had been shown to cut mother-to-child transmission in half. At this time one in five South Africans were infected with AIDS.

The talks at the White House also included regional African issues and the involvement of other African nations in solving the continent's most severe problems. But on AIDS he remained curiously stubborn.

But before this interesting Mbeki visit we had the great joy of hosting Mr. Mandela again. In July 1998 he had married Graça Machel, the widow of Mozambique's president, Samora Machel, killed in 1986 in a suspect plane crash. Machel had been a staunch ally of Mandela's African National Congress and thus a foe of South Africa's old apartheid government.

Nelson Mandela, now 79 years old, came in September 1998, before stepping down at the age of 80 as South Africa's president, thirty five years after facing death for "treason" against white minority rule. His treason: to state his ideals of democracy and equal opportunity. Some of his dreams had come true in his lifetime, and under his own leadership and example legal equality had happened as well as rights under the law for everyone in South Africa. This time he came to receive an honorary degree at Harvard University, in a ceremony dedicated solely to him. He was thus only the third person in the history of Harvard University to have been so honored – the other two being President George Washington and Prime Minister Winston Churchill. He also came to Washington D.C. to be awarded a Congressional Medal of Honor from the U.S. Congress.

While Mr. Mandela and his wife, Graça Machel, spent the first of their two nights' stay at the White House they conducted the usual busy schedule of a visit at Blair House. Mr. Mandela mostly used the basement entrance to avoid steps, and though a bit frailer than when I first met him, he radiated happiness whenever he appeared with his wife. A big fan of boxing, Mr. Mandela had invited some of our famous boxers to meet him, bellowing out to Joe Frasier: "Hello there – it's Smokin' Joe."

This second Mandela visit was shortly after President Clinton went public with his intern liaison and Congress' glee at receiving and releasing on the internet Kenneth Starr's salacious report. Mr. Mandela hosted a breakfast for Members of Congress and I said to Congressman Benjamin Gilman whom I had known for a number of years:

"You know, Congressman, I am a Republican, but I have to say this: You people are out of control up there. This has to stop. You have a majority leader who lives in a cave, a speaker who is under his thumb, and our prestige worldwide is getting ruined. I know the man over there was stupid, but you've gone too far." Mr. Gilman told me he agreed, but, of course, he would later vote for impeachment of our President.

However, the warmth and affection shown President Clinton by President Mandela seemed genuine and true. They bid each other farewell just outside the house. The two men stood on the curb facing each other, their arms entwined, Mandela talking and Clinton listening, as I believe he often had to the elder statesman who had taken such a liking to him. Mr. Clinton, in his book MY LIFE, talked about his earlier visit in South Africa when he accompanied Mr. Mandela to see his prison cell on Robben Island. This was about the time when his intern scandal was made public. Mr. Clinton had asked him if he really hated those who imprisoned him, and Mr. Mandela had replied:

"Of course I did, for many years. They took the best years of my life. They abused me physically and mentally. I didn't get to see my children grow up. I hated them. Then one day … I realized that they had already taken everything from me except my mind and my heart. Those they could not take without my permission. I decided not to give them away." Then he looked at me, smiled, and said, "And neither should you."

CHAPTER 18

EUROPE – A CONTINENT IN TRANSITION

"Peace, like war, can succeed only where there is a will to enforce it, and where there is available power to enforce it."

Franklin D. Roosevelt

Danish Ambassador Peter Dyvig was not happy; Denmark was holding the presidency of the European Union the first six months of 1993. The E.U. had always stayed at Blair House; now his prime minister had to stay in a hotel as President Clinton in his desire to focus on domestic issues had no plans to use the house for the foreseeable future. I could do nothing to change this, but the USSS could and did when they decided that Egypt's president, as referred to in Chapter 13, would not be secure in a hotel and had to stay with us.

I called Peter: "I believe the taboo has been broken. We are going to have our first foreign visit of Mr. Clinton; why don't you try again? Surely it counts for something that Denmark recognized America over two hundred years ago – and has always been a strong and loyal ally!"

Thus the first European visit in the Clinton administration was the Official Working Visit May 6-8, 1993 of Poul Nyrup Rasmussen, Prime Minister of Denmark in his role as President of the European Council, and Jacques Delors, President of the Commission of the European Union. The Danes were installed on the second and fourth floors, the E.U. visitors on the third. And one little problem was solved before arrival.

The Danish Prime Minister traveled with his fiancée, a member of the Danish Parliament, and the embassy wanted her to stay with him in the Primary Suite.

But I remembered the hullabaloo when Prime Minister Michael Manley of Jamaica, in 1992, came for his second visit. He stayed one night only, and brought with him his spokesperson, his security guard, and his fiancée, the latter causing some flutter in the dovecote of our chief of protocol who involved himself extensively in their sleeping arrangements – despite the fact that this couple were well into their senior years, the prime minister planning his fourth marriage.

He suggested she stay in the Foreign Minister's Suite on the third floor, removed from the Primary Suite, just in case the press got hold of this titillating information. Fortunately, the Jamaican ambassador took matters into his own hands. He wished me to assign a room to the lady with a convenient location enabling them to visit with each other, sight unseen, and was very happy with Room 21, directly across from the Library.

Ambassador Dyvig accepted with alacrity to do as the Jamaicans had done, and when asked by the Danish press: "Are they sleeping together?" I could with perfect honesty explain that the prime minister was in the Primary Suite, and his fiancée in Mrs. Harry S Truman's bedroom.

In July 1997 President Clinton was the guest of Queen Margrethe II on his last stop of a tour of European countries, initiating the NATO expansion. At this time Mr. Clinton was the first and only U.S. sitting president to visit Denmark, despite the more than two hundred years of diplomatic relations. My older brother, Claus, related it was a roaring success, including the President addressing a massive crowd in the old town, and receiving a bicycle by the Borough of Copenhagen – the preferred method of transportation in my native city. When I brought Claus to the White House the following Christmas the President expanded on the system whereby anyone in Copenhagen can pick up a free bicycle for the day and deposit it in designated areas after use.

As my impression had been that the European Union was mostly regarded as our commercial rival, and somewhat impotent towards the tragedy unfolding in the Balkans I was glad to be assured by the Danes that their talks at the White House and around town had been entirely satisfactory.

Prime Minister Ruud Lubbers of the Netherlands arrived January 4, 1994 for a one night stay. This prime minister I was told "has maintained that the first characteristic essential for a prime minister is not ideological drive, but the ability to forge compromise." In 2000 Ruud Lubbers was named head of the U.N.'s refugee agency, a wonderful choice.

Conflict in the Balkans was well underway during his visit. He said that European decision making had been completely paralyzed with respect to the Balkan conflict and that he would welcome greater U.S. involvement in the hope that it might stimulate more effective action from Europeans. The shocking attitude, however, of some of his own ministers who had survived Nazi occupation of their own country and seen genocide was that "there has always been trouble in the Balkans. It is no good getting involved." Later though during a visit of Prime Minister Willem Kok in February 1995, his staff told me the emphasis of all his meetings had been on the Balkans.

Wim Kok returned in September 2000. Because of our election period his foreign minister had invited both foreign policy advisors of our presidential candidates to meet with him in the Truman Study. Paul Wolfowitz enthused on Governor Bush's great liking for Harry S Truman and "how they thought alike." For one pregnant moment my eyes, as large as teacups, met those of the foreign minister, just as large as mine, and then I fled. Later when I innocently asked the minister if his meeting had gone well he commented that Wolfowitz "was stretching it a bit!"

During the latter half of the nineties enormous changes on the European continent would evolve, with an, almost for all nations, common currency launched in 1999, and a greatly expanded membership.

But the thread which seemed to weave together all our European visits at this time was the evolving tragedy of the Balkans.

In 1992 when Yugoslavia's states broke apart Bosnia's almost fifty percent Muslims declared an independent Bosnia, and consequently were attacked by the state's Orthodox Christian Serbs and Catholic Croats, residents since centuries of that country, and fearing becoming a minority group in a Muslim state. The horror and brutality of the methods used were beyond appalling. But it was not one sided, the Croatians and the Serbs went at it, as did the Muslim population, – it was a nasty little war on all sides.

The breaking apart of Yugoslavia, predicted in the former administration, now was inherited as a Clinton administration's top foreign policy priority.

During the summer of 1995 the debate raged in Congress whether to lift the United Nations Bosnia arms embargo so as to assist the Muslim population to fight. As reported by Jim Hoagland in the Washington Post July 30 Senator Joe Biden of Delaware (our current Vice-President) said: "If we do not do anything now to help them fight for themselves, when are we going to do anything? ... Do you think we would be doing that (tolerating atrocities) to a Christian population ------ I have a feeling the reason why the world has not responded in Europe is because they are Muslims – the same reason we did not respond in Europe – because they were Jews." Mr. Clinton certainly had a dilemma, particularly the vehement refusal of Colin Powell, Chairman of the Joint Chiefs, to commit U.S. forces to any form of combat in Bosnia. It evoked this commentary by former U.S. ambassador Raymond Seitz, "At the least, an American administration should convey to its own people, as well as to the international audience, that it has thought about foreign policy in an integrated fashion, and so has a sense of coherence and a sense of direction. ... It is the absence of a strategic sense that is the most conspicuous omission in the present management of America's foreign policy."

On a very personal note, I asked General John Shalikashvili, Chairman of the Joint Chiefs when he arrived at a reception: "How is it going in Bosnia, General?" He glared at me; why was I asking? "I have two nephews in the Danish U.N. contingency, Sir," I said. He remarked that the Danes had been engaged in fire that particular day. I must have gone deathly pale, and he asked for their names, went to a phone to call his office, and within an hour after leaving the party personally phoned me to assure me that my "boys" were OK. I never forgot his kindness.

Tragically, in pursuit of solutions for the Balkans, three high ranking U.S. officials and others were killed in a road accident in Bosnia on August 19, 1995. The three officials were honored in a moving ceremony at Blair House when President Jacques Chirac of France, here for a State Visit January 30, 1996, bestowed on them, posthumously, the Legion of Honor. There was not a dry eye in the Garden Room that morning among the ten relatives, and the French and American officials present, including John Deutch, CIA Director.

In public service since 1960 Jacques Chirac had served as France's prime minister several times, and as Mayor of Paris for 18 years. Fluent in English, he told me he studied at Harvard University in 1953, traveled through our country, and "flipped hamburgers" in local joints to support himself. What a difference from my very first visitor, the ice cold François Mitterrand!

Jacques Chirac was charming, outgoing, and, a true politician, shaking hands non-stop; his wife was stern, difficult to please per Mrs. Rennie and Teresinha, and rather ungracious. Yet, I had read she was an elected politician, slightly above an American country commissioner, and a hard working one.

Snow was predicted, and the French caught the usual Washington hysteria. Following the State Dinner President Chirac decided to depart so as not to miss out on his engagements the next day in Chicago. We were suddenly bereft of our guests in the wee hours. He was most apologetic, and incredibly courteous in personally explaining their dilemma to me.

Accompanying the president was U.S. ambassador Pamela Harriman who as a formidable force in democratic politics had been so helpful to the young governor, Bill Clinton, introducing him to Washington's movers and shakers, and in appreciation was named his envoy to France in May 1993. As a member of the British nobility she started out her chequered and adventurous career as the wife of Randolph Churchill, son of legendary Winston Churchill, and spent the WWII years in England working for her father-in-law. Her son with Randolph was introduced to my notice when, suddenly and sadly, in February 1997, Pamela Harriman died in Paris, following a stroke after her daily swim – at least that was the official version. I rather hoped she had died the way she had lived her life, in a blaze of passion. President Clinton, as is customary when a U.S. ambassador dies in service, sent an Air Force plane to pick up her casket, and to fly her home. I had twenty-four hours notice that we were to house the Churchills, and no idea as to who was who on the list of names. I winged it in my assignment of rooms, which supposedly included one for the girlfriend of Pamela Harriman's son. It turned out she wasn't even there.

I walked upstairs with Winston Churchill, M.P., a regular chat-terbox, and was the recipient of the following information: that Mrs. Danielson was at the Four Seasons Hotel; that Mrs. Danielson was going to be his wife; that relations were very strained in their family; that he had been separated for two years from Mrs. Churchill; that as his two women had never met, they were kept separate; that he would not be in for dinner. Then, after casting a cursory glance at the suite, he went to see his grandbabies, and ten minutes later came down the stairs carrying his suitcase, informing me sheepishly that he was mov-ing over to the Four Seasons, and would see me in the morning for his funeral meeting.

But the mother of his children, Minnie, was great as was her fami-ly including two baby girls. Born Erlangen, her ancestor was an Amer-ican banker for the Confederacy who got stuck in France during the Civil War and thus remained in Europe. I was interested to read in the newspapers later that Pamela Harriman thought so well of her daugh-ter-in-law that she left her half her fortune.

I was to see Winston Churchill a few more times as he came over for prearranged meetings, and even had to fight off his attempt to arrange a luncheon on us for his fiancée. He and his family had been honored greatly by President Clinton and offered Blair House for their sad visit to Washington. I found it tacky that he could not forgo the company of his fiancée for a few days, and play along with the program.

Seven months after the accident in Bosnia, an air force plane carrying a U.S. delegation led by Secretary of Commerce Ron Brown crashed near Dubrovnik, Croatia. The 33 Commerce Department officials and private business leaders, and a N.Y. Times reporter were on a spe-cial journey investigating how to salvage and reconstruct the devastat-ed country. I felt so sad. I first met the delightful Ron Brown in early summer 1992 when, as Chairman of the Democratic National Party, he came to meet with Chief of Protocol Jack Weinmann, and discuss how to accommodate members of the Diplomatic Corps during the Democratic Convention. The day of his funeral, the diplomatic corps gathered at the house for refreshments and security checks before boarding the buses to Washington Cathedral to join President Clinton and his cabinet. The deeply moved Belgian Ambassador told me that "just a year ago my prime minister (Dehaene) met Mr. Brown here – he was the first to reach Mrs. Brown by phone after the accident."

Richard C. Holbrooke, Assistant Secretary of State for European Affairs, former ambassador to Germany, was appointed chief negotiator and brought his skills, persuasiveness, and tendency to cut to the chase to bear in the long and difficult road to some semblance of quiet in that region in the Dayton Peace Accords in 1995. As a much deserved reward he became his nation's U.N. representative in the fall of 1999 taking over from Bill Richardson who moved to Energy, and later became governor of my home state of New Mexico.

Frequently meetings were held at Blair House dealing with this issue, and I recall particularly the Federation Forum, hosted by Secretary of State Warren Christopher on Tuesday, May 14, 1996. We arranged 12 locations, each with meeting space, office supplies, coffee service, to hold the sixty participants in addition to the self service luncheon buffet in the Jackson Place Dining and Sitting Rooms.

Secretary Christopher conducted his bilateral discussions in the Lee Drawing Room, with the Primary Suite as his holding room. The Lee Dining Room and the Conference Room were set for meetings; The Library was the Bosnia office; the Eisenhower Sitting Room the Croatia one; the Embassy Office for State Department staff; the Embassy Conference Room for general staff; and a massive set up in our Garden Room for 80 people to be used for opening and closing plenary sessions. It was a day on roller skates for our Secretary of State, moving from group to group.

But all was not about the Balkans.

When Tony Blair was elected Britains' prime minister in 1997, it seemed as if Bill Clinton had spawned a clone, the two were so alike in their governing philosophy, their modern approach, their intelligence and intellect; both were well informed, well read, and men of vision. The White House went all out for the British Official Visit in late winter of 1998. Thus Chief of Protocol Mel French met with the Social Secretary and her staff to discuss the 10 am official welcome on the South Lawn of the White House. I was listening to the details: the reviewing of the troops by both leaders and the music being played by the various military bands, when I heard myself muttering: "how about the Old Guard Fife and Drum Corps playing their happy little revolutionary tunes for this particular leader?" I was being facetious, really not thinking it would matter two hundred plus years after the revolution. But Capricia Marshall looked horrified, and I certainly managed to stop all conversation at the table. The "new" policy, to avoid playing certain tunes during a British visit, later was mentioned in Mrs. Clinton's book AN INVITATION TO THE WHITE HOUSE.

The two leaders certainly had enough on their plate to sink lesser mortals: what to do about Iraq, Bosnia, the Asian economic crisis, the European Union's preparation for a single currency, the Middle East Peace process, and Northern Ireland.

In April 1998 Bill Clinton became as popular with the Irish as 37 years earlier John F. Kennedy did just for having Irish blood. Mr. Clinton was daring, patient and committed to help effect a peace agreement between the warring factions of Northern Ireland, and brought to the negotiations a great respect for both sides of the issue. He was of course amply supported and assisted by Tony Blair, as well as Ireland's own prime minister, and former U.S. Senator George Mitchell who would prove himself indispensable in this, as later in the Middle East talks. The late Mary McGrory of the Washington Post put it eloquently: "Ireland gave Clinton a chance to be a leader. Clinton gave Ireland its last, best chance of peace." Our President vigorously pushed along the four year discussions between the less than friendly negotiation teams, calling passionately for peace, and thus imparting hope and energy to this cause. He also persuaded the British to accept America's involvement in the negotiations, thus paving the way for George Mitchell's skill and immense patience dealing with such a contentious lot. The result: that for the first time Northern Ireland's Protestant and Catholic political leaders have committed themselves to the idea of coexistence, the legacy of the Good Friday agreement.

While we were well entertained by various visits from the British and Irish, it was exceedingly interesting to observe our guests from Hungary, Romania, Bulgaria and Moldova and how hard they worked to be included in our Western community. But most of all I enjoyed welcoming for the third time Vaclav Havel, now President of the Czech Republic, here for a State Visit mid September 1998. Repeatedly hospitalized since the end of 1996, having part of one lung and a cancerous tumor removed, as well as a recent rupture of his colon, and chronic bronchitis, a heavy smoker and drinker all his life, he was frail and not in too good a shape. But he brought a new wife with him, having remarried within a year of the death of his first wife.

Dagmar, an actress, was fortyish, pretty, blond, and seemed devoted to her husband. She was often vilified in her country, as, I was told, Havel's first wife, Olga, was greatly respected for her political activism and steadfast support of her beleaguered husband before the liberation of their country. I suspect that no matter what Dagmar Havlova did she would be criticized, just as some of our own first ladies do not seem ever to meet national approval, especially for their outspokenness. For me she was a breath of fresh air, and the opposite of the unsmiling, boot clad Olga.

The president drank beer and scotch on arrival and wine with dinner with his delegation. His wife came down around 9 pm to retrieve him. They bid me goodnight, and walked up the Blair staircase, she assisting her worse-for-wear husband by pushing him up the stairs, both of them laughing delightedly like children. Half an hour later Frankie came galloping around the corner from the Front Door. His eyes were popping, and he was beating on his forehead in agitation. He stuttered: "Mrs. V, he is in there in his bathrobe, looking for his head of security."

The head of security fortunately knew enough English to understand. I took him into the Blair Dining Room and could see President Havel seated in an armchair by the Rear Drawing Room fireplace. My glimpse, before I took myself off, was of a small figure, barely clad in our white bathrobe. I advisedly say "barely" as this was wide open revealing all. I reflected that surely one's presidential authority is diminished dressed like that. Jose was present, and overheard the tongue lashing doled out to the head of security.

As Jose and I were discussing next morning's breakfast Lieutenant Waters came to tell me the latest:

The president had gone back upstairs looking for his wife. He came down into the basement, down the narrow circular backstairs where the Secret Service agent on post had intercepted him. He was intoxicated, seemed out of control, and had been taken up in the elevator by a deeply concerned agent. Also responsible for Mrs. Havlova the agent worried that she might have left the house. But she was hiding from her husband after a major quarrel and, furiously, had taken refuge with the Czech security agents in their room.

This bizarre situation was increasingly sensitive. The Secret Service agents could not barge in on her in Room 36, as if she was up to something shady, and possibly create an ugly scene. Instead they decided on going door to door casually looking for her to inform her where her husband was. He, in the meantime, had fallen asleep on the sofa outside the Embassy Offices on the second floor and was eventually coaxed into the Primary Suite by his doctor and head of security.

No more incidents took place, though the president seemed jittery and frail. His doctor appeared dismissive of the problem of mixing medication and alcohol. The Havels called for coffee, juice, fruit and cheese at 5:45 am.

President Havel's full program involved discussions regarding the entry of the Czech Republic into NATO and the European Union. During his press conference with President Clinton, who had just admitted to the nation his lying about Monica Lewinsky, Havel was asked if "our president's difficulties made you change your friendship for him?" to which he replied: "There are some phases in American life I do not understand, and there are some that I do understand – and the President referred to them a few moments ago" when President Clinton spoke about health and education.

President Havel brought with him a hand carved chest which Secretary of State Madeleine Albright had bought during her visit to the Czech Republic. This was stored in my upstairs sitting room. After a few months I called Elaine Shokas, her chief of staff, to ask if "the Secretary has forgotten she has this beautiful chest at Blair House." Within a week Mrs. Albright came to determine where the chest would fit in her Georgetown home. She apologized for leaving it in my room for so long. "No problem for me at all, Madame Secretary," I said, "it has been very useful; I hung my underwear on it." She roared with laughter and within two days sent in the movers. Despite this fun moment, I never developed the kind of association with any of the other Secretaries of State which I had enjoyed with James Baker.

However, Madeleine Albright was a tough and strong U.N. ambassador for the first Clinton term and Secretary of State for his second, and I admired her for both qualities as well as for the fact that she kept her sense of fun during those challenging years. Being deeply committed to American ideals, and the role of the United States in the world, and realizing how ignorant we are in this country she began to explain foreign policy and our obligations abroad to the American heartland. I do believe she was a marvelous salesperson for the foreign policy of Mr. Clinton. I met Madeleine Albright when, as professor of Georgetown University, she came to advise and render service during President Havel's first visit, and was touched when my husband and I were included in her diplomatic corps' receptions in the Diplomatic Reception Rooms. These generous invitations were the norm of the Clinton administrations, and while I have no doubt that Susan and James Baker would have done the same, it would rarely have been suggested to them. Madame Albright was off to a strong start, picking the brightest and most experienced diplomat as her Undersecretary of Political Affairs, career ambassador Thomas R. Pickering. I also enjoyed immensely the fact that an immigrant (she was born in Czechoslovakia), female at that, had attained that office.

In May 1998 President Clinton's push to enlarge NATO succeeded by ratification in a Republican Senate, and ensured the inclusion of Hungary, Poland and the Czech Republic in NATO, a major foreign policy achievement. It was the first of a larger expansion of our defense posture, and consequently of our democratic values.

And, for this former Dane, who had grown up looking across the Baltic Sea to the communist bloc, it was awesome. Who would have thought it possible!

Four years earlier our President was in Bruxelles addressing a NATO Summit and among other remarks said as reported in the Washington Post January 10: "We must build a new security for Europe. The old security was based on the defense of our bloc against another bloc. The new security must be found in Europe's integration – an integration of security forces, of market economies, of national democracies. That is why I have proposed that we create the Partnership for Peace (offering among other bilateral accords to East European nations which for some are stepping stones to NATO membership)... This partnership will advance a process of evolution for NATO's formal enlargement..."

In March 1999 NATO bombed Yugoslavia's air defenses to open the door to assaults on tanks, troops and military installations to disrupt the violent attacks by the Serb army on Kosovo and its Muslim inhabitants, and to break the cycle of ethnic cleansing atrocities committed against that community, and others. It was a watershed for NATO, inasmuch as what had been created as a defensive coalition now had turned into an occupying force where it was not at war. Fifty one years earlier the Soviet blockade of Berlin led to a Western airlift and focused our attention on a defense treaty with Europe, signed by 12 nations in 1949 in Washington D.C. That flying of dangerous missions to break the Soviet blockade of Berlin by allied forces 51 years ago would be repeated at this time over Yugoslavia. This latest endeavor of the alliance, preventing genocide in the former Yugoslavia, was crucial; the alliance had to prevail, and our President, better known as a peacemaker than a warrior, had to stand firm and not budge on the course he was now embarked on.

In the middle of the NATO offensive came the NATO Summit in Washington D.C. – the weekend of April 24-26, 1999, its 50th anniversary, meant to be a grand celebration. Certainly the end of the Cold War itself was a cause for celebration, as was the imminent expansion of NATO with three new members from the Soviet Bloc countries, but the prevailing mood was somewhat somber. It was renamed a commemoration.

For months leading up to this summit careful planning in Washington and Europe was going on, but not always involving serious business. On March 3, 1999 the chief of protocol hosted the NATO group from Bruxelles for a buffet dinner in the Garden Room.

45 minutes after everyone had left, a couple, the Director of the NATO Summit Task Force, and the NATO Summit Project Officer, wandered down the Blair staircase and ran into Mrs. Rennie as she was turning off lights. She asked them to wait and called Randy. "Where have you been? Everyone else has left?" "We have just been looking around upstairs," they claimed.

"In the dark?" Randy asked. "Oh, we put lights on and turned them off."

And we wondered how turning off and on the lights could make both of them disheveled and flushed.

19 chiefs of state or heads of government, their foreign ministers and defense ministers, assistants and security personnel descended on Washington, as well as 23 other leaders as observers or hopeful future

NATO members. Included were representatives from the Euro-Atlantic Partnership Council from countries as far away as Kyrgyzstan and Tajikistan. It was the largest gathering of high level government officials ever in Washington D.C. The Blair House involvement was relatively minor with several pre-planning events starting a year earlier and on the weekend itself only two events. Our gallant chief of protocol Mel French, among other duties, had the responsibility of getting the dignitaries to where they needed to be on time: moving 44 delegations in 44 motorcades, at times heading in the same direction, and required to arrive at their destination within an allotted time frame and in the assigned protocol order, and getting each person back again. Most leaders are notorious for being unable to do as they are told and have a tendency to stray. Randy, my deputy, on loan to Mel French off and on since months, was assigned responsibility for the movements around town of no less than five delegations. The assessment during and after the summit from the foreign guests about Mel French' particular responsibilities: "absolutely seamless." I shall always maintain that Mel French was the hardest working chief of protocol ever to grace that office. No detail was too small, no hour too late, no situation too tricky or difficult for her to handle beautifully, calmly, and competently.

Security arrangements were intense and complicated. Federal workers were given Friday off, so as to lighten the security burden downtown where having 100,000 less people moving about was seen as a huge plus. Everyone, regular or part time, working at Blair House had to be prelisted and preapproved by the Secret Service, and special badges were handed out to ensure access to the blocked off areas.

Our events were comparatively easy: on the Friday night, hosted by Deputy Secretary of State Strobe Talbott, NSC Director Sandy Berger invited his counterparts from the foreign security community to a reception, including many who had stayed here before with their own leaders. Simultaneously Secretary of State Albright and Secretary of Defense Cohen hosted a dinner in the Department of State for their counterparts, and President and Mrs. Clinton did the same for the leaders at the White House. On the Sunday Mrs. Clinton hosted a lunch at the house in honor of the spouses of the foreign leaders.

These arrangements had fluctuated wildly, with half of the invited guests not able to come. As a result the White House wanted the lunch in our Conference Room rather than the much larger Garden Room. At first Mrs. Clinton was delighted to try to sit around one table which was suggested when only 22 were coming. But someone had miscalculated and now there were 24 around a table seating 22. When my staff and I left Friday night three round tables were ready in the Conference Room for Mrs. Clinton, and the Garden Room was set up for the accompanying staff's buffet. The menu of Pea Soup, Salmon, and Rhubarb and Strawberry Tart with Sherbet, all of which on the menu itself would be embellished and spelt out, had been exhaustively arrived at. There were parties all over town, and our Chef and the White House Chef went over each official menu to ensure we would make no duplication. I had been requested to give a detailed description as to table settings to the White House. This presented little challenge as our choices were somewhat limited for larger groups.

I lend one of our linen tablecloth, rust colored with a check of cream, to Nancy Clark to plan her flower centerpieces to be delivered from the White House; we used a Lenox base plate in cream with a gold trellis border and the State Department seal in the middle; Lenox soup plates and cups in cream with gold border and BH initial in gold; our Tiffany china for the main course and dessert. Our crystal is Lenox Heyworth Stemware with special cut, gold rim, and BH initials in gold, and our silver the Tiffany King's pattern.

On Sunday morning my arrangements began to unravel. I was called at home by the Social Office at 8 am that Mrs. Clinton, because of the lovely sunshine, wanted to move her lunch from the Conference Room to the Garden Room with drinks and music outside in the Garden; I arrived on two wheels half an hour later. Fortunately Jose, Teresinha, Sean, and Tabitha Bullock, our new Administrative Officer, were already there. Within one hour the five of us dismantled the Garden Room and Conference Room; reset everything so the Garden Room would be the setting for Mrs. Clinton's lunch, and the Conference Room the setting for the staff buffet lunch. We ran a mile a minute, and thus christened Tabitha as a fully fledged staffer. Nothing was too much for her. She opened folding chairs, lifted tables, shifted glasses, did whatever was required. Nancy Clark per my earlier phone call added a large arrangement to the round table in the Garden Room where for the staffers' buffet I had otherwise planned to get away with a flowering plant. In the last moment the musicians were moved into the house as suddenly the wind came up and the Garden no longer seemed an attractive venue before lunch. However, for our Sean, at this particular time, this was but a drop in the bucket, so he cheerfully removed chairs he had just placed outside and reset them in our drawing-room.

Mrs. Clinton came early taking time to talk with all of us and posing for pictures with my staff. The spouses who had stayed at Blair House during their husbands' official visits greeted me warmly, but beamed at Jose who during the lunch assured me that "all is going well, Mrs. V; they are all my old girlfriends." He was one of the few who had seen them in various stages of undress serving breakfast in the Primary Suite.

I had looked forward with great pleasure to this weekend. I have always been a fervent supporter of NATO; my father served as Danish Military Representative to NATO's standing group in the mid sixties when it was still housed in the Pentagon; my older brother Claus and two nephews served NATO at various times. I grew up in a divided and devastated Europe where the creation of the alliance was viewed as a buffer against a hostile Soviet Union. The treaty which considered an attack on one of its members as an attack on all was comforting and gave peace of mind and security. In addition it constantly worked on building East-West relations through dialogue and economic, scientific and cultural cooperation. It had, remarkably, lasted 50 years.

And now, the European Union had gotten its act together, and the U.S. through its membership in NATO pursued a right course in the troubled Balkan region. A turning point came early June 1999 with Serb president Slobodan Milosevic caving in to NATO's demands, and the beginning of a peace deal for Kosovo. Bill Clinton summarized the actions of those few weeks, as mentioned in the New York Times May 23, 1999: "We are in Kosovo with our allies to stand for a Europe, within our reach for the first time, that is peaceful, undivided and free. And we are there to stand against the greatest remaining threat to that vision: instability in the Balkans, fueled by a vicious campaign of ethnic cleansing." A few days later Yugoslav military commanders started to pull out of Kosovo after 78 days of NATO bombing; and in October 2000 Serbian democratic forces ousted Slobodan Milosevic, president of Yugoslavia, following an election a few weeks before.

But dislike and hatred of Americans was a fact of life. Following a summit meeting of the Organization for Security and Cooperation in Europe in Istanbul in November 1999, Mr. Clinton paid a visit to Greece and was met by riots and demonstrators, but, typifying his attitude, commented: "Greece is the world's oldest democracy so if people want to protest they should have an opportunity to do so." Reflecting on our actions and involvement in Yugoslavia coming to the rescue of the Muslim population, I find it ironic and offensive that now, years later, the U.S. has made itself so hated in the Muslim world. It will take a wise and deliberate president to unravel that mess.

CHAPTER 19

FROM RUSSIA WITH LOVE – AND VODKA

"Tis not the eating, nor tis not the drinking
that is to be blamed, but the excess."

John Selden

I would remain fascinated, no matter how often they came, with our visitors from the former Soviet Union and its bloc countries, but always wondered, given our experiences with them, if they were all quite there! While Armenia, Azerbajian, Georgia, Turkmenistan, and repeated visits from Kazakhstan continued to fascinate, those closer to Europe remained the most interesting for me.

Stanislav Shushkevich, Chairman of the Supreme Soviet of the Republic of Belarus and Mrs. Shushkevich came July 21-23, 1993. Arriving at 7 am and finishing in the evening hours three long days later, it was like our first from Czechoslovakia: all their ministers fanned out all over town to hold meetings, and government officials streamed into the house for important and intense discussions. But they were also like the Russians and Ukrainians in that they ate everything in sight, and drank gallons of orange juice. And once the White House meeting with President Clinton was behind them they came out with their real wish: to wet their whistles with anything alcoholic which we could produce, and as they did not wish to waste a moment with this delightful and mind numbing exercise they started at breakfast.

"Jose, you are kidding!" He had just casually advised me that not only were we serving beer for breakfast, but scotch and soda with morning coffee for our Belarusian guests. Considering that their general had asked for two bottles of "vino," meaning Tio Pepe Sherry and downed these in a very short time the night before, we should not have been surprised.

Chairman Shushkevich could not have been mistaken for anything other than a former Soviet official; aging, gray, and badly dressed, he was said to rule his country by committee. We were told, discreetly, by his personal aide when he was getting ready for his scheduled meeting with Ambassador Strobe Talbott (an expert on the former Soviet Union and later Deputy Secretary of State) that he really wished to meet privately with him first, but had to make it appear as if this was a request from the American side. We played along, commented on this "request" from the Americans to his delegation, and took Ambassador Talbott straight upstairs to the Library for the one-on-one meeting. The chairman was an affable person, a former nuclear physicist fully aware of the Chernobyl's disaster on Belarus and other countries and adamant about being open about it despite the official attempt to keep this event a secret. He probably arranged his own demise by being so open, and lasted only another few years before being replaced. He was described to me also as not sufficiently innovative and decisive, qualities eminently necessary to bring such a country out from the former financial protection of the Soviet Union. He was ousted from his position in January 1994, and his country unfortunately seemed from then on to slide further into the orbit of Russia, being dominated by its communistic parliament and its hard liners.

His wife, some years younger than her husband, was so nice, the exact opposite of her neighbor from Ukraine, who could not find anything either to interest her or to enjoy in the States. But Mrs. Shushkevich went sightseeing every day, including to Mount Vernon for which expedition our kitchen packed her a picnic lunch. She went twice to the National Zoo, and was radiant upon her return, having been able to feed not only the seals in residence, but the pandas. I was so envious. She was very thin, ate sparingly and so modest in her requirements, asking for nothing as she may have had little where she came from. As the others from her part of the world, she did not go shopping. They had no funds.

A few months later, late August 1993, came the first of many visits hosted by Vice President Al Gore for his counterpart Victor Chernomyrdin, Chairman of the Council of Ministers of the Russian Federation (de facto prime minister) and Mrs. Chernomyrdin.

The Vice President was President Clinton's point man in assisting certain nations to accelerate their road to reform in all areas of government. President Clinton and President Yeltsin had created the U.S.-Russia Joint Commission in Vancouver in April 1993 to enhance cooperation in areas of space, including a joint shuttle-Mir program and science and technology, as well as incorporating earlier committees on the environment and energy, covering also an agreement to cease production of weapons-grade plutonium, important defense issues and how to apply the rule of law. But soon the Vice President would get into details such as how to label Russian foods, develop the oil fields of the Russian far east, test Russian children for lead in their blood, map the Russian Arctic, privatize Russian farmland, secure nuclear material from dismantled Russian weapons, cut the cost of treating Russian tuberculosis patients, write a Russian tax code and modernize Russia's air traffic control system, as outlined by Thomas W. Lippman of the Washington Post some years later. These were serious issues, and kept the dialogue open between the two countries regardless of strained relations from time to time.

The commission meetings here with the two principals took place at the White House Conference Center, with access from our Courtyard, and Blair House was used entirely to house the Russian party.

The one incident standing out among these hectic visits with the Vice President popping in and out for meals and meetings was when Prime Minister Chernomyrdin missed out on farewell to the staff, and more importantly, the ceremonial signing of our guest book. Chernomyrdin was expected back after his White House meeting to say goodbye and sign the guestbook before going to his luncheon party at the Russian Embassy for Vice President Gore and his departure from AAFB. However, at the White House, after the meeting with President Clinton, the Vice President jumped in the car with Chernomyrdin, and must have persuaded him to drive straight to the Russian Embassy instead of stopping by Blair House.

Randy, then Protocol Visits Officer, who had been waiting to jump in the Russian's motorcade, quickly grabbed our guestbook to have it signed before departure. Randy, who seemed to attract exciting moments in airports, such as discovering the Crown Jewels of England sitting on the tarmac, as Queen Elizabeth II's plane was beginning to wheel away, this time experienced another similar moment. Russian Minister Counsellor Edouard Malayan with our guestbook under his arm disappeared into the plane, the door closed and the steps were removed. Randy yelling, jumping up and down and swinging his arms, managed to attract some attention. After minutes of tense waiting, the steps returned to the door, the door opened and there was Mr. Malayan holding the guestbook over his head in a victory gesture. The above instance was not the only time when the signing of the guestbook and bidding farewell to the staff was somewhat cavalierly treated by this particular Russian Prime Minister, and would have happened again, had I not put my foot down. I remarked, casually, to the Russian chief of protocol how odd it was that the only leader in the world who did not deem it important to say goodbye and thank my staff was his. I asked him if perhaps I was doing something wrong in lining up the staff for the farewells, and also if he would prefer to have Chernomyrdin sign the guest book in private? From then on I had no problem, and our little farewell ceremony was written into their schedule.

Mrs. Chernomyrdin usually accompanied her husband, and gradually warmed up, in a sort of lukewarm way, to our capitalistic ways. She did not hesitate to advise us in advance that a bowl of berries such as cherries, raspberries, strawberries and blueberries, under plastic wrap, must be available in the Primary Suite every day, as well as apple juice made from green apples only; and "don't forget the dry red wine, vodka and beer;" we were also requested to have toothpaste, toothbrushes, slippers and robes available. How quickly people can get used to the good things in life; if they had only learned to be a bit more appreciative. I do not recall she ever thanked me.

President Leonid Kravchuk of Ukraine returned in March 1994, fortunately without his dour wife, and instead brought the two Olympic Gold Medal winners in skating: Viktor Petrenko and Oksana Bayul, thereby generating a flutter in all quarters, adding extra visitors to the house just to meet the young stars, including a photo opportunity for my staff. They were so handsome, smiling, shy, and so very young.

The Washington Post on March 6 noted that Ukraine "gave the Clinton administration a present as President Leonid Kravchuk left Washington after a two-day visit yesterday. It dispatched a Ukrainian train carrying an estimated 60 nuclear warheads from dismantled Soviet missiles, once aimed at the United States, on its way to a warhead graveyard in Russia. The movement of the bomb-laden train, disclosed yesterday by officials in Moscow and confirmed in Washington, signaled the formal start of Ukraine's promised denuclearization in accordance with a treaty signed in January by Kravchuk, President Clinton and Russian President Boris Yeltsin." Mr. Kravchuk naturally in return received promises of substantially increased financial aid from the U.S. government and discussed the vast problems his nation faced in privatizing and changing a government military industry to civilian use and meeting the demands of international lending agencies to open up its economic system.

During one of the Ukraine visits I went to AAFB to observe a presidential arrival, and returned to Washington on a Marine helicopter as part of the Ukrainian party. While I was on Marine Two, the Ukraine president, the U.S. chief of protocol, the foreign minister of Ukraine, and security, altogether 14, went by Marine One, first into the air, but last to land at the Washington Memorial where limousines were lined up awaiting this arrival. We all piled into the cars and five minutes later arrived at Blair House, with me galloping up the stairs in order to greet my guests.

With the new president, Leonid Kuchma came disturbing signs in Ukraine of a return to communist ways, with a slowness of economic reforms, suspension of privatization of inefficient state-run industries, and a further dismantling of individuals' rights vis-à-vis the state's. It was said that Ukraine, since 1991, had "turned from breadbasket of the region into an economic basket case." President Kuchma and his wife came for a State Visit in November 1994, and while not exactly exuding goodwill towards us capitalists, we obviously must have done something right as they did leave beaming and thankful, as did the president after his second and third visits with us in May 1997 and December 1999.

And then there was Boris Yeltsin.

President of the Russian Federation and Mrs. Yeltsin returned for a State Visit in September 1994. Visits Officer Chris Hathaway had called me after the Russians' arrival at AAFB to say that "they are so exhausted, and the president has, after first approving same, declined to ride into town with Strobe Talbott," so she expected they would go straight upstairs to bed. I guessed later than perhaps President Yeltsin did not, at that particular moment after a long journey, wish to get into discussion with our Russian speaking and very intense Deputy Secretary of State.

Despite this heads-up Jose and I decided to offer them a drink. Remembering all the preferences of the earlier visit he prepared trays with gin and tonic, scotch, beer and wine, and when the Russians saw these, their eyes lit up like a Christmas tree, and the president happily settled into a chair in the Lee Drawing-Room. President and Mrs. Yeltsin recognized all of us, and an added dimension to our changed relations came when Russian Ambassador Yuliy Mikhaylovich Vorontsov, later, asked for a special meeting with me.

"I have been instructed by my president to investigate the possibility of having a set of china made for his official representation in Moscow, and this is what he and Mrs. Yeltsin really would like," and he pointed to our Lenox china. I promptly asked Carter Cunningham, the Executive Director of the Blair House Restoration Fund, to come down and meet the ambassador. Again I blessed the foresight of Lucky Roosevelt who had requested their office space at the house making the Fund's executive director available with a moment's notice. I expect that shortly thereafter the Yeltsins would enjoy their dinners on our finest American porcelain. The Russian ambassador, by the way, was hard to pamper. When I invited him to come in to lunch he quoted a Russian proverb: "You should eat a hearty breakfast by yourself; you should share your lunch with a friend; and you should give away your dinner."

I consulted with the Russian chief-of-protocol as to with whom and when President Yeltsin would be dining, and observed him and President Yeltsin looking at the Lee Dining Room table, the president furiously making a list. I knew then my instincts had not failed me; that this president was by no means exhausted, and that we were on the right track. When I asked Mr. Yeltsin when he would like dinner served, he glared at me and said: "In ten minutes." "Certainly, Mr. President," I said, hoping to high heaven that Chef would not go into a spin. As always, Russell came through, cutting his planned roast of veal loin into medallions, thereby shortening the cooking time considerably.

And did they ever enjoy our arrangements. The president's personal staffers had insisted on preparing in our second floor kitchen some Russian delicacies of lobster, shrimp, clams on the shell, and very fatty meats to be served with our own dinner of Lobster, Scallop and Corn Chowder, Veal Medallions, Salad and Cheese, and Chocolate Hazelnut Pear Torte. All of this was washed down by gallons of vodka and wine; followed by two hours in the Garden when eight of them, including Mr. Yeltsin, consumed one and one half bottles of gin and two of Scotch; they were all rather tipsy as they staggered up to bed around 10:20 pm. During the day an enormous amount of liquor had been delivered from the Russian embassy and placed in the Primary Suite, so I suspect they continued there.

It was this night our two security officers on duty suddenly, on their screen, saw the powerful Russian president stagger down the emergency stairs, dead drunk and clad only in his briefs.

By the time the Secret Service agent on night duty found him, he was well on his way towards my office; to my eternal regret I was not there working. He was quietly led back to his bedroom, the Russian security never knowing about this little escapade which happened because their leader took a wrong turn, and for some other reasons as well.

Those of us who knew were highly amused, to the point that whenever Randy and I looked at each other the next day we would laugh out loud. The official White House welcome took place that morning on the South Lawn; a ceremony full of pomp and circumstance, and on this day, in glorious and sharp sunshine. Several of us, including protocol personnel, were watching the proceedings on television. President Yeltsin was squinting at the sunlight making several people comment how he should have worn sunglasses. However, I knew better.

He had the Mother of All Hangovers.

Later I had occasion to relate this little story to our Vice President attending a Cabinet meeting in the Jackson Place Conference Room. Al Gore was on crutches after an accident and therefore the last one to negotiate the hallway so I walked with him while telling him of our adventures. I thought he would have another fall, as he was laughing so hard tears were running down his cheeks. A few minutes later I heard him relay this to President Clinton and the Cabinet. Ron Brown, Secretary of Commerce, had his own story to tell, having received President Yeltsin in Seattle during his subsequent journey around America. "We were at lunch, with the president's personal assistant standing behind him," he told me, "and," here Ron Brown became very serious, "I have never seen anything like it. The president had a bottle of vodka handy and for every glass he downed, his aide would offer him a glass of Coca Cola. He emptied the vodka bottle during that lunch."

When President Yeltsin, on his way home, landed in Ireland for his scheduled Shannon airport visit with Irish Prime Minister Albert Reynolds it was reported in the news that he never appeared. The Prime Minister and a large group of people, including a regimental band, honor guard and flower-bearing children waited for him on the tarmac, and I heard later that President Yeltsin was out cold, stone drunk, on the floor of the airplane. Later I learned that he drank the country home of the British Prime Minister, Chequers, dry of gin during an earlier visit with John Major.

But, Yeltsin's drunken walk-about through the house naturally was not in the public domain. Presidents Clinton and Yeltsin according to all reports had fruitful talks, and at a lively press conference at the White House wrapped up their summit by signing a "partnership for economic progress" agreement which as reported by Washington Post's Ann Devroy on September 29 "lays out an agenda for establishing a normal trade relationship. They signed aid and trade deals amounting to more than $1 billion in U.S. private investment in Russia, and reached a number of agreements on U.S. assistance in helping the republic establish a tax code and other structures of a stable business environment." In addition there were agreements as to the destruction of warheads under the 1992 Strategic Arms Reduction Treaty, still to be ratified by our Congress and the formidable stumbling block of the Russian parliament. The emphasis this time was on trade and investment in contrast to President Yeltsin's visit in 1992 with President George H.W. Bush when the overriding issue was assistance and aid to Russia.

While the Yeltsin State Visit was a great success for the Clinton Administration we, though, were a bit overwhelmed by the number of bottles consumed by this group: 9.1 bottles of liquor; 26 bottles of wine; 59 bottles of beer, supplied by Blair House, but a fraction of the massive amounts of liquor carried in by the Russian staff.

The Chernomyrdins returned late January 1996 for another visit and work on the Joint Commission. Mr. Chernomyrdin was fired in the spring of 1998, but later appointed Russia's special envoy for Yugoslavia. We would hear about Chernomyrdin again during our 2000 presidential campaign when he threatened to sue George W. Bush for accusing him of stealing International Monetary Fund money.

A few months later another person tried his hand at the prime minister's slot: Yeltsin's foreign secretary, former head of the KGB, Yevgeny Primakov, became the new prime minister. Close to Mr. Gorbachev, and credited with having attempted to move Mikhail Gorbachev towards market reform as the last chance of holding together the Soviet Union he was now, seven years later, trying to put Russia's downward spiraling economy on hold. We actually had met him before when he was the guest of Mr. Reagan's defense secretary. He would last all of 8 months as prime minister in what was the increasingly volatile presidency of Boris Yeltsin.

Yevgeny Primakov was expected to come for a visit with Al Gore working on the joint U.S.-Russia Commission. The Washington Post on March 23, 1999 reported: "Mr. Primakov arrives in Washington today, barring any last minute glitches, on a quest for money."

"Barring any last minute glitches" seemed to be the operative word.

At 2:25 pm that afternoon, less than three hours before arrival I was advised that Mr. Primakov was en route back to Russia, ten minutes later this was reported by CNN. After refueling in Iceland Mr. Primakov was advised by phone by Mr. Gore that NATO likely would start the bombing of Yugoslavia during his time in Washington. Mr. Primakov promptly turned around in the air to return to Moscow, and soon thereafter was fired by President Yeltsin. We were so ready that flowers were distributed, the tea was set out, the hired waiters were in place, and only I still had to change my clothes. We felt so deflated, as did the poor young man from the Russian embassy who had so looked forward to our good food. It was akin to "being left at the altar," he said.

Boris Yeltsin was in ever increasing trouble at home, with talks of deep rooted corruption and money laundering leading straight to him and his family. On December 31, 1999 he resigned. While Boris Yeltsin vanquished communism, he probably did it to himself too. While he presided over an unprecedented period of change in his country opening Russia's doors to the west and permitting political freedom, he was less successful in shaping the new country and in building the institutions necessary to govern. He was an alcoholic, in ill health, and reportedly increasingly isolated. He announced his resignation this way: "Russia must enter the new millennium with new politicians, new faces, and new, intelligent, strong and energetic people. Russia will never return to the past. Now, Russia will always move only forward ... I am leaving. I did all I could. A new generation is relieving me, a generation of those who can do more and better." He was succeeded by Vladimir Putin a few months later.

In view of the increasing autocracy of Putin and his hostility directed at the United States, it does seem as if perhaps we missed a great opportunity to bring Russia truly into the western world. When the Soviet Union first dissolved it seemed imperative to extend as much aid as possible to get, particularly, Russia on its feet. The Gore-Chernomyrdin Commission was a proper and strong step in that direction during the two Clinton Administrations.

Because of its historical connection to Blair House, the Marshall Plan (started in the Lee Dining Room, Mr. Truman's Cabinet Room during his almost four year residence at Blair House), the primary plan of the U.S. for rebuilding and creating a strong foundation for the allied countries of Europe, and repelling communism after World War II, comes to mind.

Few Europeans in my generation are ignorant of the profound impact this brain child of Harry S Truman had on all of us whether we belonged to the victorious nations or the conquered ones of World War II. General George C. Marshall, his secretary of state in the Spring of 1947, put it eloquently in his Harvard University commencement speech: "Our policy is directed not against any country or doctrine, but against hunger, poverty, desperation and chaos. Its purpose should be the revival of a working economy in the world so as to permit the emergence of political and social conditions in which free institutions can exist."

Europe was in shambles after the Second World War, and massive funding was needed to restore this once vital continent. Years later in the Lee Dining Room, remembering how this plan laid the foundation for European postwar recovery, I suggested to a high State Department official that "following the deconsolidation of the Soviet Union perhaps a Marshall Plan was needed there." I referred to Czechoslovakian President Vaclav Havel's speech to a Joint Session of Congress on February 21, 1990 when he said: "I often hear the question: how can the United States of America help us today? My reply is as paradoxical as the whole of my life has been: you can help us most of all if you help the Soviet Union on its irreversible, but immensely complicated road to democracy. --- To put it metaphorically: the millions you give to the East today will soon return to you in the form of billions in savings." But my mild comment was dismissed as being unrealistic and impossible. When I first arrived in the USA my impression had been that it was characteristic of the American psyche to be generous, expansive, optimistic, and practical. Those elements were inherent in the concept of what came to be known as the Marshall plan, and in its execution. Unfortunately the American psyche had changed drastically. Since John F. Kennedy few statesmen would come our way, few really big thinkers existed in public life, and no one seemed to plan beyond the next election.

Although Thomas L. Friedman of NY Times Service in the International Herald Tribune early April 1993 reported the following about Russia, I believe it very much refers to all the former Soviet Union countries: "The urgency derives from the President's stated conviction that if the United States does not do what it can to bolster Mr. Yeltsin, and Russian reform falters, Mr. Clinton's ability to slash his own military budget and get his own economic program through Congress will be imperiled – indeed one cannot understand Mr. Clinton's feeling of urgency about aiding Russian reform without understanding that he sees this issue as an adjunct of his domestic agenda."

Friedman continued: "At its crudest, the White House logic goes like this: No Russian reform, no American defense cuts; no defense cuts, no chance for the Clinton administration to deliver on its pledge to halve the budget deficit in four years; no dealing with the deficit, no re-election."

But the issue was much bigger than one election; it was in our national interest to assist these nations, and particularly Russia, getting back on their feet. I only wish we had been able to do it better.

ACT IV

GEORGE W. BUSH
The President

***

COLIN POWELL
The Secretary of State

***

DONALD B. ENSENAT
The Chief of Protocol

CHAPTER 20

FINAL CURTAIN

"You can fool all the people some of the time,

and some of the people all the time, but

you cannot fool all the people all the time."

Abraham Lincoln

It was pouring rain on January 20, 2001, in stark contrast to the beautiful sunny day on which George W. Bush's father was inaugurated 12 years earlier, and I was on top of the world. Now my heart was heavy.

I had such doubts about this other George Bush who seemed but a shadow of his dad with little to show for his life. This quote of May 17, 1986 in Ronald Reagan's published diaries just about said it all: "A moment I've been dreading. George brought his ne're-do-well son around this morning and asked me to find the kid a job. Not the political one who lives in Florida. The one who hangs around here all the time looking shiftless. This so-called kid is already almost 40 and has never had a real job. Maybe I'll call Kinsley over at The New Republic and see if they'll hire him as a contributing editor or something. That looks like easy work."

The Clinton and Gore people had made such an impression on me with their humanity, intelligence, openness, and inclusion, and I was devastated that Al Gore would not be our next president.

I recall my heart sinking when I heard that James Baker was leading the effort on W.'s behalf in Florida. For sure, I thought, the odds are now favoring W. with that cunning and clever man at the helm. And December 12, 2000 is forever etched in my mind when the divided Supreme Court ruled against Gore, overturning the Florida Supreme Court decision allowing continued manual ballot recounts across the state.

I shall always remember with admiration Al Gore's statesmanlike and beautiful speech conceding to W., thus sparing the nation any more agony. I was at his residence two evenings later for an emotional farewell.

But partisanship in my position was not in the cards, and perhaps, just perhaps, surrounded by so many experienced advisors, possibly handpicked by his father, this man might just make it.

Governor Bush and a handful of his entourage had stayed with us early January to attend to transition business. While Mr. Bush was affable, his advance team was the nastiest and least pleasant of all I had ever experienced. It was hard to get a smile out of them; they reminded me of the KGB of the Ukraine, totally closed off to deviation from their smallest pronouncement. So ticked off was I by them that when they referred to George W. Bush as "The President" I reminded them that "as far as I know President Clinton is still across the street till 12 noon on January 20." Protocol wise I should have addressed George W. as Mr. President-Elect, but just couldn't; I probably would have called him President-Select so Governor he remained.

George Bush had a tight schedule, which, as far as I could tell, was never changed. One night he called me in during dinner as he had spilt on his tie: "It is my favorite tie, too." I suggested it would have to be dry-cleaned, and would it be alright for him to get it back when he returned for the Inauguration the following week, perhaps? And, "Governor, do you need another elegant tie in the meantime? I have one of President Chirac's in my drawer which I have been dying to get rid of?" I cannot believe I actually said that, but he and Karl Rove roared with laughter, and Mr. Bush assured me he had plenty of ties, "although I like President Chirac very much." Sure enough, the first question he asked me returning to Blair House before his inauguration was: "where is my tie?"

Former President and Mrs. George H.W. Bush arrived two days before their son's inauguration.

I was surprised to see them hauling their luggage up the steps themselves, and asked why Sean was not allowed to help? "Oh, we are used to doing for ourselves now," Mrs. Bush panted. "Please, please,

Mrs. Bush, let Sean do his job. He has looked forward to it all day." Finally, already well inside the house, the Bushes gave up their luggage, and Sean happily carted it away. While George H.W. Bush had aged a bit, Barbara Bush was unchanged and very happy I told her so, "and I have had seven operations since I last saw you."

Most of their grandchildren were there, the little two year olds who 12 years ago had roared around in the Garden Room in go-carts, and jumped up and down in former President Eisenhower's bed, were now teenagers who slept in, and whose rooms looked like explosions in garment factories, the worst being Room 24 where once again the Texas twins, Barbara and Jenna, stayed. Their grandfather tried to round them all up every morning to go to the various events preceding the inauguration, muttering under his breath when discovering they were still sleeping: "but this is historic; we are making history here." I took him up to show him our exercise room and told him how the seed money had come from the Korean president, really the gratuities, prohibited under federal law, for my staff, and he approved wholeheartedly, and happily succumbed to the masseuse waiting for him. He also, the first night, overhearing his son saying "I'll call Jesse Jackson right away," hissed "You'll do no such thing." I have no idea what was referred to, but in retrospect perhaps that was indicative of what was to come: a president being handled like a marionette doll.

We packed them in, had couples in the four-poster single beds, and put up extra cots. They arrived at separate times, each with their own schedule, and it was generally a lively time. Laura Bush is a nice, down-to-earth person; she wandered down into the Garden Room for lunch, in a dressing gown, with her wet hair wrapped in a towel. On January 20 exactly at 10 am, they departed to go to St. John's for service, then to the White House and on to the Capitol for the oath of office, while we had three hours to clean up after the visit and prepare for 450 guests attending the luncheon for the diplomatic corps before their viewing of the Inaugural Parade.

Shortly afterwards we were asked to do a dinner for senior White House staff hosted by Karl Rove. I was really bothered by this request. I had sent over copies of the policy and guidelines for the use of the house which did not include staff using it; in fact outside of foreign official visits it could only be used to further our foreign policy objectives and must include the President, Vice-President and/or cabinet secretaries entertaining their foreign counterparts; no fund raising or political meetings were permitted. Thus, in gross violation of our long established policy, 13 of the most visible of the President's aides in his campaign dined in the Conference Room. It was clearly, from what was overheard, a political meeting, and I wondered what they had now thought up to further mislead the American public.

While we had no other outside functions, we did have visits, my first one being a second visit of the President of the Republic of Korea and Mrs. Kim Dae-Jung; he was frailer, exclusively using the basement entrance and the elevator to get around the house. One evening President Kim hosted a dinner for the Heritage Foundation. Among the guests, and over one hour late, were U.S. Senator Mitch McConnell and his wife, Labor Secretary Elaine Chao. Randy asked me the next day who "that sleazy looking senator was?" McConnell had told off-collar jokes about Bill Clinton, and generally been rather obnoxious; "and his wife was not much better," Randy said. And the Korean president who understood English very well had looked shocked.

President Kim was not well treated at the White House as this new administration had no interest in "nation building." Mr. Bush was reluctant to aid him in his advances: his Sunshine policy (promotion of peaceful coexistence) towards North Korea.

Our new, internationally hapless President saw the world in terms of black and white, and would at all cost do everything different from his predecessor. So the diplomatic engagement which Mr. Clinton had continued with the North Koreans was closed, and the initiative by Mr. Kim, earning him the Nobel Peace Prize, was undercut. (A year later the Bush Administration finally took up this issue; but by then North Korea's dangerous road to nuclear development was well on its way and it would take another 5 years of intense diplomatic efforts to make any headway.)

I was not surprised. At all levels, including over in Protocol where the Bush appointees had begun to appear, it was evident that the preceding eight years had all but ceased to exist; somehow all of us who had served for years, in these peoples' eyes, were tainted by our association with the Clinton administrations.

In stark contrast to the eight Clinton years the new chief of protocol would dispense with any senior staff meetings, and only work through his deputy. Thus the open door, the generous spirit which pervaded the Clinton people, the inclusion which all of us had experienced, and the consequent cooperation and teamwork were gone in a flash. There was no curiosity as to how visits or events had been handled earlier in contrast to the Clintonites who always asked intelligent questions about precedence. The new deputy only met with senior staff; gave orders; rarely asked questions or saw "lower" staff; and was totally uninterested in anything said not emanating from his lips. It was clear to me immediately when I first met him that he was the type of person who kissed up (as he did to me) and viciously kicked down. The stories about him and his ability to decimate the career personnel of Protocol became legendary. He lasted six long years.

Personally, I had some career decisions to make. Adrian Cummins, my Australian husband of three years, was waiting for his immigration visa to come through; by January 2001 I had enough years in the federal government to retire; I knew that had Al Gore become president I would have remained in my position with great pleasure; but working with this new group of appointees who so openly disdained all that had happened before took the joy away.

It seemed it permeated the entire group of appointees. I recall hosting the G8, the meeting of the treasury secretaries and bank governors of the industrial nations on the eve of the World Bank meeting, and escorting our new Secretary of the Treasury to the Conference Room when Paul O'Neill turned to me and declared: "This administration is on time."

"Mr. Secretary, I do not recall that the G-8 has ever <u>not</u> been," and then I added: "I find it strange that it is suddenly as if the last eight years never happened. Of all the administrations I've worked for, the last two have been the most generous, inclusive and kind. I have not found it so with the ones before and do not expect it now either." He looked startled, but said: "I agree; did you know that Bill Clinton, on his last night as President, called me to congratulate me on this job?" Mr. O'Neill also admired my arrangement of peonies, proving he was by far too human to last long in that administration.

While I pondered my own situation and wishes I still had to take care of the leaders of Israel, Egypt, South Africa, Nigeria, Japan and Algeria.

The more interesting visits were Israel and Japan, the first because of its ruthless leader, and the second because of its irreverent and charming "Rock Star" who, it would appear, broke my jinx on his predecessors in that, after my retirement, he would return several times.

The Secret Service, taking no chances with the safety of Prime Minister Ariel Sharon, put up a tent by our front steps into which the limousine drove before unloading him. In addition all cell phones were confiscated at the entrance. Sharon was enormous and loved to eat; we supplied chocolates, cookies and fruit in his suite, as well as an extra large armchair wherever he was. Sharon was certainly appreciative, beaming, thanking me every time he saw me. Had I not studied his resume I would have been fooled into thinking he was a nice, generous, and sweet man, instead of a ruthless, tough, and take-no-prisoner sort of guy. No wonder he was able to play George W. Bush like a violin with the cowboy image of shooting first, asking questions later. And he had a willing ear. Bush, in his eagerness to do everything opposite of what Mr. Clinton had done, disengaged himself from this inconvenient area of the world, and essentially handed Mr. Sharon free hands to deal with the pesky problem of the Palestinians.

The Algerian President Abdelaziz Bouteflika's visit on July 11 was my last visitor at Blair House. The militarily backed president, facing growing social unrest shortly before had banned all public demonstrations in Algiers, though he could not avoid massive demonstrations outside Blair House during his 24 hours with us. I was so proud that several of my people when the Algerian staff complained to them about it looked at them in astonishment: "But this is a democracy and everyone has a right to speak up." I was also reminded of my own "encounter" with Algeria.

In the Spring of 1961 I sailed from Cyprus, enroute, via Marseilles, France, to Scotland where I would work for one year in the Albyn Restaurant in Queen Street. I had a not uneventful trip. I was on a small freighter, whose only passengers were an English young woman and me, and some 100 Cypriot immigrants. We arrived in the early morning hours at Marseilles, and boarded the train for Paris late that night. At that time we had been without news for 5 days. It was rather odd to find myself in the middle of what looked like an army exercise, inasmuch as the English woman and I found ourselves travelling all night with what seemed to be the entire French army! Arriving in Paris we parked our luggage and took a metro to do some serious sightseeing for the three hours at our disposal before continuing to London. Not having been in Paris before, none of us found it odd, on a Sunday, to find no traffic, no people in the streets except for tanks and soldiers, and serenely wandered around, possibly being among the few in this world who have ever seen Place de la Concorde with no movement of anybody or anything. Not until we arrived in London did we learn of the uprising in Algiers and that President de Gaulle had summoned the French army to Paris to defend the capital!

Bouteflika's government for years had been battling an armed Muslim insurgency starting after the government canceled democratic elections for Parliament when an Islamic fundamentalist party was poised to win. It was not the most charming of groups, by any means. But it was the first to the White House of an Algerian president in 16 years. I personally prepared all our information sheets in French: the rooming lists, the meal times, and the explanations as to laundry and dry cleaning.

Meanwhile in April the Executive Director of the National Security Office asked me to attend a meeting on visits; we were about 16, including the new White House Social Secretary and a representative from the Protocol Office.

Whatever was discussed that day at the White House, past precedence especially, it was clear that no Clinton program for foreign visits would be considered. The Social Secretary was explaining how the Reagans entertained during state dinners for 135 guests, and was dismissive about the Clintons and "their big tent on the South Lawn, seating 500 – really!" Everyone snickered; I could just hear how horrified they were that the hoi polloi had been invited. Even the Executive Director, a holdover from the former administration, played along.

"But, the Clintons were able to include so many more people, and it was stunningly beautiful," I said. But it was soon clear that the eight preceding years had ceased to exist. This meeting somehow became my epiphany. For months now little things about these people had accumulated in my mind: impressions of a certain arrogance; their disdain for others; the unsmiling advance team; perhaps the mere fact that when they arrived at Blair House after the "selection" by the U.S. Supreme Court and Al Gore's concession, they came as conquerors. The comparison to the arrival of the Clintons in December 1992 could not have been starker. Back then I received a glowing, happy, grateful group of people, slightly stunned and, most of all, humbled by their victory.

I thought as I was walking back across Pennsylvania Avenue that my joy and pride in my job had somehow evaporated; the accomplishments of the Clinton administrations of which we had played a hospitable part were being dismissed just like that, which meant that somehow my accomplishments over eight years on behalf of the nation were also being dismissed. Perhaps it was time to exit.

Thus early June I requested a meeting with the new Chief of Protocol Donald Ensenat, to hand him my letter announcing my retirement at the end of July and recommending Randy as my successor. As I left the office I saw him reach for the phone; this was big news; what a plum falling into his lap!

However, preceding this meeting I had carefully planned my strategy starting with its most important element: former Chief of Protocol Lucky Roosevelt. Over lunch at the Hay Adams Hotel I told her about my plans to retire and move back to Santa Fe. I asked her to support Randy Bumgardner to succeed me. Better than anyone Ambassador Roosevelt knew Randy and his abilities during the many years he worked in Protocol before coming to Blair House eight years earlier; her recommendation was crucial. Next came my letter campaign: I prepared personal letters to former President George H.W. Bush, former Secretary of State James Baker, and to Secretary of State Colin Powell advising them of my pending retirement and outlining my strong recommendation that the Blair House manager be a civil servant to provide continuity and an institutional memory, and that Randy was the best person for this; following the meeting with Ensenat, I posted my letter to Mr. Bush and Mr. Baker in Houston, and had the one to Secretary Powell hand delivered. Returning to my office I started my telephone campaign asking the Blair House Restoration Fund board members to support Randy. Little did I know that I would be so successful in this campaign that my own impending retirement after 13 years and four months, starting up the new Blair House and making it into a showcase in the world of presidential guesthouses, would slide into oblivion and that my own departure would go unacknowledged by the White House, the State Department and the Blair House Restoration Fund board. The Japanese, the Korean, and the Danish Ambassadors, though, honored me greatly by hosting farewell dinner parties for me while the Russian ambassador sent an emissary with a gift, and other ambassadors wrote me charming letters.

Over fifty letters supporting Randy were sent to the new chief of protocol. I received a charming letter from George H.W. Bush thanking me for my service to the nation, and assuring me that my strong recommendations had been passed on to the "powers that be." Closer to my retirement I paid a courtesy call on Secretary of State Colin Powell. I got all of two minutes penciled in and have always wondered if someone outside the door actually had a stop watch; and while he was prepared to sit and chat, I had more important things on my mind:

"Did you get my letter recommending Randy for my position, Mr. Secretary?" I asked him. "Yes" he said, and I continued: "and what are you doing about it, Mr. Secretary?" He shut up in his chair: "Now, wait a minute; this decision is not mine alone to make." But I continued quickly, knowing that my precious seconds were ticking: "Blair House needs continuity, Mr. Secretary, no political appointee can give it that, and you know Randy so well after all these years; this is important," and then my time with him was up. I could only cross fingers, and trust that his voice of reason, seemingly the only one around, would prevail.

Colin Powell, the much admired general, had been the voice of reason both in the Desert War and later in the Yugoslavia conflict advocating the use of military force only as a last resort. As long as he was in this cabinet I felt all was not lost. I often wondered how he managed to stay calm, collected and reasonable during the four years of the long knives out to get him. Personally I always felt he chose the wrong party; Colin Powell stands for equality in society, and surely must have found it hard going all those years with W.

Later, over Ensenat's protests, Secretary Powell made the decision that Randy Bumgardner would become the new general manager. I expect that Ambassador Ensenat never had cause to regret this, though I sometimes wondered if, in view of the very rough times ahead, Randy didn't.

But my time here was drawing to a close. I turned over certain files to Randy, particularly regarding a former president's funeral when his family would be staying at the house. I had noted the names of all white and cream roses, lilies and peonies, appropriate at such a time. Randy later told me he ordered precisely those flowers for the families of Ronald Reagan and Gerald Ford.

On my last day my staff prepared a potluck breakfast for me and gave me an original drawing of Blair House by a State Department artist, commissioned by Randy. In the afternoon they had one more surprise for me: I was escorted up to the Blair Dining Room, where my staff honored me by our traditional farewell ceremony. While I had presided over this ceremony 200 times I was now the VIP, going around the table, thanking and bidding farewell to those incredible people whose support, humor, grace, endurance, sage counsel, and loyalty had carried me along for 13 years and four months.

And in a final gracious act I was escorted out in the same manner in which Blair House staff bids farewell to the leaders of the world – through the Blair Front Door. As Lt. Waters walked with me to my car around the corner my staff was waving goodbye from the steps, just as if I had been one of the leaders of the world.

And how did I really feel when I drove away from Blair House?

I was relieved beyond words.

I said over and over again driving up Jackson Place: "I survived, I survived," thinking not only of the exposure to physical danger when in such proximity to the powerful, but also of the constant sniping, back stabbing and envy perpetrated by government colleagues.

I survived it all. I was thrown in the water and I swam.

And I was proud.

For 13 years and four months I was innkeeper of the nation's B&B, its general manager, its chatelaine, and, to some, its soul. I served four U.S. Presidents, five administrations, and six Secretaries of State; I had started up a "new" Blair House putting on it my personal stamp of hospitality, comfort, and style; and I had forged a cohesive teamwork among my staff members despite their differences in temperament, culture, attitude and language; I had brought them along with me so that while we guarded and lovingly cared for this beautiful and gracious guesthouse brimming with history, we also, together, made a substantial contribution to spreading goodwill for America around the world and thus helped furthering the interests of our nation.

Not all bad for a Danish immigrant.

And today I had, as so often before, followed the advice of my parents: "Benedicte, you say goodnight and you leave the party while the music is still playing!"

APPRECIATION

This book would not exist without the Blair House staff; it is as much about them as it is my own story. Many are mentioned throughout the book; all were important players and the book is dedicated to them. The bizarre situations in our collective lives as described throughout were handled promptly, skillfully, uncomplainingly, and invariably with great humor. I remain so proud of everyone and how we forged a cohesive team caring for and guarding this historic and beautiful guesthouse, and how, together, through our legendary hospitality we contributed to spreading goodwill for America around the world, furthering the interests of the United States.

Throughout my life I have benefitted from the actions of loving and generous people, listed below, who have influenced my life's journey. Many gave me invaluable assistance and suggestions along the way; I thank them profusely and apologize if I have left anyone out; it was done unintentionally.

Jeppe Markers and Elise Nørholm of Lindhardt & Ringhof, my publishers in Denmark, remained so supportive and helpful during the creation of the English version of my book. Guiding me through the writing process during several years, I wish to thank first and foremost author and historian Warren Sloat who was my Santa Fe advisor, writing guru, the "book doctor" who taught me how to slice and burn and rearrange; his wife June Walker who contributed sage counsel; Santa Fe authors John Pen La Farge and especially Richard McCord who set me straight in my writing style and provided advice; Frank M. Bond and James B. Alley who brought their legal opinions to certain sections; Bill Stewart who checked my Middle East chapter; Kate Lehrer in D.C. whose early suggestions and encouragement were invaluable; Janie Dimmock who never gave up on me, passing me on to George Cappannelli and, through him, to wonderful Julie Melton of The Right Type and thus to publishing of this book. I also thank Bette Ridgeway who designed my website and Andrew Neighbour who designed the covers for both the Danish and English versions; my niece Luise Valentiner who created the dachshund logo; and of course Timothy Carroll who suggested the title. I am grateful to Charles Anspach for my four years advising and counseling the Leland Stanford Mansion Foundation in Sacramento, California on protocol matters. And what would I have done without my beloved Elizabeth "Tina" Lane and her family, Jim, Cubby and Ecie, in Boulder who kept me going during my darkest days and were always there for me. I am so grateful to everyone.

I am so sad that my beloved husband, Adrian Cummins, who supported me unconditionally through the early days of creating this book, is no longer here; I have quoted him in the book, but left out his more salty Australian naval remarks. Ruth Hamory, also, is no more; she, my fairy godmother and mentor, guided me every step of the way since I arrived in America.

And of course last but not least I must mention the terrific support and encouragement I received always from President George Herbert Walker Bush and Barbara Bush, and Secretary of State Jim Baker and Susan Baker and from President Bill Clinton, Hillary Clinton, and Vice President Al Gore; they were all a joy to work for and with. And to Lucky Roosevelt an enormous thank you for having had the guts to hire me, a foreigner, for such a position and to Neboysha Brashich who sent me her way.

The photos in the book are derived courtesy of the following sources: The Ronald Reagan Presidential Foundation and Library, The George Bush Presidential Library, The William Jefferson Clinton Presidential Library, The George W. Bush White House, The U.S. Department of State, various embassies, Lynn Hornor Keith, Blair House administrative officer and unofficial photographer, and my private collection; some curatorial notes are courtesy of Candace Shireman, Blair House Curator.

And thank you, also, to the following for assistance, advice, and support:

WASHINGTON D.C.

Nancy Clark, Rex Scouten, Gary Walters and his Ushers at The White House; Bob Barnett, Pam Cicetti, David Hohman from The Clinton connection; Roy Peddicord, GSA; Marco Caceres, U.S. Senator Pete V. Domenici, Lou Gallegos, Angela Raish, Carolyn Shipley from The U.S. Senate connection; Louis Blair and Frederick Slabach of the Truman Scholarship Foundation

NEW MEXICO:

Elisabeth Alley, David and Diane Bower, Charlie Romney Brown, Kent Carnie, Mike and Helen Cerletti, Abel and Audrey Davis, E.J. Evangelos, Todd Greentree, Dick and Malie Griffith, Rickey Hardy, Donald Lamm, Janet Lowe, Karen Machon, Dheeresha and Larry Moore, Diego Mulligan, Susan and Pat Oliphant, Ambassador Frank Ortiz, Hoyt and Joy Pattison, Vic Perry, Patti Poitras, Richard and Virginia Salazar, Ambassador and Mrs. Peter Sebastian, Lea and David Soifer, Phil and Jody Sunshine, Greg Tweed, Virginia White

EUROPE:

Helle Bjerre Christensen, Patrick and Janine Erdal, Nora Jørgensen, Hans Kofoed, Jeanette Pollok-McCall, Alexander and Sorcha O'Connor, Richard O'Connor, Lisbeth Oxholm, Ambassador and Mrs. Rinaldo Petrignani, Elisabeth and Eric Pettersson, Claus Pettersson, Søren Schauser, Claus and Bodil Valentiner, Christian Valentiner, Gitte Crone Valentiner, Joakim Crone Valentiner, Luise Valentiner

AUSTRALIA:

Katherine Cummins and Richard McGregor; Julia Cummins; Andrew Cummins

OTHER FRIENDS:

Christian and Marina Brachet, Kathy Burns, Jane Buzalski, Prue Clendenning, Tom and Judy Connally, Tom Coyne, Sally Foley, Bitsey Folger, Jørgen and Gudrun Graugaard, George Griffin, Konstantine and Nancy Menghis, Tom O'Coin, Ambassador Jaime de Ojeda, Sam Rachlin, Troy Robinson, Rick Rutecki, Lisa Smith and family, Jim and Sylvia Symington, Bill Wolfe

BLAIR HOUSE CAST (list continued from page 16)
Blair House Restoration Fund Board Members and Executive Directors, an assortment of officials from agencies, their deputies, staffers and others from various presidential campaigns as well as many former U.S. chiefs of protocol; an assortment of kings, queens, princes, an emperor and empress, presidents, ministers, valets, cooks, maids, and personal aides as well as foreign ambassadors

Part time wait staff: Mustafa Akbayrak, Stelios Alexandris, Tina Berberoglu, Rodolfo Bonner, Segundo Campos, Angel Canedo, Joe Chvatal, Emilio Cola, Aurelio Conti, Regina Cortes, Janine Czarnecki, Jose Diaz, Manuel Diaz, George Dunaway, John Feist, Manuel Fernandez, Jose Ferro, Marilia Ferro, Ausilia Fuster, Mike Fuster, Vince Fuster, Harmon Goins, Lita Gomes, Francisco Gomez, Reginald Holton, Lester Jones, Jose Lopez, Ricardo Martinez, Ruben Martinez, Guiseppe Mastrangelo, Mario Ochoa, Juan Ortelli, Carlos Quintanilla, Domingo Rodriguez, Jose Rodriguez, Luisa Salvi, Mohamed Sasi, Julius Smoot, John Tan, Bashari Taweel, Pietro Telles, Norwood Williams,

Part time Kitchen Personnel: Clarence Addison, Paul Akerboom, Carlos Bracey, Mark Dohse, Mark Frieman, Twyla Fultz, Melodie Hong, Bess Klander, Ian Knox, Dave Macfarland, Jason McCarter, Sam Neal, Michael Pant, Daphne Rust, Don Trelstad, Lyle Zahorsky

Communications: Minter Boone, Richard Harrington of ATT

Interior Decorators and Curatorial Assistance:
Mark Hampton and Mario Buatta, Bill Adair of Gold Leaf Studios, Mickey Corrado, Harold Keshishian, Craig Littlewood, Craig Maue, Stephen Rice

Garden: Earl Peddicord of GSA and Messrs. Dingus Sr. and Jr. of Davey Tree and their crew

Hairdressers: Rebecca Hanks, Kelly Funk

State/Protocol Office: Barbara Adams, Pam Amaral, Chuck Angulo, JoAnn Artz, William Black, Vincent Chaverini, Frank Bright, Clem Conger, Philip Dufour, Larry Dunham, Fred DuVal, Carlos Elizondo, Mary Mel French, Richard Gookin, April Guice, Christine Hathaway, Jesse Johnson, Bill Keppler, Charles Kinn, Harlan Lee, Gene Lewis, WilloDean Lewis, Dee Lilly, Hillary Lucas, Leslie McGinty, Daphne Martinez, Mary Masserini, Bunny Murdoch, Clyde Nora, Molly Raiser, Lucky Roosevelt, Debi Schiff, Gail Serfaty, Clarence Shaw, Shirley Stewart, Maria Sotiropoulos, Cassandra Stone, Kim Townsend, Tanya Turner, John Giffen Weinmann, Mary Williams, Eve Wilks, Laura Wills, and many more

Telephone Operators: Bob Armfield, Shirley Campbell, Joan Nichols, Loraine Triplett

U.S. Secret Service: George George, Jonathan Miller, Russell Rowe, Buck Tannis and many more

Most devoted volunteers: John and Louise Beale, David Emge, William Escobe, Christina Fitz, Sally Foley, Chrissie Griffin, Jan Holderness, Sandy and Roberta Jeffries, Bill and Helen Large, Marta Marshalko, Joan Maynard, Tessa McBride, Elena Millie, Bonnie Muir, Phyllis Ottinger, Patrick and Virginia Pascoe, Anastasia Sotiropoulos, Julie Stephenson, Eleanor Tydings, Anne Lise Warga, Ross Watson and many more

Index

C

Calderón, Gloria 140
Calderón, Rafael Angel President 127, 140, 141
Callejas, Rafael President 132
Camdessus, Michel 149
Caplan, Tommy 245
Card, Jr., Andrew H. 208
Cardoso, Fernando Henrique, President 139
Carnie, Kent 25, 148, 157
Carter, Buddy 303
Carter, Jimmy President 145, 240, 278, 337, 339
Castenskiold, Christian and Cecily 119
Castleman, Sam 45, 47, 51, 81, 84, 87, 96, 113, 140, 143, 146, 162, 165, 192, 243, 273, 303
Chamorro, Pedro Joaquin 137
Chamorro, Violeta B. De President 136
Chao, Elaine 378
Charaa, Farouk Foreign Minister 277
Chaverini, Vince 96
Cheney, Dick 97-99, 154, 194, 314
Chernomyrdin, Mrs. 363, 364
Chernomyrdin, Victor Prime Minister 78, 363, 364, 369
Chirac, Jacques President 47, 348, 349, 376
Chizawa, Haruhiko 300
Choi Jong-Wook 293
Christensen, Søren Haslund 116
Christiani, Alfredo F. President 136
Christian X, King 182
Christopher, Warren Secretary of State 264, 337, 351
Churchill, Randolph 349
Churchill, Winston 350
Churchill, Winston S. Prime Minister 43, 343, 349
Ciller, Tansu Prime Minister 271, 272
Clark, Nancy 162, 358
Clinton, Bill President 98, 105, 125, 187, 211, 239-245, 247, 249, 254, 255, 257, 259, 261, 263, 264, 266, 267, 271, 272, 276-279, 282, 283, 286-290, 294-296, 298, 303-306, 308, 311, 312, 315-319, 321, 324, 325, 335, 338, 339, 343, 345, 346, 348-352, 354, 355, 357, 359-361, 363, 365, 368, 375, 376, 378-382
Clinton, Chelsea 244, 304, 314
Clinton, Hillary 149, 242, 243, 250-252, 254, 255, 270, 276, 296, 300, 303, 304, 307, 308, 314, 335, 338, 352, 357, 358
Coffelt, Leslie 7, 13

Cohen, Bill 323, 357
Collor de Mello, Fernando President 137, 139
Collor, Mrs. 137, 138
Conable, Barber 149
Conger, Clem 14, 120
Conroy, Sarah Booth 86, 301
Cooney, Michael 7
Cordovez Zegers, Diego Foreign Minister 135
Cossiga, Francesco President 171, 173
Coughlin, Mike 24, 26, 53, 65
Cowles, Fleur 52
Craighead, Kelly 246
Crawford, Officer 126
Cronkhite, Russell 28, 37, 44, 45, 49, 67, 74, 93, 96, 97, 102, 113, 132, 133, 140, 143-145, 152, 153, 198, 201, 207, 208, 242, 261, 266, 282, 295, 306, 320, 321, 358, 366, 367
Cummins, Adrian 119, 178, 379
Cunningham, Carter 62, 366

D

d'Alema, Massimo Prime Minister 175
Danielson, Mrs. 350
de Gaulle, Charles President 381
de Klerk, Frederik W. President 82, 85, 336
de Klerk, Marike 84
DeLay, Tom 308, 317
Delors, Jacques 345
De Michelis, Gianni Foreign Minister 174
Demirel, Suleyman Prime Minister 157
De Mita, Antonia 172
De Mita, Ciriaco Prime Minister 172
de Ojeda, Jaime 127
Derwinski, Edward J. 176
Deutch, John 349
Devroy, Ann 368
Diana, Princess of Wales 139
Diaz, Teresinha 50, 70, 81, 120, 137-140, 162, 164, 165, 349, 358
Dienstbier, Jiri Foreign Minister 192
Dierman, Connie 298
Dimitrios, Archbishop of Constantinople and Ecumenical Patriarch 177
Diouf, Abdou President 86
Dlouhy, Vladimir 192
Dole, Bob Senator 311, 323
Domenici, Pete V. Senator 21, 22, 26, 27, 149, 312
Dos Santos, Agustinha 53, 120, 139
Dugdale, Mrs. 111, 113
Duke, Angier Biddle 35

Duke, Robin Chandler 35, 36
DuVal, Fred 248
Dyvig, Karen 117
Dyvig, Peter 117, 345

E

Eagleburger, Larry Secretary of State 114, 137, 154, 208
Eisenhower, Dwight President 300
Eisenhower, Mamie 300
El-Baz, Osama 260
Elias, Thomas 295, 301
Elizabeth II, Queen 44, 107-114, 125, 195, 364
Ellemann-Jensen, Uffe Foreign Minister 119
Ellis, Martha Hodgson 299
Endara Galimany, Guillermo President 132
Ensenat, Donald Chief of Protocol 382
Escudero, Alberto 126
Estrada, Joseph President 287, 288
Evans, Bill 162
Eyadema, Gnassigbe President 77

F

Fahd Bin Abdulaziz Al-Saud, King 273
Feinstein, Dianne Senator 323
Fellowes, Sir Robert 110, 113
Fitzgerald, Jennifer 97
Flecha da Lima, Paulo Tarso 139
Foley, Thomas House Speaker 90, 169, 295
Forbes, Steve 193
Ford, Billy 132
Ford, Gerald President 107, 384
Fort, Arthur W. 96
Franco, Francisco President 126
Frasier, Joe 343
Frederik, Crown Prince 120
Frederik IX, King 114, 119, 120
Frei, Eduardo President 331, 333
French, Mary Mel Chief of Protocol 242, 253, 276, 282, 319, 321, 326, 351, 357
Friedman, Thomas L. 371
Funk, Kelly 328
Fuster, Jose 42, 45, 49, 53, 63, 67-69, 71, 72, 77-81, 83, 89, 90, 92, 94, 97, 109, 113, 126, 133, 136-138, 140, 143, 144, 148, 150-153, 158, 162, 168, 173, 192, 194, 196, 199, 209, 212, 242, 245, 259, 261, 266, 269, 274, 288, 289, 295, 297, 298, 304, 320, 324, 328, 337, 341, 353, 358, 359, 361, 366

G

Galbraith, Peter W. 148
Gandhi, Mahatma 287
Gates, Robert 208
Gaviria Trujillo, César President 135
Genscher, Hans Dietrich 186
Gergen, David 250
Gharbi, Hedi 152
Giffen, James 202
Gilman, Benjamin 343
Gingrich, Newt House Speaker 294, 311-315
Gonzales, Felipe Prime Minister 135
Gookin, Richard 105, 245
Gorbachev, Mikhail President 21, 180, 204, 207, 369
Gore Al, Vice President 242, 250, 263-265, 314, 342, 363, 367, 369, 375, 376, 379, 382
Grafton, Duke and Duchess of 109
Graham, Katharine 169, 190
Gustav (6) Adolf, King 116

H

Haig, Alexander Secretary of State 67, 68, 124
Hamory, Ruth 25, 50, 180
Hampton, Mark 14
Hand, Lloyd 291
Han Seung-Soo 291
Harriman, Pamela 349, 350
Harris, Julie 118
Hashimoto, Ryutaro Prime Minister 294
Hassan II, King 122-125, 205, 325, 327
Hathaway, Chris 297, 366
Haughey, Charles J. Prime Minister 175
Havel, Vaclav President 189, 191, 192, 352, 353-355, 371
Havlova, Dagmar 353, 354
Havlova, Olga 191, 192, 353
Hawke, Hazel 73
Hawke, R.J.L. Prime Minister 72, 73
Henrik, Prince 115, 117, 118
Hill, Chris 194
Hills, Carla 149
Hirohito, Emperor 296
Hoagland, Jim 85, 290, 348
Holbrooke, Richard C. 351
Hosokawa, Morihiro Prime Minister 294
Houser, Allan 299
Hussein, King 121, 261, 263, 264, 266, 267, 271, 278
Hussein, Saddam President 115, 117, 146, 154, 155

I

Ibn al-Saud, King 148
Ickes, Harold 250
Indyk, Martin 271, 276
Ingrid, Queen 114, 120
Irby, Sean 54, 74, 75, 79, 144, 166, 259, 330, 358, 376
Isa Bin Salman Al-Khalifa, Shaikh 156

J

Jabir Al-Ahmed Al-Sabah, Shaikh 146, 154
Jackson, Jesse 377
Jaharis, Michael 177
Jaidi, Abdeslam 325-327, 330
Jefferson, Thomas President 244
Jennings, Peter 149
Jiang Zemin, President 319, 322, 323, 325
Johnson, Lyndon B., Mrs. 36
Johnson, Lyndon B. President 104, 291
Juan Carlos, King 107, 125, 127, 140

K

Kaalund, Knud 183
Kaifu, Toshiki Prime Minister 165
Kandemir, Nuzhet 157
Karloutsos, Alexander Father 177
Kawior, Rabbi 144
Keating, Paul Prime Minister 287
Keith, Lynn 54, 80, 162, 180, 298
Kennedy, Edward Senator 175
Kennedy, Ethel 36
Kennedy, Jacqueline 311
Kennedy, John F. President 36, 122, 245, 352
Kennedy, Robert F. 25, 148
Keshishian, Harold 44
Khan, Genghis 197
Khan, Yaquib 147
Khokhar, Mrs. 281
Kim Dae-Jung, President 291, 292, 378
Kim Young-Sam, President 252, 289-292
King, Martin Luther 287
King of Swaziland 107
Kissinger, Henry 274, 276
Kissinger, Nancy 78
Klaus, Vaclav 193
Klavan, Rabbi 145
Klimova, Rita 191, 193
Knox, Ian 153, 277, 279, 326, 328, 329
Knuth-Winterfeldt, Ditlev Count 182
Knuth-Winterfeldt, Kield Count 182
Knuth-Winterfeldt, Trudi Countess 182

Koivisto, Mauno President 102
Kok, Willem Prime Minister 347
Konstantine, King 126
Koppel, Ted 149
Kravchuk, Antonina Mikhaylovich 199
Kravchuk, Leonid President 200, 207, 364, 365
Kuriyama, Takakazu 299

L

Lacayo, Christiana 136, 137
Lake, Anthony 264, 308
Lake, Mrs. 198
Lao An 324
Lee Hee-ho 292
Lee, Robert E. 120
Lehrer, Jim 325, 341
Lewinsky, Monica 314
Lewis, Gene 105
Lieberman, Joe Senator 90
Li Jianping 321
Lilly, Dee 309
Lincoln, Abraham President 306, 323
Lindsey, Bruce 243
Lippman, Thomas W. 282, 363
Littlewood, Craig 26
Livingston, Bob 316
Li Zhaoxing 321
Lubbers, Ruud Prime Minister 347
Lukin, Vladimir 204

M

Machel, Graça 342, 343
Machel, Samora President 342
Maher El Sayed, Ahmed 259
Major, John Prime Minister 368
Malayan, Edouard 364
Mandela, Nelson President 67, 76, 82-84, 335-338, 342, 343
Manley, Michael Prime Minister 346
Mansfield, Mike 301
Marcos, Ferdinand President 161
Marcus, Ruth 290
Margaret Rose, Princess 107, 109
Margrethe II, Queen 107, 115-120, 296, 346
Marshall, Capricia 243, 246, 254, 270, 352
Marshall, George C. 370
Masserini, Mary 135
Mattos, Lygia 140
Maue, Craig 26
Mazer, Ron 202
Mazowiecki, Tadeusz Prime Minister 193

CPSIA information can be obtained
at www.ICGtesting.com
Printed in the USA
LVHW041804230123
737762LV00017B/633/J

9 780983 576006